Organic Gardening

Organic Gardening

A Comprehensive Guide to Chemical-Free Growing

Crow and Elizabeth Miller

IDG Books Worldwide, Inc.
An International Data Group Company
Foster City, CA • Chicago, IL • Indianapolis, IN • New York, NY

IDG Books Worldwide, Inc.
An International Data Group Company
919 E. Hillsdale Boulevard
Suite 400
Foster City, CA 94404

For general information on IDG Books Worldwide's books in the U.S., please call our Consumer Customer Service department at 800-762-2974. For reseller information, including discounts and premium sales, please call our Reseller Customer Service department at 800-434-3422.

ISBN 0-02-862315-0

Cataloging in Publication Data can be obtained from the Library of Congress.

Manufactured in the United States of America

10   9   8   7   6   5   4   3   2   1

First edition

Designed by Nick Anderson

Crow's Prayer

Sowing the seed,

My hand is one with the Earth;

Wanting the seed to grow,

My Mind is one with the light;

Hoeing the crop,

My hands are one with the rain;

Having cared for the plants,

My mind is one with the air;

Hungry and Trusting,

Eating the fruit,

My body is one with the Earth;

When I rise up,

Let me rise up joyful like a bird; (a Crow)

When I fall,

Let me fall without regret like a leaf.

Contents

Contents

Contents

Contents

Contents

Contents

Introduction

Mother Nature is on time. She means for all things to go in cycles—for leaves and flowers to decay into humus, which in turn enriches the soil so that new plants will grow.

Great gardening is, in part, a matter of timing, and garden time is cyclical. Each cycle has a consistent sequence of developments in which specific events unfold. The key to a healthy garden is to carefully observe these cycles and time your planting, cultivation, and pest control activities to coincide with the natural progression of the seasons. Even harvesting is affected by timing: It is well-known that melons taste best if they have not been watered in the last 3 weeks of ripening.

The importance of the annual cycle of light and dark can be seen in the staggering of succession crops. In the spring the days become longer and the soil, air, and water temperatures begin to rise. Two rows of carrots planted 2 weeks apart in late April will mature only 1 week apart, because the later-planted crop has better conditions and will grow faster. Fall crops act the opposite way; a few days between plantings in September or October will cause a harvest delay of a week or more, since the days are growing shorter as the crop matures.

Use the timing needs of different plants to your advantage. Thinning carrots was one of the more tedious jobs in our garden. By choosing plants that work together, we are able to avoid this chore. Now we mix radish and carrot seed together, one-third radish by volume, and sow them both in the same row. The radishes break ground almost immediately, allowing us to cultivate between the rows and stop early sprouting weeds before the carrots are up. When the radishes mature a few weeks later, the harvest thins the carrots automatically. The relationship of these 2 plants makes the garden more productive.

This kind of thinking is hard to do from the seat of a tractor. The kind of garden that will put you in touch with the quiet rhythms of growth is by definition a garden of human, not industrial, scale. A personal garden needs to be small enough that you can do any major garden task in a day. Spring soil preparation, seeding, setting of transplants, and fall cleanup—none of these should take more than a single Saturday of pleasant work for the family. How big a garden is that?

Don't think of gardening as a chore. Cultivating and weeding give as much pleasure as harvesting, if you keep your garden manageable. These tasks can allow for quiet moments of observation, of close interaction with the whole community of your garden.

Organic gardening ensures that you and your plants live in a safe, nontoxic environment. By using organic methods, you create a balanced atmosphere that will grow healthy and naturally beautiful plants.

Chemical methods of gardening make plants more susceptible to disease. The chemicals do this in part by killing off organisms in the soil that protect plants from certain diseases. Organics, on the other hand, help build up the fertility of the soil, thereby creating strong and stable plants that are able to fight off insects and diseases.

If you really want to know how your garden is doing, get down on your hands and knees and look at it. Run your hand through the soil and smell it. Check the undersides of the plant leaves for insect eggs instead of just walking by and dousing them with spray. The wise grower ever renews and unites with the Earth.

Acknowledgments

We want to acknowledge Jim Willhite for his patience and understanding, and all the help he has given in the writing of this book.

PART 1

Starting an Organic Garden

Winter may be an off-season for gardening to some people, but I do not see it that way at all. What you do at this time can make or break your gardening program and activities for the rest of the year. Take Jack Frost's arrival to study and plan, and to assess last year's successes and failures.

Ask yourself these questions: Are you getting the most out of your garden? Did it yield as much the past year as you and your family could eat? Is your garden plan efficient? Does each bed grow two or possibly even three crops per season?

Do you feed your soil well enough to provide nutriment for your crops? Do you add rock fertilizers and organic nitrogen supplements to the compost pile? Do you encourage nitrogen-fixing bacteria to proliferate in your soil by rotating legumes throughout the garden?

Did you add nut and fruit trees or bushes to your garden this year? No room? How about that privet hedge that does nothing for you, but wastes your time in endless trimmings—wouldn't blueberries look better there? What about that empty spot beneath the willow? Elderberries, perhaps? How did your garden come through the drought? Did you use enough mulch to prevent damage? Did you apply it early enough? Was your problem too much, rather than too little rain? How can you improve drainage?

When you have answered these and other questions peculiar to your own situation, you will know how your garden grows.

You need to know more about what you are doing and why you do it. You should have a working knowledge of the time it takes for seeds to germinate, for plants to achieve fruitful maturity and the soil temperatures that the various seeds and plants require. This will enable you to get your gardening program started indoors on a practical schedule, moving your plants outdoors as weather conditions and the various plants' own needs permit. A program, thus maintained, will permit successive crops and a double harvest that should fill your shelves all summer and your freezer the next winter.

Every spring gardeners get a chance to start again. If you are not happy with the past year's experience, follow these steps to a new beginning.

CHAPTER 1

The Garden Game Plan

No matter how sure most of us are that we will remember all the details of our garden, the passage of time usually blurs them into a confusing jumble. The only way you can be certain to know what was planted where is to keep a garden planning and record notebook.

Soil preparation is simply a notation as to what was physically done to the soil. What types of organic fertilizers were used? What kinds of cover crops were planted? Keep track of the number of seeds and plants you used each season. Note the weather conditions in your area at different times of the year. The garden record notebook is also an excellent place to log rainfall amounts for the various months. The most easily handled notebook is a large, thick spiral one with an index. Though there are many tools for the backyard gardener, a garden notebook is an invaluable addition.

Space and Place

Before drawing your garden plan, decide how much garden you want to handle. A small garden no more than 20 × 40 feet will provide plenty of space for a variety of crops and ample opportunity for learning about gardening. In successive seasons you can expand the garden as time and resources permit.

The traditional place for vegetable gardening is in a large rectangular plot near the back property line. This style has evolved for practical reasons. A rectangular shape is easily

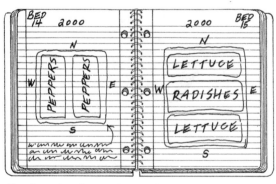

Garden planning and record notebook

fenced, cultivated, and irrigated. Moreover, woods can flourish, frosted tomato vines can sag on their stakes, and the corn stalks can turn brown, all out of public view. However, "out of sight" too often means "out of mind," and the backyard garden does not always get the timely attention it needs and deserves.

Another logical and popular place for the vegetable garden is right outside the kitchen door. This makes the garden more noticeable and invariably encourages the cook to use more vegetables and herbs.

To reconcile these two extremes, I recommend that every yard have at least some beds of salad greens and herbs near the house. But, because this little kitchen garden will be in plain view, make it beautiful with flowers, fences, and attractive bed designs. Mix vegetables and herbs with flowers in an informal way. Plenty of flowers will keep declining vegetable plants from being so obvious. Plant edibles such as rhubarb and artichokes against a foundation wall. Make a bed of red and green lettuce. Grace your patio with peppers.

Sun, Drainage, and Wind

Choose a garden spot that receives as much direct sun as you can manage, at least 6 hours of sunlight a day. Fruiting vegetables such as tomatoes, squash, peppers, eggplant, and cucumbers must have at least 7 hours. However, vegetables grown for their leafy greens or roots—such as lettuce, spinach, and carrots—will produce adequately with less sun.

If possible, your garden should be close to a water supply and located away from low or soggy areas that create poor drainage. Try, too, to keep it close to your greenhouse, compost bin, and tool shed. Slope it gently toward the east or south, as a south-facing slope warms

faster in the spring and cools slower in the fall than a flat or north-facing slope. If your garden is on a slope, run beds or rows parallel to it, rather than straight up and down the hill. The crosswise pattern will lessen runoff of soil and water during irrigation and rains.

Bare soils that are low in organic matter make prime candidates for wind erosion. During a strong gale, there is nothing to hold the soil together. With organic growing, our number one concern is the soil. In addition to erosion, an early spring wind can also cause problems with young seedlings because of the windchill factor. Take the precaution to harden off your seedlings so that they don't go directly from the greenhouse or windowsill into the garden. This way they can adapt to the outdoor soil temperature. And make sure to amend your soil with organic matter and to properly mulch (see chapter 4, "Additions and Corrections").

Maximizing Methods

In order to maximize food production in a limited amount of space, try one of the planting methods described below. Proper timing, as always, is crucial in the successful application of any of these methods. Factors such as length of growing period, above-ground growing patterns, below-ground rooting patterns, and light and nutrient needs are vitally important to know when planning an intensive garden (one that produces high yields).

Interplanting

The practice of growing two or more plants in the same bed space is called interplanting or intercropping. By choosing plants that mature at different times, the net yield of

SPECIAL CONSIDERATIONS

Mistakes can be avoided and time and energy saved if a paper plan is well-thought-out. Take into account the following factors before beginning your design:

1. Perennial crops, such as asparagus, strawberries, and rhubarb, should all be located at one side of the garden.
2. Tall-growing crops, like corn, must be kept away from small crops like beets and cucumbers to avoid excessive shading.
3. Early-planted, fast-growing, and quick-maturing crops—including radishes, spinach, lettuce, and scallions—should also be grouped together.
4. Avoid overplanting new varieties or any one vegetable at the same time. We encourage gardeners to experiment and try new varieties, but it's important not to go overboard because part of the experiment is to see how well the new varieties adapt to your type of soil and weather conditions. Also, a well-planned garden is one that uses succession planting. For example, it might be easier to plant all your green beans in one day, but you will pay dearly for that convenience at harvest time when all of your beans will be ready at the same time. In succession planting, you plant 2 rows of green beans to start and another 2 rows 3 weeks later. By doing this, you will have a steady supply of green beans throughout the summer and fall.
5. Pollination of your fruits and vegetables is encouraged by bees in your garden. They will come more readily if you provide them with sweet basil, borage, catnip, lemon balm, mint, and thyme.
6. Plants, like people, are helped by companions. Discover which plants are "companions" and plant them together (see "Grower's Glossary").
7. A living mulch blankets the soil, protecting it from the sun and moisture loss. Its dense canopy of leaves also shades the soil from sunlight-germinating dormant weed seeds.
8. Crop rotation is important as a preventive method for insect and disease control and as a way to keep the soil healthy. By growing the same plants year after year in the same soil, an increase in soilborne insect activity and a serious deficiency of nutrients will occur.
9. The foundation of maximum food production in a limited amount of space is based on precision soil management, or "P.S.M."

both crops is increased and disease and insect infestation is greatly reduced.

Corn and pole beans are two vegetables that are commonly interplanted. Plant the corn first, and when the stalks reach 5 inches high, plant pole beans at the base of each corn plant. The beans will intertwine around the corn as they grow. You can also add bush-variety squash to the mix to act as a living mulch that will conserve moisture and eliminate weed problems.

Corn and pole beans, interplanted

Succession Planting

Succession planting refers to the procedure of making several sowings of the same crop 1 or 2 weeks apart, or harvesting one crop and following it with another in the same space in a single season. Succession planting is a common space-saving method and can be easily implemented.

In conventional succession planting, you merely plant a second crop where you have just harvested a first, as in following early peas with lettuce. This is an excellent practice and it should be followed in any garden.

You can carry the idea to further advantage, however, by planting some crops before their predecessors have been harvested. Peas, for example, may be started along a fence when the soil is still too cold for beans. A few weeks later, a parallel row of pole beans may be planted with the seeds staggered to lie opposite the gaps between the growing peas. Both crops will then climb over the fence area. The peas should be picked when the

bean vines are not damp, as dampness makes them more susceptible to fungal diseases. The beans will begin yielding shortly after the pea harvest, for a longer period.

Besides following peas with beans in this way, you may plant a row of sweet corn plants along each side of any row of early bush peas or snap beans. With the corn plants spaced 2 feet apart in the rows, you will have easy access to the other crops.

Another method of succession planting is to sow different cultivars of the same plant with different maturing times together in the same rows.

Vertical-Growing: Vines and Trellises

An option most people forget about when planning a garden is planting upward, making use of vertical space instead of taking up valuable ground.

A good vertical gardener looks at a 5- × 20-foot fence and sees 100 square feet of gardening space. Any plants that vine on the ground can be trained or tied to a vertical growing area. Vining varieties of peas, beans, cucumbers, melons, squash, and tomatoes not only yield more than the bush versions, but when grown on a trellis actually take up less garden space.

Vining varieties are indeterminate in size, meaning that the plants continue to grow at their apexes, or tips, as long as the weather permits. They outlast, as well as outproduce, the bush varieties giving fruit for 4 weeks or more. Cucumbers yield for months and pole beans keep on until frost.

Growing vertically lets you plant less ground than you would need for bush varieties. It can turn unlikely nooks into garden spots. A few feet of ground along the foundation of the house or garage is enough for a crop of beans. Instead of fighting weeds along your fence, why not put in a mulched bed and a trellis?

When growing vertically, remember, too, that the principles of crop succession may apply. Any given section of fence or trellis can support more than one crop each season. Tall peas may be started first. Being a cool-weather crop, peas are finished in time for another crop like cucumbers or beans to use the trellis. Pole limas and pole string beans can go in a little later and a few inches farther from the fence.

Traditional gardeners make a tepee of four poles and sow 3 to 4 seeds at the base of each pole. This system leaves abundant space for harvesting and weeding, but it wastes growing space. Instead, sow a double row of bean seeds under a trellis at 2-inch spacings. Plant pole beans 4 to 6 inches apart. Tomato plants can be set a full foot away with cucumbers, melons, pumpkins, and squashes planted between them.

If you want to grow tomatoes, get a dozen strong plants and set them within a foot of your fence trellis in a sunny spot. Dig deep holes for the plants and leave only the tips exposed above the paper collars that you wrap around them to prevent cutworms. Apply compost, bone meal and some 4–6–4 organic fertilizer liberally over the surface.

As the plants take hold and start to grow, mulch them with hay or straw. When they begin to sprawl, prune main branches off, leaving the best two or three. Tie these to the fence with strips of cloth, being careful to take a turn loosely around each stem with the tie made at the fence end. This gives you a sling for each branch, which, like a surgical sling for a tender arm, will support it without risk of injury.

After that, all you have to do is make similar slings for the higher growth and you will have a nice crop of tomatoes.

Though it is a good idea to keep tall crops at the north end of the garden so the shorter plants get sun, you can also erect a trellis at the south end and plant crops underneath that will appreciate some shade. Lettuce, for example, planted along a fence shaded with a leaning (slanted at an angle) trellis lasts longer into the warm weather without wilting or bolting (producing seed prematurely).

Some vining plants are weak climbers. Cantaloupes, muskmelons, and watermelons all need help climbing. Even on welded-wire you have to tie up the vines. Stick to varieties with fruit less than 5 pounds or so. It is hard to keep a 20-pound watermelon airborne. Space the seed 12 to 18 inches apart to give the fruits room to grow.

In addition, muskmelons require cradles for extra support. These can be made out of cheesecloth or a similar material, spread under the fruit, and secured to the trellis. Otherwise, as melons ripen and stems begin to loosen, the fruit will fall to the ground.

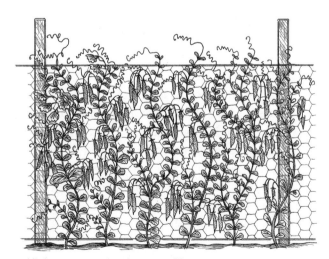

Vining peas trained up a trellis

BUILDING A TRELLIS

The trellis that I like is permanent, cheap, and versatile, constructed of several heavy posts that are strung along the top and bottom with heavy wire. Though the traditional trellis is made of chicken wire, I find it expensive and not tall enough for the big varieties. For crops like peas and beans, tie them to the wire with strings every 4 inches or so. Attach melons and squash—which are weighty crops—to the posts with welded-wire sections, twisted at the ends to seal. The 6-inch wire mesh lasts for years if you store it in the off-season. Plastic netting is strong enough for all but melons and squash and, also, lasts for years with care.

There are advantages to making a permanent trellis. You can sink the posts deeply so they are sturdy enough for any crop. You can give the soil beneath the trellis extra care over the years and be paid back in big yields. And two trellises covered with an arched top create a beautiful bower or garden gate.

Cucumbers easily climb netting without help, as they grow little curly tentacles called talons that wrap around the supports. Instead of planting them in hills, push a dozen seeds into the soil an inch or 2 from the fence or trellis. Space the seeds 6 to 12 inches apart. In a greenhouse, cucumbers can be trained up strings hung from the rafters and attached to the floor. New growth has to be wound a turn or two around the string and tied every week or so.

You will find the fruit of these cucumbers to be more uniform in color than of those that are ground-grown, without the white streaks that frequently spoil its appearance (if not its taste). Like pole beans, cucumbers keep producing as long as you pick them promptly. A daily check will assure that you get the most from your trellis—super yields from a small space.

Another possibility for trellising is Malabar spinach, a twining vine related to spinach that is grown as a hot-weather green.

If you are not yet convinced to build a trellis, consider these further benefits. The shade from trellised plants can be used to cool a porch or patio. Vegetables grown well off the ground are easier to pick, cleaner, and less prone to rot. You are less likely to injure trellised plants as you pull weeds. Try growing up!

Going to Beds

The raised bed method is a rewarding way to produce more food in a limited amount of space. It is not new; the method has been universally accepted for hundreds of years. In China it is still going strong.

Raised beds maximize food production because they utilize the "double-digging" method: A series of trenches are dug into beds in 2-foot sections and soil is replaced with a 50–50 mix of soil and compost (see chapter 2, page 21 for a detailed discussion on this method). Upon completion, each raised bed will rise 1 to 2 feet above the ground, supplying plant roots with good air circulation and drainage. The plants are laid out as a living mulch.

Broccoli in a raised bed

CREATING RAISED BEDS

To create an intensive garden in this way proceed as follows:

1. First, mark the dimensions for each raised bed with stakes and strings. To make sure that you can comfortably reach the center from any side, I recommend making the beds no more than 4 feet wide (they can be any length that you want). Leave about 3 feet between beds for walkways.

2. Using a flat shovel, dig deeply (6 to 8 inches) into the soil. Double-digging is a good way to loosen and amend uncultivated soil, and build up your beds. (See page 21.)

3. If needed, add organic fertilizer and/or compost to the planting surface and work it into the top few inches of soil as you smooth and level the surface with a steel rake. Try not to step on the bed as you work.

4. Use the back of a hoe to tamp and firm the sides and end of each raised bed so that it will keep its shape. Wait a few days before planting; this way the weeds will germinate and you can kill them easily by raking the soil. This is called pre-emergent cultivation; there will be fewer weeds to deal with later and less competition for the seeds.

5. Set seeds in multiple closely spaced rows across the width of the bed. Cross-row planting wastes less seed and is easier to thin, weed, cultivate, and harvest than traditional row planting. Plant as you normally would but, because the soil in raised beds is very loose and fertile, you can plant rows closer than seed packets suggest. Use the same spacing for distance between rows as is recommended for plants in the row. Properly spaced, mature plants will completely cover the raised bed with leaf crops just touching.

6. Plants that grow quite large should be spaced equidistantly in diagonal rows: Alternate 2 plants per row, then 3 plants, then 2, and so forth, so all have equal room to mature. Set out transplants when the soil temperature is right for that variety (ask your local nursery or Cooperative Extension). It is best to stake and prune tomatoes to one vine when they are grown this way. Cultivating close-spaced rows is easy; all work can be done from the walkways. There are a number of cultivating tools designed specifically for working between close-spaced rows.

7. Extend the growing season. Grow tunnels are good season-extenders on raised or flat planting beds. Lay black plastic mulch on the soil and cut cross-shaped slits where plants will be put in the ground. A grow tunnel or mini–growing hoop can be created with PVC plastic pipes (usually about 1 to $1^1/_2$ inches in diameter, clamped on either side of the wooden frame of the raised bed. Space the pipes about every 3 feet. Place clear greenhouse plastic over the hoop house and use it as a mini-greenhouse in the summer or spring. The sides and ends of the grow tunnel should be buried under at least 4 inches of soil and weighted down with rocks. Climbing vegetables grow upward, leaving room for crops on either side. Plant crops like spinach and lettuce that

continued

don't mind some shade in the space between the edges of the tunnel and the sides of the bed. During the summer, remove the greenhouse plastic, straighten the pipes so they point upward, and string bird netting to grow cucumbers, Malabar spinach, pole beans, etc. This is known as a trellis for raised beds.

8. Spot-plant succession crops. After harvesting a section of a bed, you can easily replant that section with another crop. Chop and turn under remaining plants right after harvest so they will break down quickly. Add organic fertilizer to feed the new crop and help break down crop residues. Prepare the seed bed deeply before you replant. As you harvest plants that are closely planted on raised beds, you make room for the remaining plants to grow.

A bed enclosed on all four sides by wood, cement, or plastic siding is called a "box garden." Box gardens are similar to traditional raised beds in that they both protrude from the soil. However, traditional beds provide better air circulation and soil drainage for plant roots, and are more efficient than box gardens. Also, moisture tends to accumulate along the sides of the box, creating waterlogged soil. Untreated wood siding (untreated wood *must* be used, as treated wood will leach arsenic into the soil) needs to be replaced every 2 years because of rotting. Cedar lasts longer, but is quite expensive.

If you wish to build a garden in a small space and your only available site is near a tree with large roots, a box garden is a good solution. Construct a box on the site in a suitable size over the tree roots, using siding between 12 to 18 inches high, and mound the soil up in the box so that it rises slightly over the siding. Most plant roots only grow between 1 to $1^1/_2$ feet deep, and in the boxed garden they will not be stymied by the tree's thick roots.

Whatever design or methods you choose, remember to keep notes in your garden journal or observation notebook.

CHAPTER 2

Tending the Soil

Before starting to plant, you will probably have to improve your soil's fertility, especially if it is a first-season garden. Of course, the first harvest will give you some indication of soil quality, but conducting a soil test is a more precise way to learn about the makeup of your soil.

Soil Analysis

Just as a doctor performs an X-ray or blood test to accurately diagnose a patient's condition, the organic farmer or gardener uses soil analysis to correctly determine the health of the soil. A healthy, balanced soil will produce hardy crops that are free of insects and disease. There are two basic procedures for testing soil available to the home gardener.

Soil Test Kit

The first and simplest method is the soil test kit. The kit, which can be purchased at garden stores, provides solutions and guides for determining the approximate content of the three major soil nutrients: N (nitrogen), P (phosphorous), and K (potash); plus a similar means of establishing the pH standing (acid/alkaline level), which is discussed further on page 19. One of the advantages in using a test kit is that it will permit you to make frequent on-the-spot tests of your soil and help you to adapt a fertilizing program to your soil's specific needs.

The test is simply performed by placing a small portion of the soil sample in a test tube and then introducing one or two reagents (a reagent is a chemical that reacts with the substance being tested and measures the soil's nutritive quality by changing color). Color charts are supplied with these kits, and you can check the color of the solution in the tube against the test chart to make various nutritive analyses.

Laboratory Method

The other way to have soil tested is to send a sample to a laboratory. For a composite sample, start at one end of the growing area and, using a soil auger (boring tool), go down about 6 to 8 inches. Remove the plug and put it in a clean container or bucket.

Walk about 12 feet in any direction and repeat this operation. On a field of an acre or more, samples can be taken several rods apart. Continue until an overall sampling has been taken from the plot.

If your growing area is quite large, a composite or mixed sample will provide more information than a spot sample. Once you have covered the area to be tested, mix the samples thoroughly in the bucket and remove one pint of soil. Label the soil sample, indicating where and when it was taken, the type of crop grown in it last season, and the type of crop to be planted this year.

Soil samples can be taken at any time of the year that weather conditions permit. Damp or wet soil will give false test readings, so make sure your soil is free of frost and fairly dry before sampling.

You can also send soil samples to us at Agri-Balance (see resource section on page 321 for contact information). We have developed a soil-testing procedure that allows us to design feeding programs based on nutritional deficiencies in the soil. See the next page for a look at our soil test.

Organic Amendments

Some soil test kits and most laboratory reports make recommendations for improving weak or deficient nutrient levels shown in the test. Growers who want their soil enriched in an environmentally safe way must translate any general or chemical recommendations into a program of natural fertilizers and organic materials that will both deliver long-lasting benefits and improve the soil's composition. Before discussing how to develop and implement an organic amendment program based on your test results, we will look at exactly what organic matter is made of and what it can do for your garden.

Organic matter is literally the lifeline of the soil and exerts the greatest influence on tilth, good drainage, and moisture-holding capacities. Fortunate is the gardener, and a rare individual he is, who has enough organic matter in his soil. The influence of organic matter on the physical and chemical properties of soil—even in small doses—cannot be overemphasized.

Clay and Sandy Soil

Organic matter makes light, sandy soils heavier and dense, clayey soils lighter. In sandy soils there is too much space around the large irregular particles; air is able to enter, but water drains through the soil too rapidly. Add a fine textured organic material to sandy soil, and the particles will lodge in the large spaces between the sand grains. This allows water to be trapped, keeping it within the reach of the roots. In effect, it makes sandy soils heavier.

Clay soils severely limit air space. Adding organic matter to heavy soils lightens them by wedging coarser organic soil particles between the small clay particles. The finer, almost decomposed, components of organic matter are sticky and act as a glue that aggregates or holds the fine clay particles together in small crumbs. This loosens up the clay and allows it to breathe.

Determine your soil type by filling a jar with a handful of soil and shaking. The following day, the soil will have settled into layers: sand on the bottom, silt in the middle,

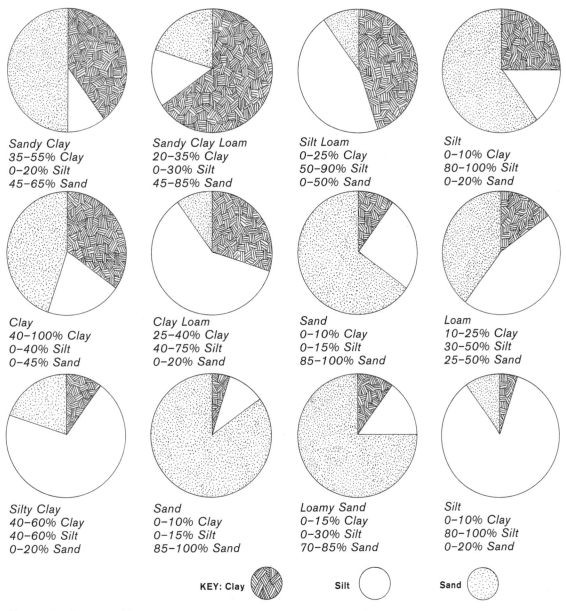

Sandy Clay
35–55% Clay
0–20% Silt
45–65% Sand

Sandy Clay Loam
20–35% Clay
0–30% Silt
45–85% Sand

Silt Loam
0–25% Clay
50–90% Silt
0–50% Sand

Silt
0–10% Clay
80–100% Silt
0–20% Sand

Clay
40–100% Clay
0–40% Silt
0–45% Sand

Clay Loam
25–40% Clay
40–75% Silt
0–20% Sand

Sand
0–10% Clay
0–15% Silt
85–100% Sand

Loam
10–25% Clay
30–50% Silt
25–50% Sand

Silty Clay
40–60% Clay
40–60% Silt
0–20% Sand

Sand
0–10% Clay
0–15% Silt
85–100% Sand

Loamy Sand
0–15% Clay
0–30% Silt
70–85% Sand

Silt
0–10% Clay
80–100% Silt
0–20% Sand

KEY: Clay   Silt   Sand

Types of soil composition

and clay on top. Use the soil diagram on page 14 to compare percentages.

In many areas, soil temperatures are also dependent on the amount of organic matter in the soil. Heavy clay soil retains moisture and admits little air to warm up the soil for seed germination and growth. Organic matter added to clay soil allows more warm air in, thus allowing the soil to respond more quickly to temperature changes. It also promotes drainage and makes it more resistant to puddling. Organic matter plays an important role

SOIL ANALYSIS FOR ORGANIC GROWING

Copyright © 1995 Agri-Balance

GROWER	SIZE OF GARDEN	FT. BY	FT.
SIZE OF FARM	LAWN/TURF	SQ. FT.	
NO. OF ACRES	LANDSCAPE	SQ. FT.	

Parts per million (PPM)
Pounds per acre. Note: An acre of soil 6-8 inches deep weighs 2,000,000 lbs.
1 PPM = 2 POUNDS PER ACRE

SOIL TEST RESULTS   DESIRED LEVELS

			DESIRED LEVELS
ORGANIC MATTER	%		5% Min.
SOIL p/H	ACID	NEUTRAL	ALKALINE

MAJOR NUTRIENTS

NITROGEN /N	PPM	250/1500 PPM
N RELEASE /HUMUS	%	5% PER YEAR
PHOSPHORUS/ P-1	PPM	50 OR MORE PPM
P-RESERVE /P-2	PPM	55 OR MORE PPM
POTASSIUM /K	PPM	150/ 200 PPM
POTASH /P20	PPM	100-200 PPM

SECONDARY NUTRIENTS

CALCIUM /Ca	PPM	750/2000 PPM
MAGNESIUM /Mg	PPM	150/250 PPM
SULFUR /S	PPM	10/ 30 PPM
SODIUM /Na	PPM	1/ 1000 PPM
HYDROGEN /H	MEG/ 100 GRAMS OF SOIL	10

MICRONUTRIENTS

ZINC /Zn	PPM	5/ 8 PPM
MANGANESE /Mn	PPM	25/ 50 PPM
IRON /Fe	PPM	18/ 50 PPM
COPPER /Cu	PPM	1.5/ 2.5 PPM
BORON /B	PPM	1.3/ 2.5 PPM
MOLYBEDENUM /Mo	PPM	2/ 7 PPM

DEFICIENT-D   LOW-L   MARGINAL-M   SUFFICIENT-S   HIGH-H

CATION EXCHANGE CAPACITY   10/ 25 DESIRED
C.E.C. BELOW 10-LOW   BETWEEN 10-15-IDEAL   ABOVE 20-SOIL PROBLEM
C.E.C. = NUTRIENT HOLDING CAPACITY

PERCENT %
BASE SATURATION ACTIVITY

K %_____ Mg %_____ Ca %_____ Na %_____H %_____

NUTRIENT RATIOS

	DESIRED RATIOS	RATIO IMBALANCE
N:S RATIO	1:10	
P-1:P-2 RATIO	2:1	
P:K RATIO	2:1	
K:Ca RATIO	10:1	
K:Mg RATIO	2:1	
K:S RATIO	2:2	
Ca:Mg RATIO RANGE OF 4:1	5:1 TO 7:1	10:1
Mn:Fe RATIO	2:02	

MEASURE OF CONDUCTIVITY

ENERGY RELEASED PER GRAM OF SOIL=ERGS_____DESIRED LEVEL 50-800 ERGS
HIGHER LEVELS ARE REQUIRED FOR TOP PRODUCTION DURING ACTIVE GROWTH PHASES
OXYGEN REDUCTION POTENTIAL=ORP_____
A SOIL rh BELOW 25 INDICATES LOW OXYGEN EQUALS LIMITED BIOLOGICAL ACTIVITY
A SOIL rH OVER 29 INDICATES TOO MUCH OXYGEN, RESULTING IN OXIDATION OF ORGANIC
MATERIAL AND LIMITING NUTRIENT AVAILABILTIY TO CROPS.

OTHER TESTS

CHLORIDES	%	SOLUBLE SALTS	PPM
SOIL TEXTURE		SAND % CLAY % LOAM %
SOIL PARTICLE SIZE		FINE / MEDIUM / LARGE
C/N RATIO_____		DESIRED LEVEL = 12:1
WATER HOLDING CAPACITY		POOR / FAIR / GOOD
COMPOST APPLICATION		20 TONS PER ACRE OR 2 LBS. PER SQ. FT.
FOLIAR SPRAY PROGRAM:		EVERY 3 WKS./ EVERY 5 WKS./4 TIMES A SEASON

MICROORGANISMS
BIOLOGICAL ACTIVITY: GOOD / FAIR / POOR / BAD   LIVING SOIL / DYING SOIL
FORMAZAN TEST FOR SOIL ENZYMES
BELOW 100/ POOR   FAIR   GOOD   ABOVE 1000/EXCELLENT

POLLUTANTS TEST   **HEAVY METALS**

NITRATES/ No3	%	MERCURY/ Hg	PPM
FUNGICIDES	%	CADMIUM/ Cd	PPM
HERBICIDES	%	CHROMIUM/ Cr	PPM
PESTICIDES	%	NICKEL/ Ni	PPM
		ARSENIC/A3	PPM
DETOXIFICATION	YES NO	LEAD/Pb	PPM
		ALUMINUM/ Al	PPM

in fertility as well, serving as food for microorganisms and small animals such as earthworms.

Organic matter eliminates or reduces crusting of the soil surface, a condition which makes it hard for seeds to push through in germination and which forces water to run off rather than permeate into the ground. It fights dusting of the soil by wind action and washing by water action. The addition of organic matter, together with gradual tilling of the subsoil, can deepen the topsoil and convert sterile builder's fill into productive soil.

What's Organic Matter?

The main sources of organic matter are animal manures, composts, mulches, and green manures. These organic fertilizers and soil amendments are available in such profusion that the categories overlap. What you cannot get in one source you can obtain in another.

Below is a list of these sources and their origins.

Recommended Treatments

Organic amendments work miracles in problem soils. They make the soil come alive as a dynamic growing medium. Adding these materials, along with regular soil testing, will almost certainly insure your gardening success. Once you analyze your soil with a test kit, the next step is to treat it according to the test results. The table on page 17 looks at some common soil deficiencies and suggests various corrections. Most of these amendments are slow-release, and should be applied in the fall. All meals, powders, and granulates are broadcast (sprinkled) over the soil as a top-dressing. Based on a soil test, you can determine application rates for your particular soil.

Getting the Right Balance

Soils in many areas contain only 1 percent organic matter; good soil should have at least 5 percent. To increase this percentage it seems logical to simply add some type of organic matter to clay or sandy soils. This, of course, is the remedy, but it is not quite that simple.

VARIOUS TYPES OF ORGANIC MATTER

ANIMAL MANURES
Horse, cow, goat, rabbit, and poultry

ANIMAL TANKAGE
Bone meal, blood meal, fish meal, leather tankage, and hoof meal

COMPOST
Municipal, commercial, and homemade

LIQUID FERTILIZERS
Fish and seaweed extracts

MINERALS
Dolomitic lime, rock phosphate, granite dust, colloidal phosphate, gypsum, and greensand

MULCHES
Leaves, hay, straw, crop residues, and sawdust

VEGETATIVE MANURES
Soybean meal, cottonseed meal, alfalfa meal, and kelp meal

SOLUTIONS FOR NUTRIENT DEFICIENCIES

NITROGEN DEFICIENCY

Nitrogen is one of the most vital elements for a productive soil and must be constantly renewed. If your soil analysis shows a low nitrogen level, start applying one or more of these rich natural sources. Most of these materials are available by mail through Peaceful Valley Farm Supply, P.O. Box 2709, Grass Valley, CA 95945. You can also call them toll-free at 1-888-784-1722.

Blood Meal

One of the richest sources of nitrogen, blood meal contains 15 percent nitrogen. The granulated crystals can be sprinkled directly on the soil or composted.

Composted Manures

Composted manure is one of the best fertilizers; relatively high in nitrogen, it should be included in any organic fertilizing program whenever available.

There are several types of animal manure to choose from, depending on availability. The following are average amounts of nutrients in pounds, per 100 pounds of manure: Cow manure—nitrogen .6, phosphorus .1, and potassium .5; hog manure—nitrogen .6, phosphorus .3, and potassium .5; horse manure—nitrogen .6, phosphorus .2, and potassium .5. Poultry manure is very high in nitrogen, with 1.1 pounds per 100 pounds. Rabbit manure is high in potassium, while sheep manure in high in phosphorus.

Before applying manure, I recommend that it be composted first. The heat of the composting process (165°F) will kill weed seeds and disease pathogens that are present in the raw manure. The composted manure should then be spread and tilled into the soil.

Linseed

Linseed is a ground meal that supplies nutrients. Use as a top dressing.

Cottonseed Meal

Cottonseed meal is especially beneficial for acid-tolerant plants such as potatoes, blueberries, etc. Use as a top dressing.

Soybean Meal

Soybean meal is a vegetarian soil amendment that is high in nitrogen. Use as a top dressing.

PHOSPHOROUS DEFICIENCY

Phosphorous plays a leading role in plant nutrition. It is essential to healthy growth, strong roots, fruit development, and disease resistance. Phosphate deficiency is considered by some agronomists to be the prime factor in limited crop production.

When a soil analysis points to a phosphorous shortage, the best sources are:

Bone Meal

Raw bone meal contains 2 to 4 percent nitrogen and 11 percent phosphorous, while steamed bone meal contains 1 to 2 percent nitrogen and up to 30 percent phosphorous. It can be applied as a side dressing (directly around plant bases) or top dressing (on the soil).

Colloidal Phosphate

This is a natural mineral product, made up of sedimentary deposits of soft phosphate with colloidal clay. It contains from 18 to 25 percent phosphoric acid. Colloidal phosphate builds up calcium and phosphorus in the soil at a faster rate than rock phosphate. Use as a top dressing.

continued

Rock Phosphate

Rock phosphate, ground to a powder, contains about 30 percent phosphoric acid. It is a slow-release nutrient, designed to build up soil calcium and phosphate. Broadcast over planting area as with other amendments.

POTASSIUM/POTASH DEFICIENCY

Potassium is an important mineral that helps plants manufacture carbohydrates. As one of the big three soil nutrients, it is essential in overcoming disease susceptibility and maintaining balanced nitrogen use. Plants lacking sufficient amounts of potash are not as resistant to extremes of heat and cold and they photosynthesize more slowly.

The following substances are good potassium suppliers:

Granite Dust

The potassium in granite dust, a slow-working and long-lasting fertilizer, helps carry carbohydrates through the plant's system to form strong stems and fight disease. Granite dust contains 11 percent potash. Use as a top dressing.

Greensand

Greensand is an under-sea mineral deposit that contains 7 percent potassium and beneficial quantities of many trace minerals, including lime and phosphorous. It has the ability to thin dense, clayey textures, and also to fatten loose, sandy aggregates. Use as a top dressing.

Wood Ash

Wood ash is another high potash source. Broad-leaved wood ashes contain as much at 10 percent potash; coniferous ashes, about 6 percent. Use as a top dressing.

Plant residues, manures, and compost also bring potash to the soil in a free and available form as they decompose.

Organic matter in the soil is made up of a number of elements including carbon and nitrogen. Soil microorganisms digest decomposing organic matter; the carbon is converted into energy, and the nitrogen is broken down into protein building blocks.

What happens to soil when we add organic matter with a high carbon to nitrogen ratio? Let's use the example of wheat straw.

Suppose we amend a clay or sandy soil with wheat straw to reach our minimum goal of 5 percent organic matter. Since the carbon is high, microorganisms feast on all of the carbon available. The microorganism population is stimulated and increases in number. As these organisms use up the carbon for energy, they also need nitrogen to take care of their own growing needs. Herein lies the problem.

If there is not enough nitrogen in the organic material, the microorganisms must borrow nitrogen from the soil supply. This puts them in direct competition with plants, which also need nitrogen. If the nitrogen in the soil cannot support both, then there may be a stunting in plant growth.

Leaves, peat moss, compost, and manure almost always contain enough nitrogen to provide for their own decay, while straw, sawdust, and grain stubble have high carbon to nitrogen ratios. In order to prevent a temporary loss of nitrogen, we must add additional nitrogen or allow at least 6 months of decomposition time before planting.

With sandy soils, cover crops or green manures really help in adding additional organic material. Plant rye or winter peas in the winter or millet in the summer. Turn this under 1 month before planting.

Soil pH Analysis

In addition to N–P–K testing, gardeners should have their soil tested for pH, or potential Hydrogen (the measure of acidity and alkalinity) at least every 3 years. The growth process naturally increases hydrogen levels in the soil, and most types of organic materials—while adding valuable humus and nutrients to the soil—also add hydrogen as a by-product of the decaying process. As hydrogen levels in the soil rise, its ability to absorb additional hydrogen decreases.

When you consider that the pH level affects the availability of nutrients, the efficiency of root cells in the absorption of nutrients and water, the solubility of toxic substances, and even the functions of soil microorganisms, it makes sense to ensure that the pH level is appropriate for the plants in your garden.

The more you know about your soil, the more productive it will be for you. Soil analysis and intelligent treatment as a follow-up can do a lot for your growing season.

Proper pH

Another important soil test is for acid/alkaline (pH) balance. The chemistry involved in determining pH value is simple.

Every element needed for plant functioning has either a negative or a positive charge. During the first part of photosynthesis, light is absorbed by the chlorophyll and divides water into negatively charged oxygen atoms bonded to positively charged hydrogen atoms.

When conditions are right (a healthy and balanced soil), the plant trades the hydrogen

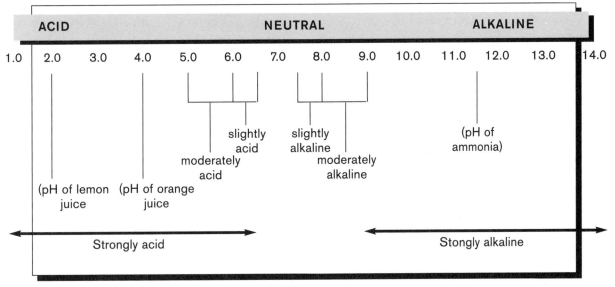

pH Scale

for equal amounts of positively charged elements like calcium and potassium. If the pH level in the plant is too low, the soil becomes over-saturated with hydrogen and is unable to absorb more. Thus, the plant becomes weak and deficiency symptoms manifest themselves. This explains why tomatoes cannot absorb calcium, even when there is adequate calcium in the soil, and blossom end rot occurs. Similarly, beets cannot grow well if they cannot obtain the trace mineral boron, another element with a positive charge.

The pH scale reads from 0 to 14, with 0 indicating extreme acidity and 14 extreme alkalinity. When a sample is neutral (7.0), the soil contains positively charged hydrogen ions at a measurement of 10.7 and negatively charged hydrogen ions at a measurement 10.7. As one factor rises the other diminishes proportionately. At a pH of 7 the plant cannot obtain iron, copper, manganese, and zinc. At the other end of the scale, pH below 5.5, elements like aluminum and manganese can be absorbed at levels high enough to have toxic effects on plants.

Optimum plant growth usually occurs in soil with a pH reading of 6.5. Potatoes prefer a more acid soil, with a pH about 5.0 to 6.0. A few crops, such as strawberries and blueberries, thrive in acid soils.

If pH is not balanced, beneficial bacteria that bring nutrients to the root systems of the plants die, creating a microbial imbalance. Nematode infestation of the root system can occur, as well as root rot and clubroot, which are caused by pathogenic fungi that destroy the roots' ability to absorb nutrients.

Help for a High pH
To correct a high pH add organic material such as compost, which will increase hydrogen in the soil as it decays; and/or add sulfur (the correct amount will be prescribed in your soil test), which reacts with hydroxide ions to produce hydrogen sulfate. This binds hydroxide in the soil.

Lime for a Low pH
An overly acidic or low pH soil can be amended with limestone. Dolomitic limestone is slower acting than high-calcium limestone, lasts longer, and adds calcium (54 percent) and magnesium (44 percent) to the soil. The limestone, applied as a top dressing, lasts 3 to 4 years.

I recommend 10 pounds per hundred square feet to raise soil pH 0.5 to 1.0 points. If your soil contains clay, you need more lime than if you have a sandy soil. The rate of application is determined by soil analysis.

Dig into It
Another way you can learn about your soil is to spend time observing it. The best way to do that is to dig.

Take a close look. Find the earthworms. You cannot really appreciate the contribution of earthworms to the soil until you see their intricate tunnels, located approximately 4 to 5 feet into the subsoil, lined with a fine casing of organic matter.

Digging is drudgery only when you use the wrong tools or try to do too much. Digging exposes the soil so you can see how it works. You can get a clear sense of its texture, its crumb size, how quickly it dries, and what sorts of obstacles lie waiting to thwart your fruits and vegetables.

Before you start digging, the soil must be cleared of weeds and grass. "Solar soilization" is the organic way to prepare soil for digging.

HOW TO DOUBLE-DIG A BED

1. Mark out a bed 3 to 4 feet wide and as long as you want. Across the width of the bed, dig a trench as wide and deep as your shovel blade. Reserve the soil in a wheelbarrow.

2. With a spading fork, break up the subsoil at the bottom of the trench to the full depth of the tines. Mix amendments into the subsoil with the fork, if needed, and leave in place. Step down into the bed to the adjacent strip of ground and dig another trench, throwing the soil into the first trench without inverting the soil layers.

3. Loosen the subsoil with the fork—amend if needed—and move on down the bed, double-digging every few feet. Fill the last trench with the reserved soil from the first trench (in the wheelbarrow).

Take a sheet of 6-millimeter plastic polyethylene and lay it over the area to be dug out 2 weeks prior to the digging. The ultraviolet rays of the sun will be magnified through the plastic, and will kill any weeds, grass, or weed seeds present.

Once the area is weed- and sod-free, it is now ready to be dug, tilled, amended, and made into a fertile bed. There are several methods to choose from, outlined on the following pages.

Double-digging

"Double-digging" is a time-tested, albeit laborious, technique for rejuvenating clayey or seriously compacted soils. If your soil is

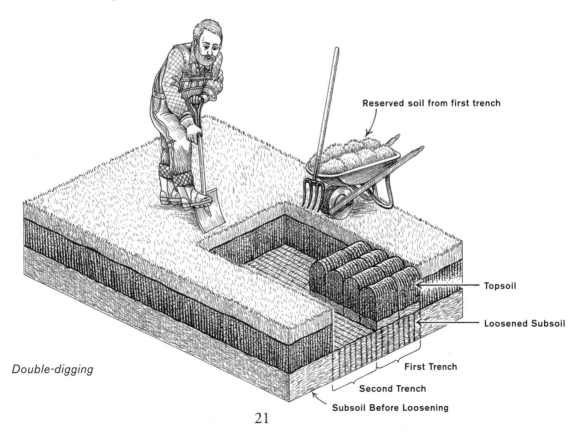

Reserved soil from first trench

Topsoil

Loosened Subsoil

First Trench

Second Trench

Subsoil Before Loosening

Double-digging

21

already workable, you can "single-dig" or till your soil as described in the next section.

When you finish double-digging, your bed will be "automatically" raised. Double-digging works by filling the soil with oxygen; in aerated soil, plants' roots grow through the soil readily and to a greater depth than usual, leading to larger root systems, a greater ability to absorb nutrients and water, and bigger, healthier plants.

After all of your hard work, don't re-compact your newly raised beds by walking on them; remember to walk on the adjacent ground so the soil level will stay permanently raised above the level of your paths.

Whether you double-dig your soil or contemplate its workings from your garden bench, one thing is certain: The soil will keep growing plants. As long as that happens, the soil-lovers among us will find an excuse to keep at least one hand in it.

CHAPTER 3

Turn to Compost

When gardeners speak of soil, they are referring to earth that looks, feels, and smells pleasant: fertile soil with good structure, depending on the extent to which the inorganic soil particles, sand, silt, clay, and humus are bound together. No matter how miserable your soil, it can be transformed into the stuff of which great gardens are made. Composting starts the process. Compost is nature recycled. It is the garden rejuvenating itself in the form of humus, as plants and other organic components decompose through microbial action.

A compost pile is teeming with microbial life as the beneficial bacteria, fungi, and protozoa go to work in this natural cauldron. This process can take place slowly or in a matter of a few weeks, depending on the materials used, their relative sizes and quantities, and how they are mixed together.

Gardener's Gold

Compost is multi-faceted, but not intended to be used as a fertilizer. In its finished form, compost offers a relatively low proportion of nutrients, yet what it does is close to magical. When applied to your garden bed as a mulch, compost reduces evaporation, inhibits weed growth, and insulates the soil from extreme temperature changes—keeping the topsoil cooler in the daytime and warmer at night. Yet compost has humble beginnings. Common, easily accessible materials such as lawn clippings, barnyard manure, and kitchen garbage decaying together in a pile will give your soil the gift of minerals and other components it needs.

Regardless of the particular ingredients, making compost is akin to making bread or beer—similar to yeast, soil-digesting bacteria need warmth, moisture, air, and something to feed on to keep them alive and growing. Almost all of the practical problems associated with making compost stem from an imbalance of these basic factors.

The traditional method, referred to as fast or hot composting, produces a lot of compost in just a few weeks. Heat is the key element

23

here. A well-constructed compost pile can reach temperatures of 160 to 170°F. In addition, a carbon to nitrogen ratio of 30–1 must be maintained, and the pile turned every 2 to 3 days over a span of 2 to 4 weeks.

Timing is crucial. Your pile is fully composted when it fails to heat up, after being turned. Then it is ready to use. Use it with a good feeling for it is your garden's natural fuel.

Remember your objective: The foundation of every successful garden is to achieve healthy soil.

Compost Basics

Anyone today can make a compost pile to add to their soil's nutritional diet. Include carrot tops, potato skins, banana peels, tea bags, coffee grounds, leaves, and grass clippings (pesticide-free, of course). You can also add manure, soil, old hay, straw, and weeds (as long as they are not in the seeding stage). There is a place and use for everything that will rot.

Compost piles are easier to manage if they are small. If you do not have much space for a compost pile, you can build mini-piles in several locations on your property or build one in a large garbage can with holes punched in the bottom. You can also purchase pre-made compost bins, or make them yourself out of plywood and chicken wire.

The top of the pile needs to be slightly concave to catch rainwater. If the rains don't come, water the pile once a week with an inch of water to help it cook.

It is best to layer what you add to the pile. Don't stack 2 feet of grass clippings on top; sandwich them between layers of manure, soil, nonanimal kitchen scraps, and lime.

COMPOSTING INGREDIENTS

Note: Use 30 parts carbon to 1 part nitrogen

HIGH-NITROGEN (GREEN) MATERIAL
Alfalfa meal
Coffee grounds
Cottonseed meal
Grass clippings
Fish meal
Manures
Soybean meal
Vegetable scraps (carrot tops, potato skins, banana peels, etc. Corn cobs are not recommended.)
Tea bags
Weeds (not in seeding stage)

HIGH-CARBON (BROWN) MATERIALS
Ashes
Ground bark (shredded tree bark)
Leaves
Sawdust
Shrub prunings
Spoiled hay
Straw
Twigs
Wood chips

DO NOT USE
Animal bones
Fat
Greasy scraps
Meat or dairy products

This prevents matting in the heap and odor problems.

Never add fat, meat, bones, or any greasy scraps to the pile. They will attract scavengers

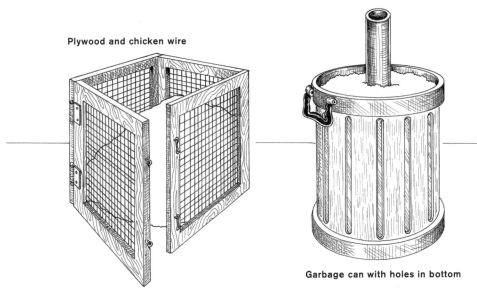

Plywood and chicken wire

Garbage can with holes in bottom

Compost bins for small spaces

and the pile will not break down properly. Do add fish meal, bone meal, or blood meal to get it to heat up.

Every 2 or 3 days take a pitchfork and turn the pile to let air circulate and help speed up the decomposition of the materials. You can also put a steel, hollow pipe in the center of the pile to let air in, or build your pile around a large fence post so that air gets into the pile.

About 2 days after you have built your first compost pile, it will start to heat. The bacteria is digesting the carbon compounds in the vegetable matter and giving off heat energy. This is a good sign! Manure tea, compost tea, or water should be added to the pile frequently.

Compost is a natural, nontoxic, and nonpolluting mulch for the garden. Earthworms love it—they will reward you by aerating your soil and providing nutrient-rich worm droppings. When spread around the base of fruit trees (see "Spread It Around" on page 28),

A SPOT OF TEA

Manure tea and compost tea can be made exactly the same way: First, fill a plastic 55-gallon container with about 41 gallons of water (so it is $^3/_4$ full), preferably rainwater. Next, take a 50-pound burlap bag and pack it with either manure or compost. Tie the top of the bag with a rope and submerge this burlap "tea bag" into the water. For the next 7 days, dunk the bag up and down as you would a tea bag for at least 15 minutes each day. At the end of the week, take the tea bag out of the container, strain the liquid through cheesecloth in order to filter out any foreign material, and pour into your sprayer or watering pail.

compost seems to increase production. It can be sprinkled on lawns and shrub beds, as well.

On my farm, I use compost for drought management and to add mulch and nutrients to the soil around vegetables and fruits.

Tomatoes, peppers, melons, and strawberries all have higher yields if I mulch with compost.

Because the compost pile is symbolic of nature's best effort to build soil and because compost is so efficient and practical in its work in the garden, it has become the heart of organic growing. It is the basic tool for the job to be done by the organic gardener: to give nature a hand and create the finest garden soil that he or she possibly can.

Composting Techniques

Most composting methods rely on the biochemical processes of aerobic or oxygenic bacteria and fungi (there is also a method that relies on anaerobic or non-oxygenic organisms that thrive in decaying organic materials, discussed on page 27). These invisible magicians produce the valuable, dark, fluffy, humus-like compost that smells like the floor of the forest. There are various ways of promoting the action of such beneficial microorganisms. These are discussed below.

In order to thrive, the organisms in the pile must be given ingredients that supply both high-carbon and high-nitrogen materials in various ratios. These include: high-carbon, "brown" substances like hay, leaves, ground bark, and twigs; and high-nitrogen, "green" material like manures, fish meal, soybean or alfalfa meals, and moderate amounts of fresh grass clippings, green weeds, and vegetable garbage (see sidebar on page 24). The final ingredients are water and warmth (aerobic bacteria require air and oxygen as well).

Method One

First, scrape or spade the grass from an area 5 feet wide by 5 feet long or more. A heap any larger would be hard to turn when it is time to fork it over to get air in.

Bacteria come up into the heap from the bare soil. After the heap has cooled, earthworms appear, too.

On the bottom, pile twigs or brush about 8 inches thick. This allows the air to circulate. Add a series of layers as follows:

1. An 8-inch layer of dry, brown, high-carbon material like leaves, straw, spoiled hay, sawdust, or wood chips.
2. A 3-inch layer of manure or other green, high-nitrogen material such as fish meal, alfalfa meal, cottonseed meal, or soybean meal.
3. A 1-inch layer of garden soil.
4. A sprinkling of rock minerals like dolomitic limestone, granite dust, and greensand to provide calcium, phosphate, and potash.

Repeat layers 1 through 4 until you build the pile up to 5 feet high.

The pile needs water, so sprinkle every second or third layer as you build the pile and water the top. A pile that is too dry will soon look white and moldy. A pile that is too wet will get soggy and smelly, so fork it open and give it more air.

You need a regular method for forking, or turning over, your compost pile. The easiest way is to move the entire pile to an adjoining bin or spot, using a large pitchfork. This should be done after the first week. (If you don't want to move the whole pile, make sure you fork it enough so that the warm insides mix sufficiently with the cool outsides—almost like stoking a fire.) Wait at least 3 weeks, fork again, and then repeat a month later. Fork once more a month afterward. This method of composting will provide fluffy, fine compost in 3 to 4 months.

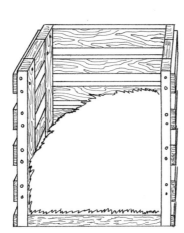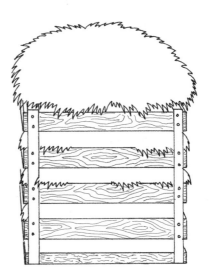

Adjoining compost bins

Method Two

In this second, easier method, you use the same materials, but pile them up slowly year after year in 3 bins. You never turn the piles, and merely add more high-nitrogen materials and soil whenever you see that nothing is happening or that something is amiss. The incorrect carbon to nitrogen ratio can really wreak havoc on your compost pile. Remember: It should be 30 carbon to 1 part nitrogen. An incorrect ratio results in putrefaction—a slimy mess that smells badly and should not be used as a soil conditioner.

The catch is that you have to wait 3 years for the materials to ripen and compost. The hazard is that you may lose many good nutrients from leaching during that period.

Method Three

A third method is very quick, but requires a lot of manpower. You need a shredder to first break the materials down into small bits to accelerate decay. Use the same ratio of 8 parts high-carbon material to 3 parts high-nitrogen material to 1 part soil. Just turn your pile every 3 days or whenever you notice that it is beginning to cool off.

Method Four

A fourth method is the anaerobic process, mentioned above, which is accomplished by microorganisms that do not require oxygen. Here those who do not like to turn piles can relax.

Put all materials inside large, dark, double plastic bags (heavy-duty garbage bags will suffice), tie them tightly, and leave them alone until the materials heat up and are eventually reduced to compost. This will take approximately 6 months, and it is important to include high-nitrogen materials (in the same 30–1 ratio). It is also possible to bury the materials in a soil-covered trench and let them rot underground.

Whichever way you go about it, composting is greatly satisfying. Even if you have no garden of your own and all you are doing is converting garbage and leaves, you know that you have avoided waste and made something of value.

Spread It Around

How should compost be applied?

About 2 to 4 inches of compost should be spread over your garden once a year. There is no danger of burning from overuse, as is the case with chemically concocted fertilizers.

If you are ambitious, you can apply it twice a year. The amount depends on the fertility of your soil (determined by a soil test) and on what and how much has been grown in it. One cubic yard of compost (27 cubic feet) weighs, on average, 1,000 pounds. This figure varies according to the materials used and the length of time composted. However, half-finished (partially decayed) compost should only be applied in the fall after harvest, not during the growing season, so that it has time to decompose.

When applying either half-finished or finished compost, first turn over the soil thoroughly and then mix the compost in with the top 5 inches. If you use a rotary tiller, you can simply spread the compost on the soil surface and go over it a couple of times to work it in.

To quickly improve the structure and fertility of poor soil, give it a thorough compost treatment in the fall. Spade it up to 12 to 18 inches deep and mix in all the half-rotted compost you have. Then leave the surface rough and cloddy so that the freezing and thawing of winter will mellow it or plant a green manure crop that will add more fertility when tilled in the spring.

Putting compost deep down in the soil gives your plants built-in protection against drought—the moisture will be held in the humus so that plant roots can drink it up in dry weather—preventing your crops from starving to death during a drought.

Vegetables and Flowers

Apply compost to your vegetables. Dig it in the fall, bury it in trenches, put it in the furrows when planting and in the holes when transplanting.

After the plants start shooting up, mix compost with equal amounts of soil and use it as a top-dressing, or heavily mulch the shoots with partially rotted compost or raw compost materials as hay, straw, sawdust, grass clippings, and shredded leaves.

Finely screened compost is excellent to spread around all growing flowers as a side-dressing. Compost tea watering is an excellent way to give your plants supplementary feeding during their growing season. Fill a can half-full of compost, add water, and let sit over night. Sprinkle liberally around the plants.

Lawns

Want a lawn that stays green all summer, has no crab grass, and rarely needs watering? Then use compost liberally when making and maintaining it.

Do you long for a thick sod with roots that go down seven inches instead of a thin weed-infested mat laying on a layer of infertile subsoil? In building a new lawn, work in large amounts of compost to a depth of at least 7 inches. The best time to make a new lawn is in the fall, but if you want to get started in the spring, till in your compost and plant Italian ryegrass, which will look quite neat all summer. Till under this green manure crop at the end of the summer and make your permanent lawn when the cool weather comes.

Feed your lawn regularly every spring. An excellent practice is to use a spike tooth motor-powered aerator. Make about 5 holes per square foot, then spread a mixture of fine finished compost and bone meal over the soil. Rake this into the holes made by the aerator. You can use a fairly thick covering of compost, just not thick enough to cover the grass. This will feed your lawn efficiently and keep it growing a dense mass of roots that laughs at droughts.

Trees and Shrubs

When planting trees and shrubs, make a mixture of equal parts compost, topsoil, and peat moss or leaf mold. After making a planting hole at least twice the size of the root ball in all directions, place the root ball in the hole and carefully fill in the mixture around the ball, tamping it down as you put in each spadeful.

Soak the ground well, then spread an inch or 2 of compost on top. A mulch of leaves or straw will keep the soil moist and control weeds.

Established shrubs should be fed yearly by working a half bushel of compost into the soil surface, then mulching with cocoa shells. When hiring up (piling) the soil around your rose bushes for winter protection, mix plenty of compost with it. They'll get a better start next spring.

The ring method is best for feeding trees. Starting in a ring about 2 feet out from the trunk, cultivate the soil shallowly to a foot beyond the drip line of the branches. Rake 1 to 2 inches of compost into the top 2 inches of soil.

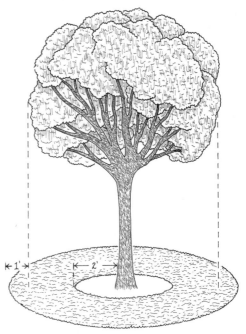

The "ring" tree-feeding method

The ring method is ideal for fruit trees, too. You can work in as much as 4 to 6 inches of compost, then apply a heavy mulch, which will continue to feed the trees. Some organic gardeners merely pile organic materials as deep as 2 feet around their fruit trees, adding more materials and a sprinkling of kelp meal as the covering decomposes.

Composting waste material is perhaps the simplest example there is of people working in harmony with nature to keep their habitat in order and ensure their own survival. The principle involved is simply the first law of good housekeeping: When you're finished using something, put it back where it belongs.

CHAPTER 4

Additions and Corrections

By growing cover crop plants, you can build up the organic matter and nutrients in the soil without the cost of organic soil amendments. Mulching acts as a buffer between the sun and the soil, conserving moisture and eliminating weed problems. Soil organisms feed on the mulch and digest it into rich organic matter. Fertilizing with slow-released organic brands may take longer and cost more, but will save you time and money in the long run because you simply need to maintain conditions, not fix symptoms.

Manure Maneuvers

One of my first choices in natural fertilizers is manure. Spread it in the fall and till it under before the first freeze. Combine it with some vegetable wastes and crops residues, and you'll get sound, healthy growth and big yields in your planting beds.

When I say manure, I mean the real thing—raw or fresh—dug, tilled, or even disked (broken up into the soil using a disc harrow) in the late fall to loosen and lighten the soil before the ground freezes. Raw manure contains such a high proportion of organic matter that this operation is sure to get the nutrients down to where they will feed the roots of next season's crops.

Yes, it's a messy job and hard work. Most years we simply spread on the manure in December, when it's easier to handle, and it helps to pin down the winter mulch of shredded leaves on our garden beds. The mulch absorbs the juices and releases them gradually into the soil, a fine way to avoid leaching, or loss of nutrients.

Late in February, just before the spring thaw, we add a smaller amount of aged manure. The first load is still visible, but greatly broken up by the snow or rain. The second spreading goes to special areas only—where the gross-feeding (gluttonous) crops, such as asparagus, rhubarb, and strawberries, are planted and more gross-feeders (cabbages, corn, tomatoes, and vine crops) will be planted in a few months.

Tilling manure

How much manure is enough? Without measuring exactly, I recommend a covering several inches think plus a second layer for plants like tomatoes. I recommend 2 tons to an acre or, for or a garden, 2 pounds per square foot.

That is quite a lot of manure—enough to maintain soil fertility and humus content by itself. You can use half that amount supplemented with liquid manure, which can be poured around the plant into the soil, and compost. Horse and poultry manure contain more nutrients, while litter and bedding (organic materials such as straw or shredded leaves) should obviously be applied more generously. As it is very hot, poultry manure must age for 6 months before adding to the compost pile. The other manures can be immediately composted.

The cost of manure may be nothing, if you are prepared to do your own hauling. Nearby horse farms will probably supply you with all that you need. If you do have to buy manure, don't consider it an extravagance, but rather an investment in the health of your garden, and therefore, yourself.

If you can't get raw manure, the dried manures (cow, sheep, and horse) sold in garden centers are adequate substitutes, although more expensive. A 50-pound bag of dried manure won't do the work of raw manure. Since it lacks bulk, you will have to mix and dig in vegetable debris. The fall is a good time to do this, or several months before the planting season. As an alternative, you can apply a mulch such as hay, straw, or leaves over the layer of dried manure.

To supplement your manuring program make use of all plant debris either for mulch or compost. This system promotes good growth and produces large yields.

Protective Coverings

A cover crop is vegetation grown to protect and build the soil during an interval when the area would otherwise lie fallow. Cover crops act as mats to hold the soil and mute the impact of failing rain by absorbing nutrients that would otherwise be lost to leaching. Their roots bore into the earth, loosening and aerating the ground and drawing up minerals from the subsoil. As a mulch, they help combat wind erosion, moderate the effects of freezing, maintain soil moisture, and control pernicious weeds and even insect pests.

It is definitely poor practice to leave the soil surface unprotected over the winter. For me, sowing a cover of winter rye provides a positive closure for the gardening year. The planting of new life rather than death by frost becomes my final act.

Winter rye should be sown in the fall. Oats and annual ryegrass are efficient soil covers too. Both need to be sown earlier than winter rye. They can be planted on the heels of midsummer crops and should be sown in the garden as a whole by Labor Day. Legumes such as clover, alfalfa, peas, beans, and vetches are also excellent choices.

Always wait 2 weeks after tilling rye and oats under before you plant legumes—or, for that matter, any vegetables, fruits, or flowers. The reason for this is that it takes 2 weeks for the nitrogen in the soil to break down the green manure (see "Turn to Green Manure" on page 34).

For soil-building, pick buckwheat. With an early start, even northern gardeners can sow and turn under 2, perhaps 3, crops a season, adding several tons of organic matter to an acre of tired land. In addition, buckwheat is a good gatherer of phosphorous and a source of calcium. Buckwheat reestablishes itself so successfully that it can wear out its welcome. It is important to till in the plants before they go to seed.

When a cover crop is turned under, it becomes a green manure.

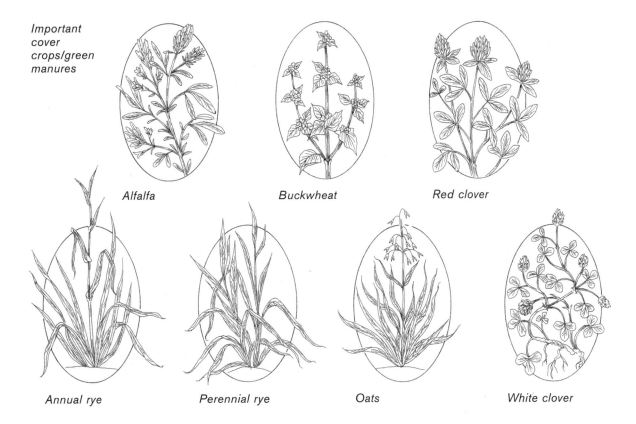

Important cover crops/green manures

Alfalfa　　*Buckwheat*　　*Red clover*

Annual rye　　*Perennial rye*　　*Oats*　　*White clover*

Turn to Green Manure

Come spring, with garden fever running high, I am eager to till in my rye cover.

I start by tilling a few sections to prepare for early plantings (I don't apply the entire green manure crop at once, as the warm weather crops can't be planted yet and I don't want to leave the soil exposed). Next, the rest of the rye is cut with a lawnmower; I give the ground a few days to air, then work the green manure into the topsoil with the tiller. I till the garden once, lengthwise, then till it again from a different direction a few days later.

As soon as the plants are turned under, bacteria begin to consume the organic matter. Microbes of various sizes and shapes devour the sugars, starches, proteins, fats, and cellulose, turning them into simpler molecules and burning up the plants' carbon in the process.

The products of this composting (including carbon dioxide, carbonic acid, and the nutrients absorbed by the microorganisms) provide sustenance to the crops that follow. As the microbes eat, they consume nitrogen from the decaying plants, from the air, and from the surrounding soil. Planting before this microbial action peaks and the bacteria begin to die can leave seedlings short of nitrogen.

The higher the carbon-to-nitrogen ratio of the cover crop, the longer it takes the plant matter to break down. Young or leguminous cover crops are relatively high in nitrogen, so they decompose most quickly.

Rye is problematic. Its ratio of carbon to nitrogen is 3 times higher than sweet clover's. To shorten the waiting period, you can plant before rye crops totally decay and feed the seedbeds a shot of nitrogen. Adding blood meal, composted hen manure, or some other nitrogen source will not only boost the new plants, but it will give the soil bacteria more nitrogen to work with, thus stimulating their productivity.

Microbes are most active in neutral or slightly alkaline soil. A dusting of lime on your soil as you are turning in the cover crop will make the soil life feel more at home.

Green manures do everything for the soil that organic matter does. They transform a plot that is too sandy, compact, or heavy into productive ground. They increase the rate at which water filters into the ground, as leaves and stems catch the rain and the roots open channels for water.

Improved soil structure, which follows green-manuring, also allows better penetration as well as retention of the moisture. Although the soil becomes more permeable, nutrients are not lost by leaching because they are absorbed by the growing crop. Many of the green manures, especially the legumes, are deep-rooted enough to reach into and effectively open the subsoil if it is heavy with poor permeability.

Cover crops and green manures add complexity to gardening, yet their contribution is enhanced with time. The sowing, decaying, and rejuvenation of a cover crop turned green manure should be ongoing, a routine part of gardening—as cyclical as life itself.

Room to Sow

The problem with green manures for most organic gardeners is where and when to sow them. If you garden intensively, there is little growing time in the year when the ground is empty long enough to establish a green manure. Even the most cold-hardy green manures like rye and vetch need to be sown before the tomatoes and peppers are finished.

A good green manure rotation requires a garden 50 to 100 percent bigger than its current size. For example, if your garden measures 20 × 40 feet, the ideal situation would be to have an adjacent green manure plot also measuring 20 × 40 feet. If you did not have enough space to double your garden (and most people do not), the next best solution would be to divide the 20 × 40 feet in half: a growing garden measuring 10 × 20 feet and a green manure plot also measuring 10 × 20 feet.

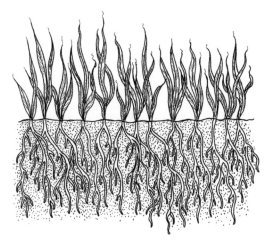

Cover crops protect and hold the soil

Here's how green manure planting might fit into a rotation: After a section with early crops (lettuce, spinach, peas) is finished, instead of planting late crops, plant a warm-season soil improver such as buckwheat or soybeans. Till it down in late summer and plant a winter-hardy cover crop such as oats or winter rye. Turn under the winter cover the following spring in time to plant your vegetables.

If your garden is small and, therefore, intensely cropped, the amount of cover-cropping and green manuring that you can do is limited.

You can grow winter cover after any of the warm weather crops. As soon as frost kills a warm-weather crop, till and smooth the area where the crop had grown and sow winter rye. Rye and winter wheat grow a lush crop of leaves in fall and produce abundant roots. By root mass, they hold the soil, and by leaf area, protect the soil from wind and raindrop impact—major causes of erosion. Rye grass winter-kills, but it still affords soil protection.

Larger gardens can be divided into zones and each year 1 zone can be used entirely for green manuring. Then, such excellent plants as buckwheat and legumes are practical for use as green manure crops.

To follow a cover crop with an early vegetable crop, the grower is faced with the need

to till in the cover crop promptly. This is because the period of temporary nitrogen tie-up engendered by incorporating a large mass of green material into the soil lasts for about 2 weeks, and one should wait 14 days or more to plant or sow an area after tilling in green manure there.

I take precautions to minimize erosion in the beds in which late vegetables remain unharvested, when the deadline for sowing cover crops has passed. After the harvest, I use the tiller to pocket the soil into depressions that trap soil particles that would otherwise be lost to erosion. The ridges that surround the pockets, or little valleys, freeze thoroughly, thus loosening the clay. They also add surface area to enhance the drying of the soil in the spring.

Then I mulch. Winter mulching holds the soil.

Once upon a time, fall plowing or rough tilling was considered to be part of ideal soil management for farm or garden. Winter "freeze and thaw" cycles do wonders for loosening rough soil, particularly clays. The rough surface exposes much soil area to the air and thus, soil dries well for spring tilling and

35

sowing. This method, called "winter fallow," does all that is claimed for it. It also does more in that it leads to loss of valuable topsoil by wind and rain erosion.

That was once upon a time. This is now. Today organic growers use cover crops, green manures, and mulches because we know just how important the soil is.

Many Mulches

To understand the value of mulch, walk through the woods in late autumn.

As the season passes, rain and snow mat the layer of leaves, evergreen needles, and bark that blanket the floor. Slowly, at the soil's surface, the litter is transformed into the quintessential plant food, humus.

Nature has devised an efficient system for recycling its debris. The decaying layer not only feeds trees and shrubs year-round, but also insulates them against summer and winter weather extremes. It anchors soil firmly in place and replenishes ground lost to wind or water. Scoop up a handful of the rich black stuff beneath it, even during a period of drought, and you will find soil more moist and friable than that of any nearby field.

When we mulch our gardens, we practice a bit of nature's alchemy. Along with compost, mulch is the organic gardener's most valued and versatile tool. During drought, 6 inches of absorbent straw ensures the survival of many plants that would surely wither in bare, baked ground. Organic mulches provide food for soil microbes which means that more plant nutrients will be available, especially nitrogen and phosphorous.

When temperatures drop below freezing for at least a part of the year, a heavy winter mulch applied to plants, after they have reached dormancy, prevents heaving during periods of alternate freezing and thawing. Whether it's a thick layer of straw or something else, mulch controls long-term weed growth more efficiently and safely than any herbicide could.

The increasing awareness of the effects of chemicals on food, water, and our soil has generated more interest in mulching. Shredders have become very popular now that people realize that they don't have to throw away leaves, grass clippings, and twigs. To save money and landfill space, some municipalities have also begun recycling tree trimmings and yard wastes.

Even with the availability of more home-grown mulches and municipal mulches, demand for processed and packaged mulch has increased. During the past several decades, an array of synthetic films, fabrics, and mats has surfaced on the market. While the plastics cannot replace organic mulches, which feed the soil as they decompose, they can enhance weed suppression and boost yields, particularly of heat-loving crops such as peppers, tomatoes, and melons.

In addition to allowing a greater degree of control over soil temperature, plastics generally retain more soil moisture. Their convenience is an advantage, especially for small growers who can't easily get hay or straw.

Traditional black plastic mulch will effectively block weed growth by excluding light. Landscapers have used it beneath wood chips to reduce maintenance and lengthen the life of the cover mulch.

The most recent wave of experiments compares the effects of reflected light from various colored plastics on plant growth and yield. For instance, tomatoes grown with red mulch yielded approximately 25 percent more marketable fruit than those grown with black plastic.

In the decades ahead, home and commercial gardeners can expect to find more mulches that bridge the gap between natural and synthetic. Some biodegradable plastics, not yet perfected for use as mulch, incorporate cornstarch or cellulose, digestible by soil microbes.

Most intriguing are the experimental plastics made from soil bacteria rather than petroleum. The all-natural plastics, produced by microorganisms in a fermentation process similar to brewing beer, nearly come full circle; researchers say the waste plastic can be fed back to microorganisms for continuous production.

Still, plastic films and fabrics only supplement the natural mulches readily available to home gardeners. After all, you cannot duplicate Mother Nature.

The Mulch Experiment

Hay mulch is best for potatoes, permitting 50 percent greater yields than those obtained with green plastic. We worked with 'Irish Cobbler' and 'Red Pontiac' potatoes, mulching them with hay and plastics respectively. As noted, the 'Irish Cobbler' came out 50 percent better under hay than the 'Red Pontiac' did under green, black, and clear plastics.

Let's see how one year's weather fitted into the overall planting program. The early spring rains encouraged vigorous, sustained growth for the first 6 to 7 weeks. The plastic-mulched potatoes ran slightly ahead of the hay group, which were somewhat retarded under the hay due to low soil temperatures. Our daily temperature records showed that soil temperature

under the mulch was 10 to 14 degrees cooler than the bare soil most of each day.

As a result, flowering was delayed on the hay-mulched plants one week, although their subsequent growth was sustained longer into the growing season. Then the weather made an about-face and turned dry. All plants were affected, except the hay-mulched spuds.

The plastic mulches did give some protection, but it was hard to keep the strips close to the plant stems. Evaporation of moisture did set in, drying the top 2 to 4 inches of the soil and causing some setbacks.

The plastic strips were 18 inches wide and butted together at the base of the plants. Still the wind and general weathering process created gaps in the coverage.

Since my purpose was to determine the relative value of hay versus the different plastic mulches on early potatoes, we planted ten 100-foot rows of 'Irish Cobblers' with hay mulch and fourteen 50-foot rows of 'Red Pontiac' with three kinds of plastic: clear, black, and green.

Spoiled hay was spread 6 to 8 inches deep over 3 rows of seed potatoes immediately after they were planted on top of the ground, not under it. Three more rows were planted in the soil and allowed to germinate and reach a sprout height of at least 8 inches before they were mulched with hay. These were the potatoes that did the best of all. Three more rows of soil-planted 'Irish Cobblers' were then left unmulched to serve as controls.

Since potatoes appear to prefer cool, moist soils, I applied the plastic mulches—clear, black, and pale green—with great anticipation because the different colors vary greatly in their effect on soil temperature.

Clear plastic lets the light rays pierce through right into the soil with practically no loss in strength. It then holds the heat inside, just like a greenhouse. There is one great drawback, however; it admits so many rays that weeds flourish underneath the plastic as well.

Black plastic soaks up the light energy, converts it to heat and then passes it along to the soil. It does not permit the weeds to grow. Black is a good heat conserver and gives it up slowly at night. That makes for uniform soil temperatures over a 24-hour period.

The pale-green plastic was the next best potato producer over the hay. I found that early potatoes handle heat well and benefit from the ability to keep things moist in the planting rows.

The hay mulch did a fair job of keeping weeds down, while the black and green plastics did very well, as expected. From the sixth week on, the weeds began coming through the hay and wild morning glory became a problem.

In my opinion, there is no doubt that the potatoes planted in soil and mulched with hay gave the best results. The 'Irish Cobblers' were the heaviest yielding, but the 'Red Pontiacs' were larger and more uniform.

The plastic-mulched spuds were larger than the controls, but their yields were not necessarily greater. As stated, green plastic was the most productive and the soil under it was by far the coolest, although it heated at about the same rate as the bare soil.

Mulch On

Mulches are wonderful for any gardener who wants what he didn't work for—a beautiful garden without serious weeds.

Mulching plants keeps soil moisture and temperature more constant; plants thrive when they endure fewer extremes. Mulches also help keep gardens weed-free by suffocating weed seedlings.

For organic gardeners, the question is not whether mulch is needed, but what kind to use and where. Mulches of once living plants are natural. A 3- to 6-inch layer of compost, straw, grass clippings, or shredded leaves between rows and around plants will stop the weeds from flourishing and keep your garden groomed. The mulch holds moisture in and fertilizes, too.

If a few weeds peek through later, they give up easily to a yank or can be smothered with more mulch. When plowed under in the fall, organic mulches change to humus by spring, providing a healthy environment for fresh seeds to settle into.

Heavily mulching the entire garden, cultivated areas, and pathways with organic matter will help keep plant roots cool and cut down on weeds and watering. Replenish as it deteriorates into the soil. Manure can be applied as mulch directly onto globe artichokes, asparagus, cabbage, cole crops, sweet corn, cucumbers, melons, and squashes. However, keep it and other high-nitrogen fertilizers away from beans, beets, carrots, parsnips, peas, sweet and white potatoes, and tomatoes. It would result in too much foliar growth at the expense of food production.

Mulching overwintering plants in the late fall or winter with slow-release and low-nitrogen well-rotted manures allows a constant gentle feeding as rains percolate through it down to plant roots. This provides for strong plants that will grow sturdily with the first spring warmth.

Grass clippings can be used for compost and mulch during any season of the year.

Because they contain so much moisture, they should be allowed to dry for several hours or days, depending on the weather, before being piled more than 2 inches thick.

Grass clippings can be spread thinly over a large area in a pinch. If they are piled thinly, however, great care should be taken not to compress or sprinkle them until they are *thoroughly* dry. Otherwise, they will form an impervious mat that will begin to spoil anaerobically (without air), smell bad, and attract garden pests.

Coffee grounds, oak leaves, and pine needles are excellent mulches for addition to compost around acid-loving plants such as azaleas, blueberries, and rhododendrons.

Shredded newspapers, too, are used for mulch. Colored and slick surfaced pages, however, are best not used, as there is still concern about the lead and other heavy metal content in certain inks still used by some newspapers. Overhead irrigation lessens the need for anchoring the paper.

The wide selection of available mulches enables us to custom-mulch our beds, borders, and landscapes for greatest productivity and beauty without harming our environment.

Mulch Time

Mulching, like pruning, is best done at the proper time to get the best results. Hay, for example, one of the most widely used mulches, becomes available in the summer, which is when it is most often applied. On annual crops, corn, and other vegetables, this is fine because the soil needs to be warmed up so the plants can get a good start and growth can be sustained.

For fruit trees and berries, early mulching is better; quite early, in fact, while the ground is still frozen. Early mulching keeps the soil cool longer and often delays blooming time for several days, enough to prevent serious fruit loss due to late frosts. Apples, pears, and strawberries especially benefit from an early mulch.

I like thick mulches: up to 8 inches of hay and 4 to 5 inches of bark or chips. While this is too thick for strawberries, it makes our fruit trees thrive.

Mulches should extend a little beyond the drip line of the tree's branches to reach the wide-spreading feeder side roots. Always bear in mind that there is as much of the tree below ground, out of sight, as there is tree above.

Mulching offers many advantages for orchards, as compared to clean cultivation (cultivating only with soil, without green manure) or sod culture (grass only). The former practice is laborious, dries the soil, and encourages washing and leaching of nutrients. Orchards in sod need mowing, which becomes difficult as the trees grow. The grass and weeds take a lot of moisture and fertility from the trees during the peak of the growing season. Furthermore, mice often proliferate in sod orchards as opposed to spring-mulched ones.

The advantages of early-spring mulching are many and should not be ignored by the beginning fruit grower or orchardist. Spring mulching promotes more even growth because it provides a uniform source of moisture, reducing the danger of trees growing in spurts after a rain and then very little in dry spells. In addition, mulched soil is loose and crumbly, permitting tender feeder roots to grow easily and rapidly. When water is needed, it soaks down easily with no runoff. Mulch for better fruits and berries.

FERTILIZER + MULCH = BETTER SOIL

Good soil contains at least 5 percent organic matter. Mulching helps the soil retain its good quality and improves it over time. Still the improvement is slow, especially at the lower root depths. Therefore, a good organic fertilizing program is important. Bone meal, kelp meal, fish meal, compost, and other balanced blended organic fertilizers worked into the top layer of soil before the first mulching improves both the soil and growth of trees.

Extra organic fertilizer may subsequently be added each spring before mulching. It need not be worked into the soil, but left for the earthworms to distribute.

Although mulch can be a considerable source of fertility, both growing and producing trees need extra food every year and lots of it to produce and mature several bushels of fruit each. Lime should be added, if necessary. Ground limestone or wood ashes spread on the top of the soil or mulch wash down quite rapidly and need not be worked into the soil.

Seafood: Seaweed Sprays

For centuries, farmers near oceans have used seaweed with very good results. One virtue of seaweed sprays is the incredible range of micronutrients they contain. Because the ocean is like a huge melting pot of the world's atmosphere, it has a tremendous array of trace elements.

Perhaps more important than just the micronutrient content of seaweeds is their unique concentration of growth hormones and plant regulators, including: auxins, gilberellins, cytokinins, and zeatin. These exotically-named compounds control, stimulate, and regulate the growth, rooting, and metabolism of plants and stimulate flower initiation.

Foliar seaweed spraying

When sprayed onto foliage, the nutrients are absorbed by the leaves and passed through a plant's xylem and phloem to be shunted throughout the plant. The cell walls of a leaf are not as solid as we might imagine. Via chelation, a chemical process that makes nutrients more easily absorbed by plants, the absorbed nutrients can pass from leaf to leaf and are translocated throughout the entire plant or tree.

Seaweed sprays are effective tools in certain farming and garden situations, including soil management. They are not, however, a replacement for incorporating organic matter into your soil. You should have a program that keeps your soil healthy and includes organic foliar feeding. All seaweed sprays are prepared by diluting a liquid concentrate or mixing a powder with water. The powdered concentrates can be stored longer, once opened, and they don't contain the chemical stabilizers or preservatives generally found in the liquids.

Liquid concentrates need to be diluted in the range of 1 ounce per gallon of water to as much as 1 teaspoon per $1/_2$ cup of water. Most seaweed extract powders are mixed in the range of $1/_4$ teaspoon to 1 teaspoon of powder for each gallon of water, making them the better buy. The advantage of the liquid concentrates is that they are much easier to mix with water.

Seaweed sprays can provide a measure of frost protection, speed up seed germination, stimulate the uptake of trace elements, increase the matter density in some crops (improving flavor), lengthen produce shelflife, limit or ward off insect and disease damage, and increase yields in some crops.

Foliar sprays are like the shots a doctor gives a patient directly into their circulatory system to quickly control the severe symptoms of a sickness. To cure the patient, the doctor may have to prescribe a more comprehensive treatment over a longer period of time. That treatment for curing the plants is to improve and balance the soil.

Soil nutrition is the key.

CHAPTER 5

Water, Water Everywhere

Managing the water supply is one of the gardener's most important chores.

Understanding how and why plants use tremendous volumes of water and how different soil conditions determine water availability is a crucial part of good garden management. The grower must build soil that holds water, garden to reduce the need to irrigate, and water at the right time and in the right amount.

Rain falls. Some of it evaporates soon after hitting the soil or a leaf. Some runs off into gutters and creeks. Some enters the ground to bind itself to individual grains of soil.

Plants, of course, take up soil moisture, but they retain little of it. At most, only 2 to 3 percent of the water entering a plant is used—at least 97 percent evaporates from the leaf surface into the atmosphere. During their peak growing cycle in midsummer, pumpkin beans absorb and transpire 10 times their weight in water a day.

Water loss on such a grand scale is a necessary part of plant growth. For photosynthesis to occur, pores on leaf surfaces must open wide, thereby exposing water-bearing inner cells to the forces of evaporation.

The sunlight that fuels plant growth claims a tool in water, which steams off the leaves and must be replaced by moisture from the soil. Wind blowing past the leaves also pulls out moisture that must be replaced.

Absorption from the soil, transpiration through the plant, evaporation into the air—the outflow of water must be replenished if growth and life are to go on.

Soil and Water

Good water practices in the garden begin, not with a twist of the faucet, but with the creation and maintenance of loamlike soil that makes moisture already present in the ground available to plants, when they need it. Less watering is necessary if plants can use more of what falls free from the sky.

Although some of you might already have an ideal loamy soil, high in organic matter and water-holding capacity, others may be starting out with sandy or clayey soils. Both of these types can be improved by the addition of decayed organic matter (leaves, grass clippings, rotted plants, and livestock manure) or humus. Chapter 2, "Tending the Soil," discusses organic matter in detail.

Humus loosens the soil and adds air space to tight clay soils, allowing water to drain to lower levels as a reserve instead of running off the top. Likewise, humus increases the moisture-holding capacity of sandy soil by giving the water something to cling to until needed by the plant.

Gardening to increase water availability in clay means devising ways to get the soil to release its water. In spring, till the clay patches extra deeply to aerate them and prevent compaction. Then shape new beds, adding a shovelful of hay or straw and manure for each shovelful of soil. Mounded in beds, the clay stays loose and aerated. Rain soaks in and stays available to plants.

The addition of air to the soil can be as effective as turning on the hose. With its excellent holding capacity, the clay acts like a drip irrigation system without the hoses and valves, storing and releasing water, when the plants call for it.

With sand, the problem is getting the soil to hang onto water long enough for roots to catch it. Till in organic matter every spring to plug the holes between the grains of sand with water-absorbing material. When plants' roots push through the sand in search of moisture, they meet these fluid-rich organic hunks and beguile the water out of them.

After getting organic matter into the soil, the next step is to get it on top of the soil as a mulch. Mulching can reduce water needs by as much as half by smothering weeds that take up and transpire moisture and by reducing evaporation of moisture directly from the soil. Mulches also cool the soil, keeping beneficial soil microorganisms active for root systems.

When the soil is no longer cold and a late spring rain has soaked it, spread a 6- to 8-inch layer of hay or straw over both the clay and sand. Be sure to replenish the mulch periodically.

The family garden is the perfect place to learn the relationship between soil and water. If you are aware of your soil types and treat them accordingly, water will be used to its greatest advantage.

Water Guards

While we all hope to be spared from drought, precautions taken against it make good gardening sense any time.

Water enables an herbaceous plant to stay upright by means of the turgor pressure in the cells from the pull of water between the points of evaporation in the leaves and the intake in the roots. This transpiration slows down when water begins to be in short supply. The plant responds by closing the pores of its leaves, the stomata.

The ill effects of drought are likely to appear soon after noon on a sunny day. Leaves begin to curl and the plant no longer looks perky and healthy.

Cucumbers in sandy soil will temporarily collapse. Lettuce, which has shallow roots, will show sagging leaves, the first sign of wilt. Dew overnight may be enough to restore the plants, but even a condition approaching wilt will seriously reduce crop yields.

Each vegetable has its own critical time, when stress is most damaging. For peas and beans it is when the plants are flowering and forming pods. For broccoli and other brassicas, such as cabbage, kale, and cauliflower, crunch time is when the heads are forming and filling out. For potatoes, it is when the tubers have already formed and tomatoes need extra attention when the blossoms are setting and the little fruits are beginning to enlarge.

Drought-weakened plants will be subject to diseases. While the weather is dry, the chances of an attack of downy mildew or late blight on potatoes is reduced, but, when the humidity goes up, the warm moist conditions are exactly right for the spores to go into action.

Aside from getting organic matter into the soil, shading the plants will cut down water loss. Although most people locate their vegetable garden where it will get a full day's sun, this is not essential. Most vegetables will do well on 6 to 8 hours of sunlight. Lettuce, beans, and parsley, for example, require as few as 3 to 5 hours. These vegetables, at least, can be planted in shadier places to protect against a dry spell. If there is none, the plants will not suffer.

Try depressed or sunken planting beds in drought times. Planting in a slight furrow will allow the plant stems to be slightly below soil level and offer some protection from wind. The furrow will also serve as a trench to accumulate a little more water around the plants.

Another way to slow transpiration is to attach shade fabric onto a light frame to serve as a barrier against wind and heat. Shade fabric is available in varying degrees of density so that you can filter the sunlight to suit your plantings.

Simple measures offer good results. Floating row covers placed over a row of seedlings will conserve moisture and let in light. A basket propped to the windward side of a plant offers some protection as well.

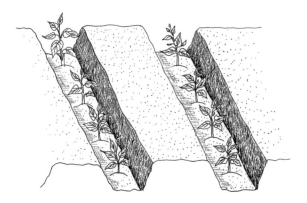

A furrow, or sunken planting bed

Well-nourished plants with strong, extensive root systems will survive drought conditions better than weak plants. Frequent side-dressings of nutrient-rich compost along the rows will supplement the organic materials dug in.

If your soil is high in iron, as indicated by a reddish-yellowish color, there is likely to be a phosphorous deficiency. In addition to increasing the amount of organic matter in the soil, an application of rock phosphate is advisable.

If the soil is acid, add limestone, preferably dolomitic lime, which will supply the extra magnesium needed for chlorophyll in the plant. Bone meal is also useful to guard plants against stress.

And don't forget that micronutrient foliage spray.

These are some of the practices that will help the gardener protect plants in the summertime, when the living is easy and the weather is dry.

Drought Outsmart

If there were a drought this summer, how would your garden grow? With the erratic weather that has been occurring, the possibility of drought should be a particularly meaningful consideration to the home gardener.

Start early in planning your garden. Consider devoting more of it to the early crops that you can enjoy before the threat of an acute drought develops. Perhaps this is the year to enlarge your asparagus bed or rhubarb section, or double the space for the pea vines or other early-maturing crops of your choice. Being practical, perhaps this is also the year to discard varieties from your list which have caused the greatest trouble and disappointment.

Take advantage of the earliest possible planting dates. Be vigilant in protecting the tender plants, if late frosts threaten. Choose varieties of seeds that have been bred especially for early planting. You can reap other rewards from early planting like avoiding certain plant insects. Early-planted squash is usually large enough to withstand an attack of the borers that come later in the season to kill weak, young plants.

If you plant radishes and cabbages as early as possible, you can avoid the peak infestation of maggots. Your early crop of peas may mature before attack by root rot or mosaic.

If the oncoming summer produces a drought, seize it as a golden opportunity to do some of the things that you have always wanted to do, but never accomplished. For one thing, you might try sprouting grains, seeds, and beans indoors. You can be sure of gathering a daily crop of crisp, fresh vegetables effortlessly, regardless of the weather.

If you are a suburbanite, this may be the time to remind yourself to reset your lawn mower to cut the grass no shorter than 3 inches high. This will minimize the browning and help the grass develop a sturdier root system.

Plan to let your lawn clippings remain where they fall. They will form a good mulch,

MINIATURE VEGETABLES AND FRUITS

In choosing seeds, consider at least some that mature quickly. These include the miniatures, several of which are very popular.

'Tom Thumb' lettuce takes only 40 days to mature whereas heads of many other varieties require nearly twice that long. The heads are compact and can be planted close together in the home garden or in window boxes. A mini-head can be served whole as an individual portion.

What would be most suitable as a companion to it in the salad bowl? 'Tiny Tim', a miniature red tomato that matures at approximately the same time. It, too, can be grown in a small amount of space, in window boxes, or even in pots, so that watering should not be a problem.

If miniatures appeal to you, consider 'Golden Midget Sweet Corn', with ears a mere 4 inches in length. Since each plant produces few ears, if you have a real love for corn, make certain that you grow enough of it to satisfy your appetite.

There are midget cucumbers, dwarf head cabbage, and diminutive muskmelons and watermelons, all maturing in far less time that their average-sized counterparts. With early maturation of these midgets, you may harvest a good share of your crop before the drought—if it occurs—becomes severe.

keep the lawn greener, and add organic matter to the soil.

If this summer produces drought, count your blessings. Some insects, as well as fungi and several plant diseases, thrive in moisture, not dryness.

INTERPLANT TO CONSERVE WATER

The interplanting of 2 crops may be beneficial in time of drought. It represents an economy of space and hence irrigation as well. I found a good drought-relief combination by planting soybeans with bush beans, the large-leafed soybeans offering shade to the latter. I also discovered that a well-mulched crop of cucumbers planted among young spruce trees seemed to thrive despite dry, hot weather. So did tomatoes close to low-branched magnolias, peppers between azaleas and onions, and beans and corn among other young ornamentals. The partial shade from the ornamentals helped the vegetables by minimizing sunscald and cracked fruit in the tomatoes, giving cucumbers attractive dark-green skins and preventing the drying out of melon leaves and vines.

If the drought fails to materialize, rejoice. Nothing is lost by planning ahead. Instead, it may provide you with some new ideas.

Watering Ways and Means

Now we know the why of watering; let's find out the when and how.

For those who want to be precise, many gauges are sold that measure soil moisture. We low-tech types use a simple device, a hole in the ground. Dig down about a foot into your garden bed and examine the soil. The top layers will be dry as expected, but, if a marble-sized hunk of soil from the bottom of the hole does not retain its shape when rolled into a ball, the ground is too dry for crops and watering is necessary.

Dig another hole in the ground, about a foot away from the plant and a little over a foot deep, to find out how much to water. Fill the hole with water, and the rate at which it drains will tell you how often you need to water. Ideally, it should take about two minutes to drain. However, if drainage is either too fast or too slow due to too much clay or sand in the soil, the remedy is the same. Dig a small area around the plant and replace the soil with compost. The root zone of most vegetables extends several feet below the surface, although most roots grow in the top foot of soil, so it is important to know the quality of that soil and correct as necessary.

To water plants adequately, the entire top foot of soil should be saturated. Shallow watering, even on a daily basis, can harm plants because it forces them to compete for space and nutrients in the upper few inches of soil and deters them from spreading downward to a potentially larger reservoir. It is better not to water at all than to water briefly and occasionally. Since plants take in virtually all of the water that they need via their roots, spraying the leaves does little more than wash the dust off. As photosynthesis during the day makes the greatest demand on roots, the soil around them should be full of water before the sun is up.

Pre-dawn watering in slow-draining soil and early morning watering in faster draining soil will keep more water available when roots need it than evening irrigation. It may take several hours for newly applied water to become available to roots, so midday watering

VEGETABLE-WATERING GUIDELINES

For watering purposes, garden vegetables can be divided into three groups:

1. The first group prefers continuous water. Lettuce, spinach, and other greens, as well as cabbage, cauliflower, celery, melons, squash, cucumbers, and onions yield best with daily morning watering.

   By midsummer the prime greens-growing season is past, but lettuce still in the ground will enjoy the cooler soil temperatures prompted by regular watering.

   Celery is one of the most water-sensitive vegetables and perhaps the only one to require almost daily watering. Drip irrigation will produce large, non-bitter stalks that withstand disease and insect attack (see the next section, "Drip Drop").

   Onions are on the frequent watering list because of taste. The bulbs have extensive roots and are able to sustain themselves through dry spells quite well, but heavily-watered onions are sweeter.

2. The second category performs well without water except at critical times of flowering and fruiting. Once tomato, bean, and pea seedlings are established, they need not be watered at all until flowering. Withholding water from them encourages the development of deep root systems, giving them access to the nutrients that lie at deeper levels in the soil.

   Sweet corn is probably the most drought-tolerant of vegetables, but it must be watered well at tasselling time. That is when to hope for a nice cloudburst or to leave the hose in the corn patch to soak the soil. Pollination, ear formation, and filling will all be improved.

3. The third type can make a good harvest with no water except rain in all but the most extraordinarily dry years.

   Root crops like carrots, beets, turnips, rutabagas, kohlrabi, parsnips, and radishes will produce nicely in years of normal rainfall without any watering at all. They put out long roots to tap deep water reserves, photosynthesize rather slowly, and lose little moisture to the wind.

   Brussels sprouts and broccoli have long growing seasons and simply wait out dry spells. Water deprivation encourages budding in most vegetables, and with these two, budding is a most desired trait.

often comes too late to help plants through the period of most demand.

Water with care. Work in sync with your crops' water needs. Take the little extra time to assess your soil's moisture. It is all part of the process of good water management in the garden.

Drip Drop

Whether your garden grows tomatoes and squash or zinnias and marigolds, whether it lays in intensive beds or long straight rows, drip irrigation can make your gardening life easier.

The object of watering is to bring the moisture level of the root zone up to a satisfactory level. Too much water can cut off necessary oxygen and wash fertilizers out of reach of the plant. Too little water can stunt growth, create a sickly plant, and, of course, cause death.

Overhead sprinklers may keep your soil moist, but frequent overhead watering tends to encourage rust, mildew, blossom damage, and many other diseases. Closely-spaced drippers can balance plant requirements by thoroughly watering the soil without wetting the leaves or blooms.

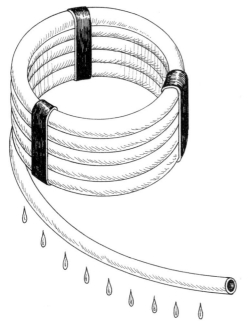

Drip irrigation hose

A $1/2$-gallon-per-hour dripper will take care of an area of about 16 inches in diameter. In coarser soil, a dripper which distills up to 1-gallon-per-hour can be used.

An entire area can be set up on one system by placing higher output drippers near plants that require more water. These should be situated about 2 inches from plant bases. All you have to do is make sure that the total output does not overload your water source. As the average hose can handle about 150 gallons of water pressure, this shouldn't be a problem.

For vegetable gardens, a good method is to set up lateral lines running the full length of the row, with drippers spaced every 12 to 20 inches, depending upon the needs of the plants. With flowers, the same spacing will work, but because flowers are so versatile, the arrangement of the bed will dictate the design of your system.

Small spray attachments or mini-sprinklers are useful in mixed landscape areas. They provide the benefits of low-volume watering, while giving a misting effect to the plants.

Drip irrigation is widely used among commercial growers, especially in orchards. The slow deep water and exact control offered by drippers encourages more productive, disease-free trees.

The changing watering needs of trees can also be easily accommodated. Saplings can start with one dripper at the base of each tree and additional drippers can be installed as the trees grow. When designing the system, plan ahead. Allow enough water for the trees when they are mature.

Fruit trees require a lot of maintenance. Installing a drip system in a home orchard gives you the flexibility to water and fertilize at the same time. By not using a sprinkler to water, you can cut down on weed and fungal growth, erosion, and over-saturation.

For container gardening from hanging baskets to oak barrels, drip irrigation is perfect. Because of their size and the porous nature of potting soils, containers need frequent watering. With a drip irrigation system all that you have to do is turn on the water for a desired period of time and enjoy effortless maintenance of beautiful plants. To make it even more comfortable, a drip system can be easily automated with a timer.

Ground covers, shrubs, planted beds, rockscapes, or any other landscape planting can be easily watered and cared for by drip irrigation with desired results. Although there are always variables, it is possible to work with them to come up with ideal conditions for your garden.

Give drip irrigation a try. You might like it.

PART 2

Growing Seasons: The Edible Organic Garden

*T*here is nothing more satisfying than enjoying the fruits of your labor. That is why organic gardening is rewarding in more ways than one. First, you can experience the satisfaction of seeing your work create life. Second, you can also enjoy eating your own produce, knowing it's grown without chemicals, pesticides, or herbicides.

We will take you through the basics of seeding, all the way to vegetable, fruit, and herb varieties and how to grow them. Once you've got the basics of planting down, you need only adjust soil nutrients according to the needs of the particular vegetable you want to grow. So, get ready to invest your time, with a rich repayment of results you can enjoy all year.

CHAPTER 6

Seed, Seeding, Seedling

There is no more mystical promise than the promise inherent in a seed. It touches something so deep within us that we can be warmed by the mere thought of it as we peruse seed catalogs in the heart of winter.

We pore over the pictures and descriptions in January to rekindle our chilled spirits with the promise of renewed life. In the spring, when we finally sow our seeds, we are awed once again. What are these seeds that hold such power? Exactly what happens between the time we sow them and the first magical show of green? How can such tiny, curled specks of life boldly shoulder aside crusted clods of soil in their eager reach for the sun?

Seed Power

A seed is the part of a flowering plant that contains an embryo, with food for that embryo and a protective covering. It is basically a ripened ovule, the result of fertilization between the plant's male and female gametes (reproductive cells).

The embryo eventually develops into a plant. As long as this embryo remains alive in the seed, the seed is said to be "viable." We take advantage of this rich, concentrated food supply when we eat beans, peas, and corn. Therein we get the carbohydrates, fats, and proteins originally meant for the developing plant.

Surrounding the embryo is the seed coat, which helps to protect the seed from physical damage and drying out. It also prevents the seed from germinating until environmental conditions are right. The most important factor for germination is the presence of sufficient moisture. Absorption of water by the seed is what triggers all of the other steps in germination. It is this essential need for water that is at the crux of all we do when we sow our seeds.

Since soil moisture increases with depth, we plant seeds as deeply as possible for their size (an approximate formula for sowing depth is to multiply the diameter of the seed by 2). Still they must not be so deep that they run out of food before reaching the surface.

Since large seeds have greater food supplies, they can be planted more deeply than small seeds, which must make do with a shallower planting. Since water is absorbed from the soil by the embryo's radicle (a rudimentary root), many seeds germinate faster if you soak them before planting to soften their coats and give the radicles a head start. As water absorption is hampered by cold, we plant seeds only when the soil is warm. If you plant too early, the seeds can rot in the ground before temperatures allow for water absorption.

As it absorbs water, the seed swells, rupturing its coat. Water activates the breakdown of the complex starch molecules that can be used by the embryo. Hormones that trigger growth and tissue development are released. The embryo develops a set of leaves called the cotyledon, which are not true leaves, but a nutrient storage apparatus for the growing seed.

The radicle then elongates and grows downward, absorbing water from greater depths. The plant, once a tiny embryo dependent upon cotyledon or endosperm for food, is now an independent entity capable of producing its own food. With the care of an organic gardener and beneficial weather it will develop into a mature and bountiful plant.

This is the botanical explanation for the working of a seed. But no explanation, no matter how technical, can ever really answer the ultimate *how*. There will always be an element of magic in the promise of a seed or the brilliance of the northern lights. There will always be an explanation we can't fully understand, but can feel in the seat of our souls.

How to Start Seed

When you grow your garden from seeds that you start, you can be absolutely sure that it's organic from start to finish. Organic seeds are genetically stronger than those chemically treated.

Seed-starting supplies

Start by ordering organic seed catalogs, which are available to you upon request. Today, you can find dozens of them listed on the Internet. They contain useful information for planning and planting your garden, such as dates of maturity, times to plant, times to transplant, when to harvest, and how far one seed packet will go.

You should also know your hardiness zone and the first and last frost dates for your area (refer to the USDA Hardiness Zone Map on page 317).

Before ordering seeds, decide what foods you and your family want to grow and how much garden you and your property can handle. Check your record notebook from the year before so that you can allow for crop rotation. Introduce a new variety of lettuce or tomatoes to perk up your salad bowl. Make your list. Start in January.

There aren't any big secrets to starting seed. All it takes is a little patience and some attention to detail.

To grow good vegetables from seed, you will need potting soil, containers, adequate light, heat, moisture, and nutrients. Let's examine each factor separately and look at the options that are available to us as gardeners.

Potting Soil

A good potting soil is free of contaminants, capable of absorbing and holding moisture, and not prone to packing and crusting. Starting seeds in ordinary garden soil isn't recommended. It tends to dry out and harden quickly and may contain weed seeds and the fungus that exposes young seedlings to "damping-off" disease.

You can buy prepared potting soil at any garden center. Formulas vary with brands, but most mixtures contain 50 percent vermiculite (an absorbent form of mica that has been puffed up by exposure to heat) and 50 percent peat moss.

If you use large amounts of potting soil and want to use a living soil mix, mixing your own is not difficult. The mix I use is composed of equal parts of peat moss, compost, vermiculite, and perlite.

To get seeds off to a good start before planting, treat them with liquid seaweed. Soak them in diluted liquid at 1 tablespoon per quart of water or powdered extract at 2 teaspoons per quart.

Various types of seed-starting pellets and cubes have become popular with some gardeners, particularly with the novice. The products are made with compressed peat that expands when water is added. You just push a seed into the medium and place the whole thing in a tray or flat. The primary advantages of these products are that they are neat and nearly foolproof: They can go right into the garden, so there is no need to transplant the seedlings from one container to another.

Note that soils high in clay tend to dry up and shrink away from pellets. To prevent this, scoop out a handful of soil and replace it with compost, making a bed to place the pellet in.

Containers

Unless you are using pellets or cubes, you will need a container to hold the soil. Plastic pots come in a variety of shapes and sizes, and are easy to clean and durable enough for several seasons' use. Find the size that is right for you and stick with it. There is also a device on the market called the Speedling™ tray, which is being used by many commercial growers. Made of Styrofoam, the trays have anywhere from 18 to 600 small cavities that look like inverted pyramids with holes in the bottom. The trays are elevated on blocks; as the seedling's taproot grows near the hole, the airflow keeps the seedlings healthy. The pyramid shape also allows the seedling to be easily slipped out of the container at transplanting time.

You can make your own growing containers, but keep in mind that not just any old thing will do. Any kind of container is alright as long as it has adequate drainage holes in it, such as cardboard egg cartons, cut-down milk containers, plastic jugs, Styrofoam cups, clay pots, plastic cell packs, and plastic growing pots or peat pots. Do not use an object that does not have adequate drainage. A popular and practical choice is the soil block.

Soil Blocks

A soil block, composed entirely of potting soil, serves as both container and growing medium for a transplant seedling. The key to this system is the tool for making soil blocks, the soil-block maker or blocker. Basically, it is an ejection mold that forms several rows of self-contained cubes out of a growing medium, separated by air spaces. Both hand and

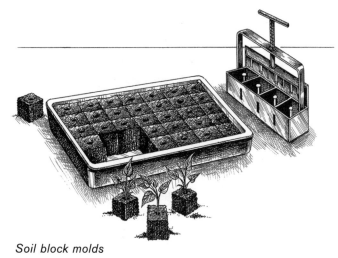

Soil block molds

machine models are available. For garden production, hand-operated models are adequate.

Plant roots, instead of circling as they do upon reaching the wall of a container, fill the block to the edges and wait. The air spaces between the blocks and the slight glazing caused by the blocker action keep the roots from growing out into other blocks. But when transplanted to the garden, the seedling quickly becomes established.

Despite being no more than a cube of growing medium, a soil block is not fragile. When first made, it is bound together by the fibrous nature of the moist ingredients. Once seeded, the block is quickly filled by the young plant's roots, thus ensuring the block's stability even during rough handling. Soil blocks can be made to accommodate any need. The block may have a small depression on the top in which a seed is planted, but blocks can also be made with a deep center hole in which to root your cuttings or transplant seedlings.

When transplants are grown, whether in blocks or pots, their rooting area is limited. Therefore, the soil in which they must grow must be specially formulated to compensate for these restricted conditions.

Because it is easier to lavish care on many seedlings sown indoors in a small space than outdoors over wide areas, starting plants in soil blocks makes good sense. Besides, seed sown in the garden is a gamble; a transplant will almost surely yield a harvest.

Seed Needs

For a healthy end product, you have to care for your seeds from the start. Here are some of the basic elements to consider as your seedlings grow.

MAKING BLOCKING MIX AND SOIL BLOCKS

The composition of blocking mix differs from ordinary potting soil because of the unique requirements of block-making. A blocking mix needs extra fibrous material to withstand being watered down to paste consistency and then formed into blocks. It also needs to be highly absorbent, because the blocks are not enclosed by a non-porous container. The basic ingredients for blocking mixes are peat moss, sand, soil, compost, and organic soil amendments.

Compost is the most important ingredient; the better the compost, the better the plants will grow. The garden soil and compost should be sifted first through a $1/2$-inch mesh screen to remove sticks, stones, and lumps.

Then, add dolomitic lime and a base organic fertilizer consisting of equal measures of fish meal (N), bone meal (P), greensand (K), and kelp meal (trace minerals). The base fertilizer provides the primary plant nutrients nitrogen, phosphorous, potassium, and minerals. The lime raises the pH of the mix. Aim for a pH of 6.5 for all the major transplants.

Add the peat moss and sand, and lastly, water must be added to wet the mix to blocking consistency. The amount of water varies depending on the initial moisture content of the ingredients. On average, to achieve a consistency wet enough for proper block-making, the ratio of water to mix by volume will be about 1 part water to every 3 parts mix. A little over $2^{1}/_{2}$ gallons of water should be added to every cubic foot of mix. Since this slurry will be much wetter than potting mixes for pots or flats, it takes some getting used to.

Spread the wet mix on a hard surface at a depth thicker than the blocks to be made. Fill the block maker by pressing it into the mix with a quick push and a twisting motion to seat the material. Lift the block maker, scrape off any excess mix against the edge of a board and place the blockmaker face down on a tray, plastic sheet, concrete floor, or other surface. Eject the blocks by pressing on the spring-loaded handle and raising the form in a smooth, even motion. After each use, dip the blocker in water to rinse.

Each block is formed with an indentation in the top to receive the seed. Sow 1 seed per block: There is a temptation to use 2, but that is not necessary.

Germination is excellent in soil blocks because of the ease with which ideal moisture and temperature conditions can be maintained. The few seeds that do not germinate are much less of a problem than thinning extra seedlings would be. Of course, if the seed is of questionable vitality, it is worth planting more than 1 seed per block. Obviously, it pays to get good organically grown seed to begin with.

The seed in the indentation on top of the block should not be covered. Studies on seed germination emphasize that oxygen is important for high-percentage seed germination. Even a thin covering of soil or potting mix can lower the germination percentage for most seeds.

The same isn't true for outside planting because another key to germination, moisture, is limited, if the surface of the soil dries out on a sunny day. The third key to high germination, heat, is best provided by using a thermostatically controlled soil-heating pad under the blocks.

Light

Nothing is as important to your seedlings as light. If you have plenty of sunny windowsills to provide them with a good, strong source, there won't be a problem. Otherwise they will grow leggy and spindly as they shoot toward the light.

If there is not enough sunlight in your house, fluorescent lights offer an excellent substitute. With them you can grow your seedlings just about anywhere.

Fluorescent tubes come in lengths ranging from 1 to 8 feet and draw about 10 watts of power for every foot of length. In general, 1 or 2 long tubes are more economical to buy and operate than a bunch of shorter ones.

Place the seedling trays on a table directly under the tubes. The seedlings should be as close to the light as possible, but there should always be at least 1 inch of space between the two. Try hanging the fixture from chains so you can adjust it as the seedlings grow. The intensity of the light falls off at the ends of the fluorescent tubes, so rotate seedlings every few days.

There is some debate as to how long the plants should remain under the lights each day, but 12 to 16 hours seems to be the consensus. It is possible for plants to get too much light, so be sure to allow them a period of darkness every day. If you turn the light on when you get up in the morning and shut it off when you go to bed, your plants will be getting sufficient light.

Heat

Vegetables germinate faster when the soil temperature (not air temperature) is 70 to 80°F. Find a good warm spot in the house for your seedlings. As with lights, heat can be too much of a good thing, so keep a soil thermometer handy to make sure your seedlings are not getting too warm. If it gets above 80°F, you're risking fungal disease.

Soil-heating cables and mats are available in a variety of sizes, and several companies

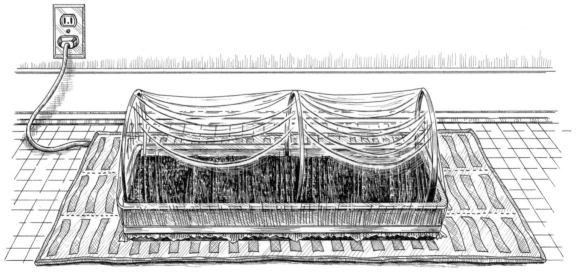

Plastic-covered seed flat placed on heat germination mat

manufacture plastic seeding trays with heating elements built in.

Water and Humidity

Everyone knows that plants need water; the trick is giving them the right amount. Too little and they will wilt. Too much and they won't be able to get oxygen from the soil. Both ways the result is the same—dead plants.

Check your seedlings daily and water them if the soil is dry. Stick your finger knuckle-deep into the soil and wiggle it; a dry soil will feel parched and crusty. A soil containing 30 percent water is ideal. After handling the flats for a while, you will be able to judge if plants need water just by their heft.

Cold water may shock sensitive young plants. Keep a container of water near your seedlings and let it come to room temperature before watering. The chlorine, which can be harmful to the plants, will evaporate as well.

Seedlings can be watered from the top, but the roots don't always get enough moisture that way. Bottom watering usually works better. If you are using flats with drain holes, simply place them in the sink in about an inch of water until the surface begins to get damp. Drain the flats and return them to their growing place.

Plants lose a lot of water through their leaves, so humidity levels can also be important. In the winter, houses can get pretty dry. If your seedlings dry out too quickly, try covering the flats with a plastic bag with air holes punched into it. If you notice a fuzzy green growth on the soil, remove the bag and run a fan near the plants to circulate the air.

If you would like a setup that looks a bit neater, most garden stores carry plastic mini-greenhouses for seedlings. The greenhouses come in lots of sizes and some even have heating cables built in. If you buy this type, you will have to watch temperatures carefully to insure that the combination of artificial and natural heat doesn't build up and cook your plants. If heat and humidity get too high, prop open one side of the clear plastic cover with a clothespin.

Nutrients

If you mix your own living potting soil with compost, there shouldn't be any need to feed the seedlings until transplanting time. However, vermiculite, perlite, peat pellets, and many commercial potting soils are devoid of nutrients. The seeds carry enough food within them to get the plant sprouted, but, after that, you will have to supply some.

When the seedlings develop their first set of true leaves (not the cotyledon, as described on page 54), feed them with fish emulsion or liquid seaweed. The best time to feed them is in the early morning, when the stomata are open.

Transplanting into the Garden

If everything goes right, your seedlings should be ready to go into the garden within 5 to 10 weeks. In preparation for this, many gardeners like to harden-off (gradually acclimatize) their plants by exposing them to limited but steadily increasing periods outside. About a week or 2 before the seedlings are to go into the garden, set them outside in the middle of the day. Gradually lengthen their time outdoors into the cooler parts of the day. Cold-frames can also be used. To work well, they need attention. If possible, place them near the house where they will not be easily forgotten. Be sure to control ventilation and check your frame once a day.

When the weather cooperates and you have a cloudy day without intense sun, it is time to transplant the healthy seedlings started in the soil blocks into your well-prepared ground. Transplanting should be done on a cloudy day or early in the morning or evening, when the sun is not too strong. Handle the seedlings very carefully, removing them from the flats and planting them one at a time.

Transplanting a seedling

Dunk each seedling's soil plug into a mixture of 20 percent fish emulsion and 80 percent seaweed extract to 1 gallon of water. This will prevent transplant shock.

After you place the plants in the soil, press the soil down around the plants; cultivate between the rows every 3 weeks, and foliar spray with the fish and seaweed emulsion once a month.

That's all, folks!

You may face other seed starting problems—cats climbing over potting benches, small children playing in the soil, burnt-out bulbs, lost labels, etc. But, if you are prepared for a few of these snafus, you are well on your way to successful plants.

Carefully sprinkling out seeds into flats and dreaming of ripe tomatoes is a wonderfully satisfying ritual of new life. It's your chance to play Mother Nature weeks before she, herself, steps into the garden for the main show.

Shop Right

If seed starting is not a possibility for you, a trip to the garden center in search of seedlings needs some forewarning.

Because of the huge assortment available, you should concentrate your efforts on choosing healthy plants and specific varieties to best fit your needs. Develop a plan before you go shopping. If you have kept notes on the previous year's planting (and you should have), now is the time to review them. Take measurements of the spots where you want to plant flowers. Note whether these areas are sunny or shady, tend to stay moist or are well drained, and what the existing plants are. Be sure to allow for growth on established plants such as roses, mums, or other perennials.

Select vegetable varieties that fit your timetable as well as your tastes. Most pepper and cabbages are designated as early-, mid-, or late-season varieties, or list the number of days until maturity on their labels.

The maturity time is calculated from the date of transplanting the seedlings into the garden and is an approximate figure that is affected by several growing conditions. Even so, you have a better chance of timing harvests by choosing varieties suited to your summer schedule. You can also extend the season

Seed, Seeding, Seedling

WHAT'S THE PROBLEM?

Seed starting is a simple process. Though a few problems can crop up, it is not hard to avoid or correct them. Here are a few of the most common dilemmas that organic gardeners face when starting seeds, along with their solutions:

Problem	Solution
Seeds were sown 3 weeks ago and there is still no sign of life.	Germination rate of seed deteriorates with age. If you have saved seed packets from previous years, it is well worth your time to do a germination test several weeks before planting. Here's how: Spread 10 to 20 seeds on a moist paper towel. Keep them warm and damp and see what percentage germinates. If fewer than 50 percent germinate within 2 weeks, buy new seeds. Most seeds need to germinate at a temperature considerably higher than their optimal growth temperature. Many vegetable plants will grow happily in a 65°F house, but some require temperatures as high as 90°F for fast germination. Buy a soil thermometer for peace of mind about seed germination temperatures. Seed packets list appropriate germination temperatures.
Seedlings come up fine, but then they flop over and die.	These plants have the dreaded damping-off disease. There are a number of fungi and bacteria that cause damping-off. All damping-off organisms are soilborne. To avoid contamination, don't use garden soil to start your seeds. Make your own seed starter using a mixture of sphagnum peat moss, vermiculite, perlite, bone meal, and compost (see section on "Potting Soil," on page 55). Also, before filling your pots and flats with potting soil, make sure the containers are clean. Damping-off disease may be spread throughout infected containers. To be safe, wash out used containers with a 5 percent bleach solution. To further discourage rot, avoid overwatering and don't let your plants get too crowded.
Seedlings are stunted and the plants are pale with yellowing leaves.	A good feeding will fix this problem. Use a balanced liquid organic fertilizer. Follow the instructions on the package. I use a fish emulsion and seaweed mix with great results. I have also had excellent results with compost tea. Beginning 2 to 3 weeks after germination, fertilize about once a week, watering the plants and the soil with the organic fertilizer of your choice.
Seedlings are tall, spindly, and floppy.	The problem is lack of light. If you are growing your plants in a window, it must be south-facing and unobstructed. Even then, you still have to turn your plants regularly to keep them from getting too lopsided. A good option is fluorescent lights (see "Light" on page 58).

by putting in a few each of early-, mid-, or late-maturing plants, instead of all one type.

The majority of plants offered through retail outlets are healthy—nearly all of them start out that way. The grower is responsible for choosing the best potting media, planting the seeds at the correct time, providing the optimum environment, fertilizing the small seedlings, and protecting them from insects and disease. If you have raised your own starter plants from seed, you know that it can be tough to handle all of these steps properly. The job becomes more complex with each additional variety.

Use your skills of observation to select the best of the group. You can get a feel of what is available by walking through the display area.

If the display appears unorganized and uncared-for, it is quite probable that the plants will be the same. Plants should be tagged for easy identification, grouped by variety, and clearly priced. Anyone who has ended up with a six-pack of jalapeño peppers instead of 'Wonder' bells or 'Pixie' cherry tomatoes instead of beefsteaks can appreciate the necessity of well-marked plants. By mid- to late summer, when this error becomes apparent, it's much too late to start a crop of what you intended to plant.

Examine a few individual plants. Are they wilted, soggy, or perfectly moist? Are the leaves green and sturdy or yellowish and drooping? Are plants bushy and compact or sparse and leggy? A few plants in poor condition can be overlooked, but if there are many it would be safest to shop another store.

Check the potting medium. Is it drawn away from the sides of the container or crusted on top? These could be signs of improper watering and possible root damage, sure to

put the plant under stress. Conversely, constantly wet conditions can be just as damaging, limiting soil oxygen. Either over- or underwatering over a period of several days can turn a healthy starter plant into a candidate for the compost pile.

Avoid weedy plants. The competition already encountered may have weakened the plant's root system, or roots may be damaged when the weeds are pulled. If many of the pots are weedy, be especially cautious when selecting unfamiliar plant varieties. If you are not sure what the plant should look like, you may end up purchasing weeds.

Shopping is more fun when all of the bedding plants are obviously healthy. If you are selecting a preplanted hanging basket or flower box which will be moved intact to a spot near home, go for the fullest, prettiest one you can find.

Look for nicely developed blooming plants in 1- to 5-gallon containers to insert in planter boxes or tubs to give instant color to entryways or to decorate for special events. If you are going to be removing the plants from their present containers to replant in the ground or a different container, it's wise to choose the smaller, more compact specimens over the larger, blooming ones.

Don't be in too great a hurry to get your purchases in the ground. Most have spent the majority of their lives in a nearly ideal greenhouse setting, protected from drying winds and temperature extremes. After a few days on the back patio, they are sufficiently hardened-off to be planted in their outdoor home. These few extra steps in selection and care before planting will pay off in dividends of sight and taste throughout the growing season.

Seed Production Methods

We who garden naturally are convinced of the superiority of organically raised vegetables, but few know how to coax those vegetables to produce high-quality seed.

There are basically four ways of producing seeds. The two most common methods of reproduction, which most of us remember from high school biology, are self-pollination (the seed being set by pollen from the plant's own male flowers) and cross-pollination (seed set by pollen from related, nearby plants). Corn, members of the onion family, and celery are examples of self-pollinators.

Vegetables like spinach and asparagus are cross-pollinators; they are dioecious, meaning that the male and female sex organs are located in separate plants. Naturally, one needs at least a loving couple of these vegetables in order to insure seed pollination.

A less common means of reproduction is performed by plants such as cabbage and kale. These so-called self-incompatible species require pollination from other plants of their own species even though individual plants produce both male and female flowers. A lonely cabbage would never set seed.

Finally, there is a very independent bunch that pollinate themselves. The male and female are contained in one flower, usually unexposed to the outer world of insects and prying eyes.

Beans and peas, for instance, have fat little full-bodied petals characteristic of the do-it-yourself pollinators. Because of their enclosed reproductive systems, hybridizers have to perform a delicate operation on the bloom to transfer pollen from one species to another. Self-pollinators usually do not pose any problems for the home gardener, and will produce seeds as robust as the parent plant.

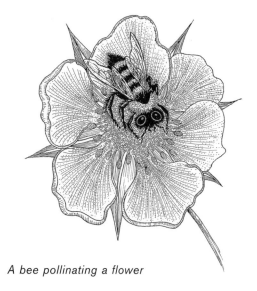

A bee pollinating a flower

Pollen Dissemination

Excluding self-pollinating plants, flying insects such as wasps, bees, and even houseflies, are the greatest assistance to the gardener hoping to produce his own seeds. Wind, water, ants, birds, and bats can all be listed as helpful agents but by far the most important external pollinator is the honeybee.

In terms of attracting pollinators, the organic gardener has a big advantage—his or

---

PLANTS THAT NEED THE
BIRDS AND THE BEES

Just how important insects are to the vegetable gardener who wants to save seeds might be realized by a partial list of plants that require external pollinators. They are:

1. All of the cabbage type crops: Brussels sprouts, cauliflower, broccoli, turnips, and radishes.
2. The melon family: cucumbers, cantaloupes, squashes, watermelons, and pumpkins.
3. The onion crops, including chives and leeks.
4. Root crops like carrots, parsley, and celery.

her land stays clear of pesticides and poisons. Because the organic garden is a zone in which nature can seek its own balance, bees are free to enter and give a hand in seed development.

When I see bumblebees, wild bees, honeybees, and various wasps hovering and zooming around my crops, I feel compensated for the relative safety that I've provided for houseflies, gnats, and even the homely moths that turn into caterpillars and compete with me for my vegetables. Even the housefly that noses around my compost sticks his busybody face into the plant flowers and does a little pollinating.

Room to Reproduce

The chief reason that commercial seed producers have better control than the backyard gardener is that the big operators have more space. Crops in the field must be isolated in order to assure that their seed remains true to type.

Spinach, for example, needs to be isolated by at least 1 mile from other members of the spinach family, such as Swiss chard and beets. Home gardeners should place a paper bag over the top of the seeds' heads to prevent them from cross-pollinating; beets, which will cross with Swiss chard, 1 mile; carrots and onions, $1/4$ mile. Lettuce requires extreme isolation for it will cross with wild varieties.

Try collecting and producing seeds for next year's garden from this year's favorite varieties. It is both satisfying and challenging to join with nature in parenting a plant from seed to harvest.

Save for Tomorrow

Saving seeds from your own garden plants allows you to have your own private seed storehouse right at hand.

One of the most important advantages of seed saving is that it lets you select plants that do well in your particular type of climate. For example, in your garden this summer you may have noticed several bean plants that seemed to have an extra-tough resistance to disease, or perhaps, a tomato plant that flourished even under near drought conditions. Saving seeds from these random standouts lets you choose qualities in a plant that you value for your own growing conditions.

Yet another consideration is that certain varieties of vegetables and fruits, like animals, are endangered or almost extinct. Many good plant varieties have already been lost forever to home gardeners. Some heirloom varieties are being kept alive only by gardeners who save and exchange seeds.

Saving seeds isn't difficult. Keep in mind that vegetables, like flowers, are divided into three categories: annuals, biennials, and perennials.

Annuals, such as peas, beans, melons, corn, etc., flower and set seed within a single growing season. Biennials, such as beets, carrots, chard, kale, etc., flower and make seed the second growing season. Perennials like chives, rhubarb, and asparagus grow for 3 or more seasons. They are propagated from seed, but usually reproduced from cuttings or root division.

Annuals are the easiest plants from which to save seed. Many staple garden crops fall into this category. Remember, however, that one variety can often cross with another variety. A walk through the garden before frost hits or cold weather sets in can help you decide which plants you would like to have back next year. Judge your parent plants based on what is important to you, such as early bearing, large fruits, drought resistance, quick germination, or extra good flavor.

Tag the parent plants to identify them and make sure that they get care for the remainder of the growing season. Keep them well-watered, mulched, and free of insects. Birds and small animals may help themselves, so tag more than one parent plant of each vegetable for diversity's sake and in case the fruit accidentally gets picked and eaten.

The text at the bottom of this page outlines how to save a wide range of seeds:

Elderly gardeners in your neighborhood can often be a rich source of information and saved seeds. Some of them may be planting old-fashioned varieties that do exceptionally well in your area.

HOW TO SAVE SEEDS

LETTUCE, RADISHES, AND SPINACH

If you are a beginner at seed-saving, start with open-pollinated (plants that can reproduce seeds), cool-weather crops such as lettuce, radishes, and spinach. These will bolt, i.e., send up a flower stalk and go to seed, when they are past their prime. Once the petals have fallen from the flowers, cut off the seed heads and hang them upside down to dry for several weeks. You can then shake off the seed into a storage container.

With these crops choose some of the later-bolting stalks for seed saving. That way next year's plants may carry the same slow-bolting qualities.

SNAP BEANS, LIMA BEANS, AND PEAS

Snap beans, lima beans, and peas generally remain pure, if different varieties like pole and bush types have been planted at least 100 feet apart. Allow the pods to dry on the plant after the leaves have turned brown. Hang the entire plant up to dry for several more weeks before shelling and storing.

PEPPERS

Pepper seeds are easy savers. The seeds are mature after the peppers have changed color to their final stage of ripeness. Allow them to turn red.

Cut the peppers open, scrape the seeds onto a plate, eat the pepper and let the seeds dry in a nonhumid, shaded place. Test them occasionally, until they break rather than bend. Sweet peppers and hot peppers can cross, but you'll have fairly pure strains if separate varieties are grown at least 50 feet apart.

TOMATOES

Saving tomato seeds takes a little more time, as tomatoes are self-pollinating. If you avoid hybrid varieties, you will be able to grow the same tomato next year from your saved seeds, even if dissimilar varieties were grown close together.

Harvest nicely ripe tomatoes from several different vines of the same variety. Cut each across the middle and gently squeeze the juice and seeds into a bowl. You will note that each tomato seed is encased in a gelatinous coating that prevents the seed from sprouting inside the tomato. Remove this coating by fermenting it. This mimics the natural rotting of fruit and has the added bonus of killing seedborne tomato diseases. Simply place the seeds in a cup of water for several days, and then strain.

continued

EGGPLANT

To save the seeds of eggplants, wait until the fruits are far past the stage when you would pick them for kitchen purposes. Seeds saved from table-ready eggplants will be immature. Eggplants ready for seed-saving are off-colored and hard. Left on the plant, purple eggplant varieties ripen to a dull-brownish color. Green varieties turn yellowish-green and white becomes golden.

Cut the ripe eggplants in half and pull the flesh away from the seeded areas. If you want to save more than a few seeds, a food processor comes in handy to mash the flesh and expose the seeds. Then air dry.

CUCUMBERS

Let cucumbers mature and become yellow on the vine. Cut the cucumber in half and scrape the seeds out of the pulp into a bowl. Save the fattest seeds. To remove their slimy coating, rub them gently around the inside of a sieve while washing them or soak them in water for 2 days. Dry in a cool spot.

If you stop picking cucumbers, their vines will stop producing fruit, so you may want to pick your seed-savers toward the end of the season.

SUMMER SQUASH

Let summer squash ripen past the tender stage. When you can't dent the squash with a fingernail, it's ready to have its seeds saved. Pick it, cut it open, and scrape the seeds into a bowl. Wash, drain, and dry.

MELONS

Save seeds of melons like cantaloupe and honeydew when you clean the cavity before eating. Spread them on a paper towel to dry for a week or two before storing.

For watermelons, eat the tasty flesh first. Put the seeds in a strainer and add a drop of dishwashing liquid to remove any sugar and saliva left on the seeds. Mix, rinse, and dry.

FLOWERS

Easy annual flowers to save seeds from include morning glories, four-o'clocks, nasturtiums, zinnias, and marigolds.

Once the petals fall, the seed pod often cracks open and exposes the seed. Simply cut the entire flower heads off of the stalks on a dry afternoon in fall. Hang them upside down in a dry place until next spring, or store them in a labeled envelope. For storage containers you can use any type of jar with a tight-fitting lid.

Many of these localized or old-fashioned (heirloom) vegetable varieties were probably planted and enjoyed by your great-grandparents. Some of our own favorites we may, in turn, want to pass along to the next generation of gardeners, our children.

CHAPTER 7

Viable Vegetables

There is nothing more rewarding than seeing the products of your labor in the form of ripe, juicy vegetables. For most people it is the main impetus for getting into natural growing in the first place. The benefits of organic growing are many, though not limited to what is served at the table.

Who doesn't enjoy relating to nature by being involved in an activity that takes place almost entirely outside? The benefits are physical, mental, and spiritual. Fresh air is an immense benefit to circulation, and quiet communion with the earth often clears our minds so we can think. Whatever your "higher power," meditation is much easier in the gentle environment of the great outdoors.

Raising vegetables provides a valuable opportunity for your family to spend quality time together planting and caring for the garden or farm. It can be shared as a hobby, or on a more serious level, as a food supply for the family.

Garden growing reaps rich rewards. I would like to share with you some specifics on the planting and care of various popular vegetables that can make your gardening easier and more fun for all.

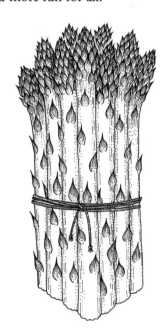

Asparagus

Though its name comes from the Latin for *sprout*, asparagus is not the first edible sprout of spring. Garlic shoots come up long before, and so do stalks of rhubarb.

Still, asparagus is truly an early crop, a perennial that starts 5 to 6 weeks before the first peas. There is not much else in the garden then, and for that reason alone they should be prized.

The only real work connected with asparagus is preparing the soil before the roots go in. The site should be sunny—6 hours of sun a day is best—well-drained, and rich. Soil must be dug deeply and loosened. If you have a heavy clay soil, lighten it with rotted leaves and/or compost.

Very early spring, when roots are dormant, is the usual time for transplanting. Late fall is permissible, too, but it may not be as easy to find roots for sale. Count on 25 roots per person, 40 to 50 if you want to can or freeze them.

The idea of deep-trench planting of asparagus was brought to this country from Europe, where blanched stalks were long esteemed. Most people think green stalks look healthier. It is a matter of personal opinion.

Deep planting takes skill; care must be taken not to smother the crowns with soil before stalks have started to grow. Therefore, the trench must be filled with soil very gradually.

Deep planting permits cultivation in very early spring over the entire surface without damage to the crown and roots. Under cultivation, asparagus is a voracious feeder. It must be to send up shoot after shoot every few days for week after week. Dig in composted manure and add a balanced organic fertilizer (4–6–4). Over winter lay on a mulch of leaves or straw.

There is an alternate method to deep planting and that's my method, which could be called shallow, not surface, planting. Make a furrow, as for peas, about 4 inches deep and spread the roots out sideways with their crowns 2 feet apart. Don't poke the roots downward. Later on they will find their way 5 to 8 feet into the subsoil.

Fill in the furrow with compost, no more than 2 inches over the plants. Firm well. A slight depression will show. This can be filled in after the growth has begun.

Asparagus crowns tend to rise up over the years. If exposed, they might be damaged by severe cold. A mulch, of course, can offset this danger.

The future care of a bed can be summed up in two words—mulch and feed. The first few years stop picking after a few weeks. Never pick thin stalks. Once the bed is vigorous and well-established, you can safely pick for 6 to 10 weeks.

I start picking in quantity on about May 1 and stop on July 4. Crowns will go on sending up shoots, but the vigor of next year's crop depends upon that top growth. Stalks measuring approximately 6 to 8 inches long are a good length for picking. The best-tasting asparagus, though, are the fat, purplish-pink spears about 3 to 5 inches in length.

Break stalks off just above the butt. Since my plants are not deep-planted, I don't need to cut below the surface, possibly injuring other shoots just forming.

When the bed is young, the space between plants can be used for intercropping. Grow things like annual flowers, Alpine strawberries, or parsley. You can also try summer lettuce, or plant a permanent 1-foot hedge of the evergreen herb winter savory.

To get more plants at no cost, you can save your own seeds. Pick the red, ripe berries on female plants. Spread them out in a protected, airy place and let dry. Keep them over winter in a dry place and soak them overnight before planting the next spring.

One of the best features of asparagus is the ease with which it is harvested, cleaned, and prepared. It can be steamed, stir-fried, or eaten raw. Just be careful not to cook the spears too long or they will turn gray and mushy.

Beets (See Swiss Chard)

Bok Choy (See Chinese Cabbage)

Broccoli

Broccoli came to America with the early Italian settlers, and has long been a favorite home-grown vegetable. Today, there are scores of varieties to choose from for planting in your garden.

For the best possible yields, select varieties that mature quickly, have large central heads, and produce many sideshoots. However, there are other variables to consider. Although 'Green Comet' produces few, if any, sideshoots, it has a large central head, matures in 40 days, and performs admirably in the spring. Another of our favorite cultivars is 'Green Duke', a heat-tolerant broccoli.

The sweetest, most tender broccoli is harvested in cool weather. Like all cole crops, broccoli prefers night temperatures of 60 to 70°F, and day temperatures below 80°F. Plant early spring and fall crops for best production. The flavor is truly enhanced after a light frost. We've found fall broccoli to be tastier than

Broccoli

spring broccoli, although we always plant a spring crop if we can get it in early enough.

When buying plants from garden centers, you have no idea how old the seedlings are, what stress they have encountered, or what diseases they may be carrying. If you start your own plants, you control all the variables. You also have a wider selection of varieties to plant.

For spring crops, start plants in a greenhouse around the first week of March. I transplant them about 3 weeks before the last expected frost. Determine the last frost date in your area and then plan when to start your own seedlings in cell packs. Early broccoli is ready to harvest in June.

The trick to producing healthy seedlings is to maintain a temperature of 60 to 65°F and to transplant them at the proper time after hardening off. The best transplants are small, 1-month-old plants. Older plants tend to be stressed and are often doomed to failure. Glossy leaves with a bluish tinge indicate that the plants are past their prime transplanting time. We direct-seed late broccoli near the end of June for harvest in the frosty days of fall.

For the best broccoli production, the most important factor is soil preparation. Broccoli requires a rich, well-drained soil replete with organic matter. We prepare the bed about 3 weeks before setting out transplants, working in as much compost and well-rotted manure as we can. This helps the soil retain moisture without becoming waterlogged.

To complete the soil recipe, we till in wood ashes or greensand, dolomitic limestone, and bone meal. Wood ashes and greensand raise the potash value in the soil; dolomitic lime adds magnesium and calcium, and neutralizes the soil to prevent clubroot (broccoli requires a pH of 6.7 to 7.5). Add 2 pounds of bone meal per 100 square feet of garden bed, and the soil is ready to welcome those transplants.

Broccoli plants, like other cole crops, have shallow root systems, so cultivation is not usually recommended. To keep the weeds down, as well as conserve soil moisture and keep the roots cool, mulch the beds with several inches of straw, leaves, or grass clippings. A sprinkling of wood ashes or scan mask, a biological insect control around the base of each plant, will also repel aphids.

A living mulch can help you use valuable garden space. Plant lettuce, spinach, and other leafy greens around the broccoli plants. The greens will shade the ground, keeping the soil cool and hindering weeds.

The scourge of the broccoli bed is the dreaded cabbage looper. The best way to control the green caterpillar is with BT (*Bacillus thuringiensis*), a natural insecticide that kills leaf-eating caterpillars and larvae. It is nontoxic to humans, animals, and beneficial insects. Infected cabbage loopers stop feeding within an hour after eating the bacteria and die within 24 hours. Spray the broccoli at weekly intervals, preferably in the early morning or evening so that the pests will eat the bacteria before they dry.

Cabbage

Let's give cabbage more respect. There is no more regal a vegetable than a well-grown cabbage, 3 feet across, its giant silvery-green or dusty purple leaves shining with health. Cabbages can take some heat, but they love the cold, which means that we can have a cabbage or two gracing the garden in more months of the year than any vegetable that I can think of. With a little planning before you plant, you can arrange your harvest according to your needs. First, free yourself from the 6-pack syndrome and grow your own transplants. Aside from giving you a much wider range of varieties from which to choose, starting cabbage from seed is easy. No other vegetable seed sprouts so readily in containers or in the ground.

Early cabbage is best started in flats, usually 4 to 6 weeks before transplanting to the garden from the greenhouse. Cabbage germinates over

CABBAGE VARIETIES

There is a lot of variation within the cabbage family. Since all of the cole or brassica (cruciferous) crops can be crossed fairly easily, nearly any combination is possible.

POINTED-HEAD

One variety is known as "pointed-head" cabbage. Pointed-heads were once quite popular; today there is only one cabbage from this group readily available, 'Early Jersey Wakefield', which has been a favorite for more than a hundred years. 'Jersey Wakefield' is still worth planting for its tender, succulent leaves, which make excellent, juicy coleslaw. These cabbages mature in 70 days. Their rapid growth also means they are a good choice for a quick fall crop.

ROUND-HEAD

Another choice is the early "round-head" cabbage, which ripens in 60 to 75 days. Early round-heads tend to be soft and juicy, which makes them excellent for eating fresh, but they will not keep long. Midseason and late round-head cabbages, sometimes called processing cabbages, are drier and are intended for slaw or sauerkraut. Midseason varieties ripen in 75 to 90 days, and late varieties take about 80 days. The best keepers will be hard, dry, and very white inside. They are the latest to ripen, taking 3 months or more to mature.

RED CABBAGE

We also raise red cabbage in our beds. For a late cabbage, this is the best choice.

These are planted in cell packs, plastic containers with several compartments filled with potting soil, used for starting seeds that are going to be transplanted into the garden. When they reach 2 to 3 inches in height, the cabbages are transplanted into rows in the garden. They are transplanted when small because there are few roots to destroy when taking them up (by roots I mean the tiny, tender feeder roots that can't be saved in transplanting).

Transplant preferably when the plants are dry and can take up water and grow, so they will not suffer much shock from the change. I always mud-in the plants by putting water in the holes to settle the soil gently around the roots.

It is better to transplant seedlings just before a rain to avoid having to water again. Once I didn't get all of the plants set before it rained and did some afterward. The difference it made in the growth of the plants was amazing; those planted after the rain were way behind the others.

FLAT HEADS

Finally, there are flat heads. This hamburger bun–shaped type produces tremendous yields of huge heads that store well. While flat heads are quickly disappearing from the American scene, they are the cabbage of choice in China where people serve wedges cut the way that we slice pie.

a wide range of soil temperatures; at 50 to 90°F the seed is up in 16 to 24 days, with seedlings that are strong enough to push gamely through rougher soils than carrots or lettuce can.

Leftover seeds won't go to waste. Cabbage seeds last a long time with no special care. If you put them in a box on top of a file cabinet or in a kitchen drawer, they will keep with good germination rates for about 5 years. Extra seed kept in sealed containers in a cool, dark place will last up to 9 years with little decline in vigor.

Plants grown for transplanting are usually set in a mixture of compost and peat, which is capable of holding a lot of water. It is surprising how little water a plant needs, when growing in the kind of rich humus that should be used to produce strong healthy plants and roots.

Putting the transplants in a cold frame first will harden them, since tender greenhouse-grown plants can't stand frost. All plants may be partially hardened while indoors by controlling the amounts of light and water that they get. The more shade and water the plants get, the more tender they will be. As the plants get larger, keep them on the dry side while giving them as much sunlight as possible so that they don't get leggy.

Remember that cabbage prefers a temperate climate on the cool side and plant accordingly. If the temperature stayed in the 60s and 70sF, cabbages would grow to huge perfection. They can take freezes down to 22°F without damage; but, when the weather is hot, cabbage flavor declines and the heads can split quickly if the soil is wet. Ideally, you want your cabbage crop to mature before daily temperatures move into the 90sF.

Although cabbages are grown as annuals, they behave like biennials in that when exposed to cold below 40°F, they start to go to seed. When figuring days to maturity remember that days when the temperature barely reaches 50°F don't count for much—the

cabbage will sit there in fine condition, but little growing takes place. During cool weather the flavor improves measurably, as sugars build up in the plant.

To get big cabbages, grow them fast. You need the plants to develop leaves quickly to power subsequent growth, so keep the soil evenly moist and fertile from planting day onwards.

Among vegetables, cabbage is one of the heaviest feeders. Apply 4 pounds of 4–6–4 organic fertilizer or fish meal, per 100 square feet. The soil should be high in organic matter and worked loosely and deeply. Cabbages do well in double-dug or well-tilled soil.

If you plan on growing big heads, set the plants about 20 inches apart. If small heads better suit your needs or the capacity of your refrigerator, set them 12 inches apart. Cabbages have many shallow roots, so don't hoe too closely to the plants. It's best to have an organic mulch around them by the time they are half-grown.

As harvest approaches, the heads become very tight and firm when you squeeze them. If for some reason you can't harvest and store them in a refrigerator, you can slow their tendency to split by pushing a shovel blade into the ground next to the stem, severing roughly half the plant's roots so they take up less water.

Carrots

Carrots are grown as annuals and biennials. When a carrot seed first germinates, it's a relative weakling. The tiny taproot and thin cotyledons (seed leaves) are easily defeated by hostile growing conditions. So it pays to make your garden as hospitable as possible for the young plants either by growing carrots in

Carrots

sandy soils, which they prefer, or if that's not possible, by loosening and de-rocking the soil.

For great carrots you should be sure that the soil is about 6.5 pH and that there is a good supply of slow-release nitrogen, phosphorous, and potash (N-P-K). Every year I apply soft rock colloidal phosphate and Sul-Po-Mag (sulfur, potassium, magnesium), as recommended by my soil test (see section on "Soil Analysis" in chapter 2, page 11). Both are slowly activated by soil microorganisms.

Other good sources of phosphorous and potash are bone meal, granite dust, wood ashes, and greensand. Again, base the amount you use on the results of your soil test. When the test indicates a need for lime, you can use wood ashes applied at 2 times the rate you would use for lime.

Despite the conventional wisdom that root crops don't need much nitrogen to grow well, I've always found that when given a good supply of it early on, carrots produce a superior crop. The stronger and more lush the foliage, the greater the chance for a fast-growing root to develop below.

Nitrogen can be obtained from many sources, but I use a commercially blended organic mix with a ratio of 3–6–3 (nitrogen–phosphorous–potassium, the 3 major nutrients) at 5 pounds per 100 square feet. Cottonseed meal, soybean meal, and other organic sources can work well, but the key is that they are all slow-released.

Go easy with the nitrogen once the plants reach 5 to 6 weeks or begin to develop pencil-sized roots. Because carrots need less nitrogen as they mature, it's easy to over-feed established plants. Too much nitrogen can result in hairy roots.

Sowing tiny carrot seeds can be frustrating. To make seeding easier, mix the seeds well with moderately fine sand. For a 20-foot row, mix a small packet with about 2 cups of sand. Then sprinkle the mixture in a shallow furrow (¼ inch deep) and cover with fine compost.

I suggest planting carrots in raised beds 4 feet wide. A 20-foot long bed can produce about 120 rows of carrots, more than enough for fresh eating and storage for a typical family. Carrots can be grown all season, but summer carrots will never have the sweet taste fall carrots do. Often, when the weather becomes hot and dry, even the best-tasting varieties will be bitter and unpalatable. Fall crops get the benefit of shorter days and cooler nights, which encourage carbohydrate and sugar storage in the roots. To get the best fall carrots, plant seeds about 60 days before the average first frost and about 80 days before the first hard frost.

The greatest mistake most gardeners make is planting carrots, then forgetting about them. Carrots don't take kindly to neglect.

When I was a beginning farmer, my farmer friend, Old Zeb, told me that every time a row of carrot seeds dried out, half the seeds would die. My experience has shown me that while the exact percentage varies, the seedlings can't push through crusted soil. A damp, loose soil always produces better stands than a dry, crusted one.

One way to keep carrot seeds healthy is to water, and then cover the soil with a layer of mulch after planting. The mulch will protect the soil from the sun, keeping it damp. Another benefit is that it will keep the night-time soil temperature warmer. Carrots' ideal germination temperature is 80°F, but they will sprout at much lower temperatures (as low as 50°F) if given enough water. After 7 to 10 days, check the soil daily by lifting some of the mulch.

A second method is to water, water, water. Check the seedbed daily to be sure the soil is damp just below the surface. When it dries out, sprinkle it until well-soaked. A water timer set for about 15 minutes provides enough moisture each day to soak a fine sandy loam. Timing, of course, will depend on your soil type.

To keep your carrots through the fall and winter, cut the tops off about $1/2$ inch from the crown and pack the cleaned roots in wooden boxes filled with damp sand. Stored in a cold root cellar (35 to 40°F), they will last well into April.

Cauliflower

Cauliflower is less tolerant to heat than most other brassica crops. If the heads mature in the heat of late spring or early summer, they are apt to be bitter, if they even head at all. The ideal time to plant cauliflower is in late

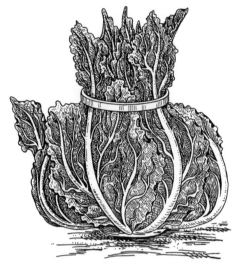

Cauliflower tied for blanching

July or August. Attempting cauliflower in spring is a gamble at best. If you can, set out transplants about a month before your last spring frost. Just remember that spring-planted cauliflower has a higher risk of failure.

To maximize your chance for success, select varieties that are quick maturing and disease-resistant. Cauliflower should be grown fast and harvested early. Besides, the plants require a lot of garden space, so you want them in and out of the garden quickly.

The real key to successful cauliflower lies in proper soil preparation. Cauliflower likes a deeply tilled soil that is rich in organic matter and contains plenty of nitrogen, which is essential for developing tasty, larger heads.

During fall garden cleanup, I plant a winter cover crop of winter rye in the cauliflower bed. In the early spring this is turned under. I also work in manure with enriched compost. A soil rich in organic matter also enhances moisture retention without waterlogging the roots. Another important consideration is soil pH. Cauliflower prefers a near neutral pH (around 6.5 to 6.8) for best production. A neutral soil also prevents club root, a disease that commonly attacks brassica crops. Be sure to have your soil tested to see if limestone is required.

Cauliflowers used for their seed are grown as biennials; if they are cultivated for eating, they are grown as annuals. I always start our own plants from seed about a month before transplanting time. I try to transplant them on a cloudy day.

It's particularly important not to disturb the root system when setting out the transplants. Any change in growth, transplant shock, drought, or high temperatures will cause the plants to bolt, forming a small button instead of a full head.

Each plant we transplant is dunked (soil plug only) in a mixture of liquid seaweed before being placed in the soil. This prevents stress and transplant shock. A successful crop of cauliflower depends on constant pampering.

Proper spacing will increase your yields significantly. I plant cauliflower in wide beds, spacing the seedlings at least 20 inches apart each way. This generous spacing produces larger heads and brings the plants to maturity faster. Crowding means less air circulation and thus a higher risk of disease problems.

If the roots don't have a constant, even supply of moisture there will be a check in heading. Cauliflower should receive 2 inches of water per week and a little more as the temperature rises. Once the plants are established in the garden, I mulch them with 6 inches of straw. An organic mulch not only retains soil moisture, but hinders weeds, keeps the soil temperature cooler, and eventually breaks down to add nutrients to the soil.

If your cauliflower wilts even when the soil is moist, you can bet that insects are attacking the root system. This is usually the dreaded cabbage root maggot. The tiny larvae burrow into the roots just beneath the soil surface, eventually killing the plants. I repel the insects by dusting the mulch with wood ashes before each watering. This also repels aphids and cutworms.

Nothing can ruin a bed of cauliflower faster than the insidious cabbage worm. The easiest way to handle these insects is to spray the plants with BT. Spray your cauliflower once a week at the first sign of the worms, applying BT in the early morning so the worms will eat it before it dries completely.

Conventional varieties of cauliflower require blanching (excluding sunlight from the developing heads) for the whitest, mildest curds. When the heads are slightly smaller than a teacup, I simply pull the larger outer leaves over the tops and bind them with rubber bands or loose twine. I check the heads every day or so to make sure that they don't overdevelop.

Normal blanching takes about a week, but it may take up to 2 weeks in fall's chillier weather. The only problem with this method is that the tied leaves often trap rainwater, which could rot the heads. To prevent this, untie the leaves on rainy days to allow the water to run off.

To avoid the chore of blanching, try some of the self-blanching varieties. Their leaves naturally curl over the head and do the job for you.

Celery

There are many good reasons for growing celery in your garden. Apart from the fact that it's a tasty vegetable, it contains large amounts of potassium and vitamin A, while at the

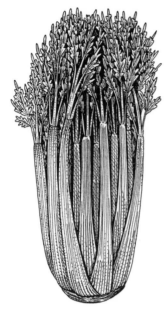

Celery

same time being calorie-free and extremely economical.

Americans love celery, yet few gardeners try to grow it. Maybe they are scared off by celery's reputation for being a difficult vegetable. True, celery isn't the easiest plant to grow, but I think its notoriety is exaggerated.

Celery demands a constant supply of moisture and nutrients, and requires a long growing season, up to 140 days of mostly cool weather. You can start your plants in February under fluorescent lights. It takes about 12 weeks for them to reach transplanting size.

To start the seedlings, I punch several holes in the bottom of 5-inch paper cups, then fill them with a mixture of equal parts of peat moss, vermiculite, compost, and perlite. Peat pots, which may be transplanted, pot and all, can be used instead of paper cups. The potting soil should be thoroughly wetted, seeds sprinkled over the top, and then covered with about $1/8$ inch of vermiculite.

Cups are then set out in foil trays that hold water and placed in a sunny spot.

In 10 days, the first seedlings begin to poke through. After the true leaves appear and they become crowded in their little pots, we transplant them into 4-inch paper pots. The roots are tightly packed and intertwined at this point, so make sure the soil is damp before you begin to work.

Tear away the paper cup and place the mass of roots and soil on its side. Hold the young plants by their leaves (not the roots), and carefully pull them apart. Now you are ready to transplant them into the 4-inch pots. Water pots now, using a mix of water and liquid fish/seaweed. Give them a good soaking, as this helps reduce plant stress transplant shock.

On a cool day in April the plants are taken out of their warm, sunny spot and planted in the garden. Keeping young plants in their paper pots, I simply cut out the bottoms with a sharp knife and set each one, pot and all, into the soil. The soil is packed firmly around and watered thoroughly with fish/seaweed mix.

For growing celery as a fall or early winter crop, count backward from the final frost date in your area and start your seeds 12 weeks before that date. Celery needs lots of water, so you have to create an environment in which the plants will flourish. Dig a trench long enough to accommodate your seedlings, figuring on 2 plants per square foot.

You should plan for 7 plants for each adult in the family. One packet of seeds can produce 400 to 500 plants, so you don't need to spend much on seed.

Because celery is a heavy feeder, enhance the soil in the trenches by filling the bottom third of the trenches with compost. Dig your trenches 12 to 15 inches deep, then pile the compost along the bottom.

Boron is a key element for celery. A deficiency will result in cracked stems. The stalks eventually become brittle, with brownish spots appearing on the leaves. If you find your soil is low in boron, you can add a very skimpy pinch of household borax to a gallon of water. Pour this mix on the soil around the base of each plant. Use no more than 1 gram for each 100 square feet of soil, or toxicity may result.

The entire trench should be deeply covered in straw mulch. Not only does this mulch help keep the celery from becoming too dark, fibrous, and bitter, it also retains moisture so the ground is always cool and damp.

Begin harvesting celery whenever the outer stalks become large enough to bother with. When you want some celery to munch on, or to add to a salad, take a sharp knife and cut just the outer stalks from several plants. These young stalks are especially crisp and nutty. Light frosts will not hurt them.

If you plan to stash a large amount of celery that has been harvested all at once, then dig up complete plants, roots and all. Plant them in boxes of earth so that the crowns are level with the soil's surface. A root cellar is good, if you have one. Water the roots, keep the boxes in darkness, and the plants should keep for 3 to 5 months.

Celtuce

How many times have you been disappointed by a lettuce crop that develops flowering stalks?

When time or conditions are ripe, nature forces lettuce into flower. Bolting, however, need not cause any disappointment when you

Celtuce

are growing celtuce, an annual. The central seed stalk is what makes celtuce most usable.

The name celtuce was given to this member of the lettuce family over 50 years ago. The intent was to convey the two uses of the vegetable: The leaves can be used just like any other lettuce, while the peeled stalk can be used as celery. However, it does not taste like celery and is not botanically related.

The leaves can be picked from the plant before the seed stalk develops. Just break the basal leaves from the central core and use them in salads. The lettuce taste is slightly stronger in celtuce leaves than in the leaves of other lettuces. It is this lack of subtlety that makes celtuce agreeable in hearty salads built around dandelion leaves, beans, asparagus, lamb's-quarters, spinach, radishes, and chunks of cauliflower.

Despite the usefulness of the leaves, celtuce comes into its own when the flower stalk forms. The stalk is the best part of the vegetable. It can be eaten fresh in a salad or cooked in a vegetable dish. It can substitute for such vegetables as asparagus, kohlrabi, broccoli, and bamboo shoots in a number of traditional dishes.

Celtuce favors cool weather, but there is no need to avoid hot weather when growing it. The seed stalk will appear more rapidly in hot weather and will probably be less well developed, but it will have the same usefulness as a stalk grown in cool weather.

As with any vegetable, fertile, moist ground, rich in humus, will cause it to grow rapidly and look and taste better. The stalks will be ready for harvest in about 85 days. Most leaf lettuce is ready in approximately 65 days.

The milky sap that gives lettuce its name (the Latin word for lettuce is *lactua*) is present in celtuce, as well. Since the sap is not very pleasant to the taste, cooks usually strip off the outside layer of the stalk and wash the stripped stalks thoroughly. Such treatment insures that none of the bitterness of the lettuce milk will be in the fresh vegetable. When boiling celtuce, however, this precaution is not necessary, as the bitter substance dissolves in the cooking water.

Stalks of celtuce, when blanched, can be frozen successfully. Overplanting of lettuce usually means wasted effort and wasted food, but since celtuce can be stored in your freezer, extra heads are not a problem.

Look for your celtuce to bolt and catch it for harvest before the flower head forms on top of the stalk—that is when your celtuce will be at its most tender and tasty stage.

Chinese Cabbage and Bok Choy (Pak Choi)

Both Chinese cabbage and bok choy are members of the mustard family, and both are

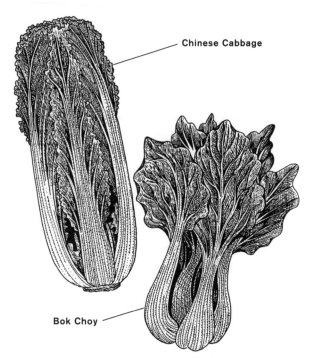

Chinese Cabbage

Bok Choy

Chinese Cabbage and Bok Choy (Pak Choi)

biennials grown as annuals. However, Chinese cabbage—including the popular napa variety—belongs to the Pekinensis group, while its relative bok choy (sometimes called pak choi or Chinese white cabbage), is part of the Chinensis group. Both are common ingredients in Oriental dishes, and add texture and nutrition to stir-fries.

Like its brassica cousins (broccoli, cabbage, kale, and cauliflower), Chinese cabbage and bok choy perform well in cool weather; they can be grown in both spring and fall, but fall crops are more dependable, maturing in the shorter days of the season.

Spring sowings encouraged by temperatures below 50°F coupled with increasing day-lengths tend to bolt (go to seed) before they reach full size. Some varieties are supposed to be bolt-resistant, but in my experience this just means they will bolt a few days later than other varieties when grown in the spring. Fall sowings, on the other hand, produce glorious specimens that wait patiently to be picked.

Both plants mature as early as 42 days from transplanting, so you can be ready for a fall harvest if you start seeds about 2 to 3 months before your first frost date. Rather than trying to germinate the seeds in midsummer's hot soil, I plant my early crops in flats in mid-July and set out the seedlings when the weather seems right. That's usually in early September, during 2 or 3 days of a cool drizzle, if possible.

Midfall weather lingers into November, so there is plenty of time for succession plantings. Home gardeners, who don't usually need a lot of Chinese cabbage all at once, can profit from succession plantings at 10 to 12 day intervals. I usually recommend 3 small plantings.

To protect seedlings from hot temperatures and voracious insects, which can continue through September, set flats in a shady area. For fall planting, choose a garden spot that is partially shaded by taller plants such as corn and will later receive full sun, when the summer crop finishes its stint. Prepare the garden site by digging in partially rotten manure at the rate of about 1 pound (about 1 shovelful) per foot of row. Rich soil keeps these cabbages growing rapidly. It should be well drained so roots will not rot in too much moisture. Soil pH of about 6.5 to 7.0 is ideal for this cole crop. A proper pH helps prevent some diseases such as clubroot.

Set plants into the garden around September 1 or about 6 weeks before the first expected fall frost. After setting plants about 10 inches apart in rows 24 inches apart, settle soil around the roots by watering them with a mix of seaweed and fish solution. This gives them a boost to get them growing.

If rain does not come, lay a soaker hose along the rows and irrigate for about 15 minutes in late morning and late afternoon. This helps keep plants cool and moist while they adjust to their garden home.

I direct-seed (sow directly in the ground instead of in cell packs) my second sowing later in September, after hurricane season gets under way. Chinese cabbage thrives on heavy rain and appreciates frequent soakings when the rains don't come.

Light frost can actually be a boon to Chinese cabbage and bok choy. It increases the sugar content of the leaves, making them very flavorful.

As with lettuces and other staples of the fall vegetable garden, polyester row covers can help extend the harvest by sheltering plants from severe cold and wind (see "Season Extenders," chapter 11, page 168). Row covers also provide excellent protection against flea beetles, one of the most troublesome insects for cabbage growers.

When shopping for "non-heading" Chinese white cabbage (bok choy), don't get confused by the multitude of spellings you may see: Pak choi, pac choi, pak choy, and sok choy are a few. All refer to the same basic type of loose-leaved Chinese white cabbages (see note on page 78). 'Pak Choy' is also the cultivar name for the most commonly grown type. 'Pak Choy' grows 8 to 14 inches tall with thick basal stalks narrowing to thin midribs. The stalks are capped with dark green spoon-shaped leaves on the plant that grow in an upright rosette resembling Swiss chard.

Green-stalked 'Shanghai Pak Choy' or 'Baby Pak Choy' has a mature length of just 6 to 8 inches. Harvested young, the entire plant may be steamed and eaten whole, as it is in southern China.

I approach insect control from the ground up. The best way to avoid insect damage on pak choy is to insure that the plants grow quickly and are healthy. Feed your plants when the seedlings have 2 leaves. Balanced growing conditions contribute to the health of the plant, enabling it to grow quickly, yet preserving the quality.

I feed my direct-seeded plants with finely crushed basaltic rock and crushed oyster shells. Another source of calcium, such as limestone, could substitute for the shells. Soil must be biologically active so that the minerals can be assimilated. I recommend topdressing the minerals with compost if your soil is poor.

Because pak choy are generally smaller than the "heading" Chinese cabbages, you can get away with closer spacing. Sometimes I direct-seed pak choy $1/2$ to 1 inch apart and later thin the plants to stand 2 inches apart. Eventually I thin the more mature plants to 4 to 6 inches apart. Use the thinnings in salad green mixes; then harvest the remaining plants at baby-, mid-, or full-size. Plants are edible even when they bolt. The blossom is delightful—similar to our broccoli.

Choosing which one of these delicious and undemanding greens to grow this spring or fall is probably the most difficult part of the job. With the many interesting, widely adapted varieties available, you, too, could find yourself putting Chinese cabbages and pak choy out front, right where they belong.

Corn

Corn has a reputation as a crop for big gardens. However, you can grow corn with ease if you avoid the biggest problem: poor pollination. To ensure proper pollination, make

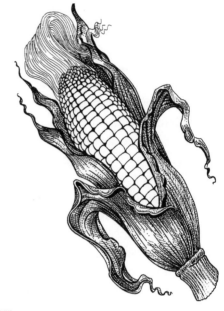

Corn

your plantings square. Rather than 2 long rows, make 5 short ones, situating the plants at equidistant spacings. The middle plants are sure to catch ample pollen.

We have all learned to forgive the over-enthusiasm of most seed catalog writers and to take a chance with some of the newer sweet corns; however, some of the entries that describe flavor have a special meaning. Here's a brief look at the story behind those words to help you read between the lines in the seed catalogs.

When ready to pick (in the milk stage), standard sweet corn and ordinary field corn are comparably sweet. What makes the standard cultivars different from ordinary corn is a single gene (called the sugary gene) that prevents the usual change of sugar to starch as the kernel matures. The sweet corn kernel shrinks as it dries because it lacks a full cargo of starch. That is also why it sprouts with less vigor than ordinary corn. The sugary gene also contributes an abundance of sugarlike substances called polysaccharides, which make these varieties creamy.

Once an ear of sweet corn is picked, the sugars rapidly change to starch. The traditional way to pick sweet corn is to start the water boiling first: that is still good advice, at least for the standard varieties.

Seedsmen rarely say what genes are in their sweet corns. If you want a standard variety, look for certain words in the catalog description, such as conventional, normal, sugar, standard, or traditional.

A few widely sold cultivars are 'Country Gentlemen', 'Golden Cross Bantam', 'Gold Cup', and 'Silver Queen'. To make several plantings, keep in mind that corn growing in midseason matures faster than corn planted either early or late in the season, when the weather is cooler. Corn grows faster in full sunlight, while beans or broccoli grow no faster in full sunlight than in half–full sunlight.

Today, there are many very early, hybrid sweet corn varieties. Early varieties do not require as much solar energy to ripen their ears, and many of them tolerate cold conditions better—some mature in less than 55 days. These seeds have to be given an early start. This requires effort on your part, because corn—no matter how early the variety—is still a tropical plant. Although corn will tolerate cooler weather, it grows best when temperatures average between 60 and 70°F. The soil must be at least 55°F, but actually, corn prefers a soil temperature between 65 and 95°F. When the soil is at 95°F, it will sprout in 3 days.

Many seed companies treat corn seed with a fungicide like Captan to overcome rot. This treatment is not for organic growers, however. Buy all your seeds from organic seed companies only for best results.

Don't even try to sprout seed in cold ground. Instead, sprout the seed inside, in a jar. When the roots emerge, plant the seeds outside. At this stage, the seed is committed to growth. With added warmth and protection from frost, it will survive. You can provide this warmth and frost protection with plastic gallon jugs. Cut out the bottoms from the jugs and place them over the spots where you've planted the sprouted seeds. Work the bottom edge into the soil and mound the soil around the sides to keep the jugs from blowing away.

You can also use the "Indian Method" of planting corn in hills. This way, you can cover 6 to 8 seeds, later thinned to 3 or 4 plants, with 1 jug. The jugs become miniature greenhouses. On a cold day, the air temperature inside may be 15 or 20°F higher than outside, and the soil within is warmer as well. The jugs also protect the plants from frost. On a hot day, we unscrew the caps to vent the jugs. This venting removes unhealthy excesses of heat and humidity.

Commercial hot caps also suffice, as long as they are vented or removed on a hot day. Large-scale growers, if they have a sandy soil which drains well, can plant corn in rows in broad, 8-inch deep trenches. They then cover the trenches with clear polyethylene to get the greenhouse effect.

In the warm, frost-proof environment, the young corn grows with vigor. It's not long before the plants are filling the space inside the jugs. By this time, we have begun to acclimate the corn to the outside environment by leaving the caps off for most of the day. When frost no longer threatens, we remove the jugs entirely.

This very early corn has a 3- to 4-week head start on the growing season. Its first ears are ripe at the beginning of summer. Then, amidst rejoicing, frolic, and fanfare, it can come to your table.

Allow more time for your early and late plantings than the seed catalog or seed packets predict, especially if your later plantings won't tolerate cross-pollination. Corn stops growing at temperatures around 50°F.

A seedling's first root grows downward rapidly and soon pushes into the subsoil. Until corn seedlings are about a foot tall, you can hoe as close as you like to them. But take care later, after the first root is safely grown. The plant sends out rings of new roots, each ring above the last. When the plant is a month or so old, its new roots are an inch or less underground.

If you keep the soil hoed and weed free for the first month, try scattering the seed of white and ladino clover. Use nitrogen-fixing bacteria on the seeds, and plant the clover among the corn. We have found that this does a good job of keeping down weeds, and the extra nitrogen supplied by the clover produces a high yield of sweet corn. Note that by adding any member of the legume family—which includes peas, beans, clovers, and alfalfa—1 acre will produce 1,000 pounds of free nitrogen in your soil to be taken up by heavy feeding nitrogen plants.

Since corn is one of the largest plants in the garden, it needs plenty of nourishment to attain good growth and sweet flavor. Leaf mulch, rock supplements, and organic fertilizer should be added, as well as a continuous supply of moisture. A humus-filled soil and plenty of compost help to retain moisture and encourage good root development. Our plants have been exceptionally sturdy, the ears large, well-filled, and good-tasting.

For summertime corn, apply a mixture of soybean and fish meal at the rate of 3 pounds per 100 square feet, then cultivate with a tiller 2 or 3 times until the cornstalks are 8 to 10 inches tall. Mulch the entire plot with a 3- to 4-inch-thick layer of straw. If the weather becomes dry earlier in the season, mulch sooner. Mulching controls weeds, keeps the soil loose after cultivation, and also encourages fast growth by conserving moisture.

Unlike field corn, sweet corn tends to grow bushy by putting forth additional growth at ground level in the form of extra stalks on the plant. If these are not removed, several cornstalks develop, none of which will bear well. You should take off these suckers as they appear and leave only the first big, sturdy stalk.

Interplant corn with pole beans or cucumbers. If you choose pole beans, plant them at the same time as the corn; for cucumbers, transplant them from cell packs. Both plants cling to the corn without any effort on your part. Also, it is a good idea to rotate your corn every year because it helps prevent soil diseases and corn smut, a fungus, and it provides for better soil nutrients, too.

There are two pests that attack sweet corn: the ear worm and the borer. The corn ear worm climbs into an ear of corn and devours the kernels. To control this worm, use the bacteria *Bacillus thuringiensis* var. *kurstaki* (*BTK*) as a biological control. Apply the granules on newly emerging silks every 3 to 4 days for 2 weeks.

To combat an infestation of European corn borers, the BT should be applied when corn plants are just reaching knee-high. Drop a few granules in each whorl, right from the can. The European corn borer bores into the stalks of corn, and will overwinter there, thus it is essential that you remove all corn stalks from your garden at the end of the growing season.

In the disease department, there are no insurmountable problems. Sweet corn is susceptible to attack from soil fungi, which results in seedling blight. To avoid this, rotate your sweet corn so populations of fungi don't build up in the soil. Corn smut is a fungus disease that can appear in the stalks, leaves, tassels, or ears. It is most commonly noticed when the ear appears to "boil" as each kernel fills with spores from the fungus. These spores are viable for 5 to 7 years. The best remedy is to keep your garden sanitary.

For harvesting, there is no question that the condition of the silk is a good indicator of when the corn is ripe: after it has turned brown. But, it does bear checking, so it's a good thing to pull one side of the husk away from the ear and see how the kernels are doing. You should harvest when the majority of the ears are full, but not overly yellow in color. The best picking is when the kernel contains the maximum amount of sugar, but hasn't started to turn tough.

Cucumber

The cucumber is an annual, and easy to grow.

Because of its short growing season (48 to 70 days from seed to picking size), it can find the warm weather that it needs in almost every garden. Being a warm-weather plant, it is very sensitive to frost and should be direct-sown only after the soil is thoroughly warmed in spring and air temperatures are 65 to 70°F.

Sow seed 1 inch deep and 4 inches apart. Fourteen days later, thin seedlings to about 12 inches apart. Cucumbers can be grown in hills. If that is not to your advantage, grow

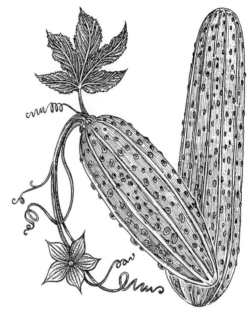

Cucumber

them in rows and train them on a trellis, pole, fence, or other support (see "Maximizing Methods," page 4, in chapter 1). This way they take up very little ground space and produce more attractive and straighter fruits. Cucumbers can also be started indoors 4 to 6 weeks before it's time to set them out as transplants (which is after frost danger has passed). Indoor-started plants are best grown in individual pots so that the roots are not disturbed when transplanting. If you are hit with an unexpected late frost, cover the new transplants with floating row covers to protect them (see chapter 11 for a general discussion on floating row-covers).

Cucumbers respond to a generous amount of organic matter such as compost in the soil, the use of a micronutrient foliage spray (seaweed and fish mix) every 3 weeks, and 4–6–4 organic fertilizer added at the rate of 4 pounds per 50 foot of row before planting.

Like most vegetables, cucumbers prefer full sun. In very hot areas, try to situate them

CUCUMBER VARIETIES

There are several types of cucumbers and cultivars within each type. Catalogs divide cucumbers into slicing and pickling varieties. Some are dual purpose.

Slicing cucumbers are cylindrical and grow up to 10 inches or longer, while pickling cucumbers are shorter and blockier. Some picklers can be harvested at different ages; the small ones are perfect for sweet pickles, and the larger ones for dills. It is true that all cucumbers should be picked in the immature stage, but a slicing variety that is just right at 8 inches long does not really have the same pickling quality as the small, sweet pickling size.

The term "gynoecium" refers to the female organs of a flower, while "monoecious" describes a species that has both male flowers and female flowers on the same plant. The new so-called "gynoecious" cucumbers grow mostly female flowers; on the "monoecious" type, male blossoms greatly outnumber the female, or fruiting, blossoms. Gynoecious cucumbers set fruit with the first flowers, set closer to the base or crown of the plant, have higher yields, and mature earlier.

Gynoecious cucumbers, however, need a male pollinator plant, and extra seeds for this purpose are included in packets of gynoecious varieties. Male plants have green seeds and female plants have beige; one male plant is needed for every 5 to 8 female plants. The male and female seeds should be planted next to each other.

There are also self-fertilizing cucumbers, which set fruit without pollination and are seedless. These varieties must be grown in an isolated area to prevent cross-pollination with other varieties. They are often grown exclusively in commercial greenhouses, but several varieties have become available to the home gardener. Check your seed catalog.

Whether eaten alone or tossed into salads, pickled or cooked, cucumbers are one of the mainstays of the kitchen and among the simplest vegetables to produce in your garden.

in an area where afternoon shade will keep the foliage from scorching.

Cucumber roots will grow to a depth of 3 feet if the soil is good. Water slowly and deeply. If the plant is under stress from lack of moisture, it just stops growing, and will pick up again when water is applied. Leaves often wilt in the middle of the day during hot spells, but check the soil for moisture below the surface.

If the first early flowers fail to set fruit, don't worry. The male flowers open first; then, about a week later, you will see the female flowers with baby cucumbers at their bases. This delayed setting shouldn't worry you, but you can avoid it by trying one of the gynoecious or self-pollinating hybrids that set fruit with the first blossoms (see box above).

Eggplant

Eggplants are perennial in the tropics. In temperate zones they continue to grow until frost, but their vigor is fragile: Cool weather, drought, or careless potting and transplanting can all ruin your crop. The plants for sale in 6-packs at supermarkets and garden centers, standing 4 inches tall in a pinch of soil, are

Eggplant

always root-bound. Their growth has been checked and they will grow poorly in the garden. You will see a big difference if you raise your own from organic seed.

There are numerous varieties of eggplant, in many different shapes and colors. We will discuss two of the most popular here: Italian eggplant, which is usually small and round and is available in varying shades of purple, white, or purple-and-white striped; and Chinese or Oriental eggplant, which is larger, more oblong, and comes in dark purple or white.

Italian Eggplant

These seeds like warmth. When the soil is 68°F, they take about 13 days to germinate, but when the temperature raises to 80°F, germination time drops to 7 days. Finally, at 88°F, the time is only 5 days. Remember, eggplant is a tropical, so you can imagine the warmth a seedling expects: it requires a temperature between 70 and 80°F. Room temperature will not do, since evaporation cools the

soil. A sunny windowsill may be fine by day, but too chilly at night.

Italian eggplant prefers nearly neutral soil, so to balance your pH use dolomitic limestone, as it is high in magnesium. Eggplants do very badly when they lack this element. Though eggplant is a heavy feeder, you can give it too much nitrogen. It will grow vigorously but set fruit rarely. Enrich your soil with compost, which releases slowly, after the plant flowers and begins to fruit, and spray with a micronutrient foliar spray (fish/seaweed) every other week.

By midsummer, your plants should be bushy looking, and when conditions are right, they will branch at every leaf. Even when bearing a half-dozen fruits, they stand erect on their woody stems, looking exotic with their gray-green 6-inch leaves, large flowers, and dark black, shiny fruit.

Harvest begins any time a fruit reaches half-size, or several inches long. Don't let the fruit mature, or it will be bitter, with hard seeds. Pick before the fruit begins to lose its shine, or its color begins to pale. You can use a fruit that has begun to dull if you pick it immediately, but why not pick the young fruit? More will be coming. Use pruners to harvest, cutting the fruit stem instead of yanking.

Oriental Eggplant

Start Oriental eggplant seeds in your greenhouse several weeks ahead of the last frost date, giving them a head start so they are about 4 to 6 inches tall when transplanted to the garden. Young eggplants are handsome with their velvety, gray-green leaves. Being tender plants, they are not transplanted until weather has warmed and the soil has lost its chill.

Oriental eggplant likes a sunny spot in the garden, but will tolerate semi-shade. These plants seem to appreciate some relief from hot summer sun and will thrive alongside taller plants that provide them shade, such as trellised cucumbers or pole beans. Eight or ten plants will produce enough fruit for the average family with an ample amount for freezing.

This Oriental import needs a sandy loam soil with plenty of humus and good moisture retaining qualities. Rich compost tilled into the soil a few weeks in advance of planting will boost production. These eggplants require a soil with a pH factor of 6.0 to 7.0, fitting in very nicely with the soil needs of many other vegetables.

Young plants should be spaced about 2 feet apart. It's advisable to immediately begin applying an organic mulch to cut down weed growth, and also to encourage the activity of earthworms, and to relieve the chore of cultivation. Adding to the mulch from time to time helps in other ways, and prevents soil from being washed away from roots.

Oriental eggplants grow tall. Usually, a 4-foot stake is sufficient, especially if plants are to remain upright while laden with fruit. Strips of old nylon pantyhose come in handy for use as ties, as they do not restrict the conduction system of the plants.

During prolonged periods of drought, even a mulch won't suffice for their need of water as eggplants must have a moderate amount of soil moisture to properly produce their fruit. When leaves continue to droop after the sun has gone down, it's time to come to the relief of the thirsty plants by giving the soil underneath them a thorough soaking. Once or twice weekly is usually enough depending on the severity of the dry spell.

Oriental eggplant fruits may reach a length of 10 to 12 inches and about 2 to $2\frac{1}{2}$ inches in diameter and still be of good texture and taste, although the recommended harvesting size is 6 to 8 inches. The only time the fruit seems to have difficulty developing is when moisture is insufficient, and then it will not be of prime quality.

Oriental eggplant is high in potassium and low in calories. However, while eggplant itself is not fattening, when combined with cheese and other rich ingredients the results can be highly caloric. If you gain a pound or two from such a delicious concoction, don't blame the eggplant.

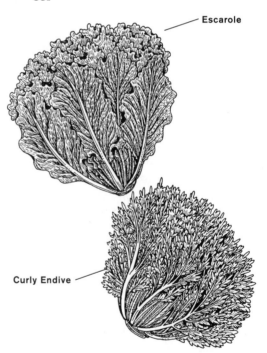

Escarole

Curly Endive

Endive

In summer, intense heat ruins lettuce, but endive keeps right on growing.

Endive is a biennial grown as an annual, and therefore does not have the same problems with long days and high heat that plague lettuce, an annual. As long as there is enough moisture in the ground, endive will thrive.

If you are not planning to grow endive in the spring, July is the perfect time to plant a fall crop of this hardy vegetable. Nearly all endive varieties available to gardeners take at least 85 to 95 days from seed to salad.

There are two types of endive. The most common is the notched, frilly-leafed curly frisée. The most cold-tolerant, curly endive is best planted in early spring and late winter.

Another type of endive, commonly marketed as escarole, has broad, thick, smoother leaves of a lighter green. Broad-leafed endive shows its stuff when the hot weather comes, and is good for late spring and summer planting.

Plan on about 5 endive plants for every adult in the family. A $1/4$-ounce packet has over 100 seeds, so you are going to have some left over. If properly stored, endive seed will be good for 5 years.

You can start the seeds on a windowsill, in a greenhouse, or under grow lights. Seeds should be planted no more than $1/4$ inch deep in a humus-rich, prewatered soil. Plant 2 or 3 seeds per inch and cover them with a light sprinkling of sand or fine compost. Within 10 to 14 days the seed should germinate.

To determine the right planting time for a late-fall harvest, count back 90 days from the first killing frost. To get an early summer harvest, you should start endive seed indoors about 8 weeks before the last frost date.

Transplant the seedlings outdoors when they are 4 weeks old. You could risk transplanting even earlier with success in most years. Once they're about 5 inches tall, endive seedlings will withstand anything short of a hard freeze.

Endive prefers a neutral or slightly acid soil. Browning on the margins of the leaves at the center of the plant indicates a calcium deficiency. These leaves ultimately turn black and die. Three pounds of either ground limestone or wood ashes per 100 square feet will serve to correct any adverse conditions.

Endive needs plenty of moisture. It can take some water stress, but if the roots are allowed to die out for a prolonged period, the leaves will turn tough and bitter.

Make sure that the plants get 2 inches of water each week. Sprinkling with a hose is just about the worst way to water endive. The way a plant is watered is more important than how much water it gets. Overhead sprinkling traps moisture inside the endive heads and that can lead to rot. I recommend drip irrigation and soaker hoses, which wet the roots deeply while the leaves stay high and dry. Otherwise, dig a trench between your rows and run water down it. A mulch of straw, leaves, hay, or grass clippings will help conserve moisture and protect the fall and winter crops from freezing.

If endive is overlooked by some gardeners, luckily it is ignored even more by insects and diseases. If your crop is rotated each year and water isn't allowed to stand in the crowns of the plants, disease should not be a concern.

Garlic

Any organic gardener who enjoys tasty foods should give garlic a try. It's easy to grow and its culinary uses are seemingly endless.

Hundreds of myths regarding its use as a folk remedy surround this member of the onion family. Just how much truth can be found in such claims?

Garlic

Louis Pasteur was perhaps the first scientist to verify that a crushed garlic clove is a potent antiseptic. More recently, research has shown that garlic extracts are effective in the treatment of colitis, anemia, asthma, and many other diseases. Researchers now know that garlic is rich in selenium, a trace element that stimulates immunity factors in the human body.

Although skeptics scoff at garlic's medicinal value, there is no denying that it's nutritional. Garlic contains all of the important vitamins except D and is high in protein, iron, calcium, phosphorous, and natural iodine.

Any gardener can grow his own garlic. It can be grown practically anywhere that has fertile, well-drained soil, plenty of sunshine, and adequate moisture. Even a pot in a windowsill will suffice. Garlic requires the same care as onions, only it needs a longer growing season, from September to July.

Elizabeth and I started growing garlic years ago, when we got tired of paying for old garlic bulbs, sprayed with a chemical sprout-retardant in shiny cellophane wrappers. The clincher came when Elizabeth opened a new package to find one bulb already sprouting into individual cloves, and planted them 2 inches deep in our garden. This was in late September, and it was the last attention our garlic received until the following spring.

By onion-planting time in March, the garlic tops were beginning to show new growth. In early June, each plant sent up a long, corkscrew shoot. As the days passed, the shoots slowly unwound until large seed heads of bulblets bobbed chest-high in the breeze.

When the seed heads' outer husks curled back, we pulled the plants and spread them over the doghouse roof to dry. Within a week, the big root bulbs were cut, clean, and strung on heavy thread for hanging in the kitchen.

The bulblets broke apart easily by rubbing them between my hands. We scattered them on a freshly turned plot of soil and raked compost over them. By midsummer, the seedlings were as thick as new grass. We transplanted 3 dozen, sticking them in tree beds and odd corners where they wouldn't take up valuable garden space.

Garlic can be used at any stage, from seedling to fully cloved bulb. For storing, however, it must be mature, or gone to seed. It can be planted in early spring and harvested that same year. But we get much larger bulbs by planting in August or early fall, and harvesting the following year, especially when planting seed buds instead of the bulb cloves. Garlic winters well in almost any climate.

I advise against planting garlic bought at the supermarket. You cannot determine if it's carrying any diseases—particularly white rot, which plagues commercial growers, and nematodes.

Some garlic is sprayed for long storage and thus is reluctant to sprout. To be safe, plant only cloves bought from reputable organic seed companies. 'German Red', 'Spanish

Roja', 'Sicilian', and 'Italian Red' garlic are all available through catalogs.

Garlic is a perennial that is grown as an annual. For truly large, delicious bulbs, prepare a site in your garden that receives full sun. Till in compost and bone meal and rake it smooth of rocks and soil clumps. Soil looseness is the key to superb garlic. If possible, plant them in raised beds.

Garlic will grow in heavy or light soil. As with any other bulbing plant, the loamier the soil, the larger the bulb. If you grow a batch in straight compost, the bulbs will be 3 times the size of those grown elsewhere.

To plant, simply separate each bulb into single cloves. Plant the cloves 5 inches apart, their pointed ends up. In the fall, bury them 4 inches deep to prevent them from heaving from the ground during the winter.

When spring arrives, the fall-planted crop resumes growth. Throughout the growing season, the plants require constant moisture. To retain soil moisture, mulch the garlic with chopped leaves or straw, when the foliage is 3 to 5 inches tall.

In July, when the plants are reaching maturity, run a finger around each bulb, being careful not to disturb the root systems. This exposes the bulbs to the sun and hot summer air, as well as allowing them more space in which to fatten up before harvest in August. Once the leaves begin yellowing, about 3 weeks before harvest, stop watering.

When the leaves of the garlic have yellowed and withered, it's time to harvest. Gently spade up the bulbs on a hot, breezy day, allowing them to dry in the sun before taking them indoors at sunset. Hang them in bunches in a cool, ventilated place such as a garage or garden shed. Curing is the secret to long storage. Allow the bulbs to cure for a

month. Then cut off the foliage, trim off the roots, and store them as you would onions in mesh bags in a cool, dark, but well-ventilated place. Don't forget to save a few bulbs for planting again next fall. With proper planning you will have enough garlic to last year-round.

If the soil is heavy, or if root systems are heavily developed, garlic can be tough to pull. By spade-forking them out, or deep-watering the bed the day before, you can save yourself the frustration of having stems pop-off beneath the ground.

Garlic requires very little cultivation or supplemental watering. It literally grows like a weed, popping up in the most unexpected places, which is another plus, since it is an ideal insect-repelling companion plant for almost any crop, takes up very little room, and actually looks ornamental in its seed stage. It doesn't even have to be harvested.

Fresh, home-grown garlic will keep for at least a year or more. String it to hang on the kitchen wall, or pile it in airy baskets on the kitchen counter. If any is left when the next crop is brought in, break the old bulbs into cloves and plant them.

You can also grow garlic in a flower pot on your kitchen windowsill. The best potting mixture is 5 cups of compost, 2 cups of perlite, 2 cups of peat moss, 1 cup of clean sand, and $1/2$ cup of bone meal. When everything is thoroughly mixed, carefully divide the garlic and plant 3 unpeeled large cloves upright with the root part on the bottom in 1 inch of soil. Then fill the 4-inch pots, covering the cloves completely.

After watering thoroughly, place the filled pots on your kitchen windowsill, which preferably has a southeast exposure with sun practically all day. For good growth about 13 hours of light is needed. It takes about 7 to 14 days—depending on the amount of sun and light—for the shoots to begin growing. Note that the shoots are tall enough to cut and eat when they are about 3 inches high. Once every 3 weeks, foliar spray, using a micronutrient mix, at the rate of 3 ounces to 1 gallon of water

As mentioned above, be sure to plant this wonderful vegetable outside, too, as it has proven itself by discouraging insects around other vegetables—especially tomatoes.

For setting between tomato plants spaced 36 inches apart in rows, dig 2 to 3 holes between the plants, each about 8 inches deep and 10 inches wide. Place about 5 inches of compost in each hole, then fill the holes to a rounded top with potting soil mix as used for the indoor garlic pots. Selected large garlic cloves are planted about 2 inches deep, watered thoroughly, and covered lightly with straw mulch.

The garlic plants should get a good watering with the liquid fish/seaweed spray every 3 to 4 weeks. Green shoots will stand up straight until autumn, when they turn yellow and fall over. The cloves form bulbs in the soil, but are small the first year. They remain in the soil all winter, until May, when the green shoots suddenly push out of the ground. By planting garlic each year, you will have sufficient amounts of organically-grown garlic for eating and for planting, while providing natural protection for the garden.

You might also try growing elephant garlic, which is actually a species of leek. The bulbs weigh up to a pound, producing huge cloves that are mild enough to eat raw.

Prepare the soil for elephant garlic in much the same way as for regular garlic. They should receive the same organic fertilizer and care. However, plant the elephant garlic cloves in mid-August. They must make root growth before cold weather sets in, and remain in the ground through the winter.

All garlic plants should be mulched with straw as a winter protection. Soil for all garlic plants must be kept in a loose, friable condition to permit the bulbs to expand and grow large, and weeds must be kept out. Regular watering should stop in late July or August for any garlic plants that are to be pulled in late September.

In spring, the garlic plants send up a center stalk, and a bud develops. Buds should be snipped off. Otherwise, if they are allowed to grow they will flower and produce seeds. The bulbs of elephant garlic do not develop into large bulbs when they develop blossoms; therefore, the garlic bulbs that are allowed to go to seed should not be pulled out. Leave them in the soil until the following year so they will grow large.

Greens

There are lots of plants that come under the heading of "greens," so we organic gardeners have plenty of crops from which to choose.

Some like beet, turnip, and rutabaga greens, while others go for purslane, spinach, French dandelion, or kale (note that beets and spinach have individual entries in this chapter, as well as the most familiar green, lettuce). Be inventive in your use of greens to enhance soups and stews, or invent nutritious and delicious salads and side dishes.

A substantial yield of greens can be had from a small garden; they don't require a lot of room to grow. I have often seen annual flower beds turned into patches of fall greens after

Turnip greens

the flowers had grown leggy or succumbed to midsummer heat.

Even amateur gardeners can make a success of growing greens, as they are among the easiest plants to raise. Greens require a soil with a pH ranging from 6.0 to 7.0, so they fit right in with other vegetables.

Most greens do best in moderately rich, well-drained soil in a sunny location. If you have sandy loam, you're in luck. Two or three weeks ahead of planting time work the soil thoroughly to loosen it and till in some compost. Work in some balanced 4–6–4 organic fertilizer. This will assure healthy plants right from the start.

Root crops, such as rutabagas, may be a disappointment in heavy soil. This is another reason for working as much compost and organic matter as possible into the soil several weeks before planting time to make it loose and friable.

Directions for planting are usually on the seed packet. Depth of planting seeds may vary some according to the texture of the soil. If soil is heavy, such as those containing quite a bit of clay, seed should not be planted over $1/4$ inch deep.

Most greens are cool weather crops and should not be expected to perform well when the weather warms up in late spring. For spring crops, it is important to sow seeds as soon as severe cold is over and the soil can be worked.

With the coming of warm weather, cold-weather greens will bolt, put up flower stalks, and lose their culinary value. By the same token, fall crops must be planted early enough to harvest before severe weather moves in.

If greens are sown in beds, the beds should be easy to reach across for weeding and thinning. Personally, I prefer row planting as the rows are easier to deal with. I can move between the rows to weed, cultivate, or harvest without fear of stepping on the plants.

Mulching plays a big part in the growing process at Spring Meadow. When plants are 4 to 6 inches high, I lay down a thick mulch of straw from the barn. This keeps rain from splashing dirt up on plants and makes for a much cleaner harvest of greens than when leaves are touching soil during heavy downpours.

By maintaining a good mulch around the plants, we manage to keep the beet and turnip roots in good shape longer than the tops when winter arrives.

Another reliable green is roquette (also called rugula and rocket). This is a vigorous plant that is more cold-resistant than most

WEED FEED

Have you ever wondered why some plants invite themselves in your garden? Ironically, it is because many of these wild species were naturalized centuries ago by our ancestors for food and medicine. I have been eating and enjoying beneficial weeds for over 20 years in addition to more traditional greens. They offer flavor, freshness, and nutritional value.

By using certain weeds as food, you "reap" the following benefits:

1. You get an early spring harvest at a time when most gardens are just getting started.
2. You increase the productivity of your garden.
3. You save money. Weeds are 100 percent free.
4. You expand your culinary horizons.

CHICKWEED

Chickweed is quite possibly the most common weed in the world. It is a small plant, rarely reaching more than 5 inches in height. Weak-stemmed, it creeps, or spreads out horizontally along the ground. Chickweed prefers rich soil, moderate shade, and cool weather.

The whole plant above ground is edible raw or cooked. Raw, it has little flavor. For this reason it is one of my favorites.

Its mild taste and crunchy texture remind me of lettuce and provide a good base for salads. It mixes well with any other more strongly flavored salad fixings such as watercress, radishes, and peppers. You can steam, boil, or sauté chickweed just like spinach. It cooks down quite a bit, so use a lot.

DANDELIONS

As is true with most Americans, dandelion's forefathers were immigrants: they were brought here by the earliest English settlers.

Dandelion was considered absolutely essential for survival and was given an honored place in the kitchen gardens of the day, providing food, medicine, and wine. Because it is an effective diuretic, dandelion was used as a cure for kidney stones, weight loss, and edema.

Dandelion is as common as crabgrass and just as much of a lawn pest. But, as a food, it is a tender taste treat, full of protein, iron, and vitamins. Every part of the dandelion, with the exception of the seeds and flower stalks, is useful. Eat the young leaves in early spring, either raw or steamed. Dig up the roots anytime, although they will be highest in nutrients in the fall. Boil them like parsnips or make dandelion teas.

Digging for Delicious Dandelions

There is a trick to getting tongue-tempting goodness out of dandelions. The method is as old as French gardening and is a small amount of pleasant work. Dig the plant up at almost any time of year, pull off the top leaves, and force them to sprout new leaves in darkness.

Dig up a plant that has 10- to 12-inch roots. Work around the edge slowly, carving it out of its matrix of soil. In soft soil a plant will come up in a minute or less.

After digging up a bushel or so of dandelions, wash them and let them rest in the shade for a few days. Once the roots have

continued

become less brittle and the leaves limp, trim the roots to an even 7 inches and pull off the old green leaves, being careful not to injure the new yellow ones at the crown (the part of the plant above the roots that protrudes through the soil).

Trim the crown with a knife, leaving a short spike of yellow-white leaves. Most often, dandelion tops split into many small crowns, particularly where they have been dug up unsuccessfully. In that case leave only 1 or 2 of the strongest looking crowns with a spike of growth and cut off all the weaker ones. That forces the plant to more vigorous growth.

Pack each plant's roots tightly in sandy potting mix in a large flowerpot or a stout box; place the container outside if weather permits. Cleaning the roots well before putting them into sand will keep stray slugs from hiding out to destroy your salad at their dark, wet leisure. Putting greater amounts of sand on top of the crowns forces them to grow more compactly and prevents the leaves from getting dried edges, which sometimes turn an unsightly brown. Additional sand on top of the crowns also produces a pleasantly crinkled leaf. When adding large amounts of sand, however, covering the tops of the roots becomes a little delicate. You don't want to break the spikes off the crowns. An inch or 2 of sand above the roots is enough.

Put a cardboard box over the container. Blocking out the light keeps the shoots white and tender. When too much light gets in, the leaves become tough and bitter, producing the kind of dandelion that should be avoided. And of course, without green leaves, the vitamin C content is low.

If the area in which the dandelions are stored is warm, the plants will be ready to eat in about 10 days. When the temperatures hover near freezing at night, more than 2 weeks will be necessary for a harvest.

When the shoots look the normal length of a dandelion leaf—about 6 inches long—they are ready for eating. They will keep coming up for 2 to 4 weeks, depending on the hardiness of the root.

Dandelions make an interesting cellar crop, if moved inside just before the hard freezes come. In that case, a 40-watt lightbulb placed at the side of the forcing box is enough to keep the temperature warm enough in cold weather. Hot frames will speed up the forcing process and the exposure to a growing lamp for a couple of days at the end of the forcing period will replace some of the vitamin C.

Sometimes you might get an extra treat if the roots produce flower heads and stems. These are just as edible as leaves and look very pretty when used as a garnish. The forced shoots are a pleasant addition to most kinds of lettuce in a mixed salad, dressed with a simple vinaigrette sauce. Should you produce more than you care to eat in a salad, braise the leaves in butter as you would Swiss chard or spinach. A touch of tarragon and lemon will bring out tastes that you never imagined existed in that weed on the front lawn.

PURSLANE

Purslane is a common garden weed that is rich in flavor and nutrients with a low-caloric content (the plant is 75 percent water, like cabbage).

Wild purslane prefers sunny spots in sandy, rich soil. It carpets the ground, rarely growing

continued

more than 5 inches high. The succulent, purplish-green leaves range from $1/2$ to 2 inches long. The tender red stems bear tiny, 5-petaled yellow flowers at their tips.

The whole plant is edible. Some purslane lovers have found that they can make use of 1 plant from June until August, just by snipping off the tips of the stems.

Raw purslane has a pleasant crunch and is a good salad green. An interesting purslane coleslaw can be made by chopping up the raw leaves and stems, mixing them with chopped carrots and other raw vegetables, and blending with a commercial coleslaw dressing.

Purslane's newfound recognition has prompted plant breeders to develop a taller, non-creeping domesticated version, which you can order from many garden seed catalogs. It has a little less bite than wild purslane.

WILD GARLIC AND WILD ONION

If you find a weed that smells strongly of garlic or onion, it is probably wild garlic or onion and is edible.

Dig up the bulb to see which one you have. Just like their domesticated relatives, wild onions are layered and wild garlic is made up of cloves. Don't be fooled by their small size; they are often more strongly flavored than domesticated varieties. Use the green shoots like chives or scallion tops.

Look for these weeds in your backyard. Try adding some to your diet. You'll be pleasantly surprised. *Bon Appétit.*

other greens. Strong-tasting and somewhat peppery, it is usually recommended for salad use, although I like it best cooked in with other greens (I like to plant a variety of greens as I have found that several flavors blended together produce a delicious dish). Roquette is ready for use in just over a month after transplanting, and will give you a good supply of tender leaves.

I have not found a better turnip for our farm than 'Tokyo Cross Hybrid'. It is an early-maturing variety, and the pure-white turnips can grow quite large without becoming pithy. Turnip leaves can also be cooked or used fresh in tossed salads. For some reason aphids don't seem to have the fondness for 'Tokyo Cross' leaves that they sometimes have for 'Purple Top' or other turnips.

Greens are a basic part of the food chain. Whether spring or fall, the best ones do not come from the supermarket. They come out of your organic garden, grown by your own hand and treated with tender loving care.

Kale

Kale is so good for you that it's astounding.

One cup of cooked kale has as much calcium as a 5-ounce glass of milk and twice the vitamin C of a medium-sized Florida orange. It's packed with vitamin A and is a great source of iron and potassium.

Kale

A biennial grown as an annual, kale grows best in cool weather when temperatures are 60 to 65°F, and will germinate when soil is as cool as 40°F. Its flavor is much better when grown in cool weather, since frost tenderizes and sweetens the thick leaves. It is best to time planting so the crop matures during cool weather and can be harvested after the first hard frost.

For a late spring or early summer crop, direct-seed or transplant kale as soon as the temperature reaches 40°F. I prefer to use transplants in order to get a jump on the growing season. The earlier I harvest, the more tender the leaves. A second crop started in late summer will be ready for harvest in late fall or early winter.

To start kale indoors, count back 10 to 15 weeks from your last spring frost date. The young plants can go outdoors 6 or more weeks before the late frost. They should be 4 to 6 weeks old at that time.

Use a porous, living potting soil mix and sow seeds about $^1/_2$ inch deep. Seeds usually germinate within 3 to 10 days. Provide the seedlings with 10 or more hours of light each day and feed them with a solution of micronutrient foliage spray once a week.

The ideal soil for kale is loose and high in organic matter, so add compost if necessary. Good drainage is also important, especially if you plan to overwinter kale. The pH should be 6.0 to 7.0. Transplant kale seedlings so deeply that only the top 4 leaves are exposed. That will prevent the plants from developing a lanky, leafless stem above ground. I usually help plants by putting a cloche around them for the first few weeks after transplanting (see page 168 in chapter 11, "Growing On"). Kale is a heavy feeder, so give it 4–6–4 organic fertilizer and use a micronutrient foliage spray every month. Mulch with organic matter such as leaves, grass clippings, or straw. Aside from suppressing weeds, it will keep the soil cool and moist.

Kale roots tend to be shallow, so moisture near the surface and roots protected from heat can mean a big difference in crop growth. Quick and steady growth produces the sweetest and most tender leaves.

Since kale takes 55 to 65 days to mature, plant fall crops 2 months before the first frost. This is one crop that shouldn't be crowded; plants need good air circulation to prevent disease problems. Because you harvest a few leaves at a time, plants will tend to sprawl more than if you let them grow to maturity and then cut the leaves off at the base.

To store kale leaves in the refrigerator, clean, pat dry, and then put them in a plastic bag. They will be fine for several weeks. You can also keep leaves in a root cellar as long as the humidity is at least 85 percent and the temperature about 34°F.

Kohlrabi

Spiny kohlrabi looks like some strange sea creature, but the bulb flesh is crisp and delicious, tasting like a cross between turnips and cabbage. Kohlrabi is a cool-season biennial, although it can tolerate some heat. It can be planted in the spring and the fall—I make sowings in early April, late May, and at the end of July. I prefer fall harvests because a few frosty nights make the bulbs even sweeter.

Usually plants are started in our solar composting greenhouse, which has proved very successful, although sometimes I direct-sow in the garden beds. Seedlings pop up in no time. Successive plantings at 2- to 4-week intervals stagger the harvest, guaranteeing a constant supply of fresh tender kohlrabi.

Plant kohlrabi in 2-foot blocks, spacing the plants about 6 inches apart each way. I plant 2 seeds per spacing, thinning to the strongest seedlings, when they are about 3 inches tall.

Kohlrabi requires the same kind of care as most other cole crops. It requires a soil that is rich in organic matter, retains moisture, yet drains readily. A light, sandy soil encourages rapid growth and the tastiest bulbs. I incorporate as much manure-enriched compost in the beds as I can spare.

Most important is mulching, which is the key to prize-winning kohlrabi. I start mulching them when they are about 5 inches tall. This assures soil moisture retention, hinders weeds, keeps the root systems cool, and prevents potential problems such as split or spindly bulbs. Keep the soil beneath the mulch moist, but not mucky.

Aside from regular waterings and spraying with a fish/seaweed solution every 2 weeks, there's nothing to do but wait for the harvest.

When direct-seeded, most varieties mature in 80 days.

Leeks

Leeks have a long harvest season and best of all, provide fresh eating in the winter.

The leek is a biennial grown as an annual, and a member of the allium or onion family. It has a false stem: Tightly clasped together, the bottom portions of its leaves form a tall, cylindrical sheaf like the pages of a rolled-up newspaper.

How much of the plant is edible depends partly on how it is cooked, but mainly on how it is grown. Some gardeners substitute tender bits of leek leaves for chopped chives. However, most of the good eating is in the stem, and with proper care, a gardener can double the stem's length.

Leek

Because of their extended growing period, I recommend transplanting leeks: sowing leeks directly in the garden will guarantee you a long season of weeding. From midwinter until spring, first sow the seeds in cell packs kept in a solar greenhouse; move the seedlings into cold frames 3 weeks later, and harden off outdoors 2 weeks before transplanting. When the seedlings are 8 to 12 inches tall and about twice as thick as a pencil, lift them with a spade or fork, pull the plants free by their leaves, and take them to the garden.

Dunking the plants in a mixture of fish and sea kelp before transplanting will soften the transition, although leeks have tough roots and suffer less transplant shock than many vegetables. When leeks reach transplanting size, they are almost 3 months old.

Use an oversized dibble to make holes $1^1/_2$ inches in diameter and 6 inches deep. Drop in a seedling and give it a shot of liquid seaweed, but don't pack soil around it. The tip of the plant should be only a few inches above ground. Sheltered by soil, the plant readily strikes root. Then it stretches up for sun, and soon the crown—the point where the leaves unclasp the stem and spread apart—pokes above the soil. Deep transplanting and tilling prompt the leek to make a far taller stem than it would without forcing. Leeks are often earthed-up to blanch their stems. Some gardeners space the plants as close as 6 inches in all directions, leaving no room for hilling, or mounding the soil around them. These leeks will be smaller, but there will be more in the harvest.

I blanch leeks by mulching them, but mulch does much more. I hate to weed, and since leeks are such a long season crop, I would have to constantly cultivate their beds if I didn't mulch. Leeks are also a thirsty crop and mulch keeps the soil moist between rainy days. The biggest advantage to mulching, however, is that it keeps leeks clean by preventing dirt from splattering crowns during rainstorms. If leeks seem demanding, keep in mind that they give big yields. Thirty or forty plants are more than enough for the average family. There is ample room for 30 plants in 1 square foot of soil. Space the plants approximately 6 inches apart in the row. In order to reserve space for hilling, don't squeeze the rows any closer than 18 inches.

Even though leeks are a long-season crop, there are cultivars that mature earlier than others. Check your seed catalog for maturing dates. Just remember that in a general way, fast-growers are generally less hardy leeks.

For an early crop, sown in mid- to late winter in cold frames, use fast-growing varieties that are ready for harvesting 70 to 85 days after transplanting. Transplant when the soil is first workable. Protected by mulch, they survive temperatures below 0°F and can yield fresh eating until spring.

The shiny black seed is small and tough, germinating in 2 to 3 weeks in cool conditions. It is best to keep the potting soil at about 60 to 65°F.

Wait until 1 to 2 weeks before the last frost to sow seed in the outdoor garden. In areas with mild winters (the kind that don't kill broccoli) sow leeks in midsummer. Since the seed does not like hot soil, it helps to get it started indoors and then sow it deeper than usual.

The early crop may suffer from the heat during the summer. A late crop needs less water and is less susceptible to stress.

Like onions, leeks can become infested by the onion thrip, which shows up in summer. Minute insects that feed on plant juices, thrips work their way into the crown and are hard to spot unless you part the leaves. On young plants, a daily spraying with a hose may control them. On mature plants simply harvest the crop.

Leeks go to seed in their second year. Plants that overwinter start growing again before the soil is workable in early spring. They stay edible until about midspring, when they send up a towering stalk topped with a globe of flowers. If you cut off the stalk when it first appears and feed the leeks with a 4–6–4 or 3–6–3 organic fertilizer, they stay edible for a longer period.

Let a few plants make seed. The leek breeds true and you can save the seed for next season. After you collect seed, carefully unearth the plants. The bulblets are at the base of the stem and can be replanted immediately at the same depth in dibble holes for a winter crop.

Wrapped in plastic bags and stored in the refrigerator, leeks keep for about a month.

Butterhead **Leaf**

Iceberg **Romaine**

Lettuce varieties

Lettuce

The basics of lettuce culture are simple.

The plant, an annual, grows to perfection pretty much on its own, when the weather is cool, and the soil is loose, fertile, high in organic matter, and receiving a steady supply of moisture. As soon as hot weather arrives, lettuce can quickly loses its succulence. Once the leaves lose their sheen and start to taste bitter, bolting to seed is imminent.

I have been growing lettuce successfully in spring, summer, and fall for many years. Each season I grow a few of all types: butterhead, leaf, crisphead, and romaine. Follow my method, and you, too, can have all of the lettuce you want for a half year or longer.

Start lettuce in foot-wide beds that are between 4 and 6 feet long. The exact size of beds isn't critical. Match them to the size of your appetite for fresh organic lettuce. (You can also start lettuce in a cold frame. See page 168 for more details.)

Before planting, scatter compost over the beds at the rate of 3 pounds per square foot (a 3-inch layer over the bed). Add in 2 1-pound coffee cans of wood ashes. Apply 4–6–4 organic fertilizer lightly over the planting bed. Dig all of the ingredients in, thoroughly mixing them to a depth of 8 inches. Then rake the bed and soak it well. Two or three days later sow your lettuce seeds.

The seeds are small. Young lettuce plants have a hard time making their way through any crust that forms on the soil. To prevent crusting, don't cover the seeds with soil. Instead, sow the seeds directly on the freshly worked soil surface.

It is typical to plant at least 3 different varieties in each bed. Broadcast the seed thickly over the whole bed—you will use the thinnings later. Neither leaf nor head lettuce will amount to much if not thinned. In cool weather thin mercilessly. Two or three weeks after seeds germinate, plunge a garden trowel into an especially crowded cluster and transplant individual seedlings to a place prepared elsewhere in the garden.

When the seedlings are bigger, pull them up by the handful. Once I've twisted off the roots, the tiny, tender leaves go into the salad bowl. Thinning continues until there is a 3-inch space between plants.

As the plants fill the spaces between them, harvest every other one, leaving a 6-inch space. When the remaining plants fill in, again harvest every other one, leaving 12 inches between plants. With most varieties, and in most years, a 12-inch spacing is ample to mature a large head. On several occasions the climate and the soil were so perfect

that I was able to grow gigantic heads of 'Ruby Salad Bowl' and 'Oak Leaf' that measured up to 25 inches across!

For midsummer lettuce, shading is crucial. Build a frame around the bed and use shading cloth or plant the lettuce in the shade of a fence or tall corn. Also, restrain yourself from thinning the midsummer beds ruthlessly. The crowded rows keep the soil soft and moist and the plants shade each other to retard bolting. Utilizing the plants this way demonstrates the "living mulch" method (see "Grower's Glossary" on page 325).

To keep the lettuce harvest steady, start a new bed every 3 to 4 weeks. As you use up early plantings, the new crop will be coming along. By making small plantings frequently, you avoid the feast-or-famine phenomenon. Instead of depleting an entire packet of seeds in one sowing, use $1/4$ or $1/3$ of the seed initially and finish the balance in later sowings.

The lettuce transplants that help provide a succession of salads also make for an attractive garden. They are nice to have on hand to fill empty spaces among flowers or herbs, or between slow-growing vegetables like cabbage, broccoli, tomatoes, and peppers.

The quickest way to get heads of lettuce on the table is to plant fast-growing leaf types, such as 'Oakleaf' and 'Black-Seeded Simpson'. They mature in just 40 to 55 days; you can start eating the thinnings in 25 days. By harvesting outer leaves and thinnings, you can get salads from the slower-growing heading types (butterheads, crispheads, red iceberg, and romaine) just as quickly as you do from leafy kinds.

Lettuce is one of the best vegetables to experiment with, since you see results fast. There are dozens upon dozens of types to try

SATISFYING SALADS

Even with the limitations of a small garden plot, you can grow all of the fixings of a good garden salad. Although it can be planted in the open ground with other early vegetables, I prefer to start my lettuce in a cold frame. I get a crop of tender, young lettuce when I transplant in April. By that time the plants are 3 to 5 inches high and they provide several fine bowlfuls of tasty greens (I simply pinch off the largest leaves).

Cabbages, too, can be started in the cold frame. Flats, boxes, cell packs, or even flower pots with drainage holes can be used for starting these salad plants in an enclosed porch which is neither too hot nor too cold.

To start my small salad garden, first, I turn the soil either with the spading fork or the tiller. Next I drive small, 1-foot stakes along both sides and across the ends of each area at 1-foot intervals. Strings attached to the stakes are run across the length of the garden to mark the 12- × 12-inch areas.

I transplant 9 plants to the square foot, using a sharpened 2-inch peg that is 6 inches long for making planting holes and for tamping down. After planting a section approximately 2 to 5 square feet, I soak the soil.

At each intersection, I plant an onion set about 2 inches deep. Cabbages and cucumbers are planted in the center row of each space. Swiss chard, very productive from spring to late fall, is planted in the outer row to give it more space and avoid over-crowding.

I thin the Swiss chard 7 to 10 inches in the row. Sometimes I pull the leaves and use them for mulch when we are unable to keep up with their heavy production.

I prefer baby head cabbages for the congested salad garden. The heads are small and firm, about 5 inches across, of superb quality, and highly resistant to bursting. More than that, they seem to have a higher resistance to cabbage worms.

Tomatoes and sweet peppers are set out in the corner areas opposite each other at the ends of the garden. Plant the beets, carrots, and turnips next to the tomatoes, in a shallow furrow about 1-inch deep made with a stick or hand trowel.

Radishes, a quick-maturing crop, may be planted in special rows with your beets and carrots. Being long, 'White Icicle' is more productive than the more colorful varieties. Radishes may also be planted as a fall crop and some may wish to try the 'Black Spanish' cultivar at that time.

Space the beet seeds about $1/2$ inch apart and cover with $1/2$ inch of soil. Thin your young plants gradually to 4- or 5-inch spacing and use the thinnings as a harvest, as the tops of beets, carrots, and turnips are high in nutritional value.

Mid-June, when the lettuce is harvested, is the time to plant the second crop of beets and carrots for fall use. Before planting, I like to work some fine compost and 4–6–4 organic fertilizer into the soil.

To insure seed germination, I take a garden hose with a nozzle to control the flow and flood the furrows. After the seeds are dropped into the furrow, I cover them with $1/2$ inch of fine compost. Where it is possible to mulch, spread straw, hay, or green lawn clippings as you can. During the hot, dry summer months, at least 2 inches of water per week will be needed and

---

continued

proper thinning of the plants will help to insure a more bountiful crop.

After the last harvest has been made in late fall, prepare your salad garden for the winter and next year's crop. I do this by first cleaning the garden and tilling under all residues. After this, I apply kelp meal, compost, and greensand. All this should be worked into the soil with a spading fork or tiller.

Finally, in full anticipation of a new crop, I rake the mulch from the soil about 3 to 5 weeks before planting time. This way the sun and spring winds may dry it for an early beginning to a new gardening year.

---

with notable differences in flavor, texture, color, and hardiness.

Lima Beans

Lima beans, hot weather annuals, sometimes seem awfully persnickety about temperature. If the soil is cool, it can be hard to get them to come up. For germination, they like high soil temperatures from 75 to 85°F. Then, if it gets too hot in summer they refuse to set pods. Lima seedlings actually grow best in weather with nights in the 70s and 80sF, but set pods better when the nights are in the 60s.

It's best to be patient, waiting until the soil temperature reaches at least 65°F before planting. If you have to get an early crop, there are several ways to go about it that work better than sticking your seed in cold soil.

Soak the seeds overnight, then place them between layers of damp paper towel and store in a warm dry place. After 4 or 5 days, when the sprouts are about an inch long, set the sprouted seeds gently in the soil 1 to 2 inches deep.

You can also start your seed in pots. I have discovered that it's worth my while to start pole beans in pots 2 to 3 weeks before the normal planting date and then transplant them. That way I can get a 2- or 3-week jump on harvesting. The plants stay in the pots several weeks after they come up, then get transplanted.

I recommend using a 4-inch pot if you are going to leave the beans potted for more than a few days after sprouts emerge. It doesn't matter what kind of pot you use.

Plants that are in the ground gain a little extra protection with hot caps or floating row covers. It takes 85 days from planting to harvest, but it's an early planting date that can give you a jump on harvesting.

If you have a limited amount of space in your garden, you should choose pole beans because you can train them to grow upward, taking air space instead of ground space. Bush varieties, on the other hand, are great if you have the extra space in your garden, and will produce earlier than pole varieties, giving you a bigger harvest.

There are some hot weather problems. Many of the large-seeded limas, like 'Fordhooks', don't release pollen when the temperature is over 90°F. Other varieties are heat tolerant. If you plant both types together, the heat-tolerant ones will pollinate the temperature-sensitive limas.

Growing the pole varieties of limas may also help you beat the heat. Many bush varieties tend to set their pods all at one time; during extended heat spells you won't get any beans at all. Pole types have a wider window of pod-set, as well as a longer harvest period. Don't cultivate the beans after they start blooming. Doing so can cause them to drop their blossoms.

Any good, well-drained garden soil with a pH of 6.0 to 6.8 will do for limas. If possible, rotate crops so that beans are not planted on land used for growing beans in the last 2 to 3 years.

Plant bush types 2 to 3 inches apart in rows about 36 inches apart. For pole varieties set seeds at least 18 inches apart in rows 42 to 60 inches apart for trellised rows or in hills around poles, if you're building tepees. This is called vertical gardening (discussed in detail on page 6 in chapter 1). Some gardeners treat pea and bean seeds with a dry bacterial culture called an "inoculant," prior to planting, to encourage nitrogen-fixing bacterial growth

on the roots to increase yields. I do not feel that there is any value to this practice: Although the beans do nodulate (form nodules on their root systems that supply nitrogen to the soil), by the time they fix any appreciable amount of nitrogen, your harvest will be over. It is better to make sure that there is sufficient nitrogen in the soil at planting time.

Erect supports for the pole types as soon after planting as possible. Bush type limas ripen in 65 to 70 days; most pole types take 75 to 85 days to begin to bear.

Mustard

Raising mustard is easy, no coddling needed. Since the plant's mission is to bolt or set seed, culture is simple and undemanding.

There are many varieties of mustard available, though most people grow the plant for their leaves, to be used in salads or stir-fries. To grow and harvest the leaves, start the plants in cell packs and transplant them when they are 3 inches tall. Transplant the seedlings 18 inches apart into 2 foot rows. When harvesting, choose the largest leaves first.

Mustard is an annual. To raise mustard for its seed, direct-sow outdoors around the last frost date, when soil temperatures reach about 55°F. Mustard seed should be sown $1/4$ inch deep and 1 inch apart in rows spaced at 18 inches.

Because mustard is a direct-seeded brassica, I place a floating row cover over the bed to keep flea beetles away. I briefly remove it to thin seedlings to stand 3 inches apart; then leave it in place until buds begin to form.

To non-farmers, a field of wild mustard (wild rape) aflame in brilliant yellow is a wondrous sight. In July the plants are a 3-foot tall mass of golden flowers, humming with honeybees. Seedpods soon take the place of flowers, after which the plants begin to dry.

By late August the maturing seedpods become increasingly brittle. To prevent shattering, harvest when the stalks begin to change from green to straw-yellow. With pruning shears, cut the stalks where the main stems branch and place on a trap or sheet. Keep soil off the trap; cleanliness here will pay off later on. Finish drying in a protected area for about 5 days or until the pods are crisp.

Don't let the next step scare you off. Cleaning seeds is simpler, quicker, and more enjoyable than the instructions will lead you to believe. My first choice for a threshing floor is the bed of a pickup truck, but any kind of wood flooring is a fine alternative.

Wrap the seed stalks in the tarp or stuff them into sturdy sacks. I use a woven plastic feed bag. On hands and knees, thump about on the bag vigorously for a few minutes, stopping to rearrange the contents a few times. This dislodges almost all of the seed.

For a more complete harvest, rub the seed stalks against a $1/4$-inch hardware cloth stretched over a wooded frame. You may already have something like this for sifting soil or compost. A sheet placed underneath

will catch the mustard seed and trash such as broken seedpods and dried leaves.

Strain through a colander to remove the biggest pieces of trash and follow with a wire kitchen strainer just large enough for the seeds to pass through. Finally, winnow by pouring seed from one bowl to another in a slight breeze or in front of a fan.

Ideally, the light seed pods and dust blow away while the heavier clean seeds drop to the bottom of the bowl. Place a sheet under the bowl in case you miscalculate height or wind speed. Expect about 1 ounce of seed from every foot of row harvested. Store the seed in a glass jar or place right in a measuring cup and proceed to the kitchen.

A traditional method for homemade grainy-style mustard is to grind the seed with fluid—a heated, acidic liquid, like vinegar, citrus juice, or wine is reputed to reduce the spiciness. I find this best done with a blender. Watching the seeds grind and absorb the liquid is entrancing. A food processor can be used instead, providing that the seed is pre-soaked; but the final product is less evenly textured.

Your own prepared mustard will find many uses, from keeping oil and vinegar dressings in suspension to enlivening cheese and mayonnaise sauces. The more mustard you make, the more uses you will find. The process lends itself so grandly to experimentation that my final advice is to record your progress, so that you can duplicate a great success.

Onions

Onions were grown in ancient Egypt, are mentioned in the Bible, and can be found in the diet of practically every nation.

Bulbing onions

This section discusses how to grow them organically for the best results both in the garden and on the table. Although onions will grow in a very wide range of soil and climatic conditions, they thrive in a soil that is well-fortified with organic matter, and need an entire day of sunshine. A deeply cultivated and well-drained garden soil is required, and is especially important for the large, Spanish varieties.

I have found that onions grow best on my farm after I have prepared the soil in fall. As I till the area deeply, I turn in at least a 4-inch layer of compost mixed with organic soil amendments—bone meal, greensand, fish meal, and kelp meal.

Another method for ensuring that your garden has sufficient humus for onions is to add shredded leaves or compost to the soil before planting. We have large quantities of leaves readily available, so I till them into our beds, using about 5 bushels of leaves for each of our 10- × 20-foot beds.

Since onions like a pH of between 6.0 to 7.0, I sprinkle crushed dolomitic limestone over the soil to counterbalance the acidity of the leaves. I also apply compost at the rate of 2 pounds per square foot or a 2-inch level over the growing bed.

Before tilling and raking this under, I apply 4–6–4 organic fertilizer at a rate of 3 pounds per 20 feet. Then I till and rake the beds until they are smooth and clod-free before planting. Onions are relatively untroubled by insects or diseases, as long as they are started in cell packs, and provided with healthy soil. As soon as shoots are up, thin the onions so that the bulbs won't touch. Then cultivate carefully between the rows.

When the onion leaves are about 4 inches high, mulch with straw. As the summer progresses, I add more mulch, pulling it over any exposed bulbs. This keeps weeds sown and helps the soil stay moist and friable.

I plant my onions around the middle of April, or sooner, depending on how soon my soil can be worked. Late frosts have no effect on onion shoots. Actually, early planting is a must in onion culture. At the time their bulbs are forming, onions must have 10 to 12 hours of daylight. If sown early, the plants will be ready to set their bulbs in June, when the days are the longest. If planted late, they overshoot this period and produce only small onions.

When buying sets (small onion bulbs that you direct-seed in the soil), it is well to remember that 1 pound will plant a 30- to 40-foot row and will produce $1/2$ to 1 bushel of onions.

Onion sets grow rapidly once established. After 6 weeks I go down the row and begin thinning them out. I relish these young plants!

Onions must have firm soil around their roots at all times. When 12 inches high, I loosen the soil slightly in the aisles to encourage good air circulation. Then I top-dress with

THE 'WHITE SWEET SPANISH' SET EXPERIMENT

Growing small onions from seed is easy enough to do. Yet in growing sets, the important thing is to keep the onions small until they are fully ripened. Otherwise, they will spoil very quickly in storage. It is possible, without taking great pains, to grow high-grade, organically grown onion sets of a variety that cannot be purchased through regular channels.

I chose 'White Sweet Spanish' onions. I sowed $1/4$ ounce of seed over a rough circle some 3 feet in diameter. After scattering the onion seed, I spindled a thin covering of peat moss over the bed, pressed that and the seed together against the soil with my feet, and watered the area thoroughly.

The seeds sprouted quickly and the small leaves filled the space so completely as to make it resemble a plot of coarse grass. The bulbs formed nicely and most of them developed to about the size of marbles by the time they were ripe.

After the tops had fallen over on the majority of the plants, I pulled those. I clipped all but a short piece of top from each with the grass shears and chose 50 of the best to store.

Up to this point I encountered no difficulties, nor had I expected to. Like gardeners, I have grown onions from seed many times and the thick planting was an obvious variation on ordinary procedures.

Storage, however, was another matter. Onions keep best in a cool, dry place and I might have found one for my sets. But I wanted my experiment to show what might be accomplished by making no extra effort. I therefore selected a convenient spot in my cellar where it was hot and dry, rather than cool and dry, and hung the bag of sets from a nail overhead.

I realized, when it was too late, that what I should have done was to divide the sets, putting half in some cooler place and leaving the rest where they were. I could then have said something definite about the effects of improper storage conditions in comparison with better methods.

As it was, all I can say is that the heat did less harm than I expected. I did not touch the sets or even the bag they were in until late April. That was when I was ready to plant any that had survived. I dumped the bag out onto the table and sat down to examine the remains. Together with a certain amount of chaff, there proved to be 40 onion sets. A few of these turned out to be a little soft, and 1 or 2 more seemed unduly dry. I had 30 prime sets out of the original 50 and these I planted at once.

---

a balanced organic fertilizer, (4–6–4), high in phosphorous, and mulch the aisles with 5 inches of grass clippings. When mulching, however, one must be careful to keep the material at least 2 inches away from the young plants. I find that my onions will not set bulbs if they are covered over with either soil or mulch. Also, the young onions are quick to rot if not exposed to air and sunlight. When weeds appear within the rows, I wait until a heavy rain falls. Then I weed while the soil is good and wet.

After mulching, the onions require no more attention other than topping. Topping consists of removing the "scape" or bloom stem. If this scape is not removed at the base, the bulb will not form and what little has formed will be of no value.

If you prefer large onions, a weekly feeding of liquid fish or seaweed after the bulbs begin to form, is very beneficial.

For the best flavor, onions should grow quickly. I have never needed to side-dress our onions, but if your soil is not rich, you should add an extra helping of compost when you thin the onions and again when bulbs start to swell.

Plant Spanish-style onions in the greenhouse in February. Set them out the first week of April, placing the transplants 4 inches apart in every direction.

A full bed of 'Sweet Sandwich' onions goes in the garden the third week of April. Although these are very strong-tasting when first harvested, they improve with age. After 3 months in storage their flavor is mild and slightly sweet.

The last week in April 'Torpedo' onions are planted. They are shaped like miniature, purple torpedoes and have a distinctive flavor that blends well with Mexican and Italian food.

During the first week in August, my onions begin to show signs of maturing by turning brown at the tips. Now is the time to go down each row and gently pull the soil away from the bulbs so that at least half of each is exposed to the air and sun.

In mid-August, I pull the onions and cure them for storage by braiding the tops together: First I plait 3 onions and then braid these strands into groups of 3 to make thick onion ropes. The ropes are then hung in a cool, airy space for 3 weeks.

Besides cultivating regular onions, you might want to try onion sets.

Onions can also be successfully grown from seed if they are started in early February in the greenhouse or indoors in flats. However, to save yourself a lot of time and effort and to insure success, grow onions sets. Not only will sets give you big onions at harvest time, but the bulbs will keep better and longer in storage.

Because onions are such robust growers, one is apt to become careless when planting. I often have a tendency just to drop the sets into furrows. Believe me, it really does pay to plant the sets correctly. Sets that are planted individually get off to a quick start. This, of course, means more and bigger onions.

There are onion growers who work the soil well, draw a line, then simply push each set into the soft soil and forget about it. Although this gives average results, I prefer to place the sets $2^1/_2$ inches apart in rows 12 inches apart, then cover them with an inch of rich soil.

After the onions are covered, I firm the soil pressing the soil particles together so they will act as a sponge in bringing up water from the subsoil to keep sets moist until adequate root systems are developed.

Perennial Onions

The familiar bulbing onions (which are biennials grown as annuals) have some desirable relatives—cousins that are perennial. Instead of producing a single bulb the first year, then going to seed the following year, these beauties keep going indefinitely. Each year they produce greens and bulbs for eating and plenty for replanting another crop, too.

Perennial onions can be grouped into several categories, each belonging to one of three groups:

1. Subtly-flavored shallots and potato onions are multiplying onions. Each

plant produces a cluster of bulbs at its base.

2. Bunching onions, also known as scallions or spring onions, reproduce at ground level. They form bigger bunches each year, but do not form large bulbs, and are harvested mainly for their stalks.

3. Egyptian tree onions divide at the base. They also form little bulbs in their flower clusters, which easily start new plants.

You plant and care for perennial onions in much the same way as you do the bulbing types. They like rich, fertile soil and hate competition from weeds. Most should be planted in fall so that their root systems can get established for early-spring growth.

Shallots

Though they closely resemble garlic in appearance, shallots have a quite delicate

Perennial onions

flavor that has earned them a reputation for continental elegance. They are very tender and cook faster than regular onions, making them perfect for sauces.

Plant individual bulbs in fall or spring. Place 4 inches apart, an inch or 2 deep, in rows 18 inches apart. Keep them watered and weeded.

You can harvest some of the greens during the summer for use in salads. The bulbs are ready when the leaves start to wither, but haven't actually collapsed.

Cure the shallots for a few days to two weeks, depending on how dry it is. Store them in clusters and braid them like onions or put them in net bags and store in a cool, dry place.

Potato Onions

Yellow potato onions were popular in home gardens until the 1940s, when the starter sets disappeared from mail-order catalogs. Many gardeners kept them going, though, and you can now get them from the Seed Savers Exchange (for a catalog, call 319-382-5990). Full-size potato onions are larger than shallots and shaped more like a flattened globe.

Potato onions produce both large and small bulbs and the two behave differently. Each small bulb that you plant will produce 1 large bulb during the next growing season. Each large bulb will produce a cluster of small bulbs.

Every fall you should plant a mixture of bulbs. Place them about 10 inches apart and 1 inch deep, and feed them well. Add some bone meal for growth.

Each large onion planted in fall will produce a spring harvest of 5 to 20 potato onions. Pull away any mulch when they begin

A POTATO ONION IS A POTATO ONION

There are quite a few theories on why potato onions are so named: It could be because they were planted in hilled soil like potatoes or planted alongside them; or perhaps because they produce a cluster of bulbs underground like potatoes do. A little more farfetched is the notion that they were carried (along with potatoes) by American settlers moving west. All of these theories are interesting, but not as interesting as the onions themselves.

to grow, so clusters can continue to develop at the soil surface.

You can harvest some of them green, but leave some until the green tops die down and small bulbs develop. Harvest those when ready. Cure them and plant them in early fall. They will be your large onions next summer.

Egyptian Tree Onions

Egyptian tree onions are easy to grow and, once established, little work to maintain. They seem immune to disease and insect pests and can be dug up from the ground at any season of the year. In the kitchen they are very versatile.

Each little bulb set in early fall grows by the following spring into a large green onion which, by the next fall, has split and formed two or three slender reeds. These will multiply the following year as well, and so on, and so on.

The Egyptian tree onion also multiplies in midsummer at the top of its stalk so that it resembles a miniature tree, hence its middle name. It is these little bulb clusters that are often used to set new plantings. However,

many people prefer to dig up and transplant an already-growing clump, either whole or separated, into individual plants.

Once established, a bed is practically no work at all and provides one with onions throughout fall, winter, and spring. Yes, winter, too, where a covering of leaves can keep the ground from freezing most of the time.

In summer, however, the onion matures into a tough, tubular stalk. Even this can be used for flavoring, if removed from the pot when the cooking is done. (For eating onions at this time of year, I depend on 'Ebenezers'. Unlike 'Ebenezers', the Egyptian never develops a big bulb at its root.)

The Egyptian onion has almost as many uses as days in the week. It can be munched raw, used in soups and stews to add flavor, and substituted for garlic in spaghetti sauce. Its tender green shoots can be snipped into potato salad.

Like string beans, Egyptian onions will grow, even thrive, in rather poor soil. Of course, a good soil and lots of water will produce better onions—naturally bigger, juicier, and finer-flavored. So-called onion soil is preferably sandy, friable, loam, not clod-like, and rich in organic matter.

My Egyptian onions are grown in a permanent, out-of-the-way bed. It's less work. Just pull a few weeds now and then and dig up the overcrowded clumps to be eaten. Of course, the bed is well-mulched.

Egyptian onions can also be grown as a row crop, in the same way as beets, carrots, or regular onions. In this case, set the little top bulbs in late summer. Mulch over winter.

Thinnings can be used the next spring for early onions, but to get the most out of your garden space, wait until the second spring before harvesting the main crop. The preceding summer, the top bulbs should have been removed to form new plantings. Cut off the tough stalks, too, and let them lie right there in the row as a mulch to decay.

Don't give up any of your old favorite onions, but experiment with some new onions too. Expand the family. Start a perennial onion patch.

Pak Choi (See Chinese Cabbage)

Peas

Some gardeners make their first mistake with peas, an early season annual, before even venturing outdoors. Whatever you do, do not Presoak pea seeds.

A lot of people still think that they can speed things up by soaking the seeds in water for a day or so before planting them out. Presoaking is like hitting the seeds with a hammer: the outside expands faster than the inside, breaking the seeds apart. Once the pregerminated seeds are in the soil, they are more susceptible to disease and rot, especially if the weather stays wet and cool. Other gardeners are overly cautious and plant their peas too late. I advise keeping a close eye on the thermometer. When the soil temperature is in the 40°F range during the day, it's time to start planting. Peas need an early start so that the pods are set before the weather gets into the 90s.

Early sowings won't do a bit of good, however, if your soil is wet and soggy. The seeds will just sit there, courting the pea's prime enemy: rot. To ensure a successful early crop, sow only in well-drained soil and plant the seeds shallowly and thickly. You will do best if you plant peas in raised beds and, for the first spring crop, sow them no more than an inch deep. If the soil is heavy, sow them $1/2$ inch deep so that the plants can become established quickly. Later sowings (when the soil is warmer and drier) can be planted more deeply (up to 2 inches), depending on the tilth of your soil.

Be sure to rotate your planting area each year. Root rot is a big problem with commercial growers because they sow peas in their earliest available land, the same field year after year. Gardeners tend to do that, too. They plant peas in the same plot, where the soil is driest and warmest. Once the root pathogen is in the soil, it's difficult to get rid of.

Peas don't need much in the way of added nutrients since they fix their own nitrogen. They will benefit from a boost of phosphorous and potassium from bone meal and greensand.

Peas do best when the pH is between 6.0 and 6.8, so acid soils should be buffered with limestone.

I recommend working in a 50–50 mix of limestone and rock phosphate at a rate of 5 pounds per 100 square feet in the fall. That way you won't tie up the trace elements in spring. Then fertilize the seedlings with a foliar seaweed-fish spray as they emerge.

A pound or 2 of 4–6–4 organic fertilizer per 100 square feet added to the soil a few days before planting in spring would also provide the necessary nutrients for good root growth and pod production.

I add coarse compost to my 5-foot-wide pea beds in the fall, turning it in by hand. In spring, as soon as the soil can be worked, I till it in.

Skimpy sowing is a common mistake that gardeners make, especially on the first spring plantings. I use a pound of seed for a 40-foot bed, planting it in a 4- to 5-inch-wide band down the middle with the seeds maybe $1/8$ to $1/4$ inch apart.

If you sow any thinner than that, you don't reap the maximum harvest. Since I need enough peas for both eating and seed saving, raising a heavy yield is crucial. Carrots and parsnips, planted on either side of peas, provide a double harvest from each bed.

Unless you're planting in a rich, loamy soil, though, $1/8$-inch spacing may be too close for comfort. Try sowing peas $1/2$ inch apart for the earliest sowing, with later plantings spaced at 1 to 2 inches in double rows 6 inches apart on either side of a trellis.

To keep peas on your plate for as long as possible, sow several plantings of quick-growing varieties throughout the spring, along with 1 or 2 plantings of a later variety. Or make just 1 spring sowing, planting 3 or 4 varieties that mature at different times.

Peas can be planted for a fall crop, as long as you sow only fast-maturing varieties. The trick to getting peas up in the summer heat is to keep the beds moist.

Still the biggest problem with late summer sowings isn't getting peas up, but keeping them growing. I've never had any trouble as long as I keep the soil moist and cool with drip irrigation and apply micronutrient foliar spray every 2 weeks.

Peppers

To enjoy the diversity of pepper varieties, start your own transplants.

Pepper seeds are slow starters. Many varieties need 80 warm days or more to yield well. The best outdoor planting time is usually a week to 10 days after the last spring frost date.

Peppers

Figure that out and then count back 8 to 10 weeks. That is when you want to start seed indoors.

Plant seeds about $1/4$ inch deep in flats, using moist, organic seed-starting material. For quick germination, keep the flat in a warm environment (at least 75°F). Seeds come up fastest in potting soil with an 80 to 90°F temperature. If your seed-starting space is 65°F or lower, they may take 2 or 3 weeks.

You can hang a lightbulb over the flats to warm things up a bit, or cover the flats with plastic to keep in warmth and moisture. Otherwise, be sure to moisten the soil with warm water periodically so seeds can swell and germinate.

When seedlings emerge, remove the lightbulb and put the plants under fluorescent lights for 12 hours a day in a warm place (70 to 80°F during the day and 65°F at night).

Mark all of your varieties clearly right from the start. The last thing you want is to find a favorite pepper near the end of the summer and have no idea what it is.

Ten days or so before you plan to set the plants outdoors, gradually harden them off.

Put them outdoors for increasing periods of time each day, starting with just an hour or 2. Peppers need organic fertilizer at transplanting time. However, be cautious. Too much nitrogen applied before planting can lead to excessive vegetative growth and low fruit yields. High amounts of nitrogen applied after planting don't lead to similar problems. Refer to your soil test results to gauge the correct amount. You want good leaf growth before fruit set.

Enrich the soil with composted cow or horse manure, rock phosphate, and greensand. Put some composted manure in the planting hole with each plant you set out.

Peppers respond to magnesium, which is why many gardeners water them with an Epsom salts solution. Use a tablespoon of the salts in a gallon of water to feed young plants. Watering or spraying plants with a fish and seaweed emulsion is also very beneficial.

Yellow, orange, and purple peppers are pretty enough to take up a spot in your flower garden. My favorite place to see them, though, is on the dinner plate. If your family has tired of raw vegetables, one of these can easily recapture their interest.

I have outlined below possible problems your pepper patch may face, and the organic solutions.

Blossom Drop

Some buds and blossoms may drop when the temperature goes over 90°F, if humidity is low. In hot summers, a straw mulch can be helpful by reducing the heat intensity. Blossom drop can also occur if temperatures fall too low—under 55°F. Again, watering is important. Keep in mind that plants produce more blossoms than they can develop into fruits, so losing a few blooms isn't serious.

> ### PERFECT PEPPER PLACEMENT
>
> When transplanting pepper plants into your bed place them closely together so that when full-grown, the leaves will touch. Two feet apart in each direction is ideal. The foliage helps shade the developing fruits from sunscald and reduces weeds.
>
> Bell pepper plants are larger than hot pepper types, so they can be spaced further apart. I suggest 15 inches as the right interval for the best bell pepper production.

Blossom End Rot

Blossom end rot is caused by insufficient calcium input when fruits are forming. Blotchy brown areas at the blossom end may also be a result of rapid growth from excessive fertilization or fluctuating water supply. Regular watering through the season and mulching after fruits form help a lot.

Insects

Insects are not a serious concern for most organic gardeners, though pepper maggots and pepper weevils may bother some pepper crops. Parasitic nematodes can control these pests.

Sunscald

Soft, light-colored, slightly wrinkled areas on both leaves and fruits that deteriorate and become discolored can result from exposure to intense direct sunlight. Employ close planting to reduce this danger.

Virus

Several viruses can attack peppers. Chief among them is the cucumber mosaic virus that is spread by aphids. Signs are leaf and fruit mottling, yellow rings, yellow spots on leaves and fruits, or stunted plants. Control aphids with insecticidal soap and use virus-resistant varieties, as listed in your seed catalog.

Potatoes

Unlike most vegetables, potatoes thrive in acid soils, so don't add any lime to your soil. In addition to raising the pH level, limestone also fosters conditions that can lead to potato scab diseases. Conversely, phosphorus is an essential mineral for tuber crops, and will ensure large, healthy yields.

Bone meal and rock phosphate are ideal sources of phosphate. Normal soils benefit from an addition of approximately 3 pounds of bonemeal or 6 pounds of rock phosphate per 100 square feet in the autumn. However, shy away from wood ashes: Like limestone, it can promote scab from high amounts of potassium, and cause the potatoes to get mealy. If your soil is alkaline, add sulfur before planting.

It is wise to buy certified organic virus-free seed potatoes, as you will end up with healthier, bigger yields. The worst source of potato seed stock is the supermarket. Supermarket potatoes may grow, but many have been treated with chemicals that inhibit sprouting.

To prepare for planting, we slice the seed into 2- to 3-ounce pieces, making sure that there are no more than 2 eyes to each piece (as a rough guide, the proper size is about the size of an egg). Smaller pieces, or those with more than 2 eyes, are a foolish economy. Since the new plants draw on the starchy reserves of the seed pieces for a good start in the garden world, the more reserves they have to draw on, the better they will grow.

After cutting seed pieces, allow the cut to cure or heal (form a skin). A freshly cut, unhealed tuber could easily rot in the soil, so put your seed in a sunny window for a week before planting. Turn them slightly each day. Besides healing the cut, the eyes will just begin to show signs of sprouting.

Plant potatoes when it is cool, from between 59 to 64°F. The seed pieces should be planted approximately 4 to 6 inches into the soil, at intervals of about 12 to 15 inches apart in each row; make the rows approximately 2 to 3 feet apart. To avoid disease and soil deficiencies, choose a site where potatoes—and other members of the nightshade family such as tomatoes, eggplants, peppers, and petunias—have not been grown for at least 3 years. (Note: Potatoes should be rotated on a 3-year program. This means you need 3 suitable sites if you want to grow potatoes every year.)

Potatoes prefer a fertile, well-drained soil. A waterlogged soil will produce rotted or sickly crops. You can loosen your soil with an application of leaf mold and seaweed. Plant as early as you can: Early planting ensures that your potatoes are well established by the time most insects and diseases arrive. And by harvesting a quick 2 to 3 months after planting, you free up garden space for a second crop or a green manure cover crop for winter.

Whenever you have to contend with freezing, get your early potatoes in the ground 3 to 4 weeks before the last expected frost. Even if the sprouts get nipped, the food reserves in the seed potato will send out new shoots, and your crop will be fine.

After several weeks or less, the first shoots will begin to emerge. Hoe the soil well around them and mound a few inches of soil up around the base of the seedlings.

The next step is to toss a thick, but loose, mulch layer over the entire patch. This keeps the potato tops from greening after they grow big enough to push to the surface. Green potatoes contain a poison called solanine, and are not safe to eat.

Some folks swear by potatoes in trenches. They draw soil around the vines as the stems grow. The theory is that the new potatoes form above the planted seed. Therefore, if you put the seed in the bottom of the trench and add soil as the vines grow, the potatoes will be encouraged. This system works, but it entails too much digging at both sowing and harvesting times.

We give our potato crop plenty of water, allowing $1/2$ inch of topsoil to dry out between soakings. After the vines flower, we watch for signs of dieback (which is when the plant dies above the soil line), indicating that the potatoes are ready for harvest.

Once the early potatoes are growing, we turn our attention to the rest of our garden. The cabbages and peas get along with the potatoes in companion situations, so we try to plant them close by. By May, the entire spring crop has been planted.

As you work your potatoes, begin to check under the first plantings. Just under the mulch or in the first inch or so of soil directly under where the stems enter the soil, are delicious quarter-sized new potatoes. They're easy to dig out with your fingers or a garden trowel if you're careful.

Let most of your potatoes mature. After the vines die back, use a 4-pronged potato fork to turn up the mature potatoes. Let them dry out on top of the soil for a few days. Once cured, they store well in boxes in a cool, damp, dark place where they will last all winter.

To grow small potatoes in a small space, follow the standard methods for growing early potatoes—essentially, just plant and harvest them as soon as possible—but sow them a little closer together.

For those of you who live in an apartment, you too can grow your own organic potatoes. Get a bushel basket, line it with plastic, and punch a few holes in the base for drainage. Put some rocks in the bottom to aid drainage as well. Next, apply a 5- to 7-inch layer of soil. You can use either a bagged potting soil, or one prepared with composted cow manure or peat moss. Be sure the pH is below 6.0.

To fertilize, use 1 part cottonseed meal, 1 part fish meal, 1 part bonemeal, 2 parts rock phosphate, and 2 parts greensand. Lay 6 to 7 pieces of seed potato on the soil, spaced 6 to 8 inches apart, then top with 3 to 5 more inches of soil. Keep your basket in a warm sunny place. As plants grow, add more soil around the stems to allow the tubers to expand. Keep well watered, and spray with a micronutrient foliar spray once a month.

Pumpkins

Pumpkins are heavy feeders, and most gardening books instruct you to give them plenty of organic plant food. But you can go one better: After you finish side-dressing early vegetables, you will probably still have a sizeable

Pumpkins

heap of compost left, at least 13 feet square and about 2 feet high.

Make a shallow depression in the center of the heap; this can be used later as a "pan" to hold water should the season prove dry. Since pumpkins are sensitive to frost, and subject to decay before germination if planted in wet, cold soil, hold off planting until the weather has settled and warmed.

Plant alternating seeds of popular cultivars like 'Jack-O'Lantern' and 'Connecticut Field' in your pumpkin patch. Seeds should be sown from 8 to 12 feet apart, as many of the varieties have long-running vines.

The male and female reproductive organs of pumpkins are located in different flowers on the same plant. The flowers are largely insect-pollinated, and that is done mostly by bees, which transfer pollen from the anthers of the male flower to the stigma of the female flower. Without this happy marriage, there is no fruit.

One thing for the small organic gardener to keep in mind is that pumpkins, especially the vining type, take up considerable room. This factor can be successfully dealt with in several clever ways: One technique is to plant cultivars such as 'Sugar Pie' or 'Tricky Jack'. These grow on compact, 4-foot bushy plants and have the added attraction of hull-less, edible seeds. Another method is to grow them on posts, poles, trellises, or interplant them with sweet corn.

Speaking of interplanting, bear in mind that when jimsonweed or thorn apple are grown near a pumpkin patch, they have a beneficial effect on crop yield, giving the pumpkins increased vigor, improved taste, and greater resistance to disease. Elizabeth and I make up a spray from equal amounts of jimsonweed and thorn apple, and spray it out on the pumpkins every 2 weeks. We never have problems with disease or insects.

Harvest your pumpkins in September and October, making sure they are fully mature. There are several tests for maturity. If you thump the pumpkin in the same way you would thump a watermelon and you hear a hollow sound, it means your Halloween vegetable is ready for harvest.

You can also test by digging into the skin with your thumbnail. If the skin is hard and resistant, the pumpkin is probably ready. However, if you lift a pumpkin and the stem end parts cleanly from the vine, you know it is definitely ready to go.

Pumpkins are a distinctly American vegetable, and their cultivation was brought to a high state of perfection by the Native Americans long before this country was settled by the Europeans. They are an excellent source of vitamin A and a fair source of vitamin C, and contain calcium, phosphorus, and iron as well. And if you didn't grow any pumpkins this year, we recommend taking the family to a pumpkin farm that lets you pick your own pumpkins. This way, you can see how they grow, and it's a fun day in the sun for you and your family.

Snap Beans

Snap beans, also known as string beans or green beans, are annuals. Bush varieties produce more of a harvest, but also take up more room in the garden, while pole varieties make use of vertical air space.

Snap beans aren't heavy feeders, but they do need a friable soil for the best germination and root development. The idea is to loosen the soil, not enrich it.

I use raised beds—measuring 4 × 15 feet—that receive full sun. A raised bed facilitates drainage and warms faster in the spring. I till the bed to a depth of 10 inches, working in some coarse sand and compost to loosen the soil. Once prepared, avoid stepping in the bed. Compacted soil hinders bean germination.

I don't fertilize the bed. Too much fertilizer often forces beans to produce lush leaf growth at the expense of pods. The compost that I use contains enough nutrients to keep the beans in good production.

Bush snap beans are the perfect succession crops. If you plant all of your beans at once, you are likely to have too much harvest at one time. It's better to space your plantings at 2-week intervals from late May until August. This offers you continuous production until the first fall frost.

Most bush snap beans mature in about 50 days. The bed that I use for early peas is the same that I use for my beans. The peas are harvested and out of the bed by mid-June, leaving plenty of time to start a succession of beans. I also plant blocks of beans as garden space becomes available, after spring crops like spinach and turnips have been harvested.

As a rule, bush beans are warm-season crops. 'Royal Burgundy' can be planted soon after the last expected frost date. Other varieties grow best between 70 and 80°F.

Below 55°F, beans suffer poor germination. It is safest to wait until soil temperature is around 65°F. If your beans don't sprout within 2 weeks after sowing, the seed has probably rotted in soil that is too wet and cold. Replanting is the only solution.

Because bush beans produce admirably in crowded conditions, I plant them in wide rows or blocks. A dense planting saves garden space, increases production, conserves soil moisture, and smothers weeds. I simply rake smooth a row about 18 inches wide; then scatter the seeds over the surface, spacing them roughly 1 to 2 inches apart. I tamp the seeds into the soil with the back of my hoe; then cover the seeds with $1^1/_2$ inches of loose soil. I don't even bother to thin the seedlings when they come up.

Once the beans are established in the bed, watering is your foremost consideration. Excessive or too little moisture may cause blossom and pod drop. The critical time for watering is during pollination and pod production.

When the seedlings pop out of the soil, I immediately mulch around the young plants to conserve soil moisture. Experience has shown that yields increase when bark mulch is used. In most garden conditions, bush beans require an inch of water each week, more during drought periods. A soaker hose or drip irrigation system is recommended. If possible, avoid watering from overhead with a hose. This disturbs blossoming and often spreads diseases like rust and mosaic. When soil is healthy and balanced, beans grow and are harvested quickly, and there is no problem with insects or diseases.

Anthracnose, bacteria, blights, and fungi are the most common diseases. Rotate the crops each year to avoid problems. Stay out of the bed when plants are wet, for this spreads disease on the foliage.

The worst insect in the bean patch is the Mexican bean beetle. Early and late plantings suffer the least from these rapacious bugs, but midseason crops can have a problem.

Rotenone (a white crystalline substance made from the roots of certain tropical pea plants) or a marigold herb spray offer some control, but it is difficult to apply these sprays to the undersides of the leaves where the larvae congregate. I usually handpick the larvae when I harvest the beans.

Some organic gardeners use marigolds, garlic, or rosemary planted around the beds to keep beetles away. This method is called companion planting (see Grower's Glossary).

Bush beans are easy to grow and produce tremendous yields, even in limited space and poor soil. No wonder these snap beans are second only to tomatoes in garden popularity.

Sorrel

If you want to harvest the first possible green from the spring garden, then sorrel is for you. A perennial member of the dock family, sorrel comes back from the roots early each spring. It produces even in the hottest weather, yet tolerates partial shade and bears continuous crops of tangy green leaves. In warm-weather areas of the country it will continue to bear year-round. Sheep's sorrel grows abundantly in clearings and meadows in the moister areas. The lance-shaped leaves can be used to pep up otherwise bland domestic salads or to nibble as thirst-quenchers while on hikes.

Sheep's sorrel responds admirably to organic methods. In the wild, leaves rarely grow over 3 inches; but, given garden conditions, they volunteer at 8 to 9 inches, very tender and tasty. It is a perfect no-work garden perennial vegetable, except for one fact: Sheep's sorrel is propagated by runners. It is not long before intertwining sorrel root systems are interfering with valuable cultivated crops. It is especially hard to deal with among the strawberries because even the tiniest piece missed in weeding seems to have the power to reinfest the whole patch.

Therefore, wild sorrel is not a desirable companion to vegetables or fruits. However, if you still want those tart, lemony leaves for salads, there is a solution. It comes in the discovery of a domesticated species that increases by clumping instead of runners and produces lance-like leaves larger than a foot long even on average soils.

Start your first seed in early spring, covering with $1/2$ inch of soil in rows 18 inches apart. When the plants are up, thin to 8 inches. With plenty of organic fertilizer, moisture, and a deep mulch during the hot summer, these plants will quickly fill the space allotted to them.

To harvest, cut or pinch off the outer green leaves, always being careful to leave a rosette of young growth to insure quick future harvests. Regular harvesting, even when you do not intend to use the produce, helps keep the crop at its tender best.

If, after a few years, they become too crowded, either turn under and sow new seed, as commercial growers do every 4 or 5 years, or divide the clumps in early spring as soon as the ground can be worked and plant again.

With that kind of care, they will reward you year after year with some of the earliest greens of the season.

Spinach

Spinach is strictly a cool-weather crop. As soon as long days and heat come, spinach refuses to produce. We have tried heavy mulches, drip-irrigation, and shady locations

Spinach

to extend its growing season into summer, but something in spinach's genetic makeup triggers the plant to send up a seed stalk as soon as those long, hot days arrive. Oddly, spinach will germinate with ground temperatures as low as 35°F, but will refuse with soil heat of 80°F. This is quite the opposite of most vegetables. It is better to grow Malabar spinach, beet greens, and Swiss chard for summer use.

Plant your spinach from early February to early May indoors, under florescent lights, and pick up again with plantings in late fall. This planting system frees us from bolting spinach and poor germination.

Spinach is both shallow-rooted and a lover of nitrogen. Plants like spinach, which need to make rapid growth for best flavor and tenderness, do better in a light soil than a heavy one. By working some compost into the top couple of inches of soil, you put the nitrogenous plant food right where it will do the most good for those shallow roots. The only other ingredient needed is a micronutrient foliar spray. It is best to plant spinach in a well-drained, sunny location. Spinach prefers full sunlight along with cool weather.

We sow the seed in ground that has been thoroughly watered a day or two previously, so that by the time the seeds are in the ground, all excess water will have percolated or evaporated, yet there will be plenty of water held in the germination zone by soil particles. As long as the soil doesn't dry out, don't water again until after the seedlings emerge. This greatly cuts down on the possibility of dampness-related diseases. After the plants are established, we water whenever the top $1/2$ inch of soil dries out. We also cultivate shallowly around the seedlings to remove weeds and promote fast growth.

From an initial sowing of 1 seed to the inch in rows a foot apart, we thin to a plant every 4 inches. I cultivate after thinning, and again at mid-growth if time permits. Handled like this, spinach becomes an easy vegetable to grow.

You can begin harvesting your spinach when you can pick enough leaves to make a meal. By successive sowings every 10 days, you have a supply all spring. I sow in rows by themselves, or between rows mapped out for large cole crops like cabbage. During the fall and winter months, pick the outer leaves as long as the plants generate rapid growth, extending the season. I have found that spinach will produce all winter when protected in a cold frame against freezing temperatures. This crop grows best between October and May, just at the time of the year when nutritious home-grown vegetables are in shortest supply.

Under the best growing conditions, plants will begin to bolt when daylight exceeds 14 to 16 hours, depending on variety. However, spinach will bolt (go to seed) even faster when grown in warm temperatures over 80°F. This is why gardeners who experience an unexpected spell of hot weather in late May will have tiny plants with just a few leaves forming a flowering stalk. Avoid this problem by planting early and using longstanding cultivars, which rapidly form large leaves, but are slow to flower.

Spinach breeders have developed some wonderful longstanding spinach cultivars. 'Melody' hybrid is one of the first. While 'Melody' doesn't bolt as quickly under longer day lengths or hot weather, it doesn't grow quite as rapidly as 'Tyee' and 'Skookum', two other hybrids. Although exact days to harvest depends on the season and the area where the spinach is grown, 'Tyee' has been harvested after 37 days. Another hybrid cultivar, 'Olympia', is even more longstanding than 'Tyee' but doesn't grow quite as fast, taking about 5 to 6 days more than 'Tyee', and 2 more days than 'Melody'.

Leaves of 'Olympia' are erect and smooth, and 'Tyee', 'Skookum', and 'Melody' leaves have few wrinkles to hold sand and soil. This is important for gardeners who experience heavy spring rains that splatter soil up onto the leaves. Heavily wrinkled or savoyed (crinkled) leaves can become so encrusted with soil that cleaning becomes a time-consuming job.

In addition to their ability to retard bolting, these hybrids are disease-resistant and tolerant to downy mildew. This mildew causes spinach to become discolored with yellow spots; in severe cases, the spots all converge, killing the plant. Unfortunately, downy mildew exists as 3 distinct races at the present time, although the second race has all but disappeared in the United States. 'Melody' is resistant to races 1 and 2, 'Tyee' is resistant to races 1 and 3, and 'Skookum' and 'Olympia' are resistant to all 3 races.

You can increase the length of your spinach harvest by using a few good growing and harvesting techniques. Spinach bolts fastest when grown under stressful conditions, including an insufficient supply of nitrogen, too little water, or overcrowding. As with many plants, a high level of nitrogen in the soil slows the development of flowers and encourages the rampant growth of leaves.

Make certain that you have enough nitrogen in your soil by adding at least 1 1/2 pounds of compost per square foot. If your plants appear to be growing slowly or are yellow-green in color, use a seaweed/fish foliar feeder once a week.

Spinach grows best in cooler temperatures—60 to 65°F is ideal— so plan to have your spinach up and growing when the temperature falls within this range in your area. Plant the seeds up to 1/2 inch deep, and 1 to 2 inches apart. Standard rows should be spaced at least 1 foot apart, but you can save space by planting a wide row, perhaps up to 2 to 2 1/2 feet. Once spinach germinates, thin it to 4 to 6 inches, since crowding encourages bolting. By competing for sunlight, nutrients, and water, weeds will slow your harvest and speed bolting, so keep your plants weed-free.

Growing a lush green crop of spinach that can be picked again and again is every spinach salad lover's dream. And that's the way it is in an organic garden.

Squash

In years gone by, all squash varieties, both summer and winter, used to be vine crops. Today, however, types have been developed that are less vining and more bushlike. These bush types can be ordered through most seed catalogs. In small gardens, bush varieties are easiest to manage.

Summer Squash

The popular annual known as summer squash prefers hot weather and cannot be planted until the air temperature hovers in the 65 to 75°F range. Most cultivars will bear fruit in 6 to 8 weeks, and most zucchini ripens in 50 days or less. You can sow squash in May and be harvesting it by July.

Summer squash requires a fertile soil. Start preparing your beds in the fall by adding a 2-inch-deep layer of composted manure and tilling it in thoroughly; supplement with organic fertilizer.

The seeds can be started early indoors, then moved to the garden around the same time as tomato transplants. Another method is to sow squash outdoors 3 weeks before the regular planting time and shield the seedlings with hotcaps. Squash that is early-seeded will ripen several weeks earlier than squash that's direct-seeded, but does not grow as quickly.

Summer care is low maintenance. Foliar spray the plants once every 3 weeks with a micronutrient fish/seaweed spray, and keep them well mulched and watered.

Summer squash should be picked before they reach maturity. To harvest, cut the fruit from the vine, leaving about 1 inch of the stem attached.

Winter Squash

Many winter squash varieties are not available in bush form, so you may have to stick to the few that are, or find a way to grow a vining squash in your small garden. 'Hubbard' is a popular winter vine variety that stores better than most squashes. If your heart is set on a 'Hubbard', plan on a vining squash.

Squash

Here are a few tips to help you manage this within a limited space:

1. Plant the squash between corn rows; it will cost you no space and the squash's prickly leaves will help keep out any 4-footed raiders.
2. Plant squash on the edge of your garden and allow the vines to trail over your lawn.
3. Once a few squash have formed, the fuzzy tops of the vines should be pinched back, or pruned.
4. Redirect vines to grow back toward the plant.
5. Try sturdy trellises for smaller varieties of winter squash. Tie up the vines carefully and, as each squash begins to develop, give it a cloth cradle tied to the trellis so its weight won't break the vine.

Bush types will grow comfortably in rows, while vining types are better off grouped in hills or planting circles.

Timing is the first thing to get right. Whether you are planting seeds or transplants, put nothing into the garden until all danger of frost has passed.

Perhaps no other crop enjoys compost as much as squash does, so work lots of it to a depth of about a foot before planting.

If you are planting in rows, allow about 4 feet of space on either side of a row. Plant 2 to 4 seeds per foot, 1 inch deep. When true leaves appear a week or 2 later, thin to 1 plant per foot.

If you are starting with transplants, put them 1 foot apart to begin. This may seem awfully tight, but experience has shown it to be the best spacing for maximum yield per given area, if not per plant.

When planting hills, remember that hills need not be mounds, but merely several plants or seeds grouped in a circle. If you have prolonged summer dry spells, or light, sandy soil that dries out quickly, design your hills as basins 1 to 2 inches below the soil level so moisture will collect where it's needed.

If you have heavy soil or plenty of wet weather, plant on mounds 3 to 5 inches high. For vining types, allow at least 6 feet between hills and plant half a dozen seeds an inch deep in each hill. Later, thin to the best 2 or 3 plants in each hill.

In several weeks, lots of bright yellow flowers will appear on your plants. All of the earliest ones are male. If you are hungry or impatient, pick some open blossoms before fruit develops, dip them in a batter, and deep fry—they are delicious. The plants will still produce more male flowers.

Female flowers, which have a swelling beneath the blossom where the fruit develops, will follow the earlier males by a week or so. Squash pollen is too heavy to float on the wind, so bees perform the pollinating ritual. Continued cold, wet weather will delay their activity, but any flowers that die unfulfilled will be replaced by many others.

Weed the young plants, being careful not to damage their shallow roots. They will shade out competitors as they grow.

Water deeply and regularly throughout the summer about 1 inch a week, unless you live in a very hot, dry area where 2 or 3 inches may be necessary. To keep in moisture and eliminate weeds all in one motion, put down organic mulch.

If you added large amounts of organic matter before planting the squash, side-dressing is not necessary. If you think that it may be needed, work in compost around plants when the vines start to run or put a handful of 4–6–4 organic fertilizer in the soil around each plant. Few crops are as easy to grow and store as winter squash. The vines wander happily, requiring little in the way of care after weeding, except an adequate moisture supply. Mature fruits and seeds come in

their own protective packaging, making storage a simple matter.

So go through your seed catalogs, pick out some squash, and get it growing.

Sweet Potatoes

Despite their name, sweet potatoes are not related to other potatoes. They are actually perennials grown as annuals, and are not a member of the nightshade family like regular potatoes.

Most sweet potato varieties need 4 frost-free months to grow to a respectable size. They grow very little when the temperature goes to 60°F or lower.

Sweet potatoes are started from 6- to 8-week-old slips or sprouts that grow out of stored sweet potatoes and develop leaves and roots. Each potato can produce a dozen or more.

You can start your own from store-purchased sweet potatoes or get some from your friends. If you do choose some from a store, do so early in the season and store them at home over the winter. Those purchased in late winter are often treated with sprout inhibitors, chemicals that are sprayed on potatoes in supermarkets (boo!). It is best to buy one of the recommended early-maturing types such as 'Porto Rico', 'Centennial', or 'Jewel'.

An easy way to start them indoors is to begin with whole potatoes. Store them in a warm, well-lit area over the winter. About 6 or 7 weeks before your last spring frost date, put them in flats filled with potting soil mix. Set the sweet potatoes about an inch under the surface.

Put flats in a warm place and keep the mix damp. When sprouts are a few inches tall, put them under fluorescent lights or in a very sunny spot. After a few weeks, if it's warm enough that they won't be subject to temperatures below 55°F, you can put them in a cold frame and nourish them with a seaweed/fish spray. By planting time, you will have strong slips with a good root structure.

Some people cut young shoots and root them in peat pots. This can cause problems later. The young plants are already forming the roots that will become potatoes. If this first development takes place in a crowded spot, the roots often twist around each other as they grow, forming distorted potatoes.

When sprouts are about 6 to 12 inches long, they are ready to plant. After frost danger is past and the garden soil has warmed, pull or cut off the slips.

If you have used certified seed potatoes or are reasonably sure that they are free of disease, you can pull off the slips with their roots attached. But if you are worried about possible infection or have noted evidence of disease on the sweet potatoes, cut the sprouts 1 inch above the potato.

Some of the slips may wither when you set them in the garden. Don't panic. Just keep them watered, spray with seaweed, and in about 2 weeks new growth will let you know that they have rooted.

Since sweet potatoes are root vegetables, they need open, loose soil in which to develop. Till or dig 8 to 12 inches down in fertile, well-drained soil.

Do not add large quantities of composted manure or other organic fertilizers. High levels of nitrogen will cause tremendous vine growth, but the vines are likely to be cracked or distorted. It helps to hill up your planting bed some 6 inches or so and plant the slips in the ridge. To increase warmth in the soil, cover the raised beds with mulch.

Firm the soil, then make a shallow depression around each plant. Water and add bone meal. Keep them watered well for the 2 or 3 weeks that it takes to get growing vigorously.

These plants develop deep root systems, so they resist drought. In prolonged dry periods, however, they should get an occasional deep watering.

If you haven't mulched, hoe away weeds until the potato plant leaves form their own weed-stifling mulch. Foliar-feed with fish emulsion and liquid seaweed once a month.

Don't water late in the season if you hope to store part of the crop. Sweet potatoes don't store well and fast growth near harvest may create growth cracks or make roots tender so they bruise easily.

Once the sweet potatoes start to fill out, they grow rapidly. If not harvested in time, they will grow to 18 inches or more in length and get stringy and tough. After the first light frost or when the temperature drops to 50°F, it's time to harvest. Once the leaf cover is partially killed off, it doesn't provide enough protection for the roots.

Sweet potatoes look fairly tough, but they're not. They bruise easily and need the tender handling usually accorded to eggs or infants. Many gardeners even wear soft gloves when handling them. Never wash them before storage. Just brush the dirt away carefully as you harvest.

Swiss Chard

Beets and Swiss chard are from the same family, and are both considered cool-weather vegetables, doing best from fall through spring.

Beets are only somewhat heat-tolerant, while deep-rooted Swiss chard is quite heat-tolerant compared with lettuce or peas, especially if your soil has plenty of organic matter. Beets are paler red and not as sweet, if grown through summer heat. Swiss chard gains amazing vigor in the cool weather of fall.

A soil that grows daffodils or gladiolus will grow beets. Plenty of compost and—unless they're grown during a very rainy season—a mulch on top of the soil contributes to their rapid growth and quality. Fairly neutral soil with pH of 6.8 is best. Good drainage is essential as with all root vegetables.

Composted manure, greensand, and bone meal dug into the soil several weeks before planting is the traditional and a reliable method of organic fertilizing. A top-dressing of wood ashes, after beets are up, adds needed potassium and helps control slugs where these are a problem.

Swiss chard needs the same kind of soil. The deeper its organic matter content and root penetration, the bigger the leaves. The top-dressing should be rich in nitrogen, such as fish meal or soybean meal. Since Swiss chard is a long-season crop, composted manure can be added several times during the life of the plant.

Swiss chard

You can pick Swiss chard leaves all year round, if you take outer ones only and let the center continue to grow. You can begin picking again in early spring before the top growth begins going to seed. After blooming, it's finished.

Beet leaves can be harvested gradually, too, and you may have your beets and eat the leaves as well. They are smaller than the chard. If you have space for both, plant both because the difference is worth it. If you have space for only one, plant beets and use the leaves, too.

Swiss chard's big leaves make a tasty dish, comparable to spinach (which is a cousin, too). Even though they feel slightly leathery compared with lettuce, they aren't tough when cooked unless old. They do not tolerate days of lying limp in the supermarket nearly as well as spinach does. That is why organic homegrown is best.

Swiss chard makes good imitation celery as well. The stalks, often an inch wide, can be substituted in almost any cooked, but not raw, celery recipe. They can also be left whole, cooked like asparagus, and covered with sauce.

Garden seed catalogs list a wide choice of early and late beet varieties—some with short or medium tall tops, round red roots, or cylindrical ones. There is even a white and golden beet strain, while a cultivar like 'Sweetheart' is so sweet that it's almost a sugar beet and tastes fine sliced raw.

Swiss chard varieties include both red- and green-foliaged types. Both red chard and beet tops bleed in boiling water, so, except for the veins (which remain slightly red-brown) the cooked vegetable is dark green.

When you sow seeds of beets and Swiss chard, you get more than you plant. They produce over a long season, yield a nutritious and flavorful crop, substitute for other vegetables, look colorfully attractive in the garden, and are easy to grow.

Tomatoes

More than 90 percent of all gardeners raise tomatoes, it is said, surely making it the most popular homegrown vegetable.

Before deciding what tomatoes to order, decide whether or not you want to stake them. The ones most frequently staked are called "indeterminate" tomatoes. They are large, late-maturing, rather vine-like, with long stems and alternating sets of flower clusters and 3 leaves.

Those unsuitable for staking are called "determinate." These plants have shorter stems than the indeterminate and fewer than 3 leaves between flower clusters. This growth pattern promotes early fruiting, which means that determinate tomatoes are almost always early or midseason plants. Staking is not necessary and pruning is not recommended.

For starting seedlings, prepare your potting soil mix. It should be well-balanced with peat moss, perlite, and compost mixed with nutrients. Sprinkle the seeds on the top of the potting soil that you have placed in cell packs. Now press down gently on the seeds and cover them lightly with soil. Water well.

Although some gardeners keep increasing fertilizer applications for young tomato plants, it is not a good idea. Too much nitrogen can make the plants shoot up and become leggy and spindly.

However, an organic fertilizer rich in kelp meal and bone meal is the right way to feed young plants. Mild organic fertilizers and cool temperatures tend to make stock, rugged plants that will grow well, once they are in their permanent place.

To prepare this place in the garden, compost should be mixed to the depth of 1 foot. This will give your plants good drainage. Tomatoes do not suffer ill effects from having their stems below ground. When you put your plants out in the garden, you can lay the stems down horizontally and cover with soil. Each plant rights itself and grows upwards toward the sun almost immediately, while roots form all along the stem and strengthen the plants.

It is possible to lose your tomatoes at planting time to cutworms. The best protection is to put a collar of cardboard around the plant, pushed 1 to 2 inches into the soil.

These insects spend the day in the soil near the surface, so you can often pick them out if you run your finger around in the soil near your plants. Wood ashes soaked in around new plants also helps to fend off cutworms, while the potassium from the ashes is also a very good fertilizer.

The best way to control disease and growth is to keep the plants cool and well-aired as soon as they are up.

Where ventilation is poor, you may get aphids on your tomato plants, especially in hot, dry weather. First, hose down the plants, which will drive off a good many. Then use a strong spray of garlic. Even Ivory soap flakes and water make a good spray. Repeat every week or after every rain. Provide better ventilation. As a last resort, use a botanical spray such as pyrethrum, rotenone, or ryania.

Tomato plants themselves are pest-repellent. You can use their leaves to lay over plants of the cabbage family to discourage cabbage butterflies from alighting and laying eggs. You can also leave self-seeded tomatoes at the rim of the garden or right along the rows of parsnips and Swiss chard to keep the woodchucks and rabbits away from the crop.

After you bring your tomatoes to maturity, give yourself a treat. Sink your teeth into a warm, juicy bite of a fresh ripe tomato. There is no better veggie than that picked at the height of nutritional value and eaten raw in the garden.

CHAPTER 8

A Feast of Fruits

When fruit gardening, your foremost goal should be variety and a long harvest season. To accomplish this, plant small numbers of each plant and care for them well. If you want more of one type of fruit, grow a second variety—these smaller patches will be easier to manage as you are learning. Most fruits are perennial plants, so pick your site well. It should be well ventilated. Incorporate lots of organic matter into the soil before planting and mulch with shredded leaves or compost every year. Prune regularly through the season to keep each branch or cane as productive as possible.

Here are some thoughts on some of the most popular fruits and how to fit them better into your garden space.

Apples

If you don't have apple trees in your backyard, now is the time to give up some of your lawn space to grow this king of the orchard.

When selecting trees for planting, be sure to choose those which are adapted to your environment and hardiness zone. As with any long-term investment, apple trees should be chosen with care. Avoid so-called bargains. Buy your trees from a reputable grower who specializes in fruit trees.

You have your choice of variety, size, and age. Familiarize yourself with these 3 variables and decide which best suit your particular requirements. The ideal time to order trees is early in the fall, when a wide variety is available.

Try to schedule the planting anytime in late October through November, after the leaves have fallen from the apple trees. If freshly dug trees are planted early enough (before April 15), planting can be done successfully in the spring. Nevertheless, soil dries up slowly at this time, and the growing season is generally well advanced by the time that the orchard soil becomes fit to work.

A more important reason for planting in the fall is that young apple trees withstand the shock of transplanting best when they are dormant, resting, as it were, from the growth which has gone on during the months before.

For pollination purposes, it is a good idea to plant at least 3 to 4 trees near one another. I prefer a triangular plan when space is limited.

Vigorous dwarf apple varieties, such as 'Baldwin', 'Macintosh', and 'York Imperial', planted 12 feet apart in fertile soil, may crowd when they reach 15 years of age. Planted 15 feet apart, however, they will not crowd even in 20 years' time. Slower growing trees, such as 'Rome Beauty', 'Winesap', and 'Golden Delicious', planted 15 feet apart, will not become overcrowded.

Apples like a well-limed soil that is rich in humus. The quality of the subsoil is often more important than that of the topsoil, however, as the roots of apple trees penetrate deeply into subsoil in search of nutrients and water. Trees will not thrive in hardpan clay, gravel, or sandy subsoil.

Cover-cropping for the larger orchard is an excellent practice for preparing the soil before planting trees. A winter cover crop of rye at $1^{1}/_{2}$ bushels per acre can be used, sowing the seed between August 20 and September 15.

Most apple growers prefer a mulch around their fruit trees. Between the first and fourth years, fruit trees are especially sensitive to competition from other vegetation. Competing growth within 5 feet of the trunk in the form of weeds, grass, or even cover-crop legumes, like alfalfa, can prevent the young trees from making normal growth. Therefore, if a cover crop is used, turn it under in early spring before the growth starts.

Though 1 pound of dry weeds or grass takes up scant nutrients from the soil, these tiny plants must process close to 800 pounds to produce that single pound of growth. When planting trees in a former lawn area, I advise keeping about a 5-foot circle around the base of the young tree free from grass and maintaining a heavy straw mulch.

Nitrogen requirements of your apple trees can easily be satisfied with spring applications of compost. Use about 5 pounds for each year of the tree's age.

Spread the organic fertilizer under the mulch in a band starting 1 foot from the trunk and extending out to the branch tips. Heavy applications of greensand, wood ashes, or other potash material should be added along with the nitrogen fertilizer to avoid creating a potassium deficiency.

To complete the feeding program, apply bone meal at about 10 to 15 pounds per tree. The best time to apply organic fertilizer is 6 to 8 weeks before the tree blooms.

Blackberries

Blackberries are far and away the heaviest-bearing of the bramble fruits, producing

Blackberries

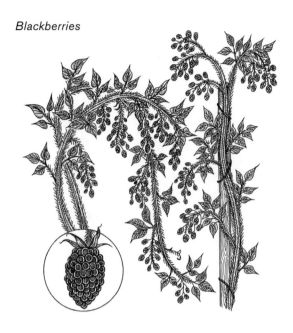

with metal or fiberglass barriers sunk a foot or more below ground level.

Blackberries are much thornier than red berries. Where space is restricted, or if you don't have the patience to pick a prickly plant, choose the new thornless varieties. Many of these are limber-stemmed and trailing in habit, so you will need to rig a wire trellis to train them up. Wait to harvest until the fruit loses its sheen and turns dull black, or it will be slightly bitter.

about twice as much as red raspberries. They ripen in midsummer, after the raspberries are finished, and are more heat-tolerant. Blackberries are robust plants that need to be restrained or they can take over your garden. Cultivate and train them as you would red raspberries (see page 142 in this chapter); however, since they throw root suckers so vigorously, you may want to confine their roots

BERRY HARVESTING

All berries—other than gooseberries—must be harvested every second day without fail. When most berries ripen, they lose their quality, becoming soft or mildewed, and they're often invaded by sap beetles or wasps.

This perishability is one of the main reasons that commercial growers find many berries troublesome crops. It is also why some of the more unfamiliar species tend to disappear from the commercial food chain and remain the special province of the organic gardener.

Blueberries

Blueberries are really a new fruit, domesticated only within the last 75 years. They probably would have been tamed sooner, if gardeners had understood their need for an acid soil. When brought from the American wilds into gardens, the fruits almost always died because the soil was limed.

One blueberry bush can do very well for you. In its fourth season it will produce a pint or so of fruit. At maturity, when it has grown

4 to 6 feet tall, the right variety can produce up to 20 pints of berries over 2 to 3 weeks. If you have room for 3 or 4 varieties, you can stretch the harvest out 8 to 10 weeks into the fall raspberry season. Though cross-pollination isn't essential, it will encourage larger fruit.

Singin' the Blues

The beauty of the blueberry plant is no surprise, considering that it is a kin to mountain laurel, rhododendron, and azalea. Besides bearing fruit, these shrubs are also ornamental. Blueberry bushes can be used in landscapes as featured shrubs or as hedges with handsome results (see "Landscaping with Blueberries" on page 131).

Blueberries need full sun for maximum production and quality, although the plants will grow and produce fruit in shaded woods as easily as they do in the wild. As with any fruit plant, choose a site with good air circulation and if possible, avoid low-lying areas where late spring frosts are likely to damage blossoms.

Blueberries are exacting in their soil requirements. Soil preparation can spell the difference between success and failure.

Test the soil to make sure that the pH level is between 4.0 and 5.4. Peat moss will help to lower the pH, but additional material might be needed.

Sulfur can be mixed with the soil to lower the pH. Mix evenly over the entire area where the bushes will be planted, since blueberries' shallow roots spread widely. Since sulfur takes time to react with the soil, it must be added a season prior to planting. Sandy soils with a pH higher than 4.5 require about $3/4$ of a pound of sulfur per square foot; loamy soils need double that rate.

Test the soil pH every few years. Whenever the pH rises above 5.2, add another $1/2$ pound of sulfur per 100 square foot.

With their fine, shallow root systems, blueberries benefit from mulching to help keep soil cool and moist, to suppress weed growth, and to eliminate the need for hoeing (which can damage roots). Good mulches include wood shavings, bark, pine needles, and straw.

You can plant in the spring or fall, though in the latter case make sure that plants are heavily mulched so they don't heave out of the soil as it freezes and thaws. The highbush, the most important blueberry species, should be planted 4 to 6 feet apart in the row with 10 feet between rows. Plant rabbit-eye blueberry (the highbush's larger Southern cousin) 15 feet apart. Note that rabbit eyes like a slightly less acidic soil, preferring a pH of 5.5 to 6.5. Their berries are almost black and not as sweet, but they can withstand summer droughts and do well in warmer climates.

Blueberry plants need only moderate amounts of organic fertilizer to maintain annual production. Nitrogen is the element needed in the largest quantity, ranging from $1/2$ ounce per year for young plants, and gradually increasing to 3 ounces per year for mature plants. Every $1^1/2$ pounds of amendments contain $1/2$ ounce of nitrogen: Cottonseed meal or blood meal are two good sources.

Double these amounts for rabbit-eye blueberries. For lowbush blueberries, a low spreading shrub with smaller, sweeter fruit, broadcast the equivalent of 10 pounds of nitrogen per 100 square feet, supplied by $1^1/2$ pounds of seed meal or a pound of fish meal. Blueberry plants, especially highbush species, will not tolerate dry soil. They need an inch or 2 of water each week during the growing

LANDSCAPING WITH BLUEBERRIES

Besides being edible, blueberries shine in the landscape. They provide color throughout the season with their shiny green leaves and lovely clusters of white flowers followed by bright blue berries that cover the plant.

In the fall, the leaves on most varieties turn a fiery red that rivals the burning bush. The leaves persist well into November in most locations.

Some varieties have been bred especially for their landscape value. 'Ornablue' has a good symmetrical form, growing thickly to 4 feet (tall and wide) with beautiful fall color. 'Novemberglow' has a lacy growth habit and comes into its own with brilliant red leaves lasting into December.

'Tophat', derived from lowbush parents, is one of the most talked about cultivars. At maturity, the bush is only 20 inches high and 24 inches in diameter, making it perfect for container growing. It is cold hardy and blooms profusely, rewarding you with a good crop of medium-sized fruit.

Landscape architects are even beginning to use lowbush blueberries as ground covers. The lowbush makes a great ground cover because it grows only 6 to 18 inches tall and spreads rapidly once established.

When choosing varieties, look at plant habit, hardiness, fruiting season, berry size, and flavor. To my mind there is no such thing as a bad-tasting blueberry, nor is there much difference in taste from one variety to another.

Pruning blueberry bushes is a breeze. Old wood has to be removed for best fruiting, but it takes the wood a long time to get old. Prune when the stems become $1^1/_2$ inches thick, which may take as long as 8 years for some plants. The idea is to remove unproductive branches.

You can spot them by their lack of fruit buds, which can easily be distinguished from leaf-buds when the leaves have fallen. The leaf buds are small and pointed, while the fruit buds are larger and round. If you prune every year, you will have to remove only 1 or 2 canes at a time.

When planting blueberries for landscaping, you may have to compromise on productivity. In a smaller yard where the bushes are part of the landscape, prune the tips of the bush lightly before buds swell in the spring as you remove the old canes.

If you are making a hedge or a border, plant them 4 to 5 feet apart in full sun. For an orchard planting, set the plants 4 feet apart in rows 6 feet apart. Small varieties can be planted much closer—$1^1/_2$ to 2 feet for lowbush varieties, 3 to 5 feet for dwarfs.

Dwarfs do especially well in containers where it's easy to give them a custom mix. Just combine peat moss and compost (up to 75 percent) with perlite in a tub or half a whiskey barrel. Blueberries need a good organic fertilizer every year. Use 4–6–4 plus kelp meal applied either all at once in the spring or in split applications—one in spring and the second just before the berries color up. Spread it in a ring just inside the edge of the leaf canopy.

Three-year-old bushes will produce a pint or two of fruit the year after they are planted. The yield should double each year until the genetic limit is reached. That will vary from one variety to the next, but it could be between 20 pints to 20 pounds per plant.

You might have to make 2 or 3 pickings over a period of 4 weeks from a single bush.

season. One inch of water translates to one gallon per young plant, and up to about eight gallons for a mature plant with a larger, deeper root system that is able to absorb more water.

Easier to grow than apples or peaches, blueberries don't usually require spraying for either pests or diseases, although the occasional aphid, leafhopper, caterpillar, or even gypsy moth may find the bushes appetizing. The few that do attack blueberries rarely get a foothold if all fruits are regularly harvested, but there are many safe organic controls available to help get rid of any of these pests (see "On Insect and Disease Control and Prevention" on page 311 of appendix A).

The worst and most common disease in home berry plantings is mummyberry, which causes berries to dry up and harden before ripening. This fungus can also damage tender young shoots. Cultural controls are often enough to remedy the problem. If mummyberry occurs, pick off and destroy all infected fruit, and keep all debris, fallen fruit, and leaves from accumulating under your bushes. The really demanding part of raising blueberries is keeping the birds away. Small-scale growers have done everything imaginable to foil the winged creatures.

They have tried foiling with foil in the form of pie pans or strips dangling from branches. Gardeners have also experimented with plastic owls and snakes, black thread draped around bushes, portable radios playing in the hedges, and plastic lines that hum in the wind. None of these methods is wholly satisfactory for keeping birds at bay. The only sure cure for birds is a bird-tight net.

Of course, the joy of backyard blueberries is the full flavor that comes from allowing the fruits not just to turn blue, but to truly ripen on the bush. Peak flavor is reached a few days after the berries turn blue. How can you tell which ones are ripe? Tickle the fruits; those that are ready will fall into your hand. Harvest the berries every other day to keep plants healthy.

Anyone who has ever sweated through a hot summer morning at a pick-your-own blueberry field or scrambled through woods and meadows collecting from the wild knows that those succulent morsels are sweeter and more fragrant than any berries you can buy at the market.

Cantaloupes

Cantaloupes have certain requirements. They like sandy loam, humus-rich soil that is close to neutral pH (6.8 to 7.0), hot weather, and room to spread.

In my garden, I set aside a bed 25 × 25 feet last June. Along each side of this bed, I planted 2 rows of peas. Down the middle I planted 4 rows consisting of radishes, lettuce, and green onions; then I planted the hills of cantaloupes down the middle of the remaining wide rows: 10 rows in all.

The peas and other early vegetables were already harvested by the time the cantaloupes needed more space. Since the soil was a heavy, acid clay that was slow to warm up in the spring, providing a warm, sandy soil was a bit of a problem. My solution was to dig a hole about 2 feet in diameter and 2 feet deep for each cantaloupe hill.

I filled the hole with alternating layers of composted horse manure, sand, and bone meal. The composted manure provided nitrogen and potassium; the bone meal, calcium and phosphorous. I mixed all of the layers together with a spading fork, except for a final layer of sand on top.

Now, I had a pocket of sandy soil rich in the organic matter (compost) that cantaloupes love. I sprinkled dolomitic limestone on top of the soil after I planted the seeds, which were spaced 2 inches apart (the depth was determined by multiplying the diameter of the seed by 2). Rain soon washed it into the soil. Preparing the soil for cantaloupes the way that I did may sound like a lot of work, but it really isn't if you just do 2 or 3 hills a day. I like to plant cantaloupes (usually 20 hills in all) over a period of a month's time so that they don't all get ripe at once.

The earliest planted hills produced the largest, sweetest melons, as they ripened during the hottest weather of July and August.

I mulch the plants with hay or straw as soon as possible after planting them. Once the mulch is in place there is no more work to do until the fruits get ripe.

One of the worst insects in the garden—certainly the worst for melons—is the striped or spotted cucumber beetle. In a bad year, this small, innocent-looking bug can all but wipe out a cantaloupe patch. Even in a good year, yields can be reduced. It will greedily devour tender young emerging plants before they have a chance to get started, feast on bigger leaves of older plants, and spread bacterial wilt from plant to plant.

Some organic gardeners recommend planting radishes around the borders of cantaloupe rows and hills to deter cucumber beetles. Presumably, the quicker growing radishes serve as cover and camouflage for the young cantaloupe seedlings or the strong odor or taste of the radishes is unpleasant to the beetles.

If spraying or dusting is needed, rotenone and/or pyrethrum are natural insecticides that will control cucumber beetles. Still, the best way to control insects and diseases is with proper soil nutrition.

Start cantaloupes indoors in cell packs about 3 to 4 weeks before the last frost date, transplanting them outside when the soil is warm. If directly seeded into the garden, they can be sown in warm soil about 1 to 3 weeks after the last frost.

Preparing rich soil, selecting genetic superstars, effective pest control, cold protection, and using yield-boosting mulches and drip irrigation: These are the ingredients for a bumper crop of cantaloupes. Planning, hard work, and some expense will be involved, but this is gardening at its best. The payoff comes at harvest when, for the first time, not only will your handcart be full but you will have to add side rails to hold the surplus of cantaloupes. Enjoy!

Elderberries

Could your garden or landscape plan use some newcomers? Do you like attractive

Elderberries

shrubs that are practically trouble-free and offer striking green foliage, big beautiful blossom clusters, and tasty, different fruit?

If you nod vigorously to both, why not do what I did? Plant some elderberry bushes.

Elderberries are dependable, vigorous plants that are extremely ornamental and abundantly rich in vitamin C. In addition, these members of the honeysuckle family are easily grown, readily propagated, and, if planted in the fall, will bear fruit by the end of the following summer. And, while shouting the praises of elderberry bushes, I can't overlook the most important factor: the healthful fresh fruit that they provide, as well as the delicious pies, jams, jellies, and wines which can be made from them.

Let's consider soil preference. Elderberries are not fussy. In fact, they thrive especially well in problem spots where the soil is partially shaded and tends to be extremely moist, but not wet.

Since the elderberry reaches a mature height of 6 to 10 feet, why not plant them where they can also serve as a practical, ornamental shrub or as a majestic fence? Or you can simply set them out in a back lot, as I did, spaced 5 feet apart, in rows spaced 15 feet apart. If my math is correct, that would mean that you would need 580 plants, if you intended to fill an acre. (An acre of fully mature plants, in full production, can be expected to yield from 4 to 5 tons.)

If you top their soil with a 6-inch mulch, it will completely suppress competing weeds and hold the moisture in nicely. However, if you plan to control weeds by cultivation only, keep the cultivation shallow since the elder roots hug the soil surface.

Elderberries prefer an acid soil. You will find that your plants respond to moderate applications of nitrogen soil amendments like fish meal or cottonseed meal. As for phosphate, use bone meal or rock phosphate. A soil test is the best way to see what your soil needs.

These shrubs also thrive on pruning. I find that since the new canes produce the largest clusters, their growth should be encouraged. Remove all old, unproductive canes in late winter, and, of course, cut off any weak, dead, or broken ones.

If your elderberry bushes should be visited by an occasional grub of the elderberry borer, quickly remove and burn all of the infected stems. This usually keeps the pests under control.

If you wish, buy just a few plants and propagate the rest from either root cuttings, cuttings of underground rhizomes, hardwood stem cuttings, leaf-bud cuttings grown under mist, or from seeds. The most common and simplest method is hardwood stem cuttings. In the winter, take as many 10-inch sections as you wish from your 1-year-old canes. Make certain that each length has 2 nodes. Then, stick them vertically into the soil 2 feet into the soil (adjusting for size) with the top node at ground level.

The cuttings will be rooted approximately 1 year later. After they root, transplant them to their permanent field positions, where they will present you with a fair-sized yield of purple-black fruit clusters the next summer. Remember to harvest the berries every other day.

Figs

Fig trees are not limited to the South. They may be grown in colder climates, if some precautions are taken to protect them.

If you have room for a fig tree in a greenhouse, more than 1 crop per year may be expected. Branches trained horizontally can save space and the protection afforded by the greenhouse will increase fig production.

Some northern gardeners dig up their trees in late fall, keep large balls of soil around the roots, and winter them in a cellar. The soil is kept moist and the plants are set outdoors again when the weather has settled in spring.

Another method is to grow the plant in a large, easily moved container that may be shifted indoors, when temperatures begin to plunge.

First, be sure that you have a good place to plant the tree. It will tolerate some shade, but will do better in open areas where it gets the full benefit of sun and rain. If there are other fruit trees in your yard, your fig tree needs to be at least 20 feet away from them. It will grow 8 or 9 feet tall and spread to even greater width when fully mature.

When you are ready to transplant, dig a hole deep enough so that the tree settles in a little lower than the previous soil line (the earth mark on the base of the tree). As with all trees, make the planting hole much larger than the tree would appear to require. Thoroughly break up the soil.

Fill the hole with a 50–50 mix of soil and compost, and water sufficiently to settle the soil around the roots.

Keep the area around the tree free of grass and weeds and don't till around it. Figs have a heavy network of roots close to the ground surface, so it is harmful to dig near them. Your fig tree should bear its first crop in 3 years.

Fig trees respond nicely to a side-dressing of compost during the spring. They can also use a good mulch to help them retain and develop their fruit during dry spells and keep weeds down. A thick mulch of hay or straw is sufficient to keep down the weeds and grass and encourage earthworms. Drought is one of the main summer deterrents to a good fig crop. Once green figs begin to shrivel and drop off, it is too late to save the crop. If you suspect that the soil is drying out too much under your fig tree—in spite of the mulch— soak the soil thoroughly at least twice a week.

Figs will grow well with or without pruning. It's a matter of deciding if you need to keep the tree restricted in size.

If you do prune, try to keep the tree to a vase shape (an upside-down triangle) with an open center. Always remove dead or crossing branches, as you do for all fruit trees.

Harvest figs when their stems wilt and their fruits droop. If they exude a milky latex, stop picking: They're not ready. A mature fig tree will yield several gallons of figs each year.

Fig trees are easy to propagate. Just before it's time for the sap to rise in the spring, select mature strong-looking branch tips for cuttings. Make them about 5 to 7 inches long. Prepare several cuttings so you'll have backup in case some fail.

With a sharp knife, cut around the nodes along the twig. Be careful to cut only through the thin outer bark, as roots develop at the cuts, giving an adequate supply of roots to support the young tree.

Place each cutting upright in fine soil with only an inch or so of its tip protruding.

Healthwise, a fig tree is a good investment. Figs are high in iron, calcium, potassium, and fiber, and are reported to be helpful in combating a number of ailments, such as anemia and fatigue. The dried fig is even higher in nutrition, yet lower in calories than a date.

Figs have been around a long time giving sustenance to Earth's creatures. Their leaves are useful, too. Remember Adam and Eve?

Gooseberries

You might not be familiar with gooseberries. Their small, slightly tart, light green fruits are wonderful for pies and jam.

Gooseberries grow on dense bushes that reach 2 to 4 feet tall without training. They

Gooseberries

leaf out in early spring. The earliest gooseberries fill the gap between the last strawberries and the first red raspberries. A mature plant can produce from 8 to 10 quarts of fruit, so 1 plant may be all you need.

Where space is extremely limited, train your gooseberry bush against a wall or fence as a fan-shaped espalier (a plant trained to grow flatly on a lattice or trellis). These make striking plants with year-round interest, and picking will be easier, too. Gooseberries trained to bamboo canes and wires can be made to grow 6 feet tall.

Gooseberries bear fruit near the base of 1-year-old shoots and on short spurs on older wood. To prune, remove about 20 percent of

A WHITE PINE WARNING

Some areas prohibit the cultivation of gooseberries as they can host the white pine blister rust disease, which is devastating to white pines and related species. Please check with your cooperative extension representative to find out if you are allowed to grow gooseberries in your region.

the oldest growth. No matter how carelessly one prunes, there is always some fruit left for harvesting; gooseberries do not have to be picked on a regular basis like other berries. So, whenever you are in the mood, pick some gooseberries.

Grapes

Grapes prefer a near neutral soil, perhaps slightly acid. The roots grow near the surface, so humus can be supplied through mulches. They do grow in low, flat soils, but quality is better when produced on sloping, well-drained soil.

Once the area is selected, dig the holes in the fall. Add a shovelful of compost, rock phosphate, greensand, and a complete organic fertilizer. I like to cover the hole and the pile of soil by its side with a temporary straw or leaf mulch, mostly because I have an aversion to bare soil and, of course, mulching prevents soil washing.

At planting time in spring, clear out the temporary mulch. The winter rains and freezes should have mellowed the mixture of soil and organic matter to ideal consistency.

Place the plant in position, spread its roots, and fill the hole with good soil, watering once or twice with at least a bucketful of water to firm the soil. Don't worry about planting depth because the vines are propagated by layering (the low stems burrow into the ground and root), rather than grafting. The size of the hole will depend on the size of the root system and the type of the soil: Clay soil requires a larger hole; while a smaller hole is best for sandy soil that filters water more easily.

In order to grow grapes, you will have to build something to keep them off the ground, such as a trellis. Keeping the vines with the fruit buds elevated reduces the risk of frost damage. This is a big advantage with seedless varieties, which are usually more vulnerable to cold. If the structure is near the house or where people gather or pass frequently, bird damage, too, will, be reduced.

You should also cut the grapes back regularly, not just to keep them from running wild, but to get a full crop of sweet fruit.

Together, the trellis and the pruning technique add up to what I call the "training system."

The curtain method of training is the system currently favored by most commercial growers. In the home landscape the curtain system is perfect if you want to make a dense-looking hedge about 6 feet tall or grow the greatest number of varieties in the least

Grape trellis

VERSATILE GRAPEVINES

Other popular ways to use grapevines in the landscape include using them as a hedge or screen to shield your yard from the street or some unwelcome view, or shaping a grapevine bower over a bench or swing to add a romantic touch to your garden.

amount of space. Yields and sugar levels will be higher, and grapevines are easier to prune, spray, and pick.

The trellis is a single wire running 6 feet above the ground, supported by 2 sturdy posts. The grapevine's trunk goes straight up to the wire, then 2 shoots extend horizontally along the wire in opposite directions to make cordons. Fruiting canes rise every 8 to 10 inches along the cordons, and shoots drape down on either side to form a curtain.

Another choice for training is the pergola, a series of sturdy poles that carry rafters and support the vines. Pergolas have open sides so that you can see through the lacy grape foliage on either side.

They are usually built to shade patios and major walkways. The structure's openness allows breezes to pass through and creates an island of comfort in a hot summer landscape. Grape yields on a pergola can be as high as or higher than with the curtain system, but grapes may not be as sweet because the jumbled shoots will shade each other.

Depending on the size of the pergola, you may be able to plant more than 1 vine. Each vine should be allotted at least 8 × 8 feet, although 10 × 10 feet would be even better. Of course, you could eventually train one vine to shade an immense area, but coverage would take several seasons.

Grapes produce fruit only on 1-year-old wood. Without pruning, the fruitful wood gets farther and farther out from the trunk with each passing season. Another good reason to prune is that grapes tend to produce too much fruit, which stresses the plant. Bud development for the following year suffers and the weakened vine is more vulnerable to winter injury.

Proper pruning removes most of the previous season's growth and with it up to 90 percent of the fruit buds. That channels the plant's energy into producing strong new growth and increases the sugar content of the remaining grapes.

When pruning, save only the healthiest canes. Ideal cane thickness is about pencil size, with buds spaced about 3 to 6 inches apart. Spindly canes are weak and unproductive, while overly thick, old, bull canes are too vegetative.

Healthy canes are reddish-brown on American varieties, and tan on hybrids. Neither type should be overly pale (which means that they haven't received enough sun), nor too black (indicating disease or winter damage). The safest time to prune is late winter, just as the buds begin to swell. That way you can assess the extent of winter damage. It doesn't hurt the vine to prune while the sap is flowing, even though the amount of bleeding may seem extreme.

If you decide to go with grapes, be versatile. Mix your flavors and stretch your harvest with early and late varieties.

Muscadines
Muscadine grapes differ from bunch grapes in several ways.

Most important from the organic viewpoint is their hardiness and disease-resistance.

They outyield and outlast bunch grapes. Yields are about 5 tons per acre and many vines are known to be over 100 years old.

The grapes are large, often $3/4$ inch in diameter. The fruit is born singly, or in small clusters of 5 to 10 grapes. The skins are fairly tough and the seeds are larger than in bunch grapes.

Muscadines do well in areas with at least 200 days of frost-free temperatures and 30 inches of rainfall per year—where temperatures rarely fall to 0°F or below. They should be of great interest to the organic world because they are so easily grown without sprays and can be processed into nutritious and tasty foods.

Two vines are necessary for pollination: a regular, heavy-bearing female type and a male or self-fertilizing variety.

The self-fertilizing varieties bear some fruit and so have largely replaced the male vines. Regular and self-fertilizing vines are available in both light and dark colors; either will cross-pollinate. Soil preparation is similar to that for bunch grapes (see page 137).

The vines can be planted to cover an arbor or set in rows and trained on a vertical or horizontal trellis. For a large planting to be grown on a horizontal trellis, vines are set about 15 × 15 feet apart. Stakes 7 feet high are placed at each plant. The vine is trained to the top of the stake, then allowed to branch out in 8 directions (like wheel spokes) on wires crisscrossed between the stakes.

For a vertical trellis-type planting, spacing is usually 17 to 20 feet apart in the rows with rows 12 feet apart. A 12- × 20-foot spacing will use 180 plants to the acre.

Each vine is trained up a temporary stake to a height of 6 feet, then lateral branches are fastened to the wires. Permanent posts are placed in the rows between the vines and strung with 1, 2, or 3 wires.

For muscadine pruning on a 2-wire vertical trellis, let the main trunk grow straight up to the top wire, then bend this trunk to form 1 of the 4 main branches. The other 3 branches are chosen a year later, from shoots off the main trunk. After a main branch has borne fruit for a number of years, it should be replaced by a younger branch. Replace only 1 at a time to avoid reducing the yield.

Each main branch will have spurs all along its length. These spurs are cut back to 3 to 4 buds each year. Grapes are grown on new growth from these spurs.

That is the only pruning that is necessary, except to keep the vines cut back so that they don't bump into each other.

Muscadines, as with most foods, are best for you when eaten fresh. To extend their usefulness, you may freeze them or make them into jellies, jams, and wine.

Mulberries

Fruiting mulberry trees originated in Asia and now thrive in many parts of the world. They are greatly favored in Italy, where nearly every garden, farm, and dooryard has at least 1 tree. Heavy fruiting varieties have been developed in Europe and the United States.

A very hardy tree, it is also easy to grow and thrives in almost any kind of soil—even sandy. Mulberries also remain relatively free from disease and insect infestation.

Most domestic and wild mulberry trees tend to grow to 25 to 30 feet tall. Rather wide-spreading, they make good shade trees. Their showers of sweet berries make them the favorite of all birds and chickens (you probably should not put them too close to a patio to avoid purple stains on your tiles or lawn furniture).

The best way to get started is to buy bare rootstock from reliable local or mail-order nurseries. The fruiting season of these trees stretches over several months. Some bear and ripen easily, while others take more time. By planting 1 of each of several varieties you can have fruit over a 6-month period. Mulberries ripen in black, red, and white. The best fruiting varieties include 'Black Persian', 'Black English', 'Thorburn', and 'Downing'. In Italy, the 'Black Persian' strain is grown extensively. In China, the East Asian white mulberry has provided leaves to the silk industry for thousands of years.

Ease of propagation is one of the mulberry's many excellent traits. You can also graft cuttings from high-producing stock onto sound native stocks and have these bear excellent crops. The tree growth is rapid and long fruiting seasons are the rule. There are early, medium, and late varieties.

Undoubtedly the very best way to draw a host of birds of all kinds to your garden is to plant 1 or more fruiting mulberry trees. Only by using a light 1-inch mesh net over smaller trees can you keep out birds. However, the trees bear so heavily and ripen over such an extended period that by picking ripe fruit daily there will usually be plenty for both birds and gardeners.

Mulberries are easily "picked" by spreading sheets under the trees and jarring fruit-laden branches. The fully ripe berries fall and the unripe ones cling. Ideal for planting along farm roads and lanes, the mulberry calls for spacing about 30 feet apart. A single tree will bear fruit, needing no cross-pollination, incidentally. Cultural methods are much the same as for peaches and apples (see individual entries in this chapter). As for pests, red spiders may do some damage to mulberry leaves. Try dusting with diatomaceous earth powder. Spruce bagworm may be controlled by hand-picking the cocoons and also by dusting with diatomaceous earth.

The fall webworm, a moth larvae, may attack trees. It lives in webbed colonies under branches and feeds during the summer. Kill it by pruning away infested branch tips.

As birds are so drawn to eating the berries that fall on the ground, there is usually no bird damage to vegetable seedlings at all. As an added plus, these birds also help to control injurious insects in the gardens.

Peaches

Peach trees are similar to apple trees in their soil and planting needs, but are highly susceptible to insects and diseases. As forewarned is forearmed, follow these preventive measures to grow perfect peaches all the time.

Bacterial Spot

The bacteria enters the tree through leaf scars that fail to mature. Therefore, help the wood to mature.

Peaches

Water the tree less after harvest. Fertilize only after the first fall freeze or in early spring.

The bacteria produces cankers on twigs and reddish spots on leaves. Infested leaves may fall, calling for the same remedy as for peach leaf curl.

Brown Rot

Overwintering in fruit spurs and cankers on twigs, the rot infects blossoms in spring and spreads by secondary infection to the fruit.

Picking fruit at the right time is vital to controlling this fungus, which can quickly ruin an entire crop. Well-timed picking gives the fungus no chance to move up a fruit stem and invade the tree. Early morning is the best time to pick ripe fruit.

Brown rot also overwinters in mummies, the shriveled remains of infected fruits. If you find any under the tree, destroy them.

Pruning cankered twigs after harvest also helps break the life cycle of this disease.

Peach Leaf Curl

Long, cool springs encourage this fungus. It can strike hard one year and not at all the next. The long-lived spores lodge in bark and wash onto the buds in spring rains.

Infected leaves fall by early summer and leaf loss weakens the tree. For an infected tree to grow new wood in time to survive the winter, you must reduce its stress. Use an organic fertilizer, but only if you can do it before June 15. Use a micronutrient foliage spray every third week and keep the tree well watered.

Peach Tree Borer

This is a dangerous pest, especially to young trees. From late summer on, the larvae feed under the bark at the base of the trunk and in the roots. Since the cocoons are less than an inch below the surface of the soil, frequent cultivation destroys many of them.

The adults begin emerging as early as June and keep appearing until fall. The female has a black body with an orange band. She lays eggs on the scaffold branches, the trunk, and the soil as far as 2 feet from the trunk. The hatched larvae make their way to the base of the trunk, bore into the tree, and begin feeding.

If you see a mixture of gum and frass (a gummy substance similar to sawdust) at the base of the trunk, that's the borer's signature. You may try surgery.

Remember, though, that large holes are often the work of larvae that have left the tree. Probe with a wire to impale the borer or open its burrow with a knife cut to locate the insect.

Remember, of course, that the first line of defense is a healthy and hardy tree and you can work toward that by giving it good care.

Perennial Canker

This fungus frequently causes limb and tree death. It enters the tree through injuries, usually buds and cambium (the layer of developing cells between wood and bark) killed by the cold, but also through untreated pruning wounds.

The cankers are oval to linear patches of darkened, cracked bark surrounded by rolls of callus. They eventually girdle the limb or trunk, killing the tree.

During warm weather, cankers may ooze gum, attracting the lesser peach tree borer, whose larvae often infect the wood near the canker.

On small limbs, prune several inches below the canker. On large limbs you will have to trim out the canker to save the limb. Burn what you remove and paint the wound with tree-wound dressing (pine tar mixed with sulfur).

Giving your trees a good site with deep, well-drained soil is the most important measure that you can take to fight canker. A healthy tree resists cold-injury.

Raspberries

There is nothing like a well-placed patch of raspberries to put the fun in the fundamentals of your first gardening season. Although first seasons have their ups and downs, it's a definite up for raspberries.

A 30-foot row of red raspberries, trained to single stems against a wall or fence, will yield about 2 quarts of fruit every other day (which is how often they should be harvested) for 4 weeks. That is more than enough raspberries for most people.

A more traditional hedge-type planting will yield twice that amount, though it takes at least twice the space. Intensively trained berries are extremely productive.

Red raspberry **Black raspberry**
Raspberries

To get the most from red raspberries, plant at least 2 kinds: a main variety for heavy early summer harvests and a fall type to close out the berry harvest.

Fall is by far the best time to prepare the raspberry bed, for the winter mellows the soil, which the berries prefer. If you must start the bed in spring, dig and fertilize this trench as early as possible. Pick a spot that faces east and is sheltered from the late-afternoon sun. Raspberries will tolerate full sun, but only if need be.

For your first raspberry patch, think small. Dig a 12- × 12-foot trench, 1 foot deep. Raspberries send out underground runners to make new plants. Since these runners can be invasive, you may want to build a wooden frame the size of the trench and bury it to ground level to keep them in check.

Fork finished compost into the bottom of the trench and turn it in with a spading fork. Replace the topsoil and cover it with 6 inches of compost. Fork this into the topsoil and let it sit over the winter months, if you are making the new bed in the fall.

Standard raspberries are fruitless the first year. "Everbearing" kinds bear both an early and late crop, and you may find some raspberries forming late in the season on the first year's growth. In the first season, allow the plants to grow without any pruning. Erect a 3-wire trellis using 3 posts, 1 at each end of the trench and 1 in the middle. Place the top wire at 5 feet, the middle wire at 3 feet, and the bottom wire at 2 feet.

Tying the canes to the trellis will prevent you from making the mistake of cutting them down to make them self-supporting. It will also allow easy access to the most fruitful buds, typically near the top of the canes.

In the early spring of the second season, when the plants are still dormant, remove all canes growing near the edges of the bed and leave about 7 or 8 of the strongest-looking canes per plant, trimmed back to a bud just above the top wire. Cut off all the rest, just above the soil level.

If the raspberry is the standard kind, these canes will produce a crop of berries as new canes grow up around them. After the crop is harvested, cut off the canes that have finished fruiting at ground level. This is also a good time to tie new canes to the trellis wires.

If the raspberry is everbearing, it will want to make an early summer and fall crop. Don't give in to it because the early crop interferes with a good fall production.

Instead, cut off all of the canes at ground level in the spring by going down the bed with the lawn mower. You can harvest bumper crops of berries late in the season, when they are most appreciated. The ideal strategy is to have a row of everbearing for late in the year, and a row of standards for early harvest.

Keep weeds down with thickly matted grass clippings, but cultivate the mulch into the soil, after killing frosts come. Every third year, spread compost over the beds when they go dormant in the fall to keep things healthy.

As for pests, the common spider mite is rarely a problem on well-watered plants. Other pests, such as the raspberry cane borer, root borer, cane maggot, and fruitworm, can be controlled by thoroughly cultivating the soil in late summer and by pruning back and destroying infested canes.

You can also save some of the young plants that emerge from underground runners. Dig them up in the spring with a trowel and start them anew, or bend the tips of the plants over and peg them to bare soil for awhile, where they will root.

Black Raspberries

Black raspberries, though closely related to the reds, have a distinctive flavor, ripen a little later, and require slightly different training.

Black raspberries spread by bending the tips of their canes to the ground where they root, leapfrogging along at 2 to 3 feet a year. New shoots arise only from the original crowns, not willy-nilly from the roots, as with the reds. In most other respects, they are very similar.

In the attempt to bend to the ground and root, the canes elongate and become thin and weak at the tips. Unless you want to start new plants, cut these raspberries back to 3 or 4 feet. They will be self-supporting with no loss of fruit potential.

Cut the old canes out, after harvest. Since black raspberries don't throw root suckers, they take much less thinning than reds.

Strawberries

Strawberries are the first fruit of the season, which may be why gardeners treasure them so.

Since your fruit garden will provide you with a variety of other berries all season long, forego everbearings in favor of main croppers. An early and a late variety will provide strawberries for 3 to 4 weeks.

I have tried every method of raising strawberries that I have heard of, and concluded that the best way to keep them healthy and bearing heavily is to grow them as an adjunct to the vegetable garden. In the bed, space them a foot apart in each direction. Strawberries should not be pruned, and vegetables make good planting companions as they excrete a substance from their root systems that makes the fruits hardier.

Renew them every year by tilling or digging under most of the plants and letting runners set in well-worked, fertile soil.

Strawberries may be plagued by strawberry weevil and are susceptible to several kinds of fungus; keep them healthy with organic methods (see "On Insect and Disease Control and Prevention" on page 311 of appendix A).

Runner

Strawberries

Home-Grown Herbs

The herb garden is a most pragmatic and versatile excerpt in your growing experience.

Herbs can be used to flavor almost any dish you can think of, teas made from herbs are flavorful and medicinally comforting, and natural healing techniques employ herbs in preventative measures and restorative therapies. Planted with the right companion, herbs also act as repellents against vegetable-attacking pests.

There is no better place to find an herb at the peak of its freshness and flavor than in your own organic garden. Include them in your growing plan and your rewards will be long-lasting. When choosing a site to plant your herbs, remember that herb gardens require the same type of soil as vegetable or flower gardens: high in organic mater and well-drained. In fact, annual herbs may be grown in the same bed as your vegetables, although perennial herbs are best given their own bed. A few feet of each of the annuals or half a dozen plants of perennials will supply enough herbs for the average family. If you don't want to have all of your herbs growing in one location, scatter some of the taller plants, such as sage, in the flower garden for an interesting variation.

The soil should be loose and well-drained; herbs are not fond of wet feet or heavy soils. If the spot you have selected is convenient to the kitchen door, but has a heavy clay soil, don't give up. Add some compost or other soil amendments that will loosen up the ground.

Fertile soil is not necessary. If you add a good organic fertilizer (4–6–4), the plants will grow more, but they will not produce the oils in their leaves that make them so wonderful for seasoning.

Still, some herbs, like basil, will look prettier if they are fertilized. Others, like chives, also do well. However, those that are native to areas of poor soil will take offense and succumb to fungus diseases, frostbite, insect attack, and other calamities that many plants suffer from when over-fertilized.

The amount of sun an herb garden needs ranges from partial sun to full sun. One more factor to consider is soil pH. Generally, herbs prefer a neutral to alkaline soil.

The Herb Garden

Once you have chosen the site, decide what herbs you want to grow. Here is a list of some of the most popular herbs to include in your kitchen herb garden for summer-long enjoyment.

Basil

Basil remains one of the most rewarding herbs to start indoors. Like tomatoes, this clove-scented annual germinates in less than a week and transplants well. And with the many varieties to choose from, you can try a different type of basil every year!

When the soil is truly warm, plant it in fairly rich soil, 1 to 2 inches deeper than the soil level in the pot or cell pack. If you fare well with tomatoes, you can grow basil and enjoy great salads and sauces all summer long.

I start my basil in cell packs and flats filled with organic potting soil mix. I make little furrows $^1/_8$ to $^1/_4$ inch deep about 2 inches apart and plant each type of basil in its own labeled furrow about 3 seeds per inch.

One flat will fit a dozen kinds of basil easily. At 3 seeds per inch you'll have enough seedlings for a small market garden. Once the seeds have germinated, I take off the plastic and put the flats 2 inches below fluorescent grow lights. Then I leave them to develop their first true leaves.

At this point, I thin the plants so they are about 2 inches apart in the rows. I also begin to feed them with a seaweed/fish foliar spray once a week. If I'm not ready to transplant the basil into gardens by the time that the plants have 4 true leaves, I then transplant each one into a 4-inch pot. When my schedule or the weather says it's time to harden them off, I put them out.

My transplants always do better when I plant them in the late afternoon or early evening. That gives the roots time to take hold before the leaves lose moisture to the hot May sun.

To give the basil a good start, fill each planting hole with compost and a little sprinkling of bone and kelp meal. After all the little plants are in place, water them well with the seaweed/fish solution. Basils will grow right up to the hard frost outdoors, if you keep them pinched. However, if you let annual basils flower and go to seed, they will figure that they've done their job and stop producing.

Basils can also be grown from cuttings. I have a Thai-type basil from a cutting growing indoors. It has purplish stems and bracts, fairly large white flowers, and smooth shiny leaves with deep veins. It's terrific added to vinegar and is very easy to propagate from cuttings.

To grow from a cutting, remove the bottom leaves from a 4- to 5-inch piece and stick it into a pot of organic potting soil. The soil for these potted plants should be much richer than the soil outdoors. A mixture of $^2/_3$ humus and $^1/_3$ sand should be just about right.

The basil roots with no more attention than occasional watering to keep the potting soil damp. If the plant leaves seem parched and crumble, the air may be too dry or the artificial sunlight too close to the foliage. Spray liquid organic fertilizer (seaweed/fish) once every 3 weeks to promote healthy indoor growth.

Taking cuttings from the basils in your garden in August or September is a much easier way of assuring yourself a winter's supply of fresh basil than trying to dig up whole plants and pot them. Most basils grow very well indoors. The Thai basil grows well under 40-watt warm and cool white fluorescent lights in a 75°F cellar.

The secret to keeping basils going is to continue pinching off the flower buds so they cannot go to seed. They will grow for years in containers, if you keep them from blooming. I also grow 'Dark Opal' basil for the wonderful pink color it gives to vinegars and jellies and because its dark leaves beautifully contrast with lighter colored plants in a mixed planting.

Lemon basil is still another favorite. Its leaves are a fresh light green and the flowers are white. Lemon basil will not tolerate the least neglect during a dry spell, but if you grow it in soil with plenty of organic matter, it will grow a foot or more taller and produce loads of flower buds and young leaves for vinegar, potpourri, and salads all season long.

I wouldn't be without cinnamon basil. It has dark green leaves, purple bracts and flowers, and purple-green stems. If you gather the flower buds with a bit of stem and a couple of

---

BASIL, BASIL, BASIL

The following is a list of some of the basil cultivars you could be growing in your garden:

'Bush Green'	'Mexican Spice'
'Genovese'	'Opal'
'Italian Red'	'Sacred'
'Large Green'	'Siam Queen' (Thai)
'Lettuce Leaf'	

---

pairs of leaves, and steep them all in white vinegar, the vinegar turns a pink violet.

Cinnamon basil seems a bit more drought-resistant than lemon basil and it grows somewhat larger. It likes soil with a lot of organic matter and is most flavorful when grown in full sun. Pinching your basil to keep it growing and bushy is the best way to harvest it. Pinch out the flower buds and one or more of the pairs of leaves behind them just above the next lower pairs of leaves. More nodes and flowers will grow from the nodes you left.

Chives

Chives add pizzazz to many dishes, and are easy to cultivate. And with their pretty purple flowers, they enliven the herb garden as well. These members of the allium family are cold hardy perennials that require a cold dormant period each year. That is why they sometimes fade away to nothing on windowsills. I accidentally left some out in cell packs one winter, and they all lived through the freezes. The ones that I coddled in the greenhouse barely made it.

The germination time for chive seeds is approximately 7 days. Start them in cell packs, 2 seeds to a pack, and transplant them when they are 5 inches tall.

Don't panic when plants disappear in the late fall. Like other bulbs, they will be back in early spring. Chives are one of the herbs that will thrive with a 4–6–4 fertilizer. Add the amendment when you cut them back in July. Always cut back to the ground to prevent brown tipspots from forming, which you will have to deal with at the next harvest. Chives also like more water than many herbs; give them a good soaking: water them when the soil moisture is below 30 percent. They prefer partial sun, 4 to 5 hours a day.

Marjoram

Sweet marjoram seeds are dustlike and cannot endure cold. They sprout in less than a week (sow the seeds indoors, in cell packs), but soon damp off if any overcrowding is encountered. Marjoram is a perennial that is grown as an annual, with a sweet aroma that is immediately evident. Keep them thinned for rapid growth, and transplant to a sunny, well-drained area when the soil is warm.

Oregano

Similar in culture to marjoram, oregano is a hardier perennial, and not as likely to damp off. The actual seeds from the really fragrant types release that familiar smell so beloved by Italian food connoisseurs.

Parsley

Although parsley belongs to the carrot family, it requires the same care as chives. It, too, likes a rich, moist soil, and can die in the summer heat.

Unlike chives, parsley is a biennial. After the first year it goes to seed and dies. Therefore, it is good to plant some every year.

Sometimes parsley will self-sow, but I have had to plant mine from seed each time.

Parsley takes 14 to 20 days to germinate. Plant 2 seeds to a cell pack and transplant when the herb reaches 4 to 5 inches in height. There are 2 different types of parsley to choose from, curly and Italian (flat) parsley. Both have the same cultivation needs, and do best in partial sun.

Rosemary

Rosemary grows slowly, but develops so attractively from seed, as opposed to cuttings, that it may be worth the wait. Due to its small seeds and sensitivity to cold, start rosemary indoors.

Germination occurs in 2 to 3 weeks. The finicky seedlings detest peat in their soil mix and overwatering at any stage.

If you do decide to propagate by cuttings, stems from the latest growth or the upper part of the older stems make the best cuttings and usually can be rooted easily late in summer or early fall. The stems should be cut with a sharp knife into 3- or 4-inch sections, each containing a set of leaves or leaf buds near its upper end. The terminal and the intermediate sections root equally well. The leaf area should be reduced by about $2/3$ by removing the larger leaves and allowing only the buds and the young leaves to remain on the upper $1/3$ of the section.

To prevent wilting, the cuttings should be placed in water as soon as they are removed from the plant.

A shallow box filled with 4 to 6 inches of clean sand and fitted with a glass cover makes a good rooting bed.

Insert the cuttings to a depth of $1/2$ to $2/3$ their length in the moist sand. Pack firmly and saturate the sand with water. Cover

Chives

Marjoram

Oregano

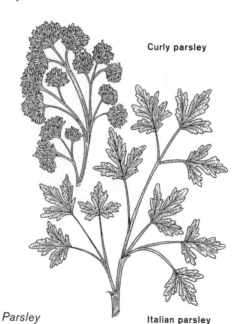

Curly parsley

Parsley   **Italian parsley**

with glass so that a $1/2$- to 1-inch opening remains along one side of the box for ventilation.

Place the box in a protected sunny place and keep moist, but not wet, at all times. The cuttings should be protected from direct sunlight by cheesecloth shading for the first week to prevent wilting. With good care, roots should appear in about 2 weeks. In 4 to 6 weeks the cuttings will be ready to pot or set in cold frames or other places where they can be protected during the winter. Early in spring the plants can be transplanted to a permanent location.

149

DRIED TO PERFECTION

The seeds, leaves, flowering tops, and sometimes the roots of different herbs are used for seasoning. The flavor of freshly-grown herbs will last long if they are dried and properly cured and stored.

The young, tender leaves can be gathered and used fresh at any time during the growing season. For winter use, however, they should be harvested when the plants begin to flower.

If the leaves are dusty or gritty, wash them with cold water, drain thoroughly before drying, and lay them on a tray or platter. Tender-leaf herbs—such as basil, rosemary, tarragon, lemon balm, and the mints—which have a high moisture content, must be dried rapidly in a well-ventilated, darkened room if they are to retain their green color. If dried too slowly, they will turn dark or moldy. For this reason, an airy attic or other dry, dark room furnishes ideal conditions for curing these herbs in a short time.

Harvesting of the seed crop is done when the plants are mature. After curing for several days in an airy room, a day or 2 in the sun before storing will insure safekeeping.

As soon as the herb leaves or seeds are dry, they should be cleaned by separating them from stems and other foreign matter. They should then be packed in airtight containers to prevent loss of the essential oils that give them their delicate flavor.

Remember that dried herbs are 4 to 5 times stronger than fresh herbs. The delicate aroma and flavor of savory herbs may easily be lost by extended cooking, chopping the leaves too finely, or grinding them in a mortar (which exposes the aromatic oils).

Rosemary

Many people keep this pleasantly pungent herb in a sunny window, year-round, fearful of losing it to a cold winter. In or out, it craves lots of light and very well-drained soil.

Thyme

Creeping thyme starts best from seeds germinated indoors. It prefers a cooler environment

Thyme

than most, thriving at around 75 to 80°F. Seedlings do not grow rapidly at first, but eventually develop into robust plants. Transplant them into a sunny, well-drained, sweet soil such as a rock garden, wall, or hillside.

Borage, caraway, coriander, and dill should be sown in peat pots or directly into the garden in early spring. Except for the biennial caraway, they are annuals that will often self-sow the following year. As is so often the case, volunteer seedlings develop into stronger plants than their parents.

Not all herbs can be grown from seeds. Others, such as French tarragon, require such particular conditions that the attempt may not be worth the effort. To expand your herb garden, purchase these herbs as plants or propagate by cuttings gleaned from a friend.

Still, you can begin a fine herb bed from seed to enjoy this summer and many seasons to come.

CHAPTER 10

Problems and Solutions

All gardeners should learn to recognize the signals that their plants are sending them. Any change in leaf or stem shape and color indicates that development is off-course and that action should be taken to correct the problem.

Different Harvests, Different Needs

Vegetable plants, in general, are grouped into 3 categories: fall-harvesting or those that need decreasing radiation; spring- and fall-harvesting, those with low-radiation requirements and tolerance; and summer-prospering, those requiring relatively high levels of radiation. These distinctions must be taken into consideration when planning and planting your garden.

Fall-Harvesting

Cauliflower will remain much the same size when grown in too much light or with too long a day length. It won't start responding until the days become shorter and the ambient day and night temperatures drop. An excess of sun also yellows and withers the foliage, and the cauliflower heads will not develop.

Therefore, cauliflower is best grown as a fall crop in most parts of the country. Although it can be grown as a winter or spring crop in the South and West, it should be started after the longest day of the year, June 21, for optimum results.

Other fall-harvesting crops are broccoli, cabbage, and pumpkins.

Spring- and Fall-Harvesting

Peas stand still when the balmy breezes blow. A spring-harvesting crop and one of the most widely grown cool-temperature vegetables, peas stop growing when the night temperatures go above 65°F. The plant remains green and the existing leaves continue to function, but no new leaves develop. No matter how much water or organic fertilizer is supplied, the plants just will not grow. Ultimately, the leaves dry on the plant and the plants die without reaching maturity.

Summer-Prospering

Tomatoes are a summer-prospering crop. When all parts of your tomato plants begin to elongate—the stems, leafstalks, and leaf blades—it means they are getting too much shade and responding to a lack of radiation. Work to get that sun around them and start them back on the prize-winning track.

Peppers and eggplant are other common summer-prospering vegetables.

LITTLE SUN, BIG YIELDS

Any vegetable plants growing in limited sunlight should be given ample space to prevent root competition and shading each other out. Fertilize moderately and with a more balanced organic nitrogen, phosphorous, and potassium ratio than you would use for rapidly developing plants in full sunlight. Water sufficiently to maintain growth, but do not flood (see watering specifics in chapter 5).

Soil Strategies

Often, sickly-looking or slow-growing plants are the result of nutritive soil deficiencies or excesses, or incorrect pH. Here are some common warning signs to help you identify what is ailing your crop, and solutions to correct the problems.

Hold the Salt

If spinach plants are stunted and bear small, dark green leaves, put the blame on excess salts, caused by over-fertilizing and excessive irrigation. Great concentrations of salts in the soil may injure the root systems and bring about iron chlorosis, causing leaf margins to appear burned and severe wilting to take place even when moisture is quite adequate. To remedy the problem, apply compost and green manure.

pH Predicament

If watermelons are on hold, blame the soil. These summer thirst-quenchers don't grow well in heavy soils, particularly ones that are too alkaline. They thrive in soil with a pH as low as 5.0. Long-term changes can be brought about by treating the soil with powdered sulfur. In the home garden it is difficult to calculate how much to add or how often. Instead of guessing, add 2 to 3 inches of peat moss or compost to the garden every year and incorporate it in into the top 6 inches of soil. The acid generated by this organic matter not only lowers the soil pH, but also renders essential elements available to plants.

When "no growth" is the problem for leaf crops, like spinach, and root crops, like beets and parsnips, an overly acidic soil is usually at fault. These grow best when the soil pH is in the range of 6.0 to 6.7, rather than in soil that is more acid. Below a pH of 6.0, such plants remain the same size for many days on end. The foliage may also be lighter green than usual and develop a purple edge, indicating a phosphorous deficiency. The surface of the soil will begin to develop a covering of moss and acid-loving weeds.

The poor growth of plants in acid soil can be corrected by applying ground dolomitic limestone. The amount of lime required to establish a specific pH level depends on both the initial pH and the type of soil. More lime is needed to change the pH of a fertile or clayey soil than a sandy soil.

Some vegetables, such as potatoes, carrots, and turnips, well tolerate a soil pH as low as 5.2. They react poorly when out of their element. In fact, injury from potato scab turns severe unless the pH is below 5.5.

Soggy Soil

Cropped carrots are a common example of root crops' sensitivity to waterlogged soils. Excess water in the spaces between soil particles reduces the soil's capacity to release carbon dioxide and to provide plants with needed oxygen. The plants are thus unable to take up sufficient water to develop rapidly. Even though ample water is available, the plants look very much like they are experiencing a water shortage: the foliage is much smaller than typical of the species; the edges of the leaves develop tan margins; and flowering and fruiting are delayed or inhibited. Improve drainage by adding sand and watering less.

When plants are not productive, often they are being asked to work out of their time frame and in unfriendly environments. They are uncomfortable and will tell you this with an exterior sign.

Let observation be the guide to your plants' health and your garden's growth. Tune in to your plants. You will learn and they will prosper.

Choosing Companions

Certain plants can protect your vegetables from insects and other pests. Other plants can harm their neighbors.

Nature grows in harmony. You, as an organic gardener, must do the same to have a healthy and productive garden. Here is some knowledge to help you choose companions among the crops.

Marigolds growing in tomato bed

Marigolds have long been grown in food gardens as a colorful, if inedible, pest control. Researchers have found that French and African marigolds do, in fact, reduce lesion nematode population in soil and even in infested plant roots. Lesion nematodes, also known as eelworms, are microscopic parasites that attack plant roots, stunting plants and causing leaves to turn yellow. Marigold roots exude 3 compounds that leach into the soil and are toxic to some nematodes, although not all nematode species are affected. Plant these pungent flowers around the pepper patch or the tomato bed, where their compounds and color will both be effective.

While the marigold-nematode connection is well-known, many gardeners do not realize that asparagus and parsley do well as a team; beans go well with potatoes, carrots, and cucumbers; and beets benefit when planted with kohlrabi and spinach. Basil planted near tomatoes, eggplant, and peppers discourages flies and flea beetles. Mustard near cabbage and cauliflower lures away worms.

Simple products made from certain plants are also known to be effective in varying degrees against plant diseases. The common geranium, with its high tannin content, reduces the effect of tobacco mosaic virus on susceptible plants such as tomatoes. Peas and wallflowers, emulsified and used as a spray, have fungicidal benefits. Garlic sprays combat plant disease with allicin, a chemical compound found in garlic extracts.

MAKE SPRAY TO SAVE SPACE

One problem with companion planting for pest control, especially when the repellent plants are largely inedible, like marigolds and nasturtiums, is that valuable garden space is taken out of food production. Planting nasturtiums among the cucumbers might repel the striped cucumber beetle, but they also take up space that could support additional vines or bushes.

Many organic gardeners simply grow their non-edible pest repellents in the ornamental garden and then convert them into sprays to protect food crops. Just about any repellent plant can be made into a spray by first running it through a blender with a little water and then straining the pulp through several thicknesses of cheesecloth.

Whether plants that make effective sprays are just as beneficial when grown as companion plants has yet to be determined under controlled laboratory conditions. However, some organic gardeners make noteworthy claims for them as such.

Garden Foes

Besides having beneficial companions, many crops are reputed to have plant enemies. Dill supposedly slows carrot growth. Tomato and kohlrabi are said to interfere with each other's growth. Others, such as potatoes and tomatoes, are more logical enemies because both are susceptible to the same blight disease. Tomatoes and apricots, both susceptible to the same wilt disease, are other examples of risky companions.

Some plants can be mutual enemies. For instance, apple tress release volatile substances that inhibit the development of potato seedlings and, in a plant world version of "an eye for an eye," potatoes release toxins that can build up in the soil and cause chemical imbalance in young apple trees and interfere with their growth.

Overall, there are many solid reasons for keeping the fruit and vegetable gardens separated by as much distance as your land will allow.

Compounds emitted from plants can also affect the soil's chemistry. Chemicals exuded from the roots of rye grass, often used as a winter cover crop in large gardens, reduce soil nitrification by up to 84 percent. Onions have a similar effect, although not so pronounced.

Inhibited nitrification does not affect the amount of nitrogen in the soil, only the soil's ability to change that nitrogen chemically into a form that can be used by plants. In the case of rye grass, the problem corrects itself, when you turn under the cover crop well ahead of spring planting time.

As with most organic planting methods, companion planting's objective is to create a natural balance. Pests and diseases cannot be totally eliminated from the garden's man-made ecosystem, but companion planting might well provide a partial solution for the gardener unwilling to resort to toxic pesticides.

The Fearsome Five Pests

The corn earworm, cucumber beetle, Mexican bean beetle, squash vine borer, and the tomato hornworm are well-known connoisseurs of warm-season crops. Unlike springtime pests such as aphids, flea beetles, and whitefly, these insects and their damage are easy to recognize. To control them however, is a real challenge.

Your best plan of attack is to strike when they are most vulnerable. Therefore, to plan your strategy, it is important to know the insects' life cycles, the crops they attack, and methods of control.

Corn Earworm

The corn earworm feeds on the foliage and fruit of corn, tomatoes, peppers, beans, and potatoes. Adult moths lay eggs on corn silks or the undersides of leaves in spring. The eggs hatch in a few days and the larvae feed on silks, leaves, and/or fruit for 3 to 4 weeks. At that point the larvae leave the ear and pupate in the soil.

BT (*Bacillus thuringiensis*) kills leaf-eating caterpillars. Slow-acting, but effective, it renders them dead in about 2 days.

Spray BT on young larvae as they are found on leaves and fruit. For corn, apply BT granules on newly emerging silks every 3 to 4 days for 2 weeks.

Deep tilling in fall exposes larvae to predators and weather.

Cucumber Beetle

The cucumber beetle overwinters as an adult in plant debris in the garden. It emerges from hiding in early summer, when temperatures are above 60°F.

The adult beetle feeds on emerging cucumber, melon, squash, corn, and bean

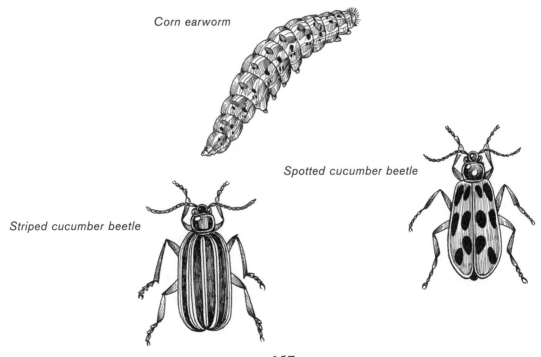

Corn earworm

Spotted cucumber beetle

Striped cucumber beetle

157

seedlings and lays eggs at the base of the plants. The eggs hatch in about 10 days.

Developing larvae feed on the roots of seedlings for about a month, then pupate. They reemerge in 3 weeks as adults.

To control the cucumber beetle, get a jump on it: Plant seedlings before temperatures reach a sustained 60°F.

Cover transplants or seedlings with fabric floating row covers and periodically check under covers for beetles emerging from the soil around the plant. Remove the covers when flowering begins. Keep plants growing vigorously by providing an adequate organic fertilizer and good water management. A healthy plant can outgrow an infestation.

Apply a spray of pyrethrum (a botanical natural insect control) to control heavy infestation. Clean the garden of plant debris in the fall to remove any overwintering beetles.

Mexican bean beetle

Mexican Bean Beetle

A relative of the ladybug, the Mexican bean beetle attacks the leaves and fruit of many types of bean plants. The $1/4$-inch-long adult emerges in spring from plant debris in the garden, begins feeding, and lays clusters of yellow oval eggs on the undersides of bean leaves.

The yellow larvae hatch in 7 days and feed on bean plants for over a month. They then pupate and reemerge as adults in 10 days.

The Pedio wasp parasitizes Mexican bean beetle pupae. Plant an early trap crop of beans. One week after you notice larvae on the trap crop, release about 200 wasps. One application of the wasps every year is best for good control.

For large plantings, spray the botanical control sabadilla (a plant in the lily family) on both sides of the leaves.

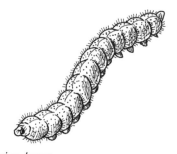

Squash vine borer

Squash Vine Borer

The squash vine borer is a destructive caterpillar that attacks stems of squash, cucumbers, and melons.

The adult of the species is a greenish-black, clear-winged moth that emerges in early summer and lays its eggs on stems and leaves. White larvae hatch within a week and bore into the stem, where they feed for a month before emerging to pupate in the soil.

Squash vine borers are one of the tougher insects to control because most people don't realize that they have an infestation until their crop is gone. In this case, prevention is the best cure. Stop moths from laying eggs on the plants by using floating row covers over emerging seedlings. Remove the covers before flowering to insure proper pollination.

Another method of prevention is the sprinkling of fresh black pepper around the roots of growing plants weekly for several weeks. Companion planting and herb sprays—many are available at garden centers—are worth a try, too.

If the stem is infected, inject 1 cubic centimeter of an undiluted liquid BT solution with a syringe above the entry hole of the borer.

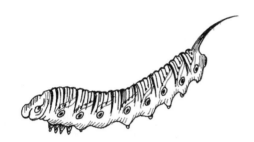

Tomato hornworm

Tomato Hornworm

The tomato hornworm is best known for its huge, green, horned caterpillar stage, when it feeds on the fruits and leaves of tomatoes, peppers, potatoes, and eggplant.

The 4-inch-wide gray adult moth emerges from its pupal stage in the soil in May or June. The green eggs, laid singly on leaf undersides, hatch in 5 to 7 days and the caterpillars immediately begin feasting. They feed mainly at night for 4 to 6 weeks before pupating.

To control tomato hornworm, spray BT as soon as you notice the larvae. Fall tilling will kill overwintering pupae in the soil.

Insects only go after plants that are weak and sick. The first and best way to solve the problem of insects is to have a healthy, balanced soil high in organic matter in order to produce strong, healthy plants.

All gardeners should be working toward that goal. Until you reach it, make use of these controls to rid your garden of the "fearsome five."

Cabbage Complaints

Cabbages aren't bothered by many insects and are able to grow fast enough to recover quickly from damage. However, they are not invulnerable. A few pests can, at times, gain the upper hand.

The aphid population can get out of control in a hot, dry spring and the cooler weather of fall. Aphids tend to cluster on the most nutritious areas of the plant—growing tips and leaf axils—which are hard to reach with sprays.

Aphid

Ladybugs or insecticidal soaps are very effective against aphids. Start spraying as soon as you see the first little pale green wedge-shaped pests.

The cabbage maggot is a small fly attracted to newly worked soil. It lays eggs at the base of a cabbage stem or on the soil nearby. The root maggots that emerge feed on the roots for 1 to several weeks. The adults can lay eggs throughout the growing season.

It's fairly easy to prevent the insect from gaining entry. Cut 6- × 6-inch squares of tar paper and punch a hole in the centers with a nail. Make a slit from the hole to one edge and slip this shield around the seedlings at planting time, making sure that it fits snugly around the stem. The adult fly won't be able to get near the stem base to lay its eggs.

Cabbage flea beetles, striped and about $1/8$ inch long, can do serious damage to young cabbage plants. They are season-long pests in most areas, with no distinct gaps between generations. They thrive in hot weather.

The best controls for them are two natural products, rotenone and pyrethrum, which are made from plants. You might also try companion planting nasturtiums, if space permits.

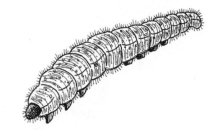

Imported cabbageworm

Several species of small pale cabbage butterflies lay tiny eggs on the undersides of cabbage leaves, from which hatch voracious cabbage-colored caterpillars. The imported cabbageworm is widespread and around from May to September. The cabbage looper and the diamond-back moth also produce small, green caterpillars that do similar damage.

All of these insects are fairly easily controlled with BT spray. For best results, apply the bacterial insect control before the worms reach $1/4$ inch in length.

Rotate members of the cabbage family each year. Avoid having them follow each other in the same part of the garden. For example, don't grow kale where broccoli was planted the year before.

Still, the best way to prevent insects and diseases is soil nutrition. Remember our motto: Healthy, balanced soil will produce healthy, balanced plants.

Seaweed Supplements

Leaf sprays of seaweed concentrate will not replace proper soil management, but foliar feeding (see a discussion of technique in chapter 4, in "Seafood: Seaweed Sprays" on page 40) is an excellent technique for bolstering the plant's health in times of stress.

One of the most important times to consider any foliar spray is in midsummer. That is when insect and disease control pressure is high. Temperatures are hot, water is scarce, and fruiting crops like peppers, eggplants, and tomatoes can lose their blossoms after a few days of stress.

Apples can suffer, too. Drought combined with a calcium deficiency in the soil can cause bitter pit in apples and blossom-end rot in tomatoes. The trace elements and growth-promoting hormones in diluted seaweed give plants a boost when they need it most.

Don't wait until leaves show signs of stress or deficiency before you apply the seaweed. If the plant is severely chlorotic or scrawny, it will be too late for the trace minerals to help the plants.

For vegetables, I recommend foliar spraying once a month. To improve the size, flavor, and health of fruit, start spraying when the fruit is small and immature and continue spraying every 2 weeks. Give your plants a dose of leaf spray whenever they are shifting gears: going from a slower mode of growth to a faster one; making flowers; setting fruit; or in the middle of an insect attack.

Consider foliar feeding whenever there are long, hot periods without rain or when temperatures begin to drop in the fall. When the soil is dry, the plants can't get as many nutrients. Foliar sprays are their vitamin supplement.

As a prophylactic against disease, try spraying 3 times a month. Seaweed sprays can help reduce the incidence of powdery mildew on cucumbers and cantaloupes and stem rust on wheat. They can also prevent peach leaf curl, a common and debilitating bacterial disease that infects peach trees.

In a garden's fertility menu there is no doubt that manure, mulch, soil amendments, and compost are the basic diet. However, foliar-feeding plays a very supportive role in any plant-nurturing strategy.

PART 3

After the Fall

Many gardeners fail to take advantage of the second half of summer. You will find, to your great relief, that crops grown in mid- to late summer are much less threatened by pests than those grown in spring. Many of the predators that despoil our gardens will have passed their nuisance period by the time the second crop is sown. We will show you how you can enjoy a wide variety of garden vegetables right up until the first frost, and even later; and the organic way to protect your soil and landscape against the freezing temperatures and snows of winter.

CHAPTER 11

Growing On

Delicious beets, tender lettuce, and sweet corn: these are just a few of the vegetables that you can continue to enjoy fresh from your garden long after Labor Day. Read further to learn how to keep your garden growing into the fall.

Late-Planted Harvests

You can have an encore performance of the tender little beets of spring, the kind that you eat—tops and all. They will come up quickly in midsummer, and, growing more slowly as the days turn cooler, be delicious right through the first half of winter. Beets can take a lot of cold weather.

Spinach is another crop that we are denied in summer, but that grows when days become shorter and nights nippier. Plant your seeds in sunny rows about $1/2$ inch deep if your soil is sandy loam, about $1/4$ deep if clay.

Pick the outside leaves, when you harvest spinach. Mulch the plants under straw after the first hard freeze.

Try for a crop of late corn. If you succeed (and I often have) you may have sweet corn well into October. If a frost takes it, what will you have lost? The frozen cornstalks cut down and spread over the bed will provide cover at first, then later—as they decay—nutrition for the soil.

Pre-germinate corn seed by soaking it overnight. You can subtract 10 days from the time of the directions on the seed packet.

I look forward every fall to the second crop of peas to be had when the weather is turning brisk. These peas combine beautifully with the tomatoes, onions, and peppers that are in season in fall to make very tasty dishes. Sow them in late July or early August.

The strawberry bed is enriched, as well as thinned, by turning under every other row of plants, together with its partly decayed mulch; first tilling north and south, then east and west. If you are growing ever-bearing strawberries, follow this treatment with a good drink of liquid organic fertilizer—a generous

LETTUCE KEEP GROWING

Although anything but a summer crop, lettuce can be stretched well into the fall by planting in late August. Fall plantings will make it possible to have extra-early crops in spring.

Lettuce is a plant that thrives in cool, not cold, weather. Throughout much of the country lettuce is most satisfying as a fall crop. As the weather turns progressively cooler, the bolting problem disappears and the quality of the leaves improves. If you can protect the plants from extreme cold, you can extend the harvest period well beyond the time when the tomatoes succumb to frost and even overwinter young plants for an early spring harvest.

The only real problem with fall and winter lettuce is that you have to start planting seeds in late summer. Sowing them seems to run contrary to the rhythms of the seasons. September is usually a time for harvesting. By then most of the seed packets have been stowed away. Still, getting into the late-summer sowing habit really pays off.

Summer sowing is best done in cell packs outdoors in a shady location. The heat of the summer sun is just too overpowering for good germination and growth. I start fall lettuce around the last week of August, or about 8 to 12 weeks before the first killing frost.

Three weeks after the seedlings sprout, I transplant them to well-prepared, moist soil in the garden beds. If the weather is hot, I shade them from intense sun for 3 to 7 days, until they are established.

Fall-harvested lettuce should be lightly fed with organic fertilizer. As the days grow shorter and temperatures drop, the plants grow more slowly and use fewer nutrients. Excessive fertilization is wasted on these plants and may cause harm.

As the temperature drops and threatens to fall below 25°F, cover the lettuce with floating row covers. Old-fashioned cold frames and polyethylene tunnels work well, too, but they demand just enough effort to dissuade many organic gardeners. Floating row covers, on the other hand, can do remarkable things for lettuce at low cost and with minimal attention. Just drape them loosely over the bed or row, then weigh them down on the sides with rocks or soil.

Once the covers go on, leave them in place. Enough light gets through to keep the plants growing. It is also warmer under the covers, so they will probably grow a little longer.

Don't worry too much about watering under floating row covers, because light levels are so low that plants are not growing fast. Go ahead and water before you cover them; then let nature do the watering. If the plants are in a cold frame, keep an eye on the soil surface and water as needed.

Harvest whole heads, rather than picking out side leaves; damaged plant tissue can become an entryway for various diseases. When you do pull back the row covers to harvest, cut several heads at a time rather than removing the covers every day.

Some varieties may, of course, grow better than others; however, the real key to success for fall picking, as I see it, is the proper use of floating row covers, not the variety.

You can't expect plants that mature in fall to make it to spring. Overwintering lettuce requires a later planting (see "Lettuce" entry in chapter 7, page 98). The rule of thumb that I use is to get the plants to 3 or 4 inches in diameter before the temperature drops below 25°F. That is when the cover should go on. As the days shorten, the

continued

Floating row cover over lettuce bed

light intensity drops, the temperature becomes too low to promote growth, and the stocky young plants go into dormancy.

In late winter, the ground under the covers will thaw much sooner than the surrounding soil and the air temperature will rise, too. The lettuce plants will burst into action, maturing in only a few weeks. You can remove the covers once you're confident that the temperature won't drop below 25°F at night.

You will have to harvest this crop quickly, though. Overwintered crops tend to bolt rapidly after they mature, in response to lengthening days. 'Winter Density' is not as daylight sensitive as most varieties, however, so it will hold longer in spring without bolting.

For anyone who is repelled by the anemic-looking iceberg from the store, a little planning and a roll of floating row cover fabric will grace your salad bowl with brilliant green, red, and bronze leaves for many months of the year.

cupful of fish and seaweed emulsion poured into the center of each plant.

Did you know that late summer is the best of all possible times to sow pansy seed? Pansies germinate best and grow most easily when there is the widest variation of temperature in a 24-hour period. Make a little seedbed with a good amount of covering compost and rake it smooth. You will have a rich assortment of well-started little plants to welcome the next spring.

While you are planning a fall harvest for yourself, why not help your garden to reincorporate its own harvest of minerals and mulch for early and rich production next spring. With the sun still warm and the days long, this is an excellent time to provide for the needs of your soil.

Remember, we are organic gardeners who return to the soil all that we take from it, plus a bonus for enrichment. Everything that we put into the soil decays quickly, and there is usually plenty of organic material on hand—grass clippings and green, mineral-rich weeds—which may be dug into the soil.

HUMUS ON RYE

Late summer is also the time to sow a cover crop on any rows from which produce has been removed and nothing has been planted to take its place (see "Protective Coverings" in chapter 4, page 32). At this season of the year it will disappear almost overnight, giving the soil nutrition and rich humus for the next planting.

For both added growing and eating rewards, plus valuable soil, make the most of that good second crop and reap late-planted harvests.

Season Extenders

Protective devices make it possible to raise the temperature of your undercover crops 10 to 20°F in cold weather. Among them are cloches, cold frames, and floating row covers.

These season-extending technologies aren't complicated. Many varieties are available for purchase.

Tent-shaped hotcap cloche

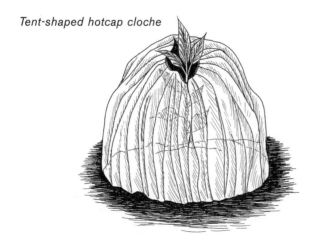

If you are creative and ambitious, you can construct some simple ones from materials that you have lying around in your garage or shed.

Cloches

A cloche is a covering, usually transparent, that is placed over plants for protection and allows the sunlight in. Cloches are good at trapping heat; the smaller the cloche, the quicker it heats up. Even on a relatively cool day, the temperature inside a cloche can soar high enough to damage your plants or promote soft, fleshy, frost-susceptible growth. To prevent this you must provide for air movement. Since this will also ward off mold and mildew, it is best to err on the side of too much ventilation.

The simplest cloche for individual plants is the cone- or tent-shaped hotcap. You can purchase inexpensive hotcaps, or make some yourself by cutting semi-circles out of the rigid material of your choice, such as a plastic milk jug, or Reemay, a type of polyester.

Cold Frames

Cold frames can stretch food budgets and break gardening rules year round. From mid- to late winter, inside a cold frame, it's spring. Transplants of tomatoes, broccoli, and cauliflower, all needing soil temperatures of 65°F or higher, can be raised in cold frames with heating cables, in hotbeds, or with only the sun and a few tricks.

A cold frame is essentially a bottomless box that is higher in the back than in the front. It is usually made of wood and is covered with glass or plastic. Some gardeners paint the interior part of the frame white to increase sunlight reflection.

Although some cold frames are complex and immovable, you can slap a simple one together with some 2- × 8- or 2- × 10-inch boards and old windows. You can also simply stack straw bales (the "sides" of the frame) around the crop that you wish to protect and lay old window sashes right above the bales. Whatever your choice, be sure that the cold frame faces south.

Black plastic transmits heat to the soil, so lay it down over the bed several weeks before sowing seeds. Remove the black plastic when you are ready to plant, then sow your seeds, and lay clear plastic over them before closing the cold frame. When your seedlings show, slit the plastic. Another early-bird ploy is germinating seeds in the house, then moving them to your cold frame once they're up. This works because most seedlings like cooler temperatures than needed by their seeds to germinate.

Hardening off is a term that means slowly toughening baby plants started inside for growing outside. Because cold frames can be open, partially open, or closed, they are prefect halfway points for growing. Once out in the frame, seedlings stay out, and there is no need to shuffle them inside during sudden cold snaps, because ready protection is there at hand.

To start, move your pots and flats from the house to your cold frame near transplanting time. Gradually let more sun, cold, wind, and dryness surround them. In 1 to 4 weeks, transplant them.

If used through the summer, your cold frames will lessen the spring rush. By midsummer, sow biennial and perennial seeds that need warm soil. Take cuttings of shrubs, trees, and houseplants at this time. Keep the soil moist and add some shade like cheesecloth.

Fall is also the time to take hardwood cuttings. We have succeeded with cuttings of forsythia, weigela, privet, junipers, and yews.

Six- to ten-inch sections with nodes at both ends, pushed to a depth of $2/3$ their length, and kept moist and mulched, should root by midspring.

During winter months, homegrown food is usually stored food. But with your garden cold frame, it can be fresh. Here's how: In late summer, boost the quality of your cold frame's soil. Then sow, using your fall frost date and days to maturity of each variety to help decide when. Plants should be $2/3$ grown by frost date.

Whether trying broccoli, lettuce, kale, corn salad, or Oriental veggies, make sure that the mature plants will fit in your garden cold frame. Special winter varieties that grow in low light and low temperatures are available from most seed companies.

Once growing, add aluminum foil under and around plants to reflect light and brighten cloudy days. Because they give off heat as they freeze, pans of water inside help moderate cold temperatures.

To work well, garden cold frames need attention. If situated near your house, they are not as easily forgotten. Choose a sunny well-drained site, unless you sow seeds in containers, in soil as fertile and balanced as that in your garden. Protected by a windbreak, a cold frame is more moist in summer and warmer in winter.

Cold-frame ventilation is far more important than weatherproofing. Low light levels, high humidity, and warmer temperatures in a stagnant environment can cause weak, leggy plants and lots of fungal growth. Heat building or cold drafts both endanger plants.

Either make a pact from the start to check your cold frame frequently, or use an automatic ventilator. Some have thermostats to set high for keeping seeds warm; low, for growing plants. On warm days, open the top of the

Cold frames

frame to allow ventilation. Ventilate cool-season crops when the temperature rises above 50 to 60°F, and warm-season crops at 70 to 80°F. A thermometer to tell you the exact temperature would be an excellent investment here. In cold weather, insulate the outside of the box with soil.

Cool-weather crops do better than warm-season crops in a cold frame. If warm-season crops were grown in the greenhouse or indoors, they will usually do better in a frame after frost. Endive, chicory, chard, radicchio, broccoli, cabbages, and radishes, however, all do well into December.

COLD-FRAME SUCCESSES

When I built the first cold frame here at Spring Meadow, I placed it in the earth facing south and banked the soil well around it. Over the years I tested the temperature both inside and outside the cold frame: In summer the thermometer readings have been 15 to 20°F cooler inside the frame than out; in winter they have been 20 to 30°F warmer. The only time that a plant became frostbitten was when some leaves of a tomato plant touched the glass on a day when the temperature dipped to 0°F.

It was February when I first installed my cold frame. I decided to start its career by making a batch of quick compost in it, to seed the flats for

continued

spring. I thought that the compost's heat would do away with whatever molds might have accumulated and that it would do no harm to the earthworms in the soil, which could tunnel down and wait out the heat.

I piled my accumulation of ground-up leaves, food scraps, and weeds, along with a little fish meal, into the cold frame. I turned it at 3-day intervals until it started to cool down, about 12 days later.

After I had forked out all of the compost that I needed for the garden, I leveled what was left in the frame, marked rows, and sowed lettuce, carrots, onions, and a row of spinach. Everything came up as though it was May (which it was in the cold frame).

Besides warmth, there was perfect humidity, and, as I was controlling it, just enough water at the right time. A straw mat placed over the glass cut down the rays of the sun when they were too much for the tiny plants.

Between the rows of early-spring produce, I placed tomatoes, peppers, eggplant, and cabbage to be set out in the garden after all danger of frost had passed. The sturdiest of these I transplanted into 4-inch pots, discarding the others.

I found that the cold frame–grown plants were stockier than similar ones grown indoors and that their roots were more luxuriant. Since the sun is above them in the cold frame, they don't have to bend to one side as they do on a windowsill, but can stretch straight up.

A shady corner of one of my cold frames made a perfect place for starting cuttings. Chrysanthemums, geraniums, and even herbs take root quickly in a box of damp sand covered with plastic.

In late spring I sowed a new planting of lettuce right in the cold frame to take the place of the garden varieties during the hot weather. I discovered that the lettuce in the cooler, shadier environment stayed crisp and tender throughout the summer.

There is nothing that gives winter-jaded spirits a better lift than a cold frame blooming with pansies and primroses, lifting their faces to the January sun against a backdrop of snow. If you would like to share that lift, make little dish gardens of them with grape hyacinths or dwarf iris. They are unsurpassed Easter gifts. It isn't at all difficult to grow them in your cold frames. Sow the seed late in August and use very rich soil so that little thinning is necessary.

Snapdragons also grow beautifully in a cold frame. Sow your seeds in March and transplant them into bands or peat pots when they are sturdy little 3-inch seedlings. You will have extra-special young plants when the time comes to set them out. Because they transplant without fuss and bloom very early, you can often predetermine the color scheme of your snapdragon bed.

If a potful of blooming tulips is the loveliest thing on earth to you, call on your cold frame again. Put your tulip pot underground (outside the frame), until rooting has started; the soil near the north side of your cold frame is the place to pick. Then put it inside the frame where the sun hits it at an angle. As the buds develop, bring it farther out into the direct rays of the sun. When the buds are all but opened, they are ready to be a beautiful addition to your home.

Think in a cold-frame-of-mind. It gets both you and your crops off to a good and early start and provides gardening pleasure all year-round.

Thanks to plastic, season extenders are now plentiful and varied. But the old-fashioned garden cold frame is still hard to beat.

Mulch

Mulch can also extend the season. For root vegetables such as carrots, winter radishes, beets, turnips, and parsnips, you really don't need to pull them up as frost approaches. Leave them in the ground, mulch them heavily, and dig as you need them. Wait to mulch until the ground is lightly frozen, or field mice might move in for the winter.

The best mulch is one that will not become packed or waterlogged. Straw or fluffy leaves are good bets. When you want to dig vegetables, remove the mulch from a small area. Dig and remove a week's supply at a time; then replace the mulch to cover any exposed food. Jerusalem artichokes, leeks, bunching onions, and salsify can also be extended this way.

Well-mulched parsley, spinach, lettuce, endive, chicory, mustard, Swiss chard, and Chinese cabbage can easily stand a light frost without any damage. Start protecting them when temperatures are expected to go below 25 to 30°F. Placing a cold frame over the top of these vegetables at frost time will extend their season a month or 2.

Brussels sprouts, kale, and collards withstand frost and freezing especially well. Prevent sunburn in the early morning by covering the leaves with burlap until the frozen leaves have warmed up. Oriental vegetables such as bok choy, siew choy, kyo mizuna, gai lohn, daikon, and michilli thrive in cold frames all winter. Cauliflower, parsley, chives, escarole, and kohlrabi are all season-extending crops as well.

Consider an alternative. Experiment with these season-extenders. Be the last on your block to harvest organic produce this year.

Sow Off-Season

Spring is always too short a season. By the time the soil thaws and dries enough to work, it is often late April or even early May. By planting spinach and brassicas off-season and following a few special cultivation tips, you could be mixing these vegetables with emerging dandelion, purslane, and lamb's-quarter leaves for a fresh, healthy dish in midspring. Meanwhile, more conventional gardeners will still be thumbing through their seed packets and wishing that the season would start.

Spinach in Spring

Spring-planted spinach is hardly up before the summer hits and then it goes to seed.

So why not plant spinach in the autumn? Seed is cheap and there are often open spaces in the garden by October. Faced with the oncoming cold, the spirit of adventure dictates that any opportunity to shrink winter's impact is worth a try.

I did that and was delightedly surprised with the results. If you plant spinach in October and can keep the soil moist for immediate germination, you can harvest the first dark green leaves before winter hits.

Spinach leaves will survive the first light frosts. They also keep for almost a month, washed and packed in plastic bags in the refrigerator, while the roots and crowns live over for a second and even bigger crop in the spring.

If you can't water and nature doesn't, or if you plant late, the seedlings will be very small going into winter. Nevertheless, to my amazement, they will survive.

Mulch is beneficial, as long as it is light enough not to smother the plants. Here is an ideal place to put the evergreen boughs after Christmas.

It is in the January thaw and the cold, dry spells of late winter that the real test comes. I advise a generous mulch of straw around the roots to keep in moisture and a light mulch of chopped leaves over the top to keep the sun from warming and drying the leaves too soon.

Once the temperature stays above freezing for long spells and the spring moisture overcomes the spring winds, the plants are ready to be harvested. This is usually by early to mid-April. At about the time the spring-planted spinach is poking its little cotyledons through the ground, fall-planted patches are producing abundantly.

For years I have used the most common spinach variety 'Bloomsdale Longstanding'. I have also used 'Winter Bloomsdale', which is hardy enough to winter over from fall sowing for an early spring crop.

After that first planting, I compared the fall-planted spinach to previous spring-planted crops. The fall-planted was thick, lush, and delicious, and did not even leave the slight aftertaste that spinach lovers overlook. There were no insects to bother it and the season stretched for weeks before the hot weather made it bolt.

I cut the plants again and again, a portion at a time, to within an inch of the crown. Each time they grew back as dark green and tender as before. By the end of May, I was too busy on the farm to keep it cut, so it finally went to seed.

Spinach seed does not retain its viability well from year to year. It is best to buy it new annually. Spinach likes cool weather to sprout, so you may have better luck by presprouting the seeds indoors in a cool place like the cellar. In any case, plant the seeds near enough to the house to keep the soil watered until they are up and growing. Otherwise, your crop may be delayed by weeks or begin to sprout only to have the dry heat return and shrivel the tender young seedlings to death.

You will also want the spinach close by in case you get an early November picking. It helps, too, in spring when rain puddles could keep you from watching the early growth. When the rest of the garden is too wet to till, you can use that frustrating waiting time to fill your table and your freezer with the first great greens of the year.

Early Brassicas

My routine for successful brassicas starts in late winter with the arrival of the seed catalogs. Of all the catalog descriptions written in small print, two stand out. The first is "disease-resistant." Most gardeners have had trouble with brassica afflictions—of which there are many. For me, the second draw is "good taste," as a good-tasting cabbage translates into one of my favorite dishes: coleslaw.

I begin my early cabbages sometime between February 20 and March 15, when I fill flats measuring 12 × 20 inches (and approximately $2^1/_2$ inches deep) with a mix of sandy garden loam, sifted compost, and dampened peat moss. Precisely the same method grows a prolific, extra-early row of kohlrabi and broccoli every summer.

To have young plants spaced accurately from the start, I mark shallow indentations, each $2^1/_2$ inches from the next, in the soil surface, and drop 3 or 4 brassica seeds into each hollow with a view to thinning later to the sturdiest single seedling per station.

Cool growing conditions produce healthy, stocky seedlings. Weather permitting, my brassicas grow outdoors in a cold frame for 4 to 6 weeks. Three weeks before the last frost date is the time to set hardy cabbages, kohlrabi, kale, and broccoli seedlings into the garden. Less hardy cauliflower should be planted around the last frost date or a week later.

Brassicas are among the garden's true gourmands. It is hardly possible to make the soil too fertile for them. Having turned a generous dressing of crumbly old cow manure into the cole crop bed the fall before, I now stir a heaping spadeful of blended compost, bone meal, fish meal, and wood ashes into the place where each seedling will go.

My early brassicas always share a 3-foot-wide garden bed. The taller broccoli sits in a row about 18 inches behind the cabbages. Both are spaced 20 inches apart in their rows.

The next step, mulching, is critical. All brassicas fall prey to root maggots, the destructive larvae of a flying insect that lays its eggs on the soil surface near stems of cabbage, broccoli, and the rest. Soon small white maggots hatch, burrow down, and, feeding as they go, riddle brassica roots with a network of tunnels.

A thick mulch (6 inches is not too much) of hay, straw, or leaves laid around young brassicas at transplanting time and snuggled right up to their little necks, has proven to be a sure root maggot deterrent. The fly simply can't get through the mulch to the base of the brassicas.

Mulching accomplished, gardeners who cultivate brassicas can relax.

Summer brings a wave of white cabbage butterflies flitting over the garden in search of the only available food. I do a search-and-squash tour of the cabbage patch, but, before they get out of hand, out comes a sprayer full of *Bacillus thuringionsis* (BT), an effective, but quickly dissipated bacterium that kills cabbage worms and various other larvae of moths or butterflies.

Root maggots

Cabbage butterfly and pupa

Vigorously growing crops can usually withstand some insect grazing. To keep them moving along, water your brassicas every week. Many times in their garden life, I treat them to a nourishing drink of fish emulsion. You can practically see a spurt of growth in the day following such a feed. After the crops are harvested, no brassicas will grow here again for 3 years. If peas or tomatoes can occupy the same garden space from one year to the next, cabbages, broccoli, and kin are one group that we rotate around the garden. This is not only because brassicas are gross feeders, but because they host many fungal, bacterial, and viral diseases that may show up as yellowed leaves of undersized or even blackened plants. Because many diseases can overwinter in the soil, strict rotation is necessary.

It is also necessary to maintain fertile soil that is close to neutral in pH (7.0). To produce neutral soil, you may need to apply limestone or wood ashes to your brassica beds. Do this in accordance with the recommendations of a soil test. In this case, guessing won't make it grow.

CHAPTER 12

Prelude to Winter

When the weatherman reports that frost is on the way, it is very important to care for your gardens. Harvest all of your summer crops. Cucumbers, tomatoes, eggplant, peppers, and the rest are all killed by a heavy frost.

After cutting, eggplant, cucumbers, and summer squash must be refrigerated. An extra refrigerator in the basement can come in very handy for these and extra fruit from the orchard.

Stored at around 70°F, tomatoes can keep for 6 weeks after harvesting. If you wrap them in tissue and store them in paper bags, you may have ripe tomatoes for 2 months or more. Be careful not to bruise the fruit.

Late onions should be lifted and sun-dried for a week. Don't forget to bring them in at night if temperatures dip below freezing. After they are cured, store onions in a cool, dry place. Hang them in a burlap bag or spread them out on dry paper.

Cabbage, broccoli, Brussels sprouts, and kale can tolerate a frost. If you have too many cabbages, stack them up in a large pile in the corner of your garden and cover with about a foot of leaves (and, if necessary, an insect trap such as netting). They will last several months that way. Chard, too, will last a month or more after frost if leaves and grass clippings are mounded around it.

Carrots, beets, parsnips, and potatoes are good keepers. Carrots and beets can be layered with sand, placed in barrels or wooden boxes, and stored in a cool place.

Winter squash must come indoors after the first frost date. Parsley will overwinter in many climates, if covered with a leaf mulch about 5 inches deep.

Preparation for Frost

If you want to spend some extra time and effort, you can delay the winter hiatus by protecting your garden from the first cold spell. Plants can be covered with bushel baskets. Old bales of hay can be formed to make a fortress around a tomato or pepper plant.

Tomato plants insulated with hay bales

Overhead sprinkling started before frost forms and continued until all ice and frost are off the plants in the morning has saved many a plant over the years. Portable cold frames are protective, too, but are limited to low-growing vegetables.

After harvesting a bed, it is desirable to mark the location of last summer's rows. Your vegetables will do better next year if you plant them in the spaces between the rows.

When harvests are complete, clear the garden of all crop residues. "Compostible" debris should be placed in the compost pile promptly. The ideal situation is to keep debris from accumulating in garden beds at all, lest they come to harbor any insect eggs or disease spores, some of which might winter over.

Winterizing the Garden

Don't just forget your garden at the end of the season—winterize it. Winterizing minimizes problems, especially soil loss, and will reward you with a larger harvest and better crops the following year.

Fall is the time to mineralize your soil. Remember, the elements of the rock powders organic gardeners use do not leach wastefully from the soil, as do chemical fertilizers. They remain in the soil until called upon by plants in ionic exchange. The clay minerals in soil, the carbon dioxide in water, the humic acid from decaying organic matter—all are made available to your plants.

In a moderate-sized garden you can afford to be generous with your rock powder additives. I suggest that you apply a high-potash granite and phosphate rock, finely ground, at the rate of 10 pounds per 100 square feet or 100 pounds to every 1,000 square feet of garden.

After you have applied these basic materials, spread a layer of compost and cover with a 4-inch layer of straw mulch. If you can get it, fairly well rotted manure is an excellent additive. Cover the garden completely.

If you are not a straw-mulcher already, late autumn is a good time to consider implementing this program. It will eliminate much of the effort of spading, tilling, weeding, and watering next season. Beneath this straw mulch the all-important biotic activity of the soil continues right along. Applying minerals in the fall and then covering them up with a good mulch speeds up the right kind of fertilization. You will find that your garden is ready to go to work earlier and more efficiently in spring.

You will also be amazed to see how much of what you put on in November is gone by April or May. Gone, that is, into the soil to give you a better garden.

A third winter soil-care method is planting a cover crop. A cover of annual rye will hold the soil against winter winds and rains, reduce nematode populations, and add needed organic matter (see "Protective Coverings" in chapter 4, page 32).

Put your garden to bed and tuck it in with these soil-building blankets that we have mentioned. It will awaken renewed and refreshed to welcome your seedlings in the spring.

Protecting the Landscape

Is your yard in winter a visual wonderland? Are there crystalline pines, rhododendrons, and boxwoods frosted with ice and snow? Is this a picture that makes you smile or do you see it as the beginning of the end of your landscape?

Planning ahead can prevent cold weather disasters. There are many protective measures that can be undertaken before the temperature falls to 32°F.

Deep and consistent watering before the onset of cold weather is probably the easiest way to forestall winter injury to trees and plants. Because evergreens keep their leaves through winter, they are particularly vulnerable to cold blasts of wind which evaporate moisture. Both evergreen and deciduous plants will benefit from a thorough soaking just before the ground freezes.

Pay special attention to container plants kept outdoors year-round. Container soil dries out almost as quickly in winter as in summer. Water generously during thaws.

Nature has produced many evergreens adaptable to regions that receive regular snowfall. Spruces and hemlocks are perfect examples, with their turned-downed main branches that quickly shed snow. Ice, followed by strong wind, can still tear off weakened branches, but these trees resist mutilation better than most.

The long, horizontal branches of pines, on the other hand, trap large amounts of ice and snow. To prevent the loss of major branches, thin the crowns of pines on a regular basis during the dormant season. Remove overlapping branches so that the center of the tree is opened, yet its natural silhouette is maintained.

An alternative method for supporting tall shrubs is to wrap the stems or branches with wire, stout twine, hemp rope, or nylon fishing line. To gently lock branches in place, wrap in a downward spiral from the top. Snow will slide off the drooping, nonspreading branches.

Deciduous trees, such as maples, with wide-spreading crowns and extensive, long branches, are prone to cracking from the weight of ice and snow. Thinning and reducing the spread help prevent winter damage and ultimately add years of life to the plant.

Brittle-stemmed trees, such as willow and silver maple, can benefit from crown reduction as well. Both of these common trees are water-loving and often situated in moist locations. Branches, therefore, may be more flexible and resistant to damage from snow overload.

Most shrubs suffer less damage than trees in winter, yet those in unsheltered sites will benefit from some protection. To guard against winter-burn, especially for truly sensitive shrubs such as boxwood and rhododendron, wrap them with burlap covers held by sturdy stakes. Loosely tie them with soft cord. Where snow-slides from a roof create havoc for plants, use sturdy wood-frame tepees to cover the shrubs.

Winter protection of some sort is necessary for hybrid roses. An economical system is to hill up the earth around the bottom 12 to 15 inches of stems, before the soil has

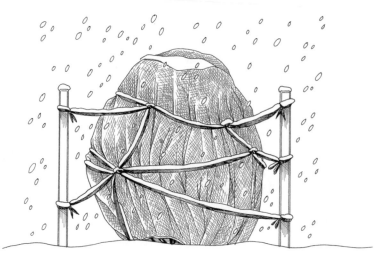

Protect against winter-burn by wrapping shrubs

frozen. Rather than take soil away from the surrounding area where it protects roots from the cold, use new soil. Pat it snugly into a cone; then prune the rose tops halfway.

After the soil has frozen slightly, mulch with pine needles or leaves. Mound soil around the base of climbing roses and wrap the canes with burlap.

Mulching your trees and shrubs will help retain soil moisture. The mulches that I use resemble the litter of fallen leaves, twigs, and other natural debris found in woods and meadows. Not only does the material preserve moisture, but it also supplies nutrients, checks erosion, moderates temperature fluctuations, and adds a tidy look.

None of these measures, of course, guarantees that all of your trees, shrubs, and perennials will make it to springtime grandeur. Plants that are not suited to their locations are apt to suffer winter damage, regardless.

However, homeowners that take the simple precautions of watering, pruning, staking, and mulching can greatly increase their plants' chances for winter survival. By winterizing your landscape in fall or early winter, you can enjoy the full beauty of all the seasons to come.

CHAPTER 13

Greenhouse Production

Peas Please

Peas thrive in cool weather, which means that they can be grown in a solar greenhouse during autumn and winter. They will germinate when soil temperatures are as low as 40°F, and their climbing ability makes them ideal for high production in small places.

If you want to raise peas in winter, use a soil mix of 1 part compost, 1 part fine washed sand, 2 parts mushroom compost, and 2 parts garden soil. Agricultural dolomite, rock phosphate, and nitrogen in the form of blood meal will complete the formula. Add these in amounts determined by the results of your soil test.

The soil should not be deficient in nitrogen. It is true that peas manufacture nitrogen, but this occurs later, after the root nodules have formed. Over the first 6 weeks, peas will grow better if they have a nitrogen supply from some source other than bacteria.

String a trellis down the middle of 24-inch-wide raised beds. Any width is fine as long as you keep at least 2 feet between each double set of rows. Plant 2 rows of peas $1^1/_2$ inches deep down the middle of the bed, 1 row on either side of the trellis. Sow each seed, by hand, 2 inches apart.

Experimentation has proven that snow peas are better than others for greenhouse production on the twin basis of speed to maturity and overall production. How long it takes for your vines to mature will depend on the average temperature and light conditions. In any event, be sure that the temperature stays above freezing at the time the peas are flowering and forming baby pods.

Edible-podded peas are ready just after the peas begin to form in the pod and the pods begin to swell. At peak they will have a sweet taste.

A couple of weeks after the first flush, you will ordinarily get a second, smaller harvest. Whether you wait for it or clear the ground for succession planting is a matter of choice.

Tomatoes

As spring approaches and the average temperature in the greenhouse begins to climb, you can start tomatoes. By the time the transplants are ready to set out in your protected environment, you will have harvested the last crop of winter peas. Perfect timing! The indoor environment will be warm enough for tomatoes, but too warm for peas, which at this time are quite able to fend for themselves outdoors.

The result is that you get your first early tomatoes at about the same time other gardeners are getting ready to plant them. Meanwhile, those outdoor-planted peas will be coming in also, thus extending your pea season to all but the hottest months of the year at little expense.

Growing vegetables in a greenhouse is a good example of maximum production within a limited space and with minimum cost.

Insects Controlled

Insects can make a mess of the leafy greens growing in a solar greenhouse. Not only is productivity set back by insect damage, but the food that you do get is not a diner's delight.

Aphids and whiteflies are two unwelcomed "houseguests." By using natural methods, you can fight them off and regain control of the premises.

The cycle starts in the fall. Even though I check over all of the transplants that I bring into the solar greenhouse and take the time to clean off every visible aphid, a strong population quite often develops by December. The pests just thrive in the moist, cool environment.

Aphid populations can explode when there is an untouched crop before them, no natural enemies in sight, and the weather is right. The first females can produce 40 offspring in a week under those conditions. The population can expand by a factor of 10 each week until the plants are overrun, usually in about a month.

One year I planted the solar greenhouses with brassicas, endive, spinach, carrots, and lettuce in mid-October. I had planted closely for high production; however, that allowed the aphids to spread like wildfire. By December 1 the plants were infested.

While waiting for the predator insects that I had sent for to arrive, I made a very effective herbal insect spray with garlic, pennyroyal, wormwood, tansy, rue, and sage. I crushed the leaves in the blender with water and a drop of liquid soap.

The day after I sprayed the infested plants with this mixture the walls were covered with aphids that had fled the vegetables. Most were trapped by the condensation on the cool surfaces and many had drowned. I wiped them off and cleaned any infested plants with soapy water.

When my order of ladybugs arrived, I released them in the solar greenhouses. After a week or so, most seemed to have hidden, but I could always find a few hunting the foliage for aphids. Many more would come out on warm, sunny days. By spring they were active all the time.

In midwinter, I also noticed many of the tiny gold bodies called "aphid mummies." The larvae of the tiny brachonid wasp had consumed the aphids, and after attaching the aphids' empty shells to the plant leaves, had pupated inside them, then hatched.

I suspect that the wasps came into the greenhouse on their own volition. This kind of predator wasp is a major parasite of the green peach aphid, which favors brassicas.

Vegetables can be grown from fall to spring in a greenhouse

You can introduce this wasp into a greenhouse by bringing in a leaf with unhatched mummies from your garden.

By midwinter, aphids were no longer a problem. I could always find a few strays, if I looked, but the greenhouse crops were now top quality. An occasional aphid is no trouble to remove at the kitchen sink, and a few aphids are even essential to maintain the predator insects. I also keep a few flowering

183

plants scattered around the solar greenhouses, in case the adult wasps need nectar or pollen to feed on. Some wasps get sap either by piercing the bodies of the aphids or by drinking from a plant where the aphids have punctured it.) Marigolds, nasturtiums, and impatiens all do well in a winter solar greenhouse.

When I start growing tomatoes, the interior climate is warmer and whitefly can become a problem. I have found that sticky yellow boards (which can be purchased at garden centers) and the predator wasps work well. Place them on the ground near the plants. Before introducing the wasps, remove all of the sticky yellow boards.

The solar greenhouse must average 75°F during the day for the predator wasps to keep whitefly in check. At 64°F the whitefly population can reproduce 10 times faster than the wasps can. At 78°F, the 2 insects breed and lay eggs at an equal rate, but the wasp is able to mature twice as fast as its host. For the wasps to establish themselves, the solar greenhouse temperatures must not fall below 55°F at night. Whitefly has never been a problem for me here at Spring Meadow, after 13 years of greenhouse growing.

You can order the *Encarsia formosa* predator wasps from an organic gardening catalog. Two to four weeks after you introduce them, you should start to see blackened forms of immature whitefly scales on the plants. The scale stage of the whitefly is the only form that the wasps will lay their eggs in, although the mature wasps will also pierce and feed directly on whitefly pupae.

Whenever you can use beneficial insects for pest deterrent, do so. They are nature's answer to control in your greenhouse, on your lawn, and in your garden.

PART 4

Year-Round Ground

*O*rganic gardening encompasses more than growing vegetables, fruits, and herbs. This section explores natural ways to cultivate and invigorate your landscape, as well as enhance its natural beauty. Whether planting foundation shrubs, trees, or flowers; starting or rebuilding a chemical-free lawn; or adding decorative elements—you will find solutions here for gardens of every size.

CHAPTER 14

Homeowner's Basics

Whether you inherited an established landscape poorly conceived and now overgrown, or moved onto a property recently leveled by a bulldozer, you can and should reshape your grounds.

Don't hold back from breaking local landscaping traditions. Define what you want your yard to do and make the changes to fit your needs.

Planning with Purpose

The best use of your property is not necessarily the planting of every square foot with grass. Yet the most common feature of home landscape is lawn grass, planted from the curb and fence lines to the foundations.

It is important to make your lawn the right size for you. Before you spread the fescue, ask yourself just how much time you want to spend on lawn care. Do you enjoy the expansiveness of green or is it taking the place of what could be a more practical planting?

On a slope, remove lawn grass altogether and use plants that don't require mowing. You can also level the area by moving the soil and building a retaining wall. Where a manicured look is not important, put a meadow of wildflowers or plants native to your area.

Foundation Plantings

You may want to incorporate low-maintenance shrub borders, ground covers (in swaths or interplanted with shrubs and trees), or a small grove of trees mixed with ferns, into your landscape design. These foundation shrubs and plantings are usually an assortment of evergreens of varying shapes from tall and thin to round and short, that merge the house with the yard. However, when planted hodge-podge without any cohesive design, you might end up with a yard that looks like a roomful of cluttered furniture.

An attractively planted landscape is as important to the beauty of a house as color, feeling, and artistic technique are to the beauty of a painting. It all depends on the choice of plants and their placement.

To avoid dull foundation plantings, use smaller plants closer to the walls of the house (3 feet away from the wall is a good rule of thumb, depending on the plants' size). They will not overgrow the space. There are hundreds of choices available, from ground covers and perennial flowers and bulbs, to head-high shrubs such as highbush blueberries or dwarf conifers.

FOUNDATION PLANTS TO TRY

Arborvitae	Rhododendron
Azalea	Rose
Dwarf evergreen	White pine
Mugo pine	

By using foundation plantings, you also create a private walk around your home. From the street, the house will still appear to be closely nestled among shrubs, but from the inside, you will be able to enjoy your shrubs at close range, which you couldn't do if they had been jammed against the foundation.

Why are evergreens so popular in foundation plantings? Shrubbery that sheds its leaves (deciduous) often appears stark and unappealing in winter, if planted right next to the house. The bare foundation will show right through the leafless shrubs. On the other hand, evergreens are "ever green" and even in the dark of winter will decorate and improve the appearance of the home.

If you have young children, it is often wise to leave the foundation planting incomplete at the back of your house where they play.

Sometimes a flower bed can be made along the foundation and, though it may get battered a bit, it will be cheerful. A rose trellis or a vine or 2 are nice along the house at the back, too.

The Front Yard

To avoid clutter (and hiding your house), it is best not to fill up your front yard with too many shade or flowering trees, unless it is large and they fill a genuine need, like screening an unwanted view. Most front yards will benefit, though, by having one lone eye-catching flowering, fruit, or unusual-foliage tree. This tree should be your absolute favorite of favorites.

Dwarf, semi-dwarf, or slow-growing types are best for this spot, especially in small yards. Consider such popular choices as white or pink dogwood, Japanese red maple, weeping Japanese cherry, flowering crab apple, or red-berried holly.

This, your special tree, often looks attractive on the street side of the front walk about halfway between the front door and the driveway, far enough out on the lawn to allow for growth without crowding the path. The object is to place the eye-catcher tree where you will see and enjoy it as you're looking out the front door, walking the front path, and coming into the driveway.

The Backyard

Everyone should have a fast-growing shade tree or 2 in the backyard. Do plant it where it is handy for you to sit under and where you can see the youngsters when they are climbing. Buy a big enough tree (at least 10 feet tall) so that you do not have to wait too many years to enjoy it. Most shade trees planted in your children's toddler years will be good for climbing during grammar-school days. Weeping willows are quite fast-growing and climb (reach mature height) well.

The backyard is also a wonderful place to plant your favorite fruit and flowering trees. Here and there along the fence or property line is often attractive.

When planting fruit trees, try to arrange them in an informal grove, perhaps with a small path running through it, underplanted with spring bulbs. If you avoid the messy ones such as peaches and plums, fruit trees can be planted in shrub borders or near walkways.

Driveways

Edges of driveways are often dead spaces in the landscape, especially in small yards. If the spot is sunny, it could be a prime area for growing fruit. You would have frequent chances to observe the tree and to better time your pruning and pest control chores. Besides yielding fruit, a hedge of blueberries, for instance, looks good all year long (see "Landscaping with Blueberries," in chapter 8, page 131). Line a long driveway with planter boxes of flowers or heat-loving vegetables. The reflected heat will make them sweet and the greenery will soften the look of the paving.

Doing your own home landscaping is a lot of fun and very rewarding. With good planning and a new outlook, you can fill your environment with the plants that you love and let nature take care of the rest.

Veiling Vines

If you have any view-spoiling areas in your landscape, conceal them with vines and climbing plants. Brick walls, neighboring eyesores, and other handicaps near your property can be transformed with an original and attractive vine treatment.

There is a vine or climbing plant for every purpose: to decorate walls and fences, beautify trellises, provide shade over arbors, or cover bare ground on steep banks and slopes. Your choice will depend on the vine's habit and what it will be used for.

Vines climb by various methods. Some, called "twining" vines, wind their stems around a vertical form such as a tree or post; others produce threadlike feelers called tendrils that grasp supports like a trellis or mesh fence. A third kind fastens itself to a wall with little disks resembling suction cups or aerial roots that grow fast on a flat surface.

Twining vines encircle their supports until a fast hold is obtained. When a twiner has been trained up a series of wires or wooden posts, the entire vine can be removed (by untwining) and laid on the ground to be pruned anytime without damaging it, even when in full leaf and actively growing.

Consider your architecture when choosing a vine. Large brick-storied buildings, for instance, are improved by such vines as Virginia creeper or English and Boston ivy. Planting such a tall, high-climbing vine on a low ranch-style house would defeat the purpose, however, since neither complements the other.

Spring is an excellent time to plant young vines. A thorough preparation of the soil along a wall or trellis where a vine is to be planted is essential because of the large leaf surface that the soil will eventually nourish.

When planting against a building, a new vine should not be placed closer than 12 inches from the wall. If it comes in a container, remove the container and keep the root ball intact. If it is burlapped, set the plant in the

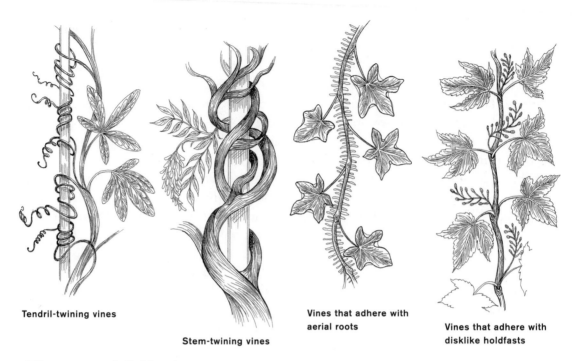

Tendril-twining vines

Stem-twining vines

Vines that adhere with aerial roots

Vines that adhere with disklike holdfasts

Different types of climbing vines

hole, and cut the strings. Leave the rest of the wrapping around the ball. Tamp soil gently but firmly around the roots.

Most vines are cold-hardy perennials, and should be fed every spring. Work compost, fish meal, and bone meal into the soil around them.

Water well to carry nourishment down to the roots. Follow with a mulch to keep the roots cool during hot summer months.

Pruning is important to keep the vines from becoming unkempt and overpowering. They should be pruned, thinned, and shaped at regular intervals. Deadwood and suckers (spindly new root growth) should be removed. Sometimes it is beneficial to cut some stems from the center of vines so that air may circulate freely through the mass.

The best pruning season for vines is before frost in early fall. This allows time for the cuts to heal and harden off.

Propagation is from stem cuttings taken in early summer, or by "layering." Cuttings about 3 inches long should be taken. The lower leaves should be removed, and the stems placed in sand and shaded from direct sunlight. As soon as they produce roots 1-inch long they can be planted individually in 4-inch pots containing a 50–50 mixture of sand and peat moss.

Layering (which is also a common form of propagation for shrubs, grapes, raspberries, and blackberries) can be accomplished by selecting a low shoot that is easily bent to the ground, then making an inch-long diagonal cut through a joint about 1 foot from the tip of the shoot. The cut area is then buried in 3 to 6 inches of soil, its branch end remaining out of the ground to form the top.

Hold down the buried section with a wooden peg and keep moist until a strong root system develops, while the other end is still attached to the main bush. Once the new

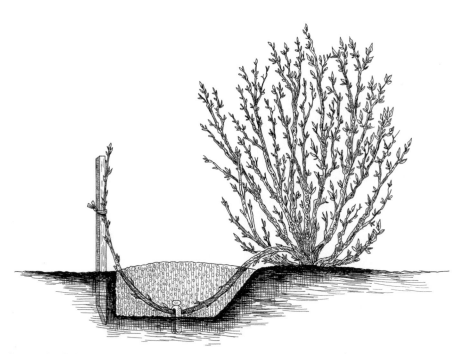

Propagating a shrub by layering

plant is formed, it is then cut from its parent, and can be transplanted wherever you wish.

Many vines are grown for their beautiful flowers, among them the passionflower, clematis, honeysuckle, climbing hydrangea, and wisteria. Perhaps the most spectacular of these is the brilliant red passionflower (*Passiflora*), a tendril vine that also fruits. Few flowers are more remarkable in appearance or more intricately formed. They are so precisely perfect as to almost seem unreal.

This section only covers a fraction of the vines and climbing plants that you can use in your landscape. Check your garden seed and plant catalogs for many other varieties from which to choose.

Mother Nature's Bounty

After selecting the more basic evergreens and flowering trees from the nurseries in your area, you will automatically begin to hunt for different or unusual things to fill the blank spaces about the home and yard.

Did you know that there are many worthwhile gifts free from the generous hand of Mother Nature just waiting to be discovered in your garden or on your grounds?

Fine-tune your sense of discovery as you approach a weedy garden row. Train yourself to weed with your eyes peeled for rewarding plant finds.

A wee scarlet maple seedling may be found among the dandelions. A Japanese yew that with time will reach skyward could now be a minute feathery sprout among the weeds in a row of carrots. Fruit tree seedlings, such as apple, peach, and cherry, are found regularly among the weeds. Blackberry and raspberry seedlings would quickly take over a vegetable patch, if not rooted out.

When you first start prospecting weeds, many plants among them will be unknown. Remove them with a garden trowel, making sure that a good ball of earth keeps the root system undisturbed. Then replant them in a 10-square-foot bed set aside as a miniature nursery for such foundlings. Water each transplant immediately, unless the soil is already wet. (Consult a plant encyclopedia in your local library or on the Web to find out what kind of treasure you have unearthed.)

Transplanting in this manner has proven successful every time I have done it. Simply because volunteer plants appear able to fend for themselves is no reason to deny them plenty of tender loving care. Leave them in their mini-nursery for about a year, after which they can either be planted in permanent sites or bartered. In a year's time they make very presentable plants for gifts, indeed. Many recipients find it difficult to believe that such desirable seedlings appeared by chance. Once informed, they invariably begin prospecting themselves.

What fascinating conversation these pieces make! The rarer the find, the greater the delight.

Attractive Ornamental Shrubs

If flowers are food for the soul, then flowering shrubs are truly a gourmet's banquet. They lend a generous touch of pleasing form, foliage, and blossoms to the most ordinary stretch of yard, enlivening every sort of landscape, foundation planting, border, or corner—even the vegetable patch.

The planting season for most ornamentals begins in October and continues until new growth appears in the spring. Early fall planting is desirable because plants set in autumn grow roots during the fall and winter months, which enable them to become established

before the weather warms. Shrubs grown in containers, however, may be planted throughout the spring and summer, provided plants are watered properly. Container-grown stock is a popular and effective method of introducing more shrubs into gardens during the growing season.

Remove the root ball from the container before planting. If roots are growing sideways out of the ball, make several vertical cuts with a knife to prevent them from continuing their circular growth. I recommend digging planting holes twice the width of the root ball to be planted and $1^{1}/_{2}$ as deep as the depth of the ball. The sides of the holes should be vertical rather than slanting.

Add compost, peat moss, or leaf mold to the excavated topsoil at the rate of 1 part peat moss to 3 parts topsoil. Mix thoroughly. Shovel sufficient backfill mixture into the bottom of the planting hole and firm so that the top of the ball will be parallel with ground level, when it is placed in the hole.

Refill the hole with the remaining mixture and firm. The mixture should cover the top of the ball slightly. Make a raised ring around the outside of the planting hole, mounding the subsoil in a circle about $2^{1}/_{2}$ inches high. Apply 2 inches of mulch from the ring to the main stem of the plant and water thoroughly.

Pruning Shrubs

Most shrubs that flower in the spring (referred to as spring-flowering shrubs) bloom from buds formed on last year's wood. To prune them before they bloom would mean cutting off the greater portion of the flower buds. Therefore, such shrubs should be pruned soon after they bloom.

Shrubs that blossom in the late spring or summer do so on new growth that has been

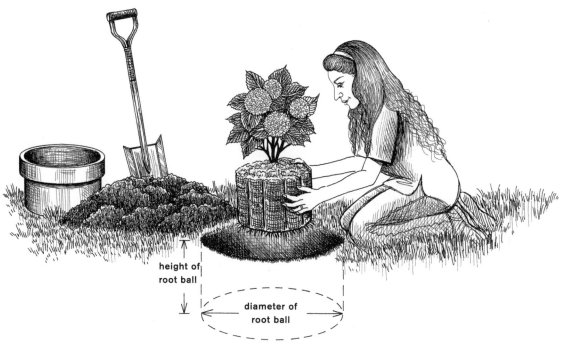

height of
root ball

diameter of
root ball

Planting container-grown shrubs

produced in the same year. This group of shrubs is pruned in early spring or the tail end of winter while still dormant.

Certain evergreens are grown for foliage that they hold during fall or winter. The time for pruning them is before spring growth.

By pruning your shrubs you not only stimulate their growth, you remove dead wood that could eventually encourage disease and infect infestation.

Shrubs to Try

One of my favorite shrubs is the burning bush, a deciduous hedge bush and hardy ornamental that goes through a series of color changes with each season. Yellow flowers in May and June are followed by gleaming red berries in late summer or fall. Its unusual cork bark adds to the winter appeal of this attention-getter. Prune when dormant.

Another beauty is the vitex 'Silver Spire', a white-flowering cultivar. It stays covered with long, pointed white flower spikes from July until severe frost. Prune in early spring or during the last weeks of winter.

Other excellent choices include the calico bush, or mountain laurel, a big pink-blossoming broad-leaved evergreen hardy down to 20°F below zero; and the unusual oleander 'Seeley Pink' patio tree, a first-year-flowering everblooming. It tolerates heat, drought, smoke, and salt spray, so it is perfect for dry, urban, or marine climates.

Don't forget 'Grootendorst', the crimson-blossoming rugosa rose. It covers its 4- to 5-foot bushes with carnation-like blooms all summer, then produces colorful, vitamin C–rich rose hips in fall (see chapter 16, page 237 , for information on rose care).

Hydrangea and pyracantha—two of the most beautiful flowering shrubs—are addressed on the following pages in greater detail.

Hydrangea

Heart-Warming Hydrangeas

Mother Nature went to a lot of trouble when she created hydrangeas. She gave many of them a border of large sterile petals around the smaller fertile ones. These act as a lure to catch the eyes of passing bees so that the smaller, real flowers may be fertilized.

Hydrangeas like their soil on the acid side. When I set out a new plant, I always dig out several spadefuls of soil and replace it with peat moss. This technique serves dual purposes: it adds to the acidity of the soil, and improves the drainage.

Although hydrangeas do better in full sun, their rich colors brighten shady or semi-shady spots. Since those places in the garden are harder to fill than the sunny ones, that is where I usually put mine.

You may decide for yourself whether you want pink or blue hydrangeas. Just prepare your soil accordingly.

If you want pink, add a little lime to the soil. If its pH is already high, leave it as it is. If you prefer blue flowers, leave acid soil as it is. If it is close to neutral (7.0), deepen its acidity with leaf mold made from oak leaves.

One year I caused 8 hydrangeas to vary in color from violet-purple to deep pink, just by varying their soil mix. I used 2 kinds of soil: one very alkaline, the other very acidic.

Down the row I went, making the first hole richly acid, adding about 10 percent of limey soil to the second, more to the third and so on, until I came to the eighth which was filled with a high pH soil. I like to fertilize my hydrangeas at the beginning of the growing season, putting fish meal and kelp meal around each shrub. Strong, healthy growth and deeper-colored blooms are the results.

Give these shrubs room when you set them out. They are long-lasting, generously spreading plants, and don't like to be crowded.

Pot them in rather small containers to start. I use a 4-inch pot. The soil is a mixture of peat, leaf mold, and compost, plus a little sand.

Never forget to water these. They grow fast and drink a lot. You will find that their flower heads are heavy. Give them support, for they shouldn't be left to the mercy of heavy rains and slashing winds.

When they look crowded, I repot in 8-inch pots. As they grow, pinch. Keep nipping a little here and there, so that they learn to be compact to fit into a pot.

Around November you will find that your little plants are ready for a rest. Put them in a cool place, preferably just above freezing. One great advantage to growing hydrangeas is that there is no trick at all to lugging them into an unheated garage or similar place to store them over the winter. Water only when they are really dry and leave them alone.

In early spring they'll start growing by themselves, indicating that it's time to bring them into a light, warm environment and feed them a little organic fertilizer rich in phosphorous (bone meal plus 4–6–4 organic fertilizer). These are the plants that react well to organic liquid fertilizer (seaweed and fish).

Admittedly, hydrangeas are a bit fussy. They require soil manipulation, lots of water, room to spread, and light. Give them these things and you will have heart-warming bloom in abundance. Their beauty will become a permanent part of your border and they will glamorize the patio.

These are not plants for lazy gardeners, but do give tremendous value in beauty and bloom for the trouble that you take with them. From full hedge plants with blossoms as big as dinner plates to thumbnail miniatures, hydrangeas are a charm and a challenge.

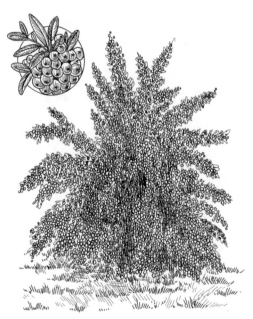

Pyracantha

Pretty Pyracantha

Pyracantha is noted for its showy masses of berries, yet often refuses to berry at all, when planted in the shade.

Ideal for foundation plantings, it is also a fast-growing, good-looking hedge that will assuredly render you privacy. Pyracantha can be used as a vine and is excellent for espalier, since its long branches can be easily trained and make tremendous growth in 1 or 2 seasons.

If you are a "hands-off" gardener, you can allow this shrub to grow naturally. It results in a rounded, wide-spreading, many-stemmed plant up to 12 feet tall.

Adaptable and accommodating, pyracantha can be planted in the spring and the fall. Be careful when making your selection. It can be extremely contrary about transplanting, so, if possible, choose container-grown plants.

If you have a neighbor who owns a pyracantha, do not hesitate to try your luck with rooting your own cuttings. July is the best time to take cuttings. For rooting, my favorite method has come to be equal parts of soil and peat moss topped with vermiculite.

Make your cuttings 3 to 5 inches long, directly below a node that is a leaf joint. Remove the lower leaves and then press the slips into your rooting mixture.

You can root several cuttings at a time in a deep box or cold frame, if you have one. I prefer to pot each cutting individually. Since pyracantha just does not like transplanting, why risk injuring roots when digging up new plants?

Water thoroughly after potting and keep the cuttings in as humid an atmosphere as possible. A large jar placed over each one will help preserve moisture. Keep pots in a place where they will not get direct sun, yet will receive good light. When I put the plants into my cold frame, I keep the sash closed most of the time, except for about 20 minutes each morning. This morning airing gives me a chance to remove any yellowed or fallen leaves.

Cuttings will root in about 8 to 10 weeks, but will not be ready to be planted out in the open until the following spring. When you feel that yours are ready to go it alone, thoroughly soak the pots in a mix of water, seaweed, and liquid fish the night before and again just before you take the cutting out. Then, soil, roots, and plants will slip out easily like a cake out of a tin.

Whether you are the kind of gardener who prunes strictly according to the calendar or when the shears are handy, you shouldn't find this plant difficult to manage. Pyracantha can be pruned anytime. The amount depends upon the use to which your shrub has been put. For a hedge, shear it closely so that later growth will be twiggy with dense foliage.

I mulch my pyrancantha year-round. For summer, a 2-inch mulch of cocoa shells is sufficient. Cocoa shells are an attractive, light brown color and will keep moisture from evaporating from the soil, while not preventing water from penetrating into the ground.

In winter you will need a deeper mulch of straw or leaves to keep plants adequately protected. Unless rainfall has been plentiful during the autumn, make sure that the planting is given at least 4 heavy soakings before frost arrives. This is important because when the ground is frozen hard, shrubs cannot draw moisture from it.

What can you plant that will get along with pyracantha? Lilac, another spring-flowering shrub, will be quite compatible, since it, too, is fond of a sunny location and an alkaline soil. Iris, carnations, or phlox are summer-blooming perennials that will make attractive foreground plantings. Among annuals, alyssum and nasturtiums make good choices.

Whether you choose pyracantha for its spring flowers, winter foliage, or autumn berries, you will enjoy it. Won't it be fun to see something so pretty growing faster than the weeds?

This is a glance at only a few of the long list of attractive plants that make yards and landscapes look the way they should. Whatever the size or mood of your garden, it is bound to be enhanced by perennial flowering shrubs.

Why not start adding some ornamentals this season that you will enjoy for years to come?

Dual-Purpose Produce

Growing space need not keep you from enjoying both attractive plants and good eating. If you have space for flower beds and borders, you can also get some eye-pleasing edibles into your landscape. Have you ever looked at a growing eggplant? The sturdy plant reaches 24 to 36 inches in height and is covered with light-green, lobed leaves. As the whorls of new leaves appear, the centers are touched with purple. The foliage alone would justify space in a flower garden, and when the delicate, lilac-colored blossoms appear, the plant is even more attractive.

For beauty of form, color, shape, and texture, the fruit of the eggplant is difficult to surpass. As a background for pink or scarlet petunias, 2 or 3 of these plants would lend an almost exotic touch, and would also supply your family all summer with delicious vegetables.

There is a dwarf edible pepper that might be the showpiece of any flower garden. It is globular in shape, about 18 inches high, and covered with tiny white blossoms for several weeks. Later in the summer it is full of cherry-sized peppers. Just imagine petunias or gold marigolds against the glossy green leaves of the plant.

Peas may be planted in areas that will later be filled in with annual flowers. Bibb lettuce rosettes bordering a rose bed may supply weeks of tossed salads.

One of the most delightful gardens that I've ever seen was outside the kitchen door of an old Amish house. The featured plants were red cabbages marching along the entire border. Before the summer was over, the cabbages were eaten and flowers soon spilled over into the empty spaces.

Savoy cabbages could be used in a corner of a flower bed. Low-growing ageratum or sweet alyssum planted in front and feathery cosmos nodding in the background would lend color to the texture of the cabbage leaves.

If you can interest your next-door neighbor in the idea of beautiful, edible borders, asparagus might be a joint project for you. A row of asparagus planted on a property line could be shared by 2 families. This would require planning and cooperation because the asparagus should not be harvested for 2 or 3 years.

However, the lacy asparagus fern, which must be allowed to grow all summer, would furnish a lovely background for flowers in the adjoining gardens. A double row of them would be dense enough for a temporary hedge, if desired.

A dwarf peach or cherry tree, when in bloom, is almost, if not quite, as beautiful as a flowering crab apple and also provides fruit to eat. Red or black raspberries have lovely blossoms and, later, berries. They will make a sturdy hedge.

Probably the most bountiful plant for edging and eating is the strawberry. Everbearing strawberry plants, kept free of runners so that they produce berries freely until frost, may be used to edge flower borders or vegetable plots.

A dozen or more strawberry plants may be tucked into a rock garden. They grow less than a foot high and blend nicely with other plants. Just be certain to place them where you can reach the berries when they are ripe.

Now that the space has been revealed, there is no reason for your not growing some produce in your patch. It does two jobs for the price of one.

Planting Don'ts

All gardeners make mistakes while establishing a landscape. Reading about some of the most frequent ones will give you the chance to learn from someone else's experience and to avoid repeating them yourself. The biggest blunders include:

Over-Fertilization of New Trees

Some people seem to think that a strong dose of organic fertilizer will make a newly planted tree grow like an old one. In using too much fertilizer, all they succeed in doing is injuring the roots and making the tree look worse than before. After planting in well-prepared soil, it is best to allow the tree time to establish itself and start normal growth before applying any kind of fertilizer—approximately 3 to 10 years, depending on the species.

Planting Broad-Leaved Evergreens in Windy Areas

If you have ever climbed mountain trails or studied pictures of windswept mountains, you will remember the sight of misshapen and tortured pines, firs, and spruces on the ridge. Often all of the needle growth forms on the side of the tree away from the wind. Still, they live, for Mother Nature has designed the needles so that the wind slips through them easily.

Therefore, in very windy yards or in almost any yard where the wind whistles around a corner or through a breezeway, a needled evergreen will often survive; yet in the same location, cold-hardy broad-leaved evergreens such as white pine, Scotch pine, and ponderosa may get battered badly each winter.

Nature just did not intend most broad-leaved evergreens to be planted in windy places. The wind treats their broad leaves much like a kite: Particularly when frozen, some leaves may be twirled off by a strong gust; other leaves may break or bend so that the veins are severed and all or part of the leaf turns brown.

These trees should be planted in sheltered locations in the yard. If you have a broad-leaved evergreen that is not doing well in a windy place, why not move it to a favorable spot? The eastern side of the house is often very good. The improvement in a year or 2 may amaze you.

Planting Directly into Clay Without Any Soil Preparation

No organic grower in his right mind would ever set out nursery-stock in the kind of clay subsoil that is often found in a new housing development, after the bulldozers have been at play. Yet, new homeowners are often stuck with this type of soil and must make the best of it.

Fully half of the dead or sick landscape plantings I have seen are caused by innocent homeowners planting new shrubbery right into heavy, poor soil. It is against nature to plant fine-rooted things in anything other

than a well-prepared, humusy, loose soil, and a waste of both time and money.

Planting Shade-Loving Shrubs in Too Much Sun

Certainly, many azaleas, rhododendrons, andromedas, hollies, and dogwoods are native to woodlands or wood-edges. In their native state they are protected from strong sun by the shade above and from strong winds by the density of the forest. If you plant them in your home yards in very windy or hot, sunny spots, they will not survive.

It is important to try to duplicate the growing conditions that prevailed in natural environments for all plants, if possible.

Mistreating Plants from Warmer, Drier Climates

Many northern homeowners fall in love with southern shrubs while on vacation and bring a few back to their homes up North. These usually "winter burn" when planted in cold, windy spots in the yard.

Yet plants such as crape myrtle and Chinese holly will grow quite far north if planted on the sunny, quiet side of the house. This is because a warm wind-sheltered area really has a climate all its own, a little touch of the South in a northern climate.

Planting Too Deep

Surface feeder roots of trees and shrubs need aeration. It is natural and good when failed leaves and twigs form a mulch over the roots in the forests. Natural mulches are loose and permit air to reach the top feeder rootlets.

It is unnatural when soil is piled over the roots, shutting out air and often causing root rot and the slow death of the tree. This smothering effect is what makes a big tree die after a year or 2, when its roots are buried by leveling operations at a new housing development.

When you first buy an evergreen, the older leaves are healthy because they were grown in good soil at the proper depth. If the new leaves that grow at your home are very small and sickly, it can be the shock of transplanting. More often, however, it is because of planting too deep.

Such sick trees should be dug up and replanted with lots of compost around the roots so that they will have something that they like to push out into. Mulch well on the top with 2 inches of leaf mold or peat moss.

Saving Overgrown Shrubbery

Why do we see so much overgrown shrubbery? The reason is quite simple.

When the homeowner is faced with a limited budget, he has two real choices in landscaping. He may start with smaller-sized plants or save the shrubbery that is there, although unattractive and/or overgrown.

The idea of saving overgrown shrubbery or moving such shrubs elsewhere in the yard just to save them is not recommended. There is no harm in weeding out undesirable plantings. It is no worse than cleaning out underbrush in the woods or mowing an abandoned lot to improve its appearance.

Plant something new, interesting, and worthwhile. Therein lies true conservation.

CHAPTER 15

Garden Art

Make your garden or yard a place you enjoy spending time in. Whether you have always wanted a Japanese-style rock garden or are trying to make the most out of a small space, there are numerous ways to beautify your natural surroundings.

Elegant Bamboo

The appearance of bamboo makes it better suited for certain landscaping uses than any other plant or shrub. Stalks of bamboo waving in the summer breeze manage to look cool even on the hottest days. Its light, airy nature makes it particularly effective when used in combination with water features such as pools, fountains, or waterfalls—even lily ponds.

A grove of bamboo is especially useful as a tall focal point, as it draws the eye to something of interest growing immediately in front of it. A shaded nook can be created by planting bamboo on 3 sides of a bench or grassy area. There are even several dwarf varieties available for border plantings to surround your flower beds or ponds.

You can also plant the smaller tropical varieties in large pots or tubs on your deck or patio. Bring the plants inside for the winter and water and feed them as you would other houseplants. Bamboo tolerates household conditions quite well. When it warms up in spring, take the pots outdoors to begin another season.

Most bamboo can be planted so as to create a light screen that doesn't completely hide whatever is behind it. Fish pole bamboo does have foliage dense enough to form a solid barrier, if that's what you need. A bamboo screen provides a lovely backdrop for a group of hardy lilies or any other main planting. If the screen gets too dense, you can thin it periodically.

The only drawback in using bamboo in landscaping is its mobility. This may seem like a strange word to describe a plant that is rooted solidly in the ground, but bamboo really isn't as stationary as it looks.

A natural screen of bamboo

Once a new clump is well established in your garden, a late-summer spirit of wanderlust invigorates the roots, prompting them to send underground runners 10 or 15 feet in all directions. In the spring, new clumps pop up where you least expect them. These new canes shoot up with incredible swiftness, attaining their full height in about a month. Some well-established bamboos can grow 3 feet in 24 hours—even faster than corn. (Japanese bamboo is considered an invasive plant in the East and Midwest, and should not be encouraged.)

This meandering pattern of growth may not be as bad as it sounds. If you don't want bamboo where some of the new canes come up in the spring, you can mow the shoots off at the ground with your lawn mower.

The root that you will receive from the nursery in late March or April looks like a fishing pole. It has small roots emerging every few inches from both sides of the main root

and a few hard buds curving up from the root. Plant the root where it will receive sun at least half of each day. Dig a trench 4 or 5 inches deep and wide enough to accommodate the side roots.

Lay the root with the buds pointing upward in the trench and cover it with 3 to 4 inches of loose soil. Water thoroughly and continue to water every 3 or 4 days, keeping the soil moist until the bamboo has sprouted.

Be patient. It may take 4 to 6 weeks for the new root to send up the first thin green shoots. When the new canes emerge, they resemble skinny, young asparagus stalks. Be very careful of these tender new shoots. Delicate, spear-shaped leaves varying from light to dark green will soon appear on the canes.

Don't expect newly planted bamboo to reach its full size for several years. Height is dependent on the age of the plant as well as the moisture that it receives during its brief annual growing season. Water generously in April and May, when the plants are growing actively. For the rest of the summer, bamboo will do quite well with the same amount of water that you give your other plants. Bamboo will add a new and exciting touch of the Far East to your garden with the added bonus of low maintenance. Its airy grace visually enhances everything in its proximity. Only your imagination can limit its use in your landscape.

Beautiful Bonsai

It is the Japanese who have mastered the bonsai art form, achieving an aesthetic microcosm with their bonsai landscapes. To achieve the bonsai ideal, you must sculpture your plant with an awareness of the integrated relationship of foliage, branches, and trunk in the container. The end result will be a living tree or shrub in a simple setting of beauty about which there is an incontrovertible rightness.

Bonsai

Coniferous evergreens are the most popular trees for bonsai. The most commonly chosen height is from 12 to 16 inches. Regardless of size, by careful training you can control the growth of the specimen by keeping it small, but healthy.

The most significant single factor by which to keep your plant to bonsai proportions is pruning. The fewer the leaves or foliage, the less the growth. Although all plants must grow to live, pruning limits the amount of new annual growth without killing them. In fact, pruning is necessary to keep the plant healthy in a small container.

Branch pruning is done to remove unwanted branches. If you are uncertain about the appearance created by the absence of a particular branch, try masking it off with a piece of cloth to get an idea of how the tree would look without it.

Leaf pruning should be carried out on a planned schedule made early in the plant's development. By doing so, trees often develop finer, more dense twigs and smaller leaves.

Root pruning is also essential. It is facilitated by the use of the traditional shallow tray as a container. At this stage, the proper pruning procedure necessitates repotting or the replanting of the specimen in its pot with new soil.

To do so remove the tree or shrub from its pot. You will see a tangled network of root hairs that have fibrous endings that you should comb out carefully with a chopstick. The root mass fills about $2/3$ of your container's width and length and about $1/3$ of its length. Brush off the soil and cut back the root mass, including any dead roots, with sharp shears.

Before replacing it in the tray, put a thin anchor wire through two spaced holes in the bottom of the tray to tie the tree to for support, after it is replanted. Put pea gravel at the bottom of the tray and add a thin layer of a soil mixture, usually of peat moss, sand, leaf mold, and natural soil. The soil mixture is critical. It is a growing medium and storage reservoir, allowing the movement of oxygen and water.

After replanting it, place the plant in a shady spot for a few weeks. Gradually move it into the sunlight (bonsai need at least 4 hours of sun a day). At this time or during the new growing period, you should fertilize it regularly with seaweed and fish. Also, water it properly because confined roots need water that is loosely held by soil particles.

In addition to pruning, tying and wiring can help you attain the desired look of naturalness. Copper wire can be used without staining or poisoning the tree. After anchoring the end of the wire in the soil at the base of the trunk, carefully wind the pliable wire upward around the trunk and then to a branch, leaving some space between the wire and the wood. Do not crush the needles or leaves. Place the winding wire loosely around the branch itself, not the small twigs and branches growing from it. Once all of the separate wires are in place (there could be a dozen or more), gently bend the branches to the design configuration that you wish. You may wire a branch at any point, but only wire the parts of the trunk or branches that you want to change to a different shape.

Often this shaping will lead to additional leaf and branch pruning. The wiring, bent and woven loosely to hold the configuration of your design, will reveal some unwanted branches in their relationship to the whole.

Depending on your chosen tree's rate of growth, you can leave the wiring in place as long as needed to reshape the tree. Sometimes it is 8 to 12 months before the tree will hold its new form, when the wire is removed.

Although you can add a rock, a piece of driftwood, or moss, remember that your miniature landscape is not intended for garish decoration. Strive for a kind of oriental simplicity.

Learn this ancient art form. Add a Japanese garden to your landscape.

Rock Gardens

A search for the true meaning and purpose of rock gardening will take us not to a library, but to a place high on the upper slopes of a great mountain. There, above the line of trees, the soil is thin and mixed with chips of rock and bits of moss. Rocks are everywhere.

The rigors of the climate have weeded out shrubs and vines, leaving only the rock plants anchored in the veins of the soil between the boulders. Some plants, like lichens, grow on the bare faces of the rocks themselves.

Long ago, skilled gardeners realized that, if the beauty of the high mountain slopes was to be captured in a sea-level garden, it was not enough to just bring in the plants. The sheltering rocks must be brought in, too.

They must be set into the ground in such a way as to re-create the compact fissures of soil, rock chips, and humus that the alpine plants found so inviting in their original homes. A few rocks scattered on the surface of a bare bank will not do.

A rock garden is truly a thing of beauty. When it does not appear pleasing, it may be because it lacks a natural look. Perhaps the gardener used overly angular blocks or quarry stones that were too close together or too far apart.

Setting stones is another art in which the Japanese excel—some gardening masters spend years refining their skills. The basic tenet of the practice is asymmetry. Begin by choosing an area that has well-drained soil, and is not too hot, dry, or overly windy. The edge of a pond or meadow is perfect, as the rock garden will provide a focal point in the landscape.

Although a slope is the most obvious place to build a rock garden, many successful ones have been made on flat ground that was scooped out to make a flowing contour. A slope signifies drainage and, if facing north, will shade the garden.

Shade and a short growing season are important to many rock garden plants. In their mountain homes, alpine plants get only a month or so of warm weather and are dormant for the rest of the year. Although you can't give them the cold, damp weather that they are used to, shade helps stimulate dormant conditions. Many successful rock gardeners cover plants with a mulch during all but the summer months to stretch their dormant period.

Make sure your site has easy access for all of the heavy moving that will take place.

Once you have chosen your site, it's time for the artistic part. Place a small rock next to a large one, so that they touch but are not lined up horizontally. Choose a medium-sized rock and place it next to the first group. Using your creative intuition, continue until you feel the outcropping looks complete. Keep in mind that too many large rocks will overwhelm the landscape, while a group of small stones will look inconsequential.

However, it is the part of the rock below the soil that is most important. You should also be more concerned about the negative spaces between the rocks, than about the rocks themselves.

ROCKERY RULES

Here are some general rules to follow in building up your garden:

1. Use quarried stone. Soft, porous rocks such as limestone are preferable to hard stones like granite. Overly-rounded rocks are difficult to fit together tightly and eventually they won't work.
2. Don't use a collection of different types of stone. You are making a rock garden, not a collection of geological specimens. Your garden will look more natural if the stones you choose are native to your area.
3. Set every rock firmly in the ground. At least $1/3$ of the stone should be buried beneath the surface so that it looks natural, and is secure.
4. Slope the top surface back into the bank behind, so that the water will flow back to the roots of your plants.
5. Don't allow overhanging rocks to keep rain off plants and roots below.

If you wish to save yourself many hours of work, make a furrow or edging along the rockery top all the way to one side to carry water laterally to a waterfall or other selected points. In a thundershower, runoff is even more important. Without edging, topsoil is constantly carried away, rocks fall out, and erosion undermines your efforts.

Another way of controlling runoff is the different placement of rocks. Larger, flatter stones placed in semi-circles will tend to hold rainwater and topsoil.

Always site plants between or close to the rocks. Place small plants at the top of the outcropping and larger ones below. Arrange them so they look natural. Where the rocks are far apart, plant dwarf and ground shrubs, which need space to grow and will offset winter bleakness.

I try to combine rocks and small trees to best advantage, placing them in close clusters at the back of the rockery, where the bank is steepest. Of course, each time any sort of plant is set, a mixture of topsoil, humus, lime, wood ashes, and bone meal goes in first.

Log cribs, hollowed-out logs used into planters, make excellent additions to a rock garden. Space the log cribs asymmetrically to integrate them naturally into the rock garden. As soon as a crib is set in place, backfill with soil. Add more soil to other parts as you plant young trees. Hemlock, fir, cedar, and Scotch pine grow wild on the land. Try to make liberal use of these.

It pays to observe nature's ways and relationships to establish plants where they like to grow. Note that fern and moss take hold on the lower side of rocks. Foxglove, a summer-flowering perennial, and bracken, a type of tall fern, seed themselves and fill in empty spaces.

Woodland and pasture plants multiply and bloom freely in an alpine garden. Delphiniums, tulips, anemones, pinks, and geraniums are included here. Ferns, aconites, and some lilies thrive in shade. Buttercups, trilliums, lady's slipper (*Cypripedium*), bog orchids, bog-stars (*Parnassia*), and primroses are suitable for moist and marshy places.

Bell flowers should be in every rock garden, as should sunroses (*Helianthemum*), which provide a mass effect of color in June and July. Rock cress is an old favorite with its woolly gray leaves and sprays of white flowers. Alyssum always attracts attention and admiration.

If you become baffled by obstinate plants, wrong exposure may be the trouble. Full sun can destroy dwarf evergreen shrubs. Dwarf shrubs and trees spread better in an open area,

A rockery filled with flowers and ferns

but a lone one near a large rock will add naturalness to the scene.

When planting the shrub, dig a hole deep enough for the roots to spread. A small wooden terrace erected around its base will enable the shrub to hold rainwater and grow stronger.

No matter how you set up your rockery, you are in for unlimited pleasure. Unlike any other garden, a rockery shows off its beauty like a stage setting. Each group of rocks or clump of flowers or evergreens provides a small scene all its own—each playing a part in an ever-changing, many-act play.

Combining the rough texture of stone with the delicate gems of alpine flowers has become one of the most interesting art forms devised by the gardener in his effort to capture and hold the beauty of nature.

Decorative Mulch

Picture a garden section devoted to shrubs, roses, and other flowering perennials. In bare, uncovered soil, the visual appeal is limited to the plants alone. Nestle a layer of auburn cocoa shell mulch around them and a whole new scene comes into view—a vista of rich color, of eye-pleasing textures and tones. A dimension of depth completes the comfortable, carpeted look. In bloom and out, your plants are more striking, and look more complete.

Mulch helps keep the garden looking well-landscaped, too. It checks weeds, stretches water supplies, and improves the view where winter chills most plant life. Along paths and fence-lines, around patios or play areas, it averts a worn-down appearance.

Mulch also works as an undercover agent. It insulates against temperature extremes and boosts soil fertility and tilth as it gradually decomposes.

Which materials are best used for landscaping with mulch? These can be as varied as the plants in your garden. It's using them with an eye to beauty besides other virtues that makes them landscaping assets.

Hay in assorted shades of brown or tan, honey-colored straw, pine needles in a kaleidoscope of changing greens, shredded leaves—all of these do the job. So do humus-rich standbys like compost and leaf mold, which lend a deep-toned healthy appearance when used as mulch.

Wood shavings and sawdust are another pair of widely available materials with landscape qualities, particularly when applied around the acid-loving berries and shrubs like azaleas or rhododendrons that they benefit. Stones and pea-sized gravel also create unusual and doubly effective mulches. Seaweeds and kelp, wherever handy to coastline gardeners, serve admirably in the dual role of soil enrichers and mulch. Other shoreline favorites include seashells, eye-catching in many garden settings and slow to break down.

Given a variety of mulches to work with, a gardener eager to do some outdoor decorating has the tools for being as creative as the fussiest interior decorator. At every turn of the yard and garden, mulch can help contrast the shapes and hues of plants or blossoms, highlighting backgrounds and vertical lines or simply blending neatly with them where desirable.

From a distance, the effect of certain mulches can be one that dramatically enhances any size or form of growing area. Up close, they easily perk up the mood of plant sites, transforming drab or detractive ground into handsome settings for every sort of growth.

How much mulch should be used? During the growing season, the thickness should be enough to prevent the growth of weeds. A thin layer of finely-shredded plant matter is more effective than unshredded loose material. A 4- to 6-inch layer of sawdust, for example, will hold down weeds as well as 8 to 10 inches of straw. So will 3 inches of cocoa shell mulch, or 4 inches of pine needles.

Leaves should be shredded and mixed with something light, like straw, to prevent soggy packing. In a mixture, unshredded leaves can be spread 8 to 12 inches deep for the winter. To offset the nitrogen shortage in sawdust and other low-nitrogen materials, add some compost, fish meal, or cottonseed meal for acid-loving plants and shrubs.

Peat moss, although not containing any nutrients, improves soil aeration and drainage, ultimately aiding plants to absorb nutrients from other materials. It can be spread 3 inches in vegetable gardens and flower beds and used as a 1-inch top dressing twice a year on established lawns. As you can see, mulches do more than sit atop the soil like a silent sentinel. Aside from creating a visual impact, they act and contribute dimension to the surroundings.

Le Petit Jardin

The little garden can be beautiful. Put to work, every square inch is fruitfully productive.

Each plant is just a few feet from all the others, so you notice things that you would overlook in a large garden. When something goes wrong, you realize it from the start, look for the cause, and then take action.

Corn is not impossible in a small garden. It is true that the leaves should touch each other for pollination, but they will when planted in triangles of 3. Quite a few of these triangles can be wedged in here and there for a vegetable that must be fresh to be worth eating.

The best of all vegetables, asparagus, is a space-taker. Yet it makes such a lovely background for the summer flowers and vegetables that I slip one in whenever there are a few inches to spare. Give it room in your garden if only to have a crop when other vegetables are scarce. You can compensate for lack of space by putting your garden to work both early and late in the growing season. Do you like early lettuce? Plant a row earlier than you would think lettuce could grow at all.

Cover it with greenhouse plastic over strong wire hoops, both ends of which are driven into the ground to form a series of arcs, about 12 inches apart. Hold the plastic down with rocks at each side or, if you have them, a couple of 2 × 4s.

I have planted lettuce in February under these mini-greenhouse tunnels and it has done well. Start in mid-September with another row. Put on the protection when the real frost threatens. You will find yourself enjoying salad greens for more months than you dreamed possible.

An advantage to this early and late gardening is that you can choose, from the entire garden, the space that your row is to occupy. I recommend a southern exposure against a protecting wall.

Another good space-saving method is to alternate garden rows and walking rows each year: This year's growing rows become next year's walking rows. The walking space is covered with mulch which is turned under in the fall, and again covered with hay, straw, grass clippings, and ground-up leaves. This is turned under early the next spring and you have rich, spongy soil all ready to receive the seeds.

When your plants are from 2 to 4 inches tall, it is time to start the process of tucking mulch around them.

Having space limitations prompted me to start growing tomatoes in large cans and buckets. A 5-gallon container with drainage holes filled with rich soil holds a well-trained and pruned tomato plant through its whole bearing period.

It has always seemed regrettable to me that we should grow tomatoes into fruitful plants only to have them destroyed when they reach their peak performance. Find a reasonably bright, cool place inside for these containers and you can stretch your tomato season right through the winter. Start these winter-into-spring tomatoes later than the others, but make sure they are bearing when you take them into the house.

Treat the Brussels sprouts that you start in a 5-gallon container the same way: Plant 3 seedlings together. They should be in a good nipping frost before they are brought in. Brussels sprouts need much less sun than tomatoes and can be grown in a place that is all but frigid. Three healthy plants will give the average family all the Brussels sprouts they want throughout the winter.

A small-space gardener necessarily becomes resourceful. I put 2 orange crates full of everbearing strawberries on the toolhouse roof. I used large plants, half a dozen to each box. I anchored the boxes firmly first, then carried up rich soil to fill them.

This was true inspiration. Since the berries were on the roof they had daylong sunshine and were deprived of their runners. I fed them liquid seaweed and fish mix at 10-day

Grow tomatoes through the winter, indoors

intervals. Strawberries are gluttons, but given organic fertilizer and water in sufficient quantities, along with unlimited light, they were very obliging about production.

Once, right in the center of one of my little gardens, I put a pool. I sunk an old wooden tub into the ground and felt that I was being very extravagant with space, to bring a little patch of blue sky into the scene. However, I made that tub pay for itself in utility as well as beauty by growing a summer's supply of watercress in it.

Did you know that it's a simple matter to root watercress from the bunch you buy at the market? Start the cress in the winter by clipping off an inch or 2 of each stem; stick the branches into a bowl that has enough sand in the bottom to hold them upright. Fill the bowl with water and put it on your windowsill.

Mist the cress with clear water every day. Once it turns warm outside, you can move the cress plants into an outdoor "tub pool" like I did, or even set them in a pond or brook. In the late fall, repeat the process again: take some cress branches from your tub pool or pond and keep them growing in your windowsill. You will have a continuous supply in the house, after frost and ice have put an end to the outdoor stock.

In your little garden, a great problem may be shade. Raise a light-loving plant a foot or 2 above the others and, in some cases, you'll double the light that it receives. You can do that by planting it in a bottomless box set on top of the soil.

Here, a special potted plant truly comes into its glory. When you lift a plant up above the others, you not only give it air and sun, but you highlight it. Without sacrificing an inch of precious room, you create a distinctive tableau. Fuschias are beautiful anywhere, but put them in a hanging basket against a white wall and the effect is breathtaking.

Flowers can make a little space into an intimate, magical garden room. Tuberous begonias are easy. Pansies in rich soil in a semi-shaded corner are beautiful. Sweet peas sharing the fence with garden peas and cucumbers are gratifying.

Don't feel that you must deprive yourself of fruit trees, even in a small area. Buy a self-pollinating tree, so that you don't need 2. Dwarf trees take very little room and bear beautifully.

You may want to investigate the possibility of espaliering a tree. Both espaliered and dwarf trees can be covered on frosty nights, as a full-sized tree cannot; often a crop can be saved by protecting blooms or fruit from freezing.

If ever there were a garden that could, it is the little garden. It could be the best garden that you ever grow, bringing you produce,

---

COMPACT COMPOSTING

With little space, we make a little garden. But, when space is your problem, where do you put your compost pile?

Take your worst problem and make it into your chief asset. It seems that garbage accumulates quickly. Buy a large wooden box, knock out its bottom and make a close-fitting, easily removable top for it. Dig a large hole not too far from your garden and fit the box over it. Then, order a thousand earthworms as your disposal unit.

They will fall on all that garbage, literally and figuratively. Add a layer of soil from time to time and a little sprinkling of water as you put in the food scraps. Cover it all with the box top.

When the worm composting box is filled, start another bottomless box over another hole. By the time that is full, the first box should be emptied, for earthworms work with speed and enthusiasm. Even in winter, business goes on as usual in the mini-compost factories. This compost is a rich plant food that will gradually rebuild your garden into a little paradise.

There are other sources of wealth, too. Pine needles are an ideal mulch for alkaline soil, at once holding in the scarce water and decaying, helping to bring down the high pH to an acceptable level. At first, I hesitated to put raw sawdust on my soil, fearing that when it started to decay, it would use up the nitrogen in the soil. Then it occurred to me to mix it with the garbage earthworm-compost and nothing could have been more satisfactory in appearance as well as performance.

pleasure, satisfaction, and a wonderful education.

CHAPTER 16

Flower Power

As discussed in the chapter on seeds, annuals flower and set seed within a single growing season, while biennials flower and make seed the second growing season. Perennials—which are usually grouped together with biennals for growing purposes—grow for three or more seasons.

Most perennial flowers do not reach "flowering size" as quickly as annuals, and usually are grown from root divisions bought in a nursery or obtained from fellow gardeners (or one's own garden) rather than from seed. There are several perennials that you can attempt to grow from seed, such as butterfly bush, purple coneflowers, and Shasta daisies; these achieve flowering size in 1 season and generally breed true. Annuals are typically started from seed; although you can buy seedlings from a nursery, it is much more expensive.

Although the majority of flowers grown from bulbs are perennials as well, they are grouped into their own category. Bulbs are essentially underground leaf buds—masses of swollen plant tissue that store energy and food for the plant. Corms, rhizomes, tubers, and tuberous roots share many similarities with bulbs, and in fact the word "bulb" is often used interchangeably to describe all subterranean storage organs.

Easy Annuals

Here are a few of the most popular and hardiest annuals to choose from. Additional annuals are profiled in the "Forever Everlastings" and "Starting Flowers from Seed" sections farther in this chapter.

Hollyhock

When starting hollyhocks, the best time to sow seeds is in late July to early August. Plant them $1/2$ inch deep in flats and 1 inch apart. As the seedlings emerge, thin out to 2 inches apart. Transfer them to composition pots (large ceramic planters), if they grow too large before fall, or let them remain in flats in the

Hollyhock

In the fall, cut down the old stalks. This is one way to discourage rust-scale that sometimes forms on established plants.

Remove them to the compost pile, unless you want to let a few stalks remain for reseeding. For livelier, more colorful plants, it is best to plant new seeds every few years.

Portulaca

The single, semi-double, and double varieties of portulaca are all members of the widespread purslane family. While small, they have great charm, many uses, and an uncanny ability to transform a poor, sandy spot into a thick carpet of green foliage and colorful flowers.

The rugged little plants grow well in ordinary garden soil, but prefer a mixture of garden loam, leaf mold, and coarse sand. Although they do reasonably well in partial shade, the flowers will bloom only in a location that is in full sun and is well-drained.

Even though you may not be able to grow any other flower in a particular spot on your

cold frame until spring, covered with a light mulch of straw.

Soil should be well-supplied with humus, so apply compost to build up your organic matter. Since hollyhocks prefer a near neutral soil (pH 6.8 to 7.5), you should take a test and add limestone, if needed.

Cultivate beds to a depth of 6 to 8 inches. If your plants are fairly large by fall, you can set them out into their permanent locations. They like full sun.

Transplants should be spaced 12 to 15 inches apart and kept well-watered to help them get established. Once transplanted, either in spring or fall, do not disturb, as the taproot that forms on the full-grown plant makes it difficult to move it to another area.

With the right culture you will be able to enjoy blooms from your plants all summer. To encourage a succession of flowers, pick off old blossoms as well as any seedpods that may form.

grounds, you will more than likely succeed with portulaca. Its seeds need moisture while germinating, but once the plants become established, they can withstand desert-like conditions for long periods of time.

Although portulaca performs well in a poor soil, it does much better on one fortified with composted manure and leaf mold turned in a few weeks before planting time. Three weeks before I sow portulaca seed I work the soil well to a depth of at least 7 inches. Because my soil is naturally sandy, good drainage is provided without adding coarse sand.

If possible, plant in direct sunlight, no matter how hot the location becomes in mid-summer. Portulaca seed is almost as fine as that of petunias. If just sown loosely, the planting will probably consist of little more than thick, scattered clumps.

To prevent uneven sowings, I place the seed in a small paper bag, then drop in handfuls of dry soil. After giving the bag a good shaking, I broadcast the mixture over the worked area, then rake it gently into the top $1/4$-inch layer of soil with an iron rake. No other cover is necessary.

If no rain is in sight, I wet the entire planted area thoroughly with a fine spray from the garden hose. I make certain that the soil remains reasonably moist until germination takes place.

After the plants are about an inch tall, they are on their own, except for a weekly watering if a long dry spell should hit.

If seed is mixed with soil or sand before planting, thinning portulaca is usually not necessary; it depends on how you want to use them. If you grow them mainly for their colorful flowers, space them 4 to 6 inches apart in all directions for better bloom. If you prefer a thick ground cover, the closer the

plants, the better. Because of their low, creeping habit, portulaca varieties are excellent for rock gardens, borders around the base of lampposts, and as turf in hot, dry spots where grass refuses to catch on or a sandy embankment needs cover to prevent soil erosion.

Shortly after portulaca plants sprout, they begin to spread and bloom, continuing until frost even though old blossoms and seed heads are not removed. In fact, it is wise to allow seed heads to remain as this is the plant's means of self-sowing for the coming year.

Portulaca is a flower that has been grown and enjoyed in gardens for many generations. It is known by several different names such as purslane, sun plant, or rose moss.

One spring my grandmother planted a packet of seeds beside our garden gate. Much to my childhood delight, every spring after that the spot abounded in portulaca blossoms of brilliant yellow, pink, and scarlet.

If you have a problem spot in your garden or just don't have much time to devote to flowers, brighten your surroundings with masses of cheerful portulaca.

Sunflower

It seems an irony that the sunflower, native to North America, should have been so long ignored, when it is such an attractive and useful plant. In addition to the tasty seeds, which can be eaten, made into tea, or distilled into cooking oil, the other parts of the plant are also utile.

The whole plant can be used for forage: Most livestock relish the plants and poultry will eat the seed. Sunflower petals make a safe, natural dye. Bees go into ecstasy over the large yellow blossoms, as they yield both nectar and pollen.

Sunflower

Sunflowers may be planted a couple of weeks before corn, due to their ability to withstand light frosts while the plants are still small. The soil should be prepared deeply, as with corn, because the sunflower needs to root deeply in order not to topple over when heavy winds blow, especially if the ground is saturated during a windy thunderstorm. The soil should be fairly rich, too, to achieve those monster 20-inch-plus heads.

Sunflowers are sown about $1/2$ inch deep in rows about 3 feet apart. The large varieties should be thinned to about 2 feet apart in the row and the smaller ones to 1 foot apart. One of the agreeable things about sunflowers is their ability to control many invasive plants, as their large leaves shade out sun-loving weeds.

Although sunflowers are mostly pest-free, there are a couple of pests that may be troublesome in some years. A borer, similar in action to a squash borer, eats a tunnel through the stalk, and, as you might expect, the top may wilt or collapse. You can slit the stem and remove this critter. Sanitation is vital in preventing a buildup of these insects. Either dispose of the remaining stalks in the fall, or use them for feed.

Other than the borers, the only other consistent pests might be wild birds, who think that you have planted these cafeteria-style feeders just for them. They gobble the seeds before you have a chance to harvest them.

One possible way to thwart the birds is to cut the still-somewhat-green, but filled-out seeds and dry them under cover, such as hanging them from the rafters in an attic or barn or spreading out the heads in a warm, dry varmint-free place.

If you searched for a food that is packed with proper nutrition, it would be hard to surpass the sunflower seed kernel. It is loaded with B vitamins, calcium, phosphorous, and iron and surprisingly contains traces of many of the other important vitamins as well. Protein content is 20 percent and oil content is 27 percent. The oil turns rancid very slowly compared with the other oils, due to its lack of linoleic acid, one of the culprits that cause early rancidity.

Picking Perennials

How are you supposed to choose from the flowering favorites that are on the perennial list? Many require very specific growing conditions; these requirements should help you in deciding. If you are like most gardeners today, low maintenance is also a consideration. Here are some easy-care perennials that have stood the test of time, and can provide a full season of shifting textures and abundant color.

Let's walk through the season according to bloom time. As blooming varies from place to place, year to year and variety to variety, the sequence may change in your garden. Plant hardiness zones are indicated for each entry; refer to the zone map on page 317 to confirm the correct zone for your area.

The soil must be well-drained. Wet soils promote bacterial soft rot, a disease that causes rhizomes to decay, producing a foul odor when broken.

Iris should be planted about an inch deep and 18 inches apart. Lift and divide them about every 4 seasons in July or August. (Note: This section addresses irises that grow from rhizomes or fibrous roots; for bulbous iris, see page 230.)

There are many types of iris; among the most popular are bearded, Japanese, and Siberian. Because they come in so many colors—from blues and pinks, to intense violets and yellows—they are a natural to scatter among other flowers with similar colors. These can continue the color scheme, after the iris flowers have faded.

Iris
Zones 3–10

Iris is my first choice. There are countless species and cultivars to choose from; by staggering a variety of plantings, you can have irises blooming in your garden from spring through fall. Most species require full sun; while some plants may survive in light shade, they will flower less or not at all.

Peony
Zones 2–10

Peony gets my vote as the most outstanding herbaceous perennial. The lush white, pink, or yellow flowers are gorgeous in the spring and its foliage remains attractive all season.

Disregard any notion that peonies are too fussy to handle and too hard to grow. The peony shouldn't cause more work than any other garden plant. Although peonies don't ask for much, location is important. They grow best in full sun and rich, well-drained soil.

Just keep in mind that August or early September is the ideal time for planting new peonies and dividing old ones. Peonies usually resist transplanting and may take a little while to reestablish themselves. Don't move or divide plants unless absolutely necessary. When plants become so gigantic that flower production begins to lose vigor, then these plants will need division.

The reddish buds on the tuberous roots should be set about an inch below the surface of the soil.

In a mixed border, peonies may be planted 2 feet apart. It takes 3 years for roots to become fully established and begin flowering. Once established, plants may remain in place for 15 to 20 years without division.

Sometimes, in older established yards where shade trees take over, peonies convert from flowering to a green foliage plant. The key is to avoid planting peonies in overly or potentially shady spots, such as too close to large trees, tall shrubs, or a wall.

When ordering new peonies, in addition to the big double-bloom plants, ask for those with single and semi-double flowers and

DIVIDING AND PLANTING LARGE PEONIES

1. Cut the tops back almost to the ground. Never cut the peony foliage back when it's green—wait until the foliage begins browning.
2. Drive a spading fork or spade into the ground to the full depth of the roots and continue all around the outside of the clump, gently loosening and prying the plant up.
3. Take the entire plant out, roots and all.
4. Wash the roots with a garden hose to see what needs to be divided. Allow the plant to set a few hours to become less brittle and more pliable for root division. Don't be tempted to transplant the entire clump.
5. Examine the washed roots to locate 3 to 5 "eyes" (small protuberances on the roots that eventually form buds) for each division. Even when purchasing new plants, make sure to buy those with enough eyes for better blooms.
6. While waiting for the roots to become pliable enough for cutting, take advantage of the time to prepare the soil and holes for the cuttings or new plants. Dig the hole 2 to 3 feet all the way around.

   Then refill the lower half with topsoil that has been amended with some organic matter such as compost. Use this soil base because a hard impervious subsoil will restrict root systems, development, and proper drainage.
7. Set the cuttings or plants in the prepared holes, and add a good organic fertilizer (4–6–4, plus bone meal) but avoid a high-nitrogen-content fertilizer. Fill the rest of the hole with good soil and mound for settling. Dampening the layers will help settling.

   Proper root depth is important for large healthy blooms. The eyes should not be covered with more than 2 to 3 inches of soil. Firm the soil around the roots to contact the soil and eliminate air pockets.

Japanese types with extra-large flowers. When the flowers appear in June, occasionally check for faded blooms that need deadheading. Letting them go to seed will use up the energy plants require for new root growth. After the blooming season, you get an extra bonus with peonies: The foliage remains in the garden as a handsome decorative bush for the rest of the summer and fall. Use a few peony leaves to make background arrangements for your cut flowers.

Some of the larger-blooming cultivars may cause their stems to topple over; these should be supported with stakes or peony rings.

If you have ever heard stories that ants may destroy peony buds at blooming, you needn't worry. They merely like the sweet syrup on the buds. Use a solution of rotonone, an organic spray, to get rid of them.

If you use these few precautionary measures when dividing and maintaining your peony bushes, you will be rewarded with big, beautiful, colorful flowers in your garden next spring.

Primrose
Zones 5–8

Primroses like shade; not the deep sunless shade of the north side of the house, but a thin, dappled blending of light and shadow with protection from the noonday sun's beating rays.

They like their soil rich, deep, and moist. I mix compost with peat moss and some leaf mold and add this to my primrose bed. I also add cottonseed meal, bone meal, and greensand. You would think that amount of organic fertilizer would satisfy any plant. However, I have found that liquid organic fertilizer (seaweed and fish) poured over the roots of each

Primrose

plant just as it is coming into bud, will give a deeper, richer color to the blooms.

With primroses growing in your garden, why not try to raise a few from seed? They germinate easily and grow quickly. About every other year the bees are not yet around to pollinate my earliest primroses, so I do the job myself, using a camel's-hair brush to transfer the pollen from one flower to the stigma of another. Do it when both flowers are in full bloom.

Be sure to mark your seed parent plant. If you think you can remember which it is without marking, I assure you that you can't.

If it is late enough in the season to have the competition of the bees in your germinating efforts, it is advisable to slip a paper bag over the flower after you have brushed pollen on it. In about a month, the seed pod will have ripened and will begin to burst at the top.

Remove the paper bag; clean the foreign material away and let the seeds dry in an airy place. These seeds can be stored until winter or the next spring, or they can be planted immediately.

No matter how you have obtained your seeds, the pre-sowing treatment is the same. Just put a drop of water into the seed packet and put it in the freezing compartment of the refrigerator. Let it freeze for 3 or 4 days, then remove and thaw. Put in another drop or 2 of water and freeze again. I do this 3 times. That alternate chilling and warming is nature's way of preparing the seed for germinating.

Sow them in flats provided with good drainage. My seed-sowing mixture is $1/4$ compost, $1/4$ peat moss, $1/4$ leaf mold, and $1/4$ perlite plus a little fine sand. Scatter the seed on top of the soil and water it in.

From experience I have learned not to cover the seed with soil. I put a square of heavy cloth over the flats which I dampen often. I put my flats in a warm place that is bright, but without direct sun. I water them, if and when it becomes necessary, by quickly immersing in a pan of water.

The soil should not be allowed to dry out, but it should never be sopping wet. The seedlings usually appear in about 10 days, though it may take as long as 2 to 3 weeks.

Transplant your seedlings into small pots when they develop true leaves. I use the same soil mixture that I did for germination. After 4 weeks in the pots they are ready to be set out in the garden.

Primroses will come into bloom in spring, a year after the seed is sown. If you have a cool greenhouse or a cold frame, you can cut that time to 10 months or less, sowing your seed in the fall and getting bloom the following spring.

Primrose plants multiply rapidly and so must be divided often. You have your choice of 2 times of the year to do this. It may be done right after they bloom, or it may be put

off until late summer. I prefer to do it immediately. I always have a long list of people who have asked for plants, and, if I do it then, there is little chance of giving a blue plant to the gardener who requested a deep pink, or a purple primrose to the person who is dreaming of a white one.

Grow primroses to greet the growing season. These sparkling flowers can brighten the end of winter and start a colorful spring in your garden.

Delphinium
Zones 4–7

A few seeds from a package are the beginning of delphinium life. If you have tried growing delphiniums from seed before, but without too much success, try my method. It works.

In the spring, I half-fill an ice-cube tray with water and place four seeds in each of the fourteen small compartments, then freeze. When the water is frozen solid, I add more water and leave them to freeze for 48 hours.

(Don't use old seeds, they simply will not germinate.)

I remove the ice cubes and plant them in a flat containing 1 part sand, 1 part peat moss, 1 part perlite, and 1 part compost. Cover the cubes with $1/4$ inch of the potting mixture. I put the flat in a cool, dark place down in the cellar. Temperatures should be between 45 and 50°F. Poor germination results when the thermometer rises about 55°F.

After spending about 2 months in the cellar, they are ready for transplanting. The soil in my flower bed is well-drained, friable, and loamy. Before transplanting the seedlings, I dig holes 2 feet apart and place a handful of bone meal at the bottom of each hole, working it well into the soil.

The watering is done when the plants are set where they can receive plenty of sunshine, but some protection from strong winds.

I cultivate the plants constantly with a hoe, staking them as they grow tall. In fact, my plants are approximately 3 feet high when I start to use individual stakes to support the large flowering spikes, which bloom from late spring to early summer.

After blooming, I cut the plants back just below the flower cluster. If this stem eventually becomes unsightly, it can be cut back within a few inches of the soil.

During their dormant period in the winter, I avoid watering and cultivating. When spring comes, I feed the plants organic fertilizer (4–6–4) and water generously. They reward me with a second crop of blooms in the fall. To keep the plants flowering, no seed should be allowed to form. Cut out the faded spikes nearly down to the ground to prevent seeding.

A delphinium's life span is long. It continues indefinitely where crown rot is not serious. This disease can be discouraged by covering the crowns with ashes in winter.

Once established, these hardy plants do not require much prewinter coddling except in very cold climates. They are much more likely to suffer from poor drainage than from low temperatures.

Perhaps no other seed rewards you so well for your trouble. Their stately spike-like clusters of blue, purple or white stand proudly against a fence or provide a majestic backdrop to a mixed border; delphiniums delight the eye with their full splendor during a long season.

Oriental Poppy
Zones 3–9

Oriental poppy is not well-suited for all locations. Still, its large dramatic flowers of hot orange, red, pink, or white with black centers, which bloom from late spring to early summer, make it one of the most dramatic perennials in the garden. Once they are established, they should be left undisturbed for many years.

Because Oriental poppies tolerate shade, plant them about 15 inches apart where they get morning and afternoon sun, but are shaded from intense heat. The plants need plenty of moisture in spring and through flowering. Then, keep the soil on the dry side after flowering, during dormancy, and in winter. Therefore, drainage must be perfect.

Given the right location and drainage, the Oriental poppy will stay pest-free. If they die in a few years, it is probably because they were planted in poorly drained soil that remained too wet in winter.

Fuchsia

Daylily
Zones 3–10

Cheerful, ubiquitous daylilies bloom from early to midsummer in a multitude of colors. They flower best in full sun, but can take light shade. Spacing depends on the variety. Most need at least 2 feet between them, as well as a well-drained soil enriched with lots of organic matter. Divide in the fall.

Fabulous Fuchsias
Zones 3–10

Fuchsias are tender shrubby perennials that bloom bountifully throughout the summer, but succumb to frost in the fall.

After the first frost, I cover the flower bed with an inch of soil, then mound a covering of straw over it. In early spring I gently lift the cover here and there along the row, checking the progress of the new life coming up from the roots. Then I carefully reposition the straw, leaving it in place until all danger of frost is gone, at which time it is removed (all but the partially decayed layer at the bottom).

About June 1, when the flower buds are heavy, I go down the rows scattering 2 inches of compost.

Here at Spring Meadow we have a bright, unheated room where fuchsias live happily throughout the winter. Once a week I take the plants to the sink and wash all of their leaves, front and back, and let them drain and dry before I take them back to their place in the sun. I have never found any sign of insect life on my indoor fuchsias, and credit this fact to my weekly dunking.

Nothing is easier to propagate than a fuchsia. Just break off 3 or 4 inches of stem, remove any leaves that would be under the soil level, and plant, preferably in sand.

I like to cover my cuttings with a plastic bag turned upside-down over it to keep the sand moist. Leave it in a bright place, but out of direct sunlight, and within 10 to 14 days you will have new little plants.

I use a potting soil mixture consisting of equal amounts of peat moss, perlite, compost, and sand. Fuschias like their soil quite acidic. They are not bright-sun flowers, but neither do they like deep shade. I grow mine successfully in hanging baskets on my south porch where they have all the sun there is until noon, and, after that, open shade for the rest of the day.

To my thinking, fuchsias and geraniums are perfect companions. Each likes rich, porous soil, grows luxuriantly throughout a long season, and they get along with a minimum of fussing.

Even colorwise they go together, for both come in rich, bold shades and soft pastels. Since they can be grown together as potted plants, and usually are, you can change the pots around until you get the color combination that pleases you, then leave it for a summer of undemanding beauty.

At the end of the season I bring in my potted fuchsias, cut them back to 2 or 3 inches on each branch, and store them in a cool room. They don't need any care through the winter, just a slight dampening from time to time to keep their wood from becoming brittle.

Sometime in February I repot them in rich soil, water well, and put them where it's bright and cool. They grow quickly and soon give me all the cuttings that I need for my summer stock.

For winter blooming it is a good idea to take your cuttings in late July or August. Once rooted, I pot them firmly and set them back a little from the glass in a sunny window, for the August sun can be very bright. Now there is nothing left to do but to nip each branch until the plants assume the proportions of a butterball.

As soon as your plants show roots at the drainage hole, repot 2 sizes larger. If the place where it stands tends to become dry and hot, mist the plants every day with a sprayer.

Have you ever tried to make a fuchsia tree? Fuchsias grow so quickly that you can have a nice one in short order.

For these I use rooted cuttings coaxing them along by changing them from one pot to another as their roots grow. Tie the main stem to a stick about 4 feet tall, pinching off all the side branches. Don't remove the leaves along this main stem; your plants need them for growth.

When the tree reaches the size of your preference, pinch the tip to induce branching. Then pinch these branches after they've grown a few inches. Soon you will have a nice bushy head that will cover itself with flowers.

I like to make 2 of these trees, putting them on either side of the walk for bright accents above the other flowers.

Do you want a plant that seems to delight in being alive, grows like a teenager, and blossoms all over itself? Then grow fuchsias. You, the butterflies, and the hummingbirds will all be delighted.

Butterfly Weed
Zones 3–10

Butterfly weed thrives during the summer in dry locations. It is spectacular as a single specimen, but may also be used in groupings.

Its clustered flowers are usually a clear bright orange, but red, light orange, and yellow types have been developed. It grows about 2 feet tall, and is loved by butterflies.

Set plants out in spring or fall as young seedlings. Once established, plants are best left undisturbed. Soils that remain fairly dry and have a low fertility are most suitable.

Rose Mallow
Zones 5–8

Rose mallow is undoubtedly one of the most spectacular-looking and easily-grown perennials. Its white, pink, rose, or crimson flowers bloom in late summer, and may reach from 5 to 6 inches in diameter.

Once established, this hibiscus grows larger each year, reaching a height of 4 to 5 feet, and becomes almost as wide as it is tall; therefore, it should be planted in the back of your perennial bed. Dwarf varieties are also available.

Rose mallow is outstanding in wet soils, although it tolerates drier conditions. Roots should be planted in spring about 3 inches below the surface. Space plants about 3 feet apart.

It is essentially pest-free.

Chrysanthemum
Zones 4–10

I enjoy mums for their attractive foliage from May to fall, then throughout bloom from September until frost. Mums are available in almost every color in the rainbow.

Most of the chrysanthemums blooming in fall will go dormant when the weather turns cold, then resume growing in spring. Still, some won't make it, even though mums are supposed to be hardy perennials.

Inadequate snow cover, extreme cold, heaved roots, and the absence of a thick organic mulch all contribute to their demise. Dormant mums mulched with 4 to 6 inches of chopped leaves or straw are those most likely to live through the winter.

Chrysanthemum

To insure that your mums will be around a long time, multiply them by division and propagate by root cuttings.

A quick way to divide a year-old mum clump is to look down at it and imagine that it's a big pie. Then take a sharp shovel and cut the mum pie in half vertically and horizontally. Next, cut each of the quarters in half, winding up with 8 chunks.

Dig up each of these sections and plant them elsewhere in the garden in a hole enriched with compost. Snip out at soil level any hard, woody stems and all but 4 to 5 of the young succulent ones. Tamp down the soil and water.

Another way to divide an existing clump is to insert a shovel to its full depth into the soil around 2 sides of the plant. Make a third insertion on another side, angling it to get under the root ball. Lift the whole clump up and out of the hole. Loosen the soil around the roots with a trowel. On the outer rim of the root ball you will notice lots of new shoots with small, young hair roots. Snip these rooted stems from the mother plant and place them in water for later planting. Because of the large number of young rooted stems that can be taken from the periphery of a year-old mum clump, you don't even need to bother with any of the woody center portion. Compost it instead.

To get even more plants, when new growth comes up on the old plants in the spring cut the top 3 or 4 inches of each shoot off with a sharp knife, and root it in sand or vermiculite in shallow flowerpots. The cut should be made about $1/8$ to $1/4$ inch below a leaf node. A straight horizontal cut is better than a slanting one as the little rootlets come out all around the straight cut stem.

Use a pencil to make holes in which to insert the cuttings, rather than just pushing them down into the rooting medium. The sand or vermiculite must be kept uniformly moist during the several weeks that it takes the roots to form. I find that covering the flats in which cuttings are planted with clear plastic sheeting helps to keep them from drying out.

Rooting should ordinarily take from 2 to 4 weeks. The ideal temperature for promoting root growth is between 60 and 65°F, but unless one has a greenhouse with temperature control, it is impossible to maintain rigid temperature control.

If cuttings do not form roots within 3 to 4 weeks, they will scarcely ever make healthy new plants. If they stay in the rooting mixture after roots form, they become starved, spindly, and wood-stemmed. Such plants will never produce prime blossoms.

It would be better to dump cuttings which don't root quickly or which have been neglected after they acquire roots and start again. Cuttings may be taken anytime up until mid-May.

The soil in which chrysanthemums are to be grown should be prepared well in advance. In addition to nitrogen for growth of foliage, mums need phosphorous and potash to produce strong root systems and large clear-colored flowers.

Bone meal is an excellent source of phosphorous, but, since it is slow-acting, it should be applied to the soil the fall before planting mums the following spring. Wood ashes and potash rock or greensand are good sources of potash (see Special K on page 231), or you can use 4–6–4 balanced blended organic fertilizer.

I spread compost, wood ashes, bone meal, kelp meal, and fish meal on the beds and work these materials in to a depth of 8 to 10 inches in the late autumn. In the spring, additional compost is added and the soil cultivated lightly several weeks prior to planting the rooted cuttings.

When a rooted cutting is planted in May it is hard for a novice to visualize how much space the mature plant will require by fall. Planting rooted cuttings 25 inches apart seems like a tremendous waste of space. Yet a mum in flower needs at least that much room and some of the large flowered varieties require even more. Set the little plants the same depth as they were inserted in the rooting mix.

When I line out cuttings, I plant them close, about 7 inches apart. But the close spacing is temporary. About a month after planting, every other seedling is transplanted to another part of the garden or potted. A few weeks later half the remaining mums are again separated, providing a full 25 inches between plants.

Pinching makes chrysanthemums compact and bushy (pinching is just another name for pruning with your fingers, removing about an inch of stem per pinch). Start pinching the tips of rooted cuttings when they reach 6 inches. They will develop additional stems from the leaf nodes below the pinch. By late July when pinching should stop, the single stem, a rooted cutting planted back in May, will have developed hundreds of stems with buds forming on its tips.

With organic fertilizer, compost, and abundant water, chrysanthemums, even the so-called low growers, tend to get top heavy. It's disappointing to nurture the plants from their infancy to maturity, have them come into full bud, and then see them topple over from the sheer weight of their blooms. Add some wind and a driving rain and your prize mums will be flat on the ground.

To preclude floppy chrysanthemums, I support the taller ones with twigs pruned from my fruit trees. Insert them in the ground around the plants, when they are half grown. As the mums continue to leaf out during the summer their foliage soon hides the branches.

I have no doubt that the methods above will bring such superior results that they will be well worth the effort.

There are countless other perennials you can choose from, including garden phlox, blanketflower, bleeding-heart, black-eyed Susans, hosta, asters, yarrow, penstemon, spike gayfeather (*Liatris*), and perennial sweet pea.

As you begin to grow and work with perennials, you will find it easier to select new ones and add them to your list.

Forever Everlastings

Everlastings are flowers that, when air-dried, look almost as beautiful as they did when alive.

Many of these plants have papery bracts (modified leaves) that take the position of petals in other flowers. The true flowers of everlastings tend to be tiny, nearly insignificant, and clustered tightly together, encircled by the plant's colorful bracts.

All everlastings can be started from seed and should be planted outside as seedlings as soon as all danger of frost has passed. Keep your seedlings moist, but don't overwater.

Perennial varieties may not bloom until the second season. Annuals should start producing flowers by mid- or late summer, depending on the weather.

Gather the flowers of everlastings when they are in bud or just before they reach their peak. Arrange the flowers in small bundles, tie with some string, and hang upside down in a dark, airy place to dry. Flowers continue to mature as they dry. Don't waste your time picking flowers in full bloom, because by the time that they finish drying, they will be past their prime and not worth displaying.

Everlastings that have thin, non-woody flower stalks can be wired to make them more sturdy. Cut the stem off $1/2$ inch below the flower head. Then, insert a piece of #24 straight green floral wire up through the stem just into the head of the flower. As the flower head and stem dry, they will shrink and the flower should hold fast.

If, for some reason, the wire doesn't hold, drive the wire up through the flower head. Using small, needle-nosed pliers, bend a small crook in the end of the wire and pull the wire back down until the crook disappears and just catches in the flower head. Wired flowers can be dried standing in a large container.

Here are some of the everlastings that can brighten your home.

Globe Amaranth

This annual is on the short side, 1¹/₂ feet tall with grayish green leaves and stems. The bracts are arranged in a cone shape with the tiny, true flowers hiding among the bracts like seeds in a pine cone.

Globe amaranth comes in many colors, including white, purple, lavender, rose, and orange.

Love-in-a-mist

Love-in-a-mist is an annual reaching about 1¹/₂ feet tall. It has lovely blue, purple, white, or pink flowers that remind me a little of bachelor's buttons, another plant that can be dried. It gets its name from its fennel-like foliage that curls and gracefully surrounds the flowers.

Pearly Everlasting

Pearly everlasting is a 2-foot-tall perennial with cut leaves and woody stems covered with white hairs. The flower heads have a daisy-like appearance with white bracts surrounding tiny yellow flowers.

Although the flower heads are only about the size of a fingertip, sometimes there are as many as 20 heads clustered together on each stem. Therefore, quantity makes up for the lack of size. Cut the stems long, defoliate, and hang to dry.

Sea Lavender

Sea Lavender is a 2-foot-tall perennial with spatulate leaves in basal rosettes. It grows in sandy soil in salt marshes.

Sea lavender puts out a woody flower stalk with tiny, pale lavender, tubular flowers. Just cut and dry.

Statice

Statice is an annual with scalloped, hairy leaves in basal rosettes. Two-foot-tall, winged branches that sport papery, tubular flowers originate from the center of the rosette.

Much attention has been paid to developing strong varieties in an interesting range of flower colors.

Strawflowers

Strawflowers are probably the best-known everlastings. These annuals grow 2 to 3 feet high. They have dark, lance-shaped leaves below 2-inch-wide flowers.

The true flowers are yellow and gathered in clusters. They are surrounded by several rows of bracts in various colors, including red, yellow, orange, and shades of pink and white.

Sunray

Sunray is another annual that resembles the strawflower. Like the strawflower, this 2-foot-tall plant has yellow flowers surrounded by papery bracts limited to shades of pink and white.

Winged Everlasting

Winged everlasting, a perennial grown as an annual, likes sandy soil. It produces oval basal leaves that give way to long, winged branches. These wings are an interesting part of the branch and should not be removed.

There are many other plants that could fall into the category of everlastings. If you start with those I've mentioned, you should have plenty of flowers for both fresh and dried arrangements, enough to last year-round.

Starting Flowers from Seed

Flower seeds come in a vast array of shapes and sizes. Some, like petunia seeds, are dust-like; others are large and easily handled. Some need special attention, while others can be simply sown outdoors with care.

You must first determine whether the seeds can be sown directly in the flower beds or if they should be given a jump on the season indoors. For example, snapdragons, verbena, double-flowered petunias (all annuals), and asters (a perennial) must make considerable growth before flowering. Since this growth is rather slow, a backward extension of the growing season into late winter is of definite benefit in obtaining an early and long-blooming season in the flower garden.

Extremely fine seeds, such as petunias, are best started indoors because of the difficulties associated with their size. Tender seeds that require a long period in the soil to germinate also benefit from the controlled conditions indoors. Though such easily handled, fast-growing kinds as marigolds and zinnias (both annuals) do not actually require an early start, they, too, would be helped from an indoor planting. One group, however, should not be attempted indoors. The hardy annuals, such as larkspur, bachelor's buttons, clarkia, and California poppy should be sown directly in the garden as soon as the soil can be worked. They require a long, cool period in order to break dormancy and obtain a maximum percentage of germination.

Although most indoor-started seeds germinate best in daytime temperatures of about 70°F, the seedlings should not be subjected to a higher temperature, and fare best when the thermometer drops 15 to 20° at night (they do well in a cold frame). Warm-weather plants grow slowly at these temperatures, but will produce the sturdy plants desired for transplanting outdoors. Higher temperatures coupled with a low light level

indoors produce tall, spindly plants not equipped to withstand weather conditions in the open garden.

Perhaps the most common mistake with getting a head start on the outdoor season is attempting to extend it too far backward. In a greenhouse, with proper conditions and plenty of space, there are no complications, since the plants can be successfully grown to full size, if necessary. In your house, however, the combined effects of heat, poor light, and lack of space can easily lead to disaster.

When to start seeds can be determined by the length of time required for germination, rate of growth, and the earliest date that the plants can be set outdoors (printed on the back of seed packets or in catalogs). The general rule is to start seeds about 6 weeks before the safe outdoor planting date. Slow-growing species do better with as many as 10 weeks of indoor growth, while rapid growers need only 4 weeks.

With all seeds, wherever they are sown, the critical factor is always moisture. Once seeds have been subjected to moisture, they must not be allowed to become dry again.

For maximum results with the least attention, the containers of soil with their seeds should be set in a situation just warm enough for germination and covered with a sheet of clear plastic or glass to conserve moisture. It is equally important to watch for the first sign of germination. At that point immediately remove the cover and bring the seedlings to strong light.

Seedlings grown indoors, even with the recommended cool temperature, are not equipped to withstand a sudden transfer to outdoor conditions. They must be gradually hardened-off, either in a cold frame or by setting them in some sheltered location outdoors during the day and when mild weather is expected at night. After a week to 10 days of this treatment, they will be ready for their permanent place in the garden.

Into the Garden

Once the seedlings are in the garden, your responsibilities will shift: There is no low light problem outdoors, and the improved air circulation lessens the danger of damping-off. Except for determining the proper time for seed-sowing as determined by weather conditions and the tenderness of the species, give most of your attention to providing and conserving the necessary moisture. Toward this end there are several practical suggestions:

1. Incorporate a quantity of organic matter and compost in the top inch of your soil; it will maintain a more even moisture supply for longer periods of time than soil low in organic content. It also prevents heavy rains from packing the soil so tightly that seedlings have difficulty emerging.

   In addition, light soil permits slightly deeper sowing of seeds without cutting off the necessary air supply, thus placing the seeds closer to the zone of continuous moisture.

2. Do not be in a hurry to sow seed of the more tender species. Germinate them indoors and wait to plant the seedlings until the ground is thoroughly warm. Time will actually be saved, since germination will be much faster than in cool soil and often much sooner than the number of days given in catalogs.

   Do not be misled by the air temperature. Under a warm sun, the top of the soil feels warm, but wait until the next morning before the sun is up and recheck: in the spring, even after several warm nights, the soil will be cold before dawn.

   The wetter the soil, the longer it remains cool because of constant evaporation. Even with the danger of frost past, there is nothing to be gained by sowing warm-season plants in cool soil.

3. "Sow thin, thin quick." Whoever coined that succinct advice had the benefit of seedlings in mind. Both indoors and in the garden, crowded seedlings increase the risk of poor growth or complete failure.

   Clusters of seedlings are difficult to thin without damaging the delicate roots of those that remain. Sow seeds thinly in the beginning and thin out the excess as soon as possible so that the seedlings initially stand at least 1 inch apart. Future thinning proceeds with growth so that any removal of excess plants does not interfere with the expanding root systems of those that remain.

There is never any gardening thrill greater than bringing your own seedling to bloom. In this adventure it pays to start with the best seeds available. Though most seeds are classified only as to general type, i.e., cactus, formal, pompon, etc., they have been saved from choice, named varieties. The chances for germination are much better than if cheap mixtures are purchased.

A seed is the vital link between growing seasons of the plant species that ultimately grows and flowers from it. Among all flowering plants, the one dominant characteristic is this ability to produce seeds to perpetuate the species. It is up to us to make the best use of this characteristic, if our gardens are to get the most value from flower seeds.

Give them the right conditions for germination. Make sure that the seeds don't dry out. Do a good job of transplanting, hardening-off tender seedlings before setting them in their outdoor location. This way you can be sure that your flower seeds will develop into the highlights of your garden.

The right start, either indoors or out in the garden, is the key to making your flower garden better than ever.

Pre-Seeding Procedures for Perennials

One year, losses from severe winterkill, overcrowding by more belligerent plants, and neglecting to divide and reset took away a number of species from my garden that I consider essential to a good perennial border. The following spring I ordered some new seeds and prepared a bed.

The seeding was done the first week in June. Prior to this I had started perennials in cold frames in February and March and had also made fall plantings in September.

By the first week in July I was able to transplant some of the perennials to their permanent beds, while we were getting some nice rains.

SOME PERENNIALS YOU CAN GROW FROM SEED

Chrysanthemum	Hosta
Delphinium	Lady's-mantle
Digitalis	Phlox
Hibiscus	

Growing certain perennials from seed is neither difficult nor expensive. There are, however, 4 requirements or rules that must be observed by all from the rank beginner to the experienced green thumb. These are the following:

1. Make a well-prepared level seedbed of good organic soil. Notice the emphasis on "level." Fine seed, and much seed is fine, must be planted very shallowly. Even a slight slope will erode with the hard rains common in spring and valuable seed will be washed out or covered too deeply. So select the spot for your seedbed with this in mind.

2. Prepare soil carefully, leaving no clods, and firm it well. Laying down a board and walking on it several times until the whole bed is flattened is the best way to accomplish this. You could also wait for a good rain to settle the soil.

3. Never let the surface of the bed dry out. Make the bed within easy reach of the garden hose, so that it may be thoroughly showered every day with a fine spray of water.

4. Secure fresh seed from a reliable garden seed catalog. Do not depend on a packet of seeds from your local supermarket. Flower seeds are very short-lived and many will sprout only the first year. No reliable seed company will send out old seeds and most guarantee satisfaction. Another advantage in ordering from a garden seed catalog is that you have a big variety to choose from, including many new introductions of almost every species—it may have been one of these that you admired so much elsewhere.

STUNNING STANDING CYPRESS

Not all garden seed catalogs list gilia or standing cypress (*Ipomopsis rubra*), but it is one of the most striking plants in the border, when in bloom. The *rubra* variety will grow from 4 to 6 feet high with great spikes of scarlet blooms. It is not difficult to grow, if it is planted where water will pool over its crown during the first year of its growth.

It is not a long-lived perennial and perhaps should be treated as a biennial with new seed planted each year. Once started, it will reseed itself.

Just remember to set the plants on higher ground and do not let leaves mat on it during the winter. Small branches may be placed on the plants before the leaves drift over them to protect them over winter.

By watching the plants and the weather, I am able to transplant all of the seedlings that I have places for by August, keeping them watered. Thus, they become well-established during the fall growing season, and ready for immediate growth when spring arrives.

Blooming Bulbs

Contrary to popular belief, you can force potted spring bulbs into bloom again the following winter. I've been doing it for years with freesias, narcissi, and tulips.

My method is to continue watering the plants after they have stopped flowering. Once the foliage has died back, I stop watering, put the pots in a dark place, and let the plants lie dormant until fall. Begin watering the bulbs again in October to bring them into bloom once more between December and

February. Don't forget the liquid seaweed fertilizer for a boost during growth. You can use the same technique for forcing all bulbs into bloom out of season.

New Bulbs

When you receive a shipment of bulbs, store them in the refrigerator until you are ready to force them. Then pot the bulbs up in good soil, if you want to enjoy them again next year.

Because a bulb stores its own food, the soil shouldn't be too rich. I use a mix of equal parts sand, peat moss, potting soil, and vermiculite with a tablespoon of bone meal per pot. Keep the soil fairly loose below the bulbs so the roots can grow through it easily.

Set the bulbs in the pot so they're almost touching for the finest display of flowers. Then just cover each bulb with soil and firm it down so it doesn't burst out with the vigor of growing. Once the bulbs are potted, don't let the soil around them dry out, but make sure that they are not standing in water.

When you grow many different species of bulbs, they naturally tend to come into bloom at different times (from 33 to 107 days after planting). You can get the same effect from a single variety by staggering planting dates, potting up one set of bulbs every 2 weeks or so. Alternatively, you can plant different varieties with an eye on the length of time to flowering, so that they all bloom at about the same time.

Whether you are forcing a hyacinth or a star-of-Bethlehem, light and temperature make all the difference between lanky, flowerless plants and stocky, dark green foliage studded with blooms. When you've potted your bulbs, set them in a cold, dark place until they've put down strong roots. Keep them where the temperature stays between 40 and 50°F.

After 4 to 13 weeks, depending on the kind of bulb, shoot growth will begin. That's a sign that it is time to move the pots into a sunny area. After the shoots have greened up, give them full sun in a cool window.

Temperatures much above 60°F will cause fast growth and few flowers. When the flower buds are ready to open, move them out of direct sunlight for longer bloom, usually 1 to almost 3 weeks.

One of my favorite blooms is the highly fragrant dwarf Iris, whose compact foliage and colorful blue flowers with yellow markings make them splendid pot plants. They bloom 65 days after planting and create a beautiful centerpiece.

Most memorable of all are the freesias whose delicate arching sprays will fill a room with glorious fragrance. They are profuse and colorful, ranging from white through lilac, yellow, and scarlet with bicolors available. Freesias make lovely cut flowers as well as stunning pot plants.

Don't let this winter go by without blooming bulbs to cheer you in its dreary days.

More Forceful Methods

If, like me, you're a gardener for whom spring never comes early enough, try arranging your own private preview of the season by potting a few bulbs for forcing.

A good potting soil mix for starting bulbs is 1 part peat moss, 1 part sand, 1 part perlite, and 1 part compost with a good sprinkle of bone meal. I use a clay pot 8 inches deep and 8 inches across the top.

Before potting, be forewarned by these few forcing don'ts:

1. Don't compact the soil. A thump on the table will settle it and the roots can penetrate better.
2. Don't twist bulbs into the soil. You may damage the basal plate from which the roots emerge.
3. Don't crowd too many bulbs into one container. Roots seeking room may heave the bulbs right up out of the soil.
4. Don't sprinkle newly planted bulbs—saturate them. This will be their last water for many weeks.

After labeling, store the pots in either a cold frame with the glass removed or a trench deep enough so that they're covered at least 1 foot deep. I used to slog through January snows to the cold frame near the garden. Now I get pots out of cold storage from a handy trench dug beside the garage.

I cover the trench with a thick layer of pine needles, leaves, and straw. As an extra precaution, I lay a piece of window screening over all, weighting it down with a light layer of soil to discourage mice and chipmunks who like to nibble on tulips and crocuses.

Bulbs can also be stored in an unheated garage where the temperature does not drop to freezing, nor go above 50°F.

After about 6 weeks have elapsed, remove the covering in the trench or cold frame to see if the smaller bulbs are rooted. If the bulbs do not come loose with a gentle tug, or you see yellow sprouts, they can be brought indoors.

I begin to remove the large bulbs from their trench early in January, moving them into the cellar until the potting soil thaws. Next they are moved upstairs to dim light for a day, then placed near a window. In another day or 2 they are placed in direct sunlight.

I check every couple of days to make sure that the soil is moist, but not soggy. I turn the pot frequently so growth is symmetrical.

In a couple of weeks the buds show color. I mist them with a sprayer to substitute for the moist atmosphere of springtime. If you can't keep your living area on the cool side, move the plants to the cellar at night to prolong flower freshness.

Hyacinth bloom should be out of the neck of the bulb before you put it into strong light. Otherwise, it tends to blossom down in the crevice at the base of the leaves, instead of unfolding at the top of a nice sturdy stalk. Slip a cone made of a twist of heavy paper over the bloom and you can coax it upward. When you see the florets ready to unfold, remove the cone.

If you want to experiment, dig up a few of those grape hyacinths from your garden border for forcing, too. They may not do as well as fresh ones, but there's little to lose and they may surprise you.

I first learned that these miniature blue thimbles had a lovely fragrance when I grew them indoors. *Scillas* and wood hyacinths force well, too.

Bulbs that you want to save for planting outdoors will need water, sunlight, and a light feeding with fish and seaweed emulsion after their flowers have faded. As the weather warms, they can be knocked from pots and set outside or left to ripen in the pot, dried off, then planted in the fall.

Special K

Many gardeners seem to have success with daffodils, crocuses, dahlias, and many other spring-, summer-, and fall-blooming bulbs only the first year after planting. During the

BULB BUDDIES

When planted together, bulbs and perennials can stretch the blooming season from before spring thaw to the edge of fall's first frost.

Spring-flowering bulbs work particularly well as companion plants to perennials simply because most of them come up and bloom much earlier. Still, the joining of bulbs and perennial mix goes even deeper—down to the roots to be exact. Bulbs are generally planted from 4 to 8 inches deep. Therefore, their root systems do not directly compete with those of many perennials, which usually do not go that far down.

Mixing bulbs into a perennial bed is also the solution to hiding leftover foliage that remains after bloom. As the bulbs finish blooming, the perennials' vigorous growth hides their foliage from view. You should never remove the bulb foliage until it yellows and falls over because it is busy producing sugar for next year's blooms.

Beyond the aesthetics of this pairing, perennials provide near ideal conditions for their bulb buddies, after they've bloomed. Perennials shade bulbs from the hot summer sun and suck up available moisture during the summer and into fall just when most bulbs need to be cool and dry.

Peonies, bulbous iris, and daylilies, for example, make excellent companions for daffodils. Their foliage hides maturing daffodil leaves, provides wonderful color after the daffodils are

continued

gone, and helps to shade the daffodil bulbs as the sun gets warmer.

When choosing a site, consider where you will enjoy this garden the most. It could be the focal point for your gaze out the kitchen window or a welcome border that greets visitors along your driveway. Pick a spot that is not too wet. If you do not have a choice, however, some bulb types such as *Camassia* and *Scilla* can tolerate moist soil.

When it comes to moisture, try to find the middle ground: Avoid extremely dry sites and extremely wet sites. Good drainage is important. Still, do not ignore the moisture-retaining quality of the soil, which is just as important because bulbs do not root deeply.

Light is another important consideration. If bulbs do not get enough light, they will be too leggy. Most bulbs prefer full sun, but can tolerate up to a half day of shade.

Compost is all that you need to improve soil structure and provide slow-release nutrition for the new planting. One of the neat things about combinations of bulbs and perennials is that they're not too fussy. Just create the best growing site that you can.

In new gardens, plant bulbs first and perennials second. You may want to mark where bulbs are planted and draw a map to make it easy to add to your new bed in seasons to come. In already established perennial beds, plant bulbs around the base of perennials, when the perennials become dormant in fall.

To protect bulbs that voles find irresistible, such as lily, crocus, and tulip, put a handful of sharp, crushed gravel about the size of peas into the planting hole. Voles have a hard time going through the gravel.

Mulch newly planted bulbs, preferably with pine needles. Mulching helps to maintain constant soil temperatures and keep bulbs from emerging too early. Mulch will also help prevent premature sprouting in warm winters and protect sprouts that do pop up too soon from frost damage.

Bulbs like to receive a yearly supplement of potash. Wood ashes are one good source, but be careful. Ashes are somewhat alkaline and bulbs usually prefer neutral soil (a pH of 7.0). Greensand is also an excellent source of potash and trace elements and is an alternative, if your soil is already alkaline (see "Special K" on page 231).

Use bone meal or rock phosphate to add phosphate, and fish or cottonseed meal to raise nitrogen levels. Fertilize in the fall when bulbs feed to fuel new roots. Stick to low amounts of slow-release nitrogen, so you don't encourage unwanted fall leaf growth.

Bulbs and perennials may seem like the odd couple, but can be beautiful companions that will bring pleasure through the season.

---

years that follow, the size and amount of bloom gradually diminish, until the plants finally wear themselves out and disappear completely.

If this seems to be your problem, first get your soil tested. You will no doubt find out that your soil is low in potash (K).

To better understand the necessity of potash in bulb growing, let's look at what it does for plants. Potash is necessary for the development of strong plants. It is chiefly responsible for the plant's manufacture of carbohydrates, both sugars and starches, acting as a catalyst for this process.

When potash is used as a fertilizer for bulbs, carbohydrate production (which helps build plant cells) is intensified. As the plant grows bigger, it produces a greater root system that is capable of extracting a larger amount of plant food from the soil to store in the bulb for next year's growth.

Potash is also capable of counteracting excess quantities of nitrogen in the soil, resulting from the overuse of manures. Too much nitrogen can cause plants to lose their resistance to disease.

Potash rock is a good source of potash. Because potash rock does not burn the roots of plants, you may use as much as you like. About $2^1/_2$ pounds per 100 square feet will do in an average garden soil. Potash can be used on any type of soil without the danger of upsetting the nutrient balance. It is wise to remember that you must use organic matter along with the potash for maximum results. Organic matter will increase the bacteria population, which will act upon the potash in greater force and quickly turn it into food nutrients for immediate use by plants.

If you prefer, you may add the potash rock to your compost pile in the spring. Then turn it back into your beds along with the compost in the fall.

Granite dust is another source of potash, containing the minerals mica and potash feldspar. Its potash content ranges from 3 to 5 percent. Granite dust is a valuable addition to any soil for three reasons: It is inexpensive; it contains many valuable trace elements needed in all soils for proper growth; and it will not leave any harmful chemical residues to poison the soil, regardless of how often it is used.

Granite dust may be applied to the soil while you are working the beds. Used as a top-dressing or added to the compost pile, 10 pounds per 100 square feet is sufficient. About 6 to 8 pounds will do it for a tulip border 25 feet long and 4 feet wide, or a round bed 14 feet in diameter.

Greensand is still another source of potash to use in growing bulbs. It has been used for generations in organic soil building. Greensand is actually an undersea deposit composed mostly of glauconite, a silicate of iron and potassium. It has about 6 to 8 percent available potash and at least 30 trace elements, all of which are important to the growth and health of plants.

Greensand is fine so it needs no further processing before it can be used. About $1/_2$ pound per square foot of garden soil yields excellent results. Although it may be applied at any time without endangering plants, it is best when applied while working the soil. If desired, greensand may also be used as a top-dressing under mulch or added to the compost pile to be returned to the soil later.

It is greatly satisfying to produce huge, strong bulbs and tubers in your garden each year—they will grow into healthy plants that will bloom well and multiply quickly to increase your gardening pleasure.

The extensive use of potash and compost will keep your bulbs blooming beautifully every spring, summer, and fall. For the best results, lift and divide bulbs every 2 years in autumn. Then replant them after reworking the garden bed.

Doing Dahlias

Not many people try growing dahlias from seed, but I have found them interesting and simple to grow in this way. Dwarf strains can be flowered in a single season as easily as any annual. The same is true of the larger types, if seeds are given a running start on the season indoors.

Dahlia

Dahlias provide a glorious burst of late summer and fall color in exquisite shades and assorted sizes. Since seedlings rarely come true to color or form, growing your own dahlias from seed as well as tuber is an intriguing task.

Start with seeds along with a few tubers, initially, for cross-pollination. Most mail-order suppliers provide only the seeds, but several provide tubers for large dahlias. If a tuber begins sprouting before you plant it, place it in a plastic bag with slightly dampened peat moss and refrigerate. Root growth may continue, but sprouting will not.

Start seed indoors 4 to 8 weeks before the last frost. Soak compressed peat moss pellets until they expand to their full 2-inch height.

Use a fingernail to dig under the top indentation in each pellet and insert a single seed horizontally. Cover the seeds with a pinch of loose peat moss and place the pellets in a south-facing windowsill where the temperature will be 65 to 75°F.

Water lightly to keep the peat moss from drying out, but avoid soaking. Seedlings appear within a week to 10 days with about 80 percent germination.

When a seedling shows several pairs of leaves and roots beginning to protrude from the base of the pellet, set the seedling in a 4-inch peat pot. Set the space around the pellet with loose peat moss.

Dahlias need full sun to partial shade, but do well in a wide climate range. They perform best in a light, sandy loam, but almost any type of soil rich in organic matter with good drainage and a pH of 6.5 works well.

To prepare soil for easy root penetration, work the area to a depth of about 12 inches at least 3 weeks before actual planting time. Turn in as much organic matter—such as compost or leaf mold and bone meal—as you can, since dahlias are heavy feeders. Also, make liberal use of rock phosphate and greensand, especially if your soil tests low in nutrients.

Before setting out plants in May, rework the beds slightly, then mark off planting locations with an *X*. Hammer 5- to 6-foot stakes into the ground at 3- to 4-foot intervals to ease spacing for plant maintenance. Use higher stakes for taller species and tighter spacing for dwarf varieties.

Drop the seedling peat pots into a hole dug at the base of each stake, so that the top of the pot is at ground level. Lay the tubers horizontally 4 to 6 inches below soil level with the sprouting eye pointed upward and placed no more than 4 inches from the stake.

Cover with several inches of soil and peat moss. Water until the soil is well-soaked down to a depth of 8 inches. The morning after planting, I fill each hole with a mix of liquid seaweed and fish, which gets both the seedlings and the tubers off to a good start.

Once the plants break surface, growth is rapid and should be kept that way by frequent waterings and feedings. Water deeply about once a week during the early morning hours, more often if leaves are drooping or yellowing.

Fill in the remainder of each hole with compost as plants gain height. After the plants are at least 1 foot tall, tie the central stalk loosely to its stake at 12- to 18-inch intervals.

By July 15 surface roots begin to develop, so all cultivation must stop. I hill the rows like corn at this time, loosen the soil in the rows, then scatter 4–6–4 organic fertilizer on the entire bed. Over this goes 6 inches of straw mulch.

Although pruning and disbudding can increase the size of flowers and yield stronger plants, I generally avoid the extra effort of constant snipping. Most of my plants grow 4 to 5 feet high. Dahlias have their share of pests, but healthy dahlias are the result of healthy soil and they will resist attacks. Keep debris such as weeds, brush, and boards away from flower beds. Slugs attack young dahlias. Use floating row-covers or traps to control them. Handpicking will control borers and Japanese beetles, but if infestations are severe, use BT against the borer and milky spore for the beetles.

Spider mites and earwigs also enjoy a snack of dahlias. Flush the mites with a good blast of water or insecticidal soap. To trap earwigs, which seek daytime shade, prop up jar-lids, lip-side down, so that they will crawl in. Check traps during the day and squash the earwigs.

Dahlias are great for seed-saving. Some plants bear as many as 100 flowers and some pods yield up to 40 seeds. Some of the biggest flowers, however, may provide just 5 to 15 seeds. Although still-green seed pods can be removed for indoor drying, I prefer to leave the pods attached for natural drying. This yields better seeds, even though some seeds fall out. Take the seed pods indoors before the first frost and keep them in sealed glass containers for long-term storage. Seeds remain viable for at least 5 years.

Dig the tubers after the first major fall frost. As soon as heavy frost blackens the foliage, cut off 3 inches above ground level. Then lift the tubers a week later. When lifting, force a garden fork into the soil all around the cluster, slightly loosening the clump as you go. Do not shake off excess soil, as this is needed to help protect the tubers in storage.

Bring tubers into an outdoor building to finish curing. After 2 weeks cut the stems back to within 2 inches of the tubers. Pack loosely in boxes or barrels, filling in with dry sand or peat moss to prevent shriveling.

Store in a cold room, where temperatures remain just above freezing. Remove from storage in April and place on damp burlap in a warm room to encourage sprouting for a new season of dahlia beauty.

Hardy Hyacinths

You do not need many hyacinth bulbs in order to produce a large number of new bulblets. I have obtained as many as 45 good-sized bulblets from just 5 mature bulbs.

If you would like to grow these bulbs to sell, propagate a few each spring so that you will eventually have a large number of maturing ones.

There are two methods by which you can force a single hyacinth bulb to produce 5 to 10 bulblets in just 2 months. The first is called scooping. It produces more, but smaller bulblets than the other method.

Scooping is accomplished with a kitchen tool called a melon-ball maker. This is pressed

Hyacinth

against the very bottom of the bulb within the circle created by the dried root stubs and twisted once to remove a scoopful of bulb tissue.

The procedure exposes the inner leaf scales, which aid in the production of bulblets that appear within this opening and around the root area. Scooping can also be done satisfactorily with a sharp pocketknife.

The other method (which I prefer) is called scoring. It yields fewer, but bigger, bulblets, and is easier than the first.

Simply turn each bulb upside down on a cutting board and make 2 crisscrossed incisions, each $1/2$ inch deep, across the bottom. You can make as many as 3 or 4 incisions, if you like, but I find that 2 is usually sufficient.

After I cut across the bottom of each bulb, I gently pry the cuts apart a little so that the new bulblets will not have difficulty growing within these incisions as they often do.

The best time to propagate hyacinth bulbs, I have found, is in late spring after the foliage has turned yellow. You can either use

hyacinth bulbs that have been growing in your garden or purchase special varieties and colors the fall before.

I buy my bulbs in the fall, then plant them in my border to add color and fragrance in spring. After their foliage turns yellow, I take them up and hill them in the garden for a week or so until they ripen. Then I bring them in, remove all foliage and roots, and plant them in open trays in a warm, dry room to cure. This curing is very important and must not be omitted. If not completely cured before scoring, hyacinth bulbs will rot when replaced in the soil.

When replanting, I place the scored bulbs upside down and cover them with 4 inches of compost that has been firmed gently to eliminate air pockets. A mulch applied over the spot aids in retaining moisture and in keeping the soil cool.

Around the end of September, I push the mulch aside and remove the bulbs carefully with a gardening spade. After inspecting and counting the bulblets, I replant them, still upside down, in a well-protected spot in the border gardens. They are planted the same depth as before, then mulched heavily after the soil freezes hard.

The following spring, the spot is thickly covered with hyacinth foliage, but no bloom. After this foliage turns yellow, I again take up these propagated bulbs.

By now, most of the bulblets are as round as a dime, or bigger, and are easy to handle. All are removed from the mother bulb and replanted in a bed rich in compost, 2 inches apart in all directions and 4 inches deep.

After they reach blooming stage (in 2 or 3 years), I transplant them to stand 6 inches apart in a border garden fortified with compost, greensand, and bone meal. Fed and planted this way, hyacinth bulbs will go on blooming beautifully for years with little or no care except a feeding of liquid fish and seaweed.

Rite for Roses

Take care of your roses and they will reward you with their beauty and fragrance well into late fall, long after most other flowers have stopped blooming.

How much should you water them? Roses will survive with a minimum of this precious liquid, but with the right amount your flowers will have more substance, better color, and longer keeping qualities. Plants will be healthier and better able to survive the rigors of winter, too.

There are a lot of ways to water the rose garden. You may have an automatic sprinkler system, soaker hoses laid on the ground, or an overhead sprinkler. Whichever you choose depends upon your preference and budget.

Just make sure that you water in the morning, especially if you are watering overhead. Mildew is especially prevalent in fall as nights become cool, although days are still warm. If foliage sits wet through an already humid night, disease will spread more quickly.

Although you can start to withhold water in the fall, be sure to keep irrigating, if days are still hot and dry. When it starts to cool off, watering can slow down to about 1 inch every 2 weeks. Be sure that plants do not go through the winter bone dry, as they will suffer greatly from cold damage, if they do.

Fertilizing is always an important aspect of rose growing. Like anything else, it can be harmful if overdone. A good rule of thumb is to not fertilize later than 8 weeks before the first expected fall frost. Determine the correct fertilizer based on your soil test. Roses need a

well-drained soil high in organic matter, slightly acidic (from 6.4 to 6.5).

Late fertilization causes lush, soft growth which will not have a chance to harden-off before winter. This new growth will not make it through the winter. Still you can and should fertilize with bone meal, which is high in phosphorous for deep root growth, and kelp meal in the fall.

It is important that rose bushes go into winter as healthily as possible. This way they will be better able to fight off winter injury. So, take a good look at your plants and make sure there are no problems.

If the summer has been hot and dry, your roses are more susceptible to mites. Look carefully for their signs: full, reddish leaves, small black spots on the undersides of foliage, and webbing. If you have mites, use rotenone, a safe, organic insect control. Strong water sprays, especially on the underside of leaves, will also keep the mites from returning.

If blackspot has been a problem during the summer, clean up as many of the fallen leaves as you can before winter. Blackspot spores overwinter on canes, in the ground, and just about any other place that they can find.

As the leaves start to fall from your trees, especially if they are oak leaves, rake them into the rose beds. They make an excellent winter mulch, allowing water and air to pass through, but keeping the ground at an even temperature and well-insulated.

When spring comes, don't remove the leaves; instead, leave them in place. By the time it gets hot, they will have crumbled into small pieces, forming an attractive and useful mulch. The ground will be cooler, more even in temperature and freer of weeds.

As autumn turns to winter, think of preparing your roses for the cold. If your plants are very tall, prune them back by almost $^1/_3$ to prevent wind damage. Waiting to prune later in the season will encourage growth that will not harden-off before freezing temperatures.

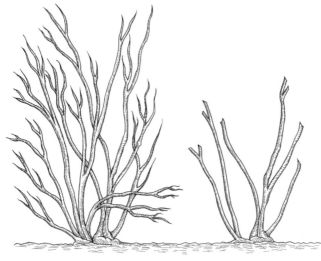

Rose bush, before and after pruning for winter

Fall planting of roses is superior to planting the following spring. Plants will be larger and bloom sooner, when the roots are allowed to develop through winter. Roots will grow until the soil temperature dips below 30°F, which is long after the leaves have fallen and the tops of the plants have been hit by frost. Be sure to water well after planting and apply protection to keep the canes moist until new growth starts in the spring.

Proper rose care in fall will insure a better rose garden next spring. You will enjoy the vibrancy of the last rose of summer and maybe even the last one of fall.

Well-Contained Growing

Confidentially, I've always been a window box fan. I love to see the bright boxes of gaily-colored geraniums and ivy gracing the fronts of the houses that I pass. Until recently, though, I never realized the vast, practically unlimited possibility of organic gardening in containers.

It must be stressed that in container gardening, you have to grow strictly organic: Your soil must be rich and it must not pack.

Equal parts of soil, sand, and humus material (such as compost, leaf mold, or peat moss), plus generous amounts of composted horse manure and bone meal make a wonderfully fertile soil. I work on the theory that the more tightly crowded a container is with plants, the better they thrive and bloom, provided that the soil is right.

I recommend mulching all plants grown in containers with semi-finished compost, peat moss, or cocoa shells for most plants; use pine needles or oak leaf mold for acid lovers.

Once the organic end of my project is taken care of, I give my imagination free rein in thinking up decorative uses for planters. Window boxes don't have to be restricted to just windows. Festoon a front porch, for example, with a continuous row of plant boxes. When choosing plants, I like to include at least 2 colors in each planter, preferably in varying tints. Light and dark blue or red with white is very attractive, as is the contrast of brilliant yellow and red with bright blue and white.

In a box or container that is viewed from one side only, I put the taller plants in the rear, lower ones in front of these, and let trailing plants cascade over the rim. Boxes that are seen from 2 or more sides should have the tallest plants in the center. In large boxes, it is best to intermix tall and medium-height plants so you don't get a step effect.

Selecting the plants themselves is easy. In consulting your flower seed catalogs, there are four things to consider: color, season of bloom, height, and exposure.

In shady northern exposures, I favor tuberous begonias, browallia, fuchsias, gloxinias, impatiens, caladiums, crotons, ferns, torenias, balsam, forget-me-nots, and abutilon. Partly shaded or eastern or western locations that miss the hot midday sun are planted with lobelias, wax begonias, fancy-leaved caladiums, and impatiens.

Hundreds of plants will thrive in containers receiving full sun. I often combine pansies and geraniums, or blue ageratums and white petunias; for a red and gold blend I prefer marigolds and lantanas. Miniature roses, dwarf zinnias, pompon dahlias, primroses, snapdragons, sweet alyssum, and calendulas are some of my other favorites.

Careful study of your seed catalogs will enable you to map out a plan for 3-season beauty. In spring, you can have bulbs, cineraria, pansies, primroses, English daisies, and azaleas. For summer the annuals offer unlimited choices. Fall inspires a combination such as coleus and mums.

The biggest trick is to keep a supply of plants growing to blooming size in a suitable spot in your backyard. This takes careful

---

CONTAINER CUISINE

Don't forget that you can also grow many organic edibles in containers and planters. Chard, lettuce, beets, spinach, and other greens do well in containers. Herbs are very easy to grow in planters. Strawberries do fine in tubs, barrels, boxes, or pyramids. And, of course, there are window-box tomatoes and other miniatures especially suited to container growth.

---

planning, but will give you spectacular color from crocus time until frost.

Planter and container gardening is truly an art, and it is an art worth learning. The range of plant material is endless, indeed. Many plants seem to show up to much better advantage when grown in containers rather than the ground.

This method of organic gardening can be practiced anywhere—on a porch, windowsill, terrace, or city rooftop. When the weather changes, you can bring the plants indoors to prolong your growing pleasure. Whether planter or container gardening, you don't have to spend all of your time or money to make your home a beautiful, fruitful, and happy place.

CHAPTER 17

Getting a Lawn

Is your lawn a black hole of gardening, endlessly sucking in your time, energy, and money? You fertilize, mow, water, mow, spread pesticides, mow, and mow some more? Well, it doesn't have to be that way. A lawn is a complex community of plants, insects, and microorganisms, and the more we understand it, the easier it is to successfully maintain. Sure, organic lawn care is work, but at least we are not working against ourselves—and the environment—with toxic chemicals. And even mowing is almost pleasant when the lawn is healthy and green.

There are four basic elements to organic lawn maintenance: fertilization, liming, irrigation, and mowing. Done properly, these practices all work together to produce a dense, green turf with few common problems such as pests or thatch. Done improperly, they can work at cross-purposes, making trouble for both you and your lawn.

Let's look at each one of these aspects individually and see how they affect lawn quality.

Fertilization

Proper organic fertilization takes time, but can reduce mowing chores—as well as the temptation to use pesticides and herbicides—while making for a prettier and hardier lawn.

The object of fertilizing is to encourage vigorous root growth without stimulating too much leaf growth. Strong roots sustain a healthy lawn that will resist drought, pests, and diseases, while excessive leaf growth just means mowing.

Before you start fertilizing find out how fertile your lawn already is. Take a soil sample and bring it to Spring Meadow or another local soil testing laboratory you find in the phone book—we will test it and tell you the proper organic fertilizer to use on your lawn. This way you will get the best results and save money by not putting down more than your lawn requires.

The test results will indicate what formula of organic fertilizer is best for your conditions and how much to apply.

241

Fall is the best time to fertilize cool-season grasses—such as bluegrass, tall fescue, and rye—in order to develop strong root systems. For these types of lawns—especially those with nutrient-poor soil—split the desired amount of organic fertilizers over 2 monthly fall fertilizations, starting in September and ending in October. Please refer to page 248 in this chapter for more information on applying fertizer.

Liming

Contrary to popular belief, not all lawns need lime every year. Lime is only necessary when the pH of your soil drops to an undesirable level. A soil pH in the range of 7.0 to 7.5 favors most varieties of turf grasses.

Soil testing is the only way to know your soil's pH. Since you have already tested your soil for fertility, all you need do is check those results, which will include soil pH. Many soil test results also specify how much lime to apply.

Spread lime in the fall of the year, as it takes about 2 months to change the pH. If more than 50 pounds of lime per 1,000 square feet is required, split the amount into separate applications applied several months apart.

Irrigation

It doesn't hurt a lawn to go brown in mid-summer. All it means is that the grasses are dormant, waiting for fall rains.

If you must have a lush green outdoor carpet through the summer, you will probably have to water. Should you choose to do so, remember this rule: Water deeply and water regularly for 3 to 4 hours at a time—once a week for heavy soil, and every other day for sandy soil. Deep watering—enough to wet 6 inches into the soil—encourages roots to grow downward, instead of staying near the surface. Surface-rooted plants require more frequent watering. This results in a constantly moist surface that encourages weeds to germinate and disease to spread. Deep roots stay cooler and are less likely to go dormant in summer's heat. Most lawns require about 1 inch of water per week to continue growing.

Regular watering keeps the lawn from fluctuating between periods of dormancy and growth several times per season, which can weaken the turf. If you forget to water your lawn one week and it turns brown, let it stay that way until it naturally comes out of dormancy with the return of regular rains. The lawn may not look pretty, but it will be healthier than if you continued to water it sporadically.

Cool-season grasses such as bluegrass, tall fescue, and rye suffer the most in times of drought. Keep your lawn aerated and de-thatched to make it more accessible to water. (Thatch is the natural layer of decayed plant parts that accumulates between the grass blades and the soil.) Aeration should be done in spring before reseeding and fertilizing.

Dethatching should be done when thatch builds up to $1/2$ inch or more. Cool-season grasses should be dethatched in the fall while they are actively growing. Dethatching machines can be purchased at home centers or rented by the day. A dethatcher looks like a lawn mower, and pulls up the old, dead roots, a.k.a. the thatch. That is raked up and added to your compost pile.

Mowing

Mowing heights affect the health of the grass roots. During time of high temperatures and

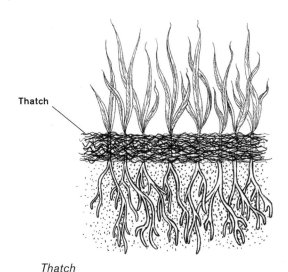

Thatch

Thatch

little moisture, mow your lawn taller than usual. Raise your mower height to 3 inches and mow often (see "Mowing" in the yearly lawn care program on page 259).

A lot of clippings fall on your lawn when you mow. Short clippings fall to the crown to form a moisture holding mulch. They also provide nutrients.

Annual weed grasses such as crabgrass can be crowded out of your lawn by healthy grass mowed high and fertilized with a 3–6–3 organic fertilizer (see "How to Control Crabgrass Organically" on page 251).

I am always amazed at the intertwining of all aspects of organic lawn care. Mowing heights affect the health of grass roots, as does the timing of fertilization (which can affect how much mowing is necessary), and so on. Knowledge of these interactions will give you a green and healthy lawn now and for all seasons.

Using the Right Varieties of Grass

The trouble with most lawns is that they are usually planted with bluegrass, a fine-textured,

DEALING WITH DROUGHT

In times of drought, water only when actually needed. Too much water deprives the soil of air. Let lawns show some stress before watering—this gives them time to grow deeper roots and makes them more drought tolerant. Signs of drought in turf include a gray cast to the normally dark green color and footprints that remain after walking across it.

If you have to make a choice, choose to water trees over lawns, vegetables, or flowers. Shrubs and trees are stressed for water when their leaves curl upward during morning or evening. Allow water from a hose or soaker to trickle overnight at their base. Mulch trees and shrubs with shredded bark or composted organic material. Try to avoid black plastic as it can restrict air movement.

To restore drought-damaged trees, try to build up the root system. Give young trees a light application of a complete organic fertilizer just before mulching. Avoid stimulating top growth with a high-nitrogen fertilizer until the root system has a chance to recover.

You can have a successful season even if Mother Nature is less than cooperative. Precautions taken in times of drought make good gardening sense any time. Everyday conservation of water should be a goal for all.

deep green grass that has very shallow roots. In fact, about 75 percent of its root growth is in the top 5 inches of soil, making bluegrass quick to dry out and even quicker to form a thick layer of thatch that can cause disease, and eventually choke your lawn to death.

The answer lies in saying goodbye to the blues and hello to grasses that can help you create a vibrant, thick, green lawn with less thatch, less watering, more disease resistance, and in many cases, less mowing.

Fescues

Fine fescues are a versatile family of grasses and good choices whether your lawn must tolerate northern cold or southern heat. It is an especially good alternative for shady lawns or if you want less maintenance without tearing up your existing turf. Fine-leaved and hard fescues are well suited to overseeding to improve thin turf in shady spots. Fine fescue is shade and drought tolerant, has good insect resistance, and also germinates rapidly. Best of all, fine fescues don't require much organic fertilizer and need less mowing than bluegrass or rye.

Tall fescue, a cool-season grass, has always been praised for its drought resistance and ability to perform in poor soils. A fast grower, the secret is its deep root system. Descended from pasture grass, newer varieties have been bred for a finer texture and darker color. These new varieties can tolerate full sun or medium shade, and can even beat out some weeds.

Another plus of tall fescue is that it's quicker to germinate than bluegrass, although you will have to water it heavily the first summer. And its less-aggressive sideways growth habit means that it is more likely to stay out of flower beds and gardens; however, because tall fescue doesn't spread with underground runners like rye and bluegrass, it doesn't recover as quickly from traffic damage. It also doesn't do well when competing with bluegrass, so to get the maximum benefit from tall fescue you should tear up what you have and start fresh.

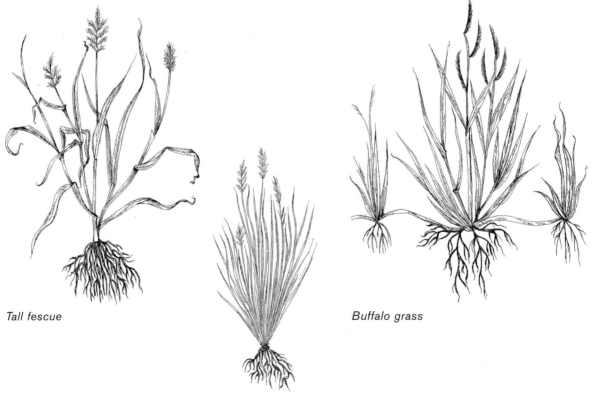

Tall fescue

Fine fescue

Buffalo grass

Buffalo Grass

Used for turf cover since the 1930s, buffalo grass is a slow-growing, warm-season grass well-adapted to dry weather. Newly developed varieties are bred for darker color and low growth, and are durable in scorching sun and drought conditions. These grasses require minimal irrigation (about once a month during the summer, instead of several times a week like bluegrass), mowing, and fertilizing. A typical homeowner with a buffalo grass lawn would need to mow and water only a few times during the growing season. Left uncut, the grass only grows 4 to 8 inches tall, and the grass can tolerate cold weather as well, maintaining a pleasing color. Buffalo grass can be planted by plugs, sprigs, sod, or seed.

Starting a New Lawn from Scratch

Knowing how grass grows, plus some fundamental pointers on planting and maintenance, lets even a novice succeed at starting a new lawn. Essentially, a new grass plant springs from a seed so small that it takes millions of them to make a pound. Once in contact with wet soil, the seed starts absorbing moisture, the tiny embryo begins to grow, and in a week or two a root tip brakes through the seed coat and pushes down into the soil. About the same time, a bud shoot breaks out and starts up toward the sunlight. After this critical period of germination, when the soil surface must be kept moist (or the embryo may not survive), the grass plant is launched into life and then pretty much is on its own.

New lawns are best started in the fall—late August to late October—because most grasses get growing in autumn's cool weather

---

ENDOPHYTE-ENHANCED GRASSES

Many of the new tall fescue and perennial rye varieties currently being developed contain endophytes, parasitic plants that grow within other plants. In this case, the grasses contain friendly naturally-occurring fungi that resist insect damage. As the seed germinates, the fungus grows into the plant and continues to live as the grass matures. Endophytes are most effective against surface-feeding insects such as aphids, cutworms, chinch bugs, and sod webworms. Endophyte-enhanced cultivars have also shown increased heat and drought tolerance, as well as an enhanced ability to repel weeds and recover rapidly from injury.

And there is an added benefit: Planting endophyte-enhanced lawns reduces the need for pesticides. Sure, we know that avoiding toxic agricultural chemicals is important to our health, soil, and water, but did you know that those chemicals also reduce earthworm populations in a lawn by 60 to 99 percent? Earthworms keep your lawn and garden healthy by mixing thatch with soil and providing plant nutrients, as well as conditioning your lawn's soil as it passes through their digestive system. Earthworms are critical to the long-term stability of a turf grass ecosystem.

---

and become well-established by spring. Other advantages include faster germination in the late season's warm soil; adequate rainfall and cool nights; development of more extensive root systems better able to withstand dry, hot weather in summer months; and the absence of competition from weeds or pests that enter their dormant period with the advent of fall.

INSTRUCTIONS FOR SEEDING A NEW LAWN

1. Till the soil to a depth of 6 to 8 inches. Don't work the soil too deep. A good stand of grass can be obtained even in 2 to 3 inches of good organic soil, if there is good drainage. Besides good drainage, grass soil needs air. Tight, heavy clay needs loosening with organic supplements. Aerate with a spike-tooth tool. (Note: If you are reseeding, first spread peat moss, use an aerator, and rake surface soil loose.)

2. Perform a soil test to determine pH and fertilizer needs.

3. Smooth and grade the seedbed until it is uniform.

4. Apply a peat moss mulch at the rate of 2 pounds per 1,000 square feet. To insure uniform coverage, spread half the grass seed in one direction, and the remainder in the opposite direction.

5. Firm the soil by rolling or raking lightly.

6. Keep the soil moistened, but not soaked, until growth is evident. This may mean watering twice a day where rainfall is sparse. At first, give light daily sprinklings, using a mist water spray so as not to wash out seeds. After 10 weeks, start irrigating more heavily: established lawns should be watered only when thoroughly dry, then given enough to penetrate deeply, to encourage root growth.

Like other plants, healthy lawn grass needs a sturdy foundation and a loose porous soil into which air, water, and roots can penetrate, along with an adequate supply of rich, natural food. While good grass can overcome many obstacles, it can't successfully compete against lifeless soil or an environment that remains constantly unfavorable.

You don't have to be an expert to grow a fine lawn. But you do have to adhere to sensible practices. In addition to caring for the soil, the construction of the lawn is crucial, including how it is graded and drained and how the seedbed is prepared. Your selection of grasses, and how and when they are planted, is also an important factor. Maintenance—which includes soil testing, fertilizing, mowing, watering, and the organic control of weeds, thatch, diseases, and insects—must be ongoing.

Choose grass seed carefully. No one type or mixture is ideal everywhere. The variety or blend that will do the best job for you depends on many factors: where you live, the type of soil you have, and how much sun or shade your lawn receives.

When fertilizing, keep in mind that the greatest lawn needs a balance of nutrients to spur healthful growth. Choose one of the many balanced organic lawn fertilizers now on the market. These fertilizers are richer, longer-lasting, and most importantly, ecologically safer than chemicals.

Rebuilding Your Worn-Out Lawn

If your lawn is only half-alive, it can be coaxed back to an allover, lush green growth by simply reseeding the worn-out areas in the spring or fall. Or if there are little bald patches in your lawn, a little time to repair them is all that is needed to make your neighbors "green" with envy.

Getting a Lawn

Reseeding worn-out or bare areas of your lawn

1. Cultivate bald areas to a 5-inch depth.

2. Rake smooth.

3. Spread compost and mix with soil. Rake smooth again and top with soil.

4. Fertilize with a spreader.

5. Sow seed by hand or spreader.

Most importantly, your patching efforts can save you up to 50 percent of the time and energy it would take you to rebuild an entire new lawn from scratch.

When the weather is right and the soil not too wet, dig into those worn spots with a spading fork. Sink the fork to a 5-inch depth with your foot and, as you lift out the soil, flip it over and let it drop with a force that will break up large lumps. Cultivate each bald area in this way, then rake them all smooth, removing any sticks and stones that might have come up.

Work a good amount of compost into the areas you have cultivated, mixing it with the soil. The more compost you can work in, the better. Your careful toil will pay off next summer by giving your seed beds moisture-holding qualities during dry periods that your area may experience. Rake the areas smooth, and top them off with the soil from your existing lawn.

You can now give your entire lawn its usual organic spring feeding, with the proper organic lawn fertilizer (see "Fertilization" on page 241). Make sure your organic fertilizer is spread over your worn areas as well, using a spreader, to prepare them for the sowing that is to come.

Be sure you use a high-quality lawn seed mixture to reseed the worn-out areas. If you have large-enough spots, use your seed-spreader to put down your seed; otherwise broadcast the seed by hand, first going north-to-south, then east-to-west, to make sure the patch is covered evenly. About 10 seeds per square inch is ideal.

Use a metal rake to lightly sow the seeds into the soil, and tamp the soil firmly with the soles of your shoes, a roller, or the end of the rake.

The next step, watering, is one of the most important in encouraging your seeds to sprout. Use a fine spray, and once you start irrigating your seeded areas, make sure they are not allowed to dry out. Otherwise, the seeds will not germinate and your efforts will have been in vain. The seeds will require daily watering until they become strong and lush. In about 7 to 21 days you will see green fuzz appear, and with coaxing it will continue to grow.

To protect your seed areas against children or dogs, cover them with a light straw mulch or floating row-covers. Should your established lawn require mowing before your wornout spots are filled in, mark off the newly seeded areas with stakes and string as a protective measure.

Another good reseeding trick is to spread seed over bare spots during the winter, when they are frozen hard. Subsequent freezing and thawing will work the seed down, and it will start growing by early spring.

Reseeding bare spots can rescue your carpet of grass, giving you a full, green cover with half the work. All it takes to keep your lawn handsome and healthy is adequate ventilation and drainage, plus good soil structure, the right seed, and organic lawn fertilizer.

If you are planting a new lawn this fall or rejuvenating an old one, get down to grass tacks. Do it right from the start, for an organic lawn you can really live with.

Fall Feeding

Lawn care can be a burden, especially for the home gardener who doesn't want to be weeding and feeding the lawn when his beans are ready for harvesting or he has to do battle with potato bugs. When fertilizing organically,

1 fertilization a year can be ample for healthy soils. It is best to do this in the fall. The cooler days and nights are better for root development than the warm spring days that prompt a flush of heavy top growth.

Fall fertilizing encourages plants' roots to develop both sideways and deeper into the soil. The roots obtain nutrients from a wider area; thus, they build reserves that are a basis for good growth the next year. An organic fertilizer blended specifically for lawn application, such as an N–P–K of 12–8–6, 10–8–4, or 8–2–4, is preferable to an all-purpose fertilizer of 5–10–10 or 10–10–10.

Organic lawn fertilizers are best applied at the rate of 1 pound of pure nitrogen (N) per 1,000 square feet of lawn. This means that a 50-pound bag of 12–8–6 organic lawn fertilizer, which contains 12 percent or 6 pounds of nitrogen, will cover about 6,000 square feet.

Most lawn fertilizer spreaders are calibrated to spread 1 pound of nitrogen per 1,000 square feet, if you set the number on the discharge opening to correspond to the percentage of nitrogen in the fertilizer that you are applying.

If you are in doubt about the settings on your spreader, mark off a 1,000-square-foot area of lawn. Weigh out the appropriate amount of fertilizer (so that it contains the equivalent of 1 pound of actual nitrogen), and experiment with the settings on your spreader to see how much fertilizer is discharged. For example, for a 50-pound bag of 12–8–6 organic fertilizer, which contains 6 pounds of actual nitrogen, you would use $1/6$ of a bag or about 8.3 pounds.

Start with a small discharge opening (you can enlarge it if you have fertilizer left over). If you see that you start running out of fertilizer before covering 1,000 square feet, reset the opening to a smaller calibration.

Alternative Lawns

An alternative lawn utilizes ground covers that either work with or replace grass to reduce or eliminate lawn work and add variety. Low-growing plants that have good strong root habits, plus the ability to spread and hold down soil without getting big and out of hand, are collectively referred to as "ground covers."

A number of such plants have been combined to produce ecologically sound lawn mixes: Herbal and floral mixes are two of the most popular. They usually include nitrogen-fixing plants, such as clover; plants that stay green in hot weather; plants that do well in cool weather; and some support plants. The latter act as fillers until the other plants get started, lasting only until the herbal or floral lawn is established, and then dying or becoming crowded out. Many of the plants in these mixes flower at least once a year, making them much more colorful than grass; and most of these mixes need less mowing than pure grass, as well as requiring less fertilizer and no pesticides.

Herbal Lawn Mixes

A blend of slow-growing dwarf grasses and herbs like chamomile, sweet alyssum, yarrow, and strawberry clover has an appealing combination of textures and releases a sweet fragrance when mowed (note that both yarrow and sweet alyssum are flowering herbs that are included in both herbal and floral mixes). An herbal lawn needs less water and fertilizer than grass alone, and you only have to mow once every 3 to 4 weeks.

To create an herbal lawn, you don't have to start from scratch with bare soil. You can seed white clover into an existing lawn to provide nitrogen that will fertilize the grass. Use an inoculated, locally adapted clover variety and rake out any grass thatch before seeding it in early fall.

The soft, dense carpet of Roman chamomile's fine yellow-green foliage is not unlike Irish moss in appearances. But while Irish moss can't take traffic and is used mainly to fill the space between stepping stones on a path, chamomile takes wear well enough to *be* a path. Undisturbed, chamomile can grow to be about 9 inches tall, but light foot traffic keeps it low enough to make mowing unnecessary. And the yellow-centered flowers that rise above the mat add an interesting touch. It's fast to spread too; individual plants that are set in place 6 inches apart will fill in solidly in a single season.

Sweet alyssum is a good ground cover that is tolerant of dry soil and attractive in bloom. Once established it reseeds itself well.

Thyme isn't just for the kitchen anymore: Several types make for great ground covers as alternative lawns. They grow low, spread quickly, and sport flowers ranging from light lemon yellow to deep grayish green. Originally native to dry regions, most thymes not only grow well in dry, poor soil, they absolutely require such hardships to develop their best flavor.

Yarrow, a component of some alternative lawn mixes, can also be grown as a lawn all by itself. Yarrow can withstand light foot traffic; plants in well-traveled areas will simply be smaller than elsewhere.

Woolly yarrow has especially attractive small silvery plumes, and its soothing scent could well make lawn mowing a pleasant experience.

Floral Lawn Mixes

Here you can fill your lawn with the tiny, colorful flowers of baby-blue-eyes, pink English daisy, sweet alyssum, and yarrow amidst slow-growing dwarf grasses. After mowing, most of the flowers rebloom within 5 days. This is a beautiful look that's easy and economical to care for. Just think of all the money you will save, the chores you can skip (yearly thatching and aeration), and the toxic lawn chemicals you can avoid.

Partial shade, rich moist soil, and plenty of water are what violets need, so they are not the right choice for every yard. But for a ground cover with delicate, sweet, old-fashioned fragrance, they are hard to surpass. Violets are clump formers: The deeper the shade, the farther apart the clumps. They spread very well, both by creeping runners and profuse seeds. Despite their name, they also come in shades of blue, pink, white, and yellow.

Other Ground Covers

You are probably familiar with such common, reliable ground covers as myrtle, pachysandra, and English ivy. They all form tight mats within a few years after planting, and myrtle has pleasant little blue flowers rising above its dark, shiny leaves in spring. All of them are quite easy to propagate by lifting and dividing, so you need only a moderate number of plants to get started. Once established, ground covers like these can take the place of grass in shady areas where lawns struggle or will not grow.

Quite a few herbs can be grown as independent ground covers, including mother-of-thyme, which grows to about 1 inch high with small purplish flowers that bloom all summer. It will thrive in either sun or shade, stays a long time once established, and is easily propagated by dividing.

There is also creeping speedwell, which grows to about 4 inches in a mossy, prostrate mat in sunny places. Its blue flowers come and go in May, and can be very attractive when planted with spring bulbs. Speedwell will seed itself, or you can propagate it by dividing.

Easy division of these plants begins with a sharp-edged trowel or spade, which you thrust down to sever the rooted shoots, suckers, or offshoots of the mother plant. It is rarely necessary to slice through the main plant as you do in dividing perennial clumps. Since the little plantlets are very sensitive to shock, take up all of the roots that you can, and transfer them to well-prepared ground. The best time to do this is early spring, but if the soil is moist enough, you must be sure that there is enough growing time left before frost for the transplant to reestablish itself well.

Cuttings are a favorite method for propagating. Easiest are plants like English ivy or moneywort. Cut a length of 2 or more nodes off the top of a stem and insert in a good rooting medium like moist sand, or a 50–50 mix of sand and peat moss. Cuttings from shrubby plants like thyme, called "softwood" cuttings, are taken from the current year's growth when they snap easily if you bend them. Take lengths of about 6 inches, but see that there are at least 2 nodes or places where buds form on each stem. Remove all the lower leaves to reduce transpiration and loss of water, and put the end in the moist rooting medium up to the second node.

LAND OF THE LAWNLESS

For those who have very limited garden space, why not do away with a lawn entirely? Turn your whole yard into fruit, vegetable, and flower beds. Or you can dig circles here and there and set such handsome food plants as tomatoes, green peppers, or onions in them. That way you can have your lawn and eat it too.

As soon as you feel the tug of roots when you try to pull out the cuttings, it is time to transplant to a richer growing mixture containing more garden soil, or to put the new plants out in the garden where you want them.

Ground covers are so attractive that they sometimes look good enough to eat. In fact, if you want to, you can grow blueberries or box huckleberries anywhere you can keep the soil acid enough to suit them. Along many roadsides and steep embankments you may see tall ground covers of fine edible daylilies, whose early shoots are so tender and tasty, and whose buds and flowers make good eating.

How to Control Crabgrass Organically

Lawn weeds were not always such a problem. Before the days of power mowers and suburban developments the average person confined their grass-producing efforts to a small patch in front of their house, which they would liberally dose with manure donated by the family horse or cow.

An occasional cutting with a scythe or sickle allowed the grass to grow at a reasonable height. "Good" lawn grasses grew well on this plot because a healthy, fertile soil gave them the strength they needed to crowd out weeds.

The real secret of crabgrass control is contained in this simple formula: Crabgrass and

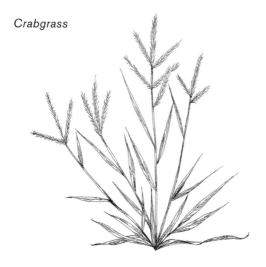

Crabgrass

lawn grasses thrive on different sets of growing conditions. You can encourage the weed, or discourage it by altering its environment.

Lawn grasses require fertile soil, preferably no less than 6 inches deep and rich in humus. They need to be cut properly; perennial ryegrass, one of the most common "good" grasses, grows 6 feet high in its normal habitat. When trimmed down to 1 to $1^1/_2$ inches, it will not flourish. So, during the hot summer months when weeds take hold, trim your grass to a height of 3 inches. Also, at this time of the summer you should spray your lawn with a micronutrient foliar spray (fish and seaweed mix) 2 times a month in July and August.

Crabgrass has a different set of likes: It only grows well in poor, undernourished soil. Crabgrass cannot compete with lawn grasses planted in fertile soil. Also, it likes to grow low to the ground, and is not stunted by low

CRABGRASS CONTROL

1. If you have a lawn sweeper, use it after several midsummer mowings to pick up crabgrass seeds that will sprout next year.
2. Put the clippings in your compost pile.
3. Aerate your soil as much as possible; don't be afraid to really shake up your soil because air and moisture are needed below the surface to give encouragement to good grass roots.
4. Have your lawn's soil tested so you will know how to balance the right nutrients in the soil to feed your lawn's needs (see "Fertilization" and "Liming" on pages 241 and 242).

5. Now comes the most important step, the creation of a good soil structure. I cannot stress enough how important it is to improve soil tilth and structure. The only practical way to do this is to spread 1 inch of compost in early spring, and again in the fall. In addition, use an organic lawn dethatcher in spring and fall. This way thatch is broken down, decomposed, and turned into rich organic matter. Note: The more organic matter in your lawn, the less watering it will need.

mowing. Quite the contrary, low mowing gives crabgrass the room it needs to spread out and grow strongly.

The program is simple. Work to make your lawn a better place for the good lawn grasses to grow.

Crabgrass begins sprouting in early spring and grows very slowly until the hot days of July and August, which is when most homeowners notice they have a problem. A product you may want to try, called A-Maizing Lawn™, is an organic preemergence weed control. A by-product of corn syrup, its main ingredient is also used in pet food and chicken feed—which means your kids and pets can play on the lawn right after you apply it (see page tk for application instructions).

Soon after sprouting, weeds send out secondary feeder roots, which are especially adept at drawing nutrients from the soil. A-Maizing Lawn stops these feeder roots from developing, and seedlings quickly die. Apply this only twice a year and control emerging crabgrass and other lawn weeds without using toxic chemicals. Note: For more information on this product call Gardens Alive at 812-537-8650.

The Organic Lawn: No Diseases, No Chemicals

Organic lawn methods can prevent or limit disease and pest attacks before they destroy your lawn. If it is healthy and self-sustainably strong from the start, your lawn will throw off these attacks successfully.

Don't overpamper a lawn with extra waterings that it doesn't really need, or booster feedings of fertilizers that make it too easy for grass plants to get their food. When this happens (and it happens all too frequently) your lawn doesn't develop strong, deep-delving roots that reach out into the soil for the nutrients that are available there.

Fighting Lawn Disease

Don't be too concerned with drought and its possible effects on your lawn. Almost all midsummer fungal lawn diseases are caused by overwatering. Grass plants require more air and oxygen during hot, dry summer days. But in the humid midsummer, the air is moist and the grass is covered much of the night and part of the day with clinging, strangling droplets of moisture. The soil itself can be clogged with water, choking off the roots by depriving them of air.

Causes of Lawn Fungal Disease

There are two lawn diseases that can be relieved by water; gray leaf mold and fairy ring (which can be accompanied by miniature toadstools). Other fungal diseases—such as brown patch, leaf spot, dollarspot, snow mold, and pythium blight—have many possible causes. These include: poor circulation of air over the lawn, waterlogged soil or poor soil drainage, overstimulation of grasses with fertilizers during the summer, thatch buildup, strong soil acidity, and inadequate root systems caused by overfeeding and scalping (mowing the lawn too short). Use disease suppressive organisms for all (see "Microbial Disease Control" on page 258 for specific instructions). Lawns should be mowed once a week at 3 inches using a mulch mower.

Correcting poor soil drainage and maintaining adequate aeration build a strong healthy lawn because these practices encourage stronger, deeper grass roots, and top growth. Keep in mind that watering late in the evening may be good for the person who does the watering, but it is very bad for the lawn; the grass remains wet through the night, which directly encourages mold and fungus.

Close mowing is another mistake that encourages diseases. Such shaving weakens the grass, and facilitates the production of more succulent and tender leaf growth, which is vulnerable to fungus. Many diseases attack lower leaves first. But on lawns cut at the proper height of 3 inches, new leaves are formed as quickly as the lower ones are infected, and no permanent damage will ensue.

In addition, close cutting encourages shallow root systems because about 95 percent of all food taken in is absorbed by the grass blades through the process of photosynthesis. When you cut your lawn down to the soil line, food production virtually ceases, and the plants' root system is weakened.

Applying fertilizer to speed summer growth is another practice that can lead to lawn trouble. During the summer, tender young leaf blades are particularly vulnerable to fungus diseases because the prevailing temperature and moisture conditions favor their enemies. During the months of July and August you should spray your lawn with a micronutrient foliar spray 2 times a month to prevent summer brown-out in your lawn, but do not fertilize. (To make your own micronutrient spray, mix 3 ounces of fish and seaweed extract to every gallon of water.) Just fertilize in early spring with a 7–5–5 organic fertilizer, and again in the fall with 4–6–4 organic fertilizer. This stimulates growth during these two seasons when danger from disease is reduced.

It must also be stressed that adequate liming is a valuable aid in the prevention of diseases. Turf that is grown on acid soil is much more susceptible to disease disorders than a lawn that is raised on a pH of 7.0, a neutral base. When needed, use dolomitic limestone with 54 percent calcium and 42 percent magnesium.

Grubs and Their Rubs

If your lawn starts to wilt, turn brown, and die in patches during late spring or late summer, is it due to lack of water or could the problem be something else?

Give a tug on the grass plants. If they can be pulled up with very little resistance and the sod rolled back like a carpet, look closely at the root zone.

You will, most likely, find white or off-white colored worms curled into a C shape about 2 inches below the soil. These are grubs feeding on the roots of the grass.

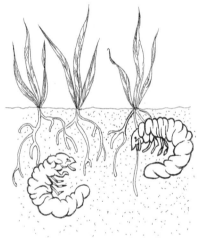

Grub

White grubs, an inclusive term for many different species, have hard brown heads, 6 legs immediately behind their heads, and a dark area in the rear. If they are mature, they can vary in length from $3/4$ to $1 1/4$ inches.

There are numerous lawn-infesting white grubs that are similar in appearance. Some of the most common are the larval stages of the May beetle, the masked chafer beetle, and the

Japanese beetle. It is important to know which one you are dealing with in order to control it.

Identification is made by looking closely at the "raster pattern," the arrangement of the spines on the underside of the last segment of the grub's body. You will have to uncurl the grub to see this pattern and maybe use a magnifying glass. Another way to identify the species is to put the larvae in a jar and see what type of adult emerges. Visit the library and compare your grub or beetle with the photographs in a good insect guidebook.

The time of year that a grub feeds is another clue as to its variety. The May beetle or June bug larvae feed at the grass root zone in the spring. The feeding usually begins in May and continues through early October, depending upon whether the larvae are first, second, or third generation.

Since the masked chafer also feeds during some of these same months in the spring and fall, categorization may be difficult. Visual examination of the raster pattern is important in this case.

Japanese beetle eggs hatch in late July and the larvae feed into August, September, and October. They feed again in April and May before emerging from the ground as adults.

First, decide if you really do have a problem. Your lawn can handle a small number of grubs if it is otherwise healthy.

Using a spade, cut a 1-foot square of sod on 3 sides to a depth of 4 to 5 inches. Then carefully fold it back, scraping the roots so that you can count the larvae. Do this in several places to determine where the infestation is heaviest.

Having fewer than 4 or more grubs per square foot in the spring might not do much damage to the lawn. However, during the dry weather of summer this number could cause damage to an already stressed lawn. If you find 10 to 12 grubs per square foot, you are probably already seeing large areas of brown, and action must be taken.

Organically there are 2 ways to go: milky spore disease; and a biological insect control that is safe for people, pets, and plants. The milky spore disease is totally harmless to the soil, water, beneficial insects, plants, animals, and humans.

If you are using the milky spore disease bacteria for Japanese beetles, you can apply this powdered treatment at any time except when the ground is frozen or the wind is blowing. Try to apply it as soon as you see the grubs in the spring or late summer. Sprinkle 10 ounces to every 2,200 square feet.

It will begin working when the environment is moist and warm. Milky spore is not a quick-acting insect control. It may take a season or two for its impact to show, but it will last for about 30 years.

Biological insect control employs the use of microscopic nematodes. They begin killing grubs within the first 24 hours after application.

Once the nematodes enter the insect pest, they release bacteria that kill the host. The nematodes then feed on the decaying insect, breeding and depositing their eggs. The new generation hatches and bursts out of the host insect to begin seeking out new prey and continue the lifecycle. To make your lawn less attractive to grubs, keep it thatch-free. Water deeply and infrequently to encourage deep root growth. Use a good balanced organic lawn fertilizer and raise the mowing height for summer to $2^{1}/_{2}$ to 3 inches.

A healthy organic lawn is the best defense against grubs.

COMPLETE ORGANIC MAINTENANCE PROGRAM

Here is a schedule, season-by-season, of how to maintain your organic lawn.

FALL PROGRAM

Start anytime from September 15 to October 25, later if weather is mild. First, take soil samples, as directed. Send them to us as soon as possible, so we can calculate the right feeding program.

Mechanical Thatching: This is a one-time-only procedure. Perform this before applying biological thatch control. By using biological thatch control every fall and spring, your lawn will never need mechanical thatching again. Apply biological thatch control when soil temperatures are between 50 and 80°F.

Detoxification: Detoxify turf. This should be done if lawns have been maintained chemically in the past. The product we recommend is called Micatrol™. Number of applications will be determined by how toxic the soil is, according to a pollutants test. Normally, 1 to 2 applications over a 6-month period will eliminate all toxins. This procedure can be done either in the fall or spring, depending on when the lawn is started.

Plug Aeration: Plug aeration is the mechanical removal of plugs from your lawn to encourage deeper root growth and help maintain proper thatch levels in the lawn. Lawns should be plug aerated every fall and spring to increase oxygen flow to the roots of plants, eliminate compaction, and allow compost to be added to the soil to build up organic matter. It is important to use an aerating machine that actually pulls cores of soil out of the ground rather than simply punching holes into your lawn. Such machines can be rented or purchased through lawn-care centers. Rake up and remove plugs and add them to your compost pile.

Fill holes with compost. Note: Compost should be of good quality. In-vessel composting (made indoors) is the best because it is made in a controlled environment. If using wind-row made compost (compost arranged in long rows), make sure it was heated to the right temperature (160°F) to kill weed seeds, and that it has been covered so that wind-borne weed seeds are not present. Using top-quality compost is not only important to soil management, but also for weed control.

After top dressing lawn with compost, seed with 'White Dutch' clover at the rate of $1/2$ pound per 1,000 square feet. Inoculate seeds with nitrogen-fixing bacteria. 'White Dutch' clover provides free nitrogen for lawns (150 pounds of nitrogen per acre). Also, clover fixes nitrogen from the air—up to $1/3$ the amount of nitrogen your lawn needs. Clover sprouts fast and grows so dependably that it is a valuable aid in starting new lawns.

With drought resistant clover in your lawn, you will spend less money on organic fertilizers. Clover grows vigorously even in poor clay subsoil around new home construction. Also, mid-September is the ideal time to do over-seeding of lawn grasses, filling in the bare spots when necessary. Two to three weeks after seeds germinate, apply an organic preemergent for weed control (see A-Maizing Lawn™, on page 253).

Organic Weed Control: Organic preemergent weed control helps you control crabgrass, dandelions, and other pesky weeds. You can

continued

now weed and feed your lawn organically with just 1 application in the spring and 1 in the fall. A by-product of corn syrup production, organic pre-emergent weed control eliminates germinating weeds. By applying organic preemergent weed control in the early spring and fall, you can reduce germination of dandelions and other broadleaf weeds by as much as 90 percent. At the same time, you will provide your lawn with the complementary balance of nitrogen and other nutrients the grass needs for strong root growth, stress resistance, and a beautiful green appearance.

We recommend that you apply 10 to 20 pounds per 1,000 square feet when mild early spring weather encourages weed seeds to germinate. Yearly spring and fall applications at 10 pounds per 1,000 square feet provide even better control. Application rates as high as 80 pounds per 1,000 square feet will not harm your grass. In fact, the percentage of weed control increases with higher application rates. Water deeply after application. Pre-emergent weed control is granulated for use in either drop or broadcast spreaders. It is not toxic to humans or pets. People and animals can enter the treated area immediately after application.

Microbial Monitoring: Turf samples should be analyzed for living components to determine the correct microbial ratios and rates of disease-suppressive organisms required. For monitoring, we recommend using BBC Laboratories or Soil Food Web, Inc.

Microbial Applications: About 2 weeks after applying the organic pre-emergent weed control, foliage-spray turf area with microbial concentrate and enzymes every spring and fall.

Organic Feeding Program: Apply fall fertilizer as recommended by soil test, and lime if needed (see "Liming" on page tk).

FALL AND EARLY WINTER CARE
September to December
Shrubs: Foliage-feed using Drammatica Fish Kelp™ or Kelp Plus™ on shrubs. Also use a leaf mulch (shredded leaves are better than grass clippings) placed around shrubbery to prevent winter evaporation. Monitor soil moisture around plants; water if necessary. Soil should have a 35- to 40-percent moisture content. Feed all acid-loving shrubs using cottonseed meal at the rate of 5 pounds per 100 square feet.

Trees: Fall and spring is the time for root-feeding your trees. Make 4 holes (north, south, east, and west) 2 to 3 feet from the tree trunk, around the tree. Make the holes 18 inches deep and 1 inch wide. Mix Drammatica Fish Kelp™ or Aggrand™ at the rate of 4 ounces to 1 gallon of water. Pour 1 quart of this mixture down each hole, and then pack the holes with compost. Compost will slowly release nutrients and build up organic matter. Place holes in different spots each year around the tree.

When trees become dormant in winter, spray them with lime–sulfur dormant oil. This suffocates insects and their eggs, and destroys any fungus disease organisms present that may winter over in the cracks and crevices of the tree. Follow this procedure in mid-March also.

SPRING PROGRAM
March to April
March 10–20, apply lime–sulfur dormant oil to trees. Remove winter mulch from around shrubs and compost mulch. Top dress compost around

continued

shrubs and beds at a rate of 2 pounds per square foot (a 2-inch layer).

April

Spring cleanup, root feed trees. Trees also benefit from mycorrizhal inoculant for root-zone injection. MycorTree™ mycorrhizal injectable tree and shrub inoculant combines a proprietary "cocktail" of spores of beneficial endo- and ecto-mycorrhizal fungi with natural wetting properties of yucca plant extract to achieve rapid, effective inoculation of trees and shrubs. It is designed for use with soil injection equipment and is effective for all tree and shrub species except rhododendrons, azaleas, and laurels. This product is available from Plant Health Inc., at 516-338-8786.

Foliar-spray shrubs with fish–seaweed mix. Plug aeration and top dress turf with compost, adding organic matter to the soil.

Mid- to Late April

Apply organic preemergent weed control, biological thatch control, and organic fertilizers as recommended for your particular garden or property.

Mid-May

Starting at this time, shrubs, perennials, and small trees should also be foliage-sprayed with fish kelp–micronutrient preparation once every 30 days, ending in mid-September or early October. Note: After following this feeding program for shrubs, if there are any problems or lack of vigor and growth, take soil samples and send them in for analysis.

Early to Late May

Apply insect control, first year only. It will keep working as long as no chemicals are used.

Insect Control: Apply milky spore disease powder at the rate of 10 ounces per 25,000 square feet. Milky spore is a naturally occurring microscopic bacteria (*Bacillus popillae*) that kills grubs, including Japanese beetle larvae, before they grow into ravenous adults. Simply apply the powder in a grid pattern on your lawn, making your lawn environment lethal to grubs. It continues to work for up to 30 years, with just 1 application, and is safe for people, pets, and beneficial soil organisms. Also apply parasitic nematodes at the rate of 250 million per 8,000 square feet for controlling grubs, chinch bugs, sodweb worms, and 250 other soilborne insects. First year application only.

Microbial Disease Control: Apply biological fungicides and parasitic fungi. Biological fungicides and parasitic fungi are beneficial microbes, disease-suppressing organisms that protect turf from soilborne pathogens such as pythium, botyrtis, fusarium, phytophthora, and more. These are nontoxic, environmentally safe products that contain live strains of beneficial soil fungi and bacteria that colonize plant roots to provide preventive biological protection against harmful soilborne diseases. Only when absolutely necessary, use mineral fungicides. While these products are considered safe and acceptable for organic production, we feel they should be used only as a last resort. Most fungus disease problems can be corrected with biological fungicides or cultural modifications, such as growing resistant varieties, irrigation, humidity management, plant and soil nutrition, etc. Note: Biological thatch controls, applied in spring and fall, eliminate an unhealthy soil environment where diseases breed and turn thatch into organic matter.

continued

Late May to Early June

Microbial Application: Foliage-spray turf area with microbial concentrate and enzymes every spring and fall.

SUMMER PROGRAM

Starting in late May and every 18 days through June, July, August, and ending in September, foliage-spray turf, using the micronutrient Drammatica Fish Kelp™. By following this procedure, you will eliminate the stresses that cause summer brown-out, and keep your lawn green and healthy throughout the hot, humid months. It will also allow you to cut back on irrigation.

Mid-June

Take tissue samples for nutrient analysis and send to Agri-Balance for interpretation. This is part of their feeding program evaluation. Agri-Balance is a nonprofit educational outreach program that converts chemical lawns, gardens, and farms to 100 percent organic methods. It was founded by the authors of this book in 1985. We offer a free helpline at 516-725-5725.

July to August

Apply biological fungicides once a month in the first year and every third year thereafter, to maintain microbial balance against fungus pathogens.

Mowing: I recommend that lawn should be mowed at 3 inches all the time and never cut more than $1/3$ of the grass height. Mowing should be done once a week or once every 2 weeks, depending on rate of growth. I also recommend the use of a mulching type mower; if using a regular mower, leave grass clippings lay. Always use a sharp blade that cuts, not rips, grass blades. The best time to mow is late afternoon, 5 P.M. until dark. Rotate mowing directions; the first week go straight up and down; the second week, from side to side; the third week, up and down at a 45° angle. Maintain this rotation system. "Preventing a problem is the best solution." After each mowing, spray the undercarriage and wheels of your mower with a 5-percent-Clorox and water solution. This will prevent disease pathogens from spreading from one lawn to the next.

Irrigation: You must monitor soil moisture levels, compaction, and water retention. Depending on the amount of rainfall and organic matter content in the soil, you should water only once a week for 3 to 4 hours an area (approximately 4 inches of water penetration). During hot dry weather in July and August, water every fourth day, 3 to 4 hours at a time, to a 4-inch penetration of the root system. The best time to water is from 6 A.M. to 10 A.M., or if that is not possible, from 4 P.M. to 8 P.M. Never water between the hours of 11 A.M. and 4 P.M.: Because of high plant transpiration during the afternoon, 50 percent of the moisture will return into the atmosphere and you will only waste water. As there are many different types of soil conditions, you must adjust your irrigation methods to suit your needs. Note: There is portable testing equipment available for monitoring moisture levels and water retention, and also for testing soil compaction. The equipment can be bought at gardening centers or through supply catalogs.

CHAPTER 18

Tree Techniques

Trees should be fed, just like your vegetable-producing and ornamental plants. Fall through early winter is the time to do this.

It doesn't matter what kind of trees you have—whether they are nut, fruit-bearing, evergreen, or deciduous ornamentals, get out your soil amendments and make up your own organic fertilizer. If you don't want to mix your own cottonseed meal, granite dust, kelp meal, fish meal, bone meal, compost, and rock phosphate, you can buy a balanced blended organic fertilizer: I recommend those with N–P–K ratios of 4–6–4, 3–8–3, or 7–7–7. Either way, start feeding your trees.

Some people argue that most trees appear to do very well in the forest, where they obviously are not fed by anyone. The trees on your grounds, in your landscape, are growing in an artificial environment. It is up to you to make them feel at home by creating the conditions that they have been used to for thousands of years.

There is no turf or grass in the forest, only the forest floor, rich in decayed leaves and organic litter. Most homeowners install a healthy, vigorous lawn over their trees' root systems to rob them of the water and nutrients they need. Many organic gardeners haul away their leaves to the compost pile or spread them around smaller plants.

This is what your trees are up against: loss of the growing conditions that they require in order to flourish in a healthy state, plus competition from plants that normally do not grow in the forest. But, admittedly, the beauty of trees greatly enhances your property, so it is up to you to keep them happy and well by giving them the nutrients they need.

Deep-Feeding

Since a tree's root system cannot reach out for nutrients quickly and efficiently like a vegetable or flowering plant, *you* have to help the tree eat. Primarily it's a matter of placing organic fertilizers where the roots can reach and absorb them.

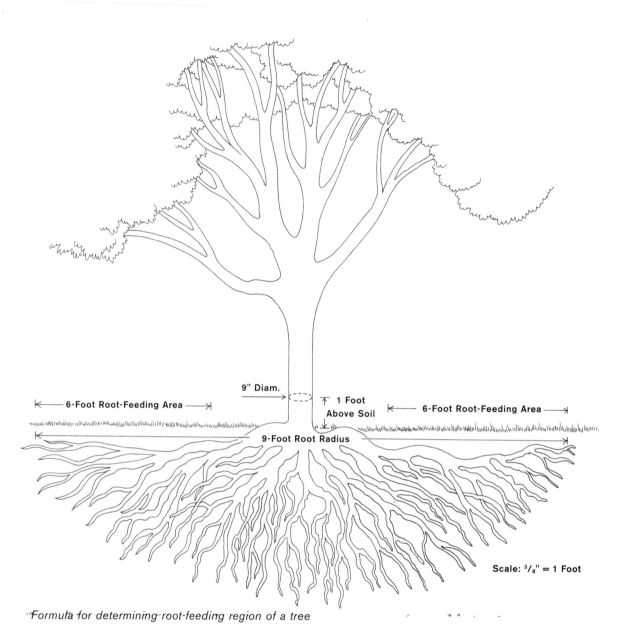

Formula for determining root-feeding region of a tree

Nutrients are absorbed by the smallest roots. The feeding roots usually occupy the outer band of a circular area whose circumference lies just beyond the spread of the outermost branches. The width of this band is equal to about $^2/_3$ of the radius of the circle.

With most trees, few feeding roots lie within the $^1/_3$ of the circle closest to the center. A rule-of-thumb method for determining the root-feeding region is as follows: The radical spread of the entire root area in feet is equal to the diameter of the tree (1 foot above the soil) in inches. For example, a tree whose diameter 1 foot above the ground is 9 inches will have most of its roots within a 9-foot radius from its center, and its feeding roots in the outer 6-foot-wide band.

My method of feeding a tree calls for making holes in the sod or turf and then placing the organic fertilizer in the holes 12 to 15 inches down, close to the tree's feeder roots. I believe that broadcasting (surface fertilizing) fertilizer to trees, except the shallow-rooted evergreens, is a waste of time and money. By thickening the turf, broadcasting also tends to lessen the tree root's water and air supply.

PRO-FEEDING

The standard professional method of tree feeding is to thrust food below the soil to where the roots run, or even lower, to attract roots downward and improve their grip on the ground. When the tree is large (too big to foliar-spray), a series of holes is tapped in the ground, north, south, east, and west at the tree's dripline (the area below the outermost circumference of the branches). I punch the 12- to 15-inch holes into the soil with a 3-foot pipe or crowbar, spacing them at 2-foot intervals. The holes are filled with such organic nutrients as rock phosphate, fish, and kelp meal and then plugged with compost. This method may be strenuous, but it will bring the kind of results that you want.

Besides fall–early winter root-feeding, you should foliar-spray at 3-week intervals with micronutrient spray (fish-seaweed mix) throughout the spring growing season. Mulching with straw, pine needles, or leaves is also a recommended fall practice, particularly with evergreens. Such mulches prevent wide fluctuations in soil temperature and help the soil hold moisture. The mulch can be left on all winter and then worked into the soil in the spring.

Revival of the Fittest

Many a weeping, suckering (suckers, or "water sprouts," are shoots that sprout out of the trunk and roots that suck energy out of the tree), and mournful-looking fruit tree can be easily rejuvenated with a little patience, good old elbow grease, a lot of sweat, and a bit of skill. Still, some are just not worth saving. Before you get out the pruning saw, take time to examine the tree carefully.

The first thing that I look for is the state of the trunk. Is it hollow, broken, rotten, or split? The trunk has to be able to support heavy crops of fruit and hold the tree upright even in the strongest winds.

Many older trees may have branches that have already split, when the tree's trunk rotted because of improper pruning decades earlier. When faced with such a tree, look at the upright portion carefully to see if it is centered enough to be restored to an evenly balanced canopy.

Check for early signs of a rotten trunk. By tapping the trunk with a board, you can hear rot before you can see it.

Get a section of a 2 × 4 that is about 3 feet long. Swing it out 2 to 3 feet and tap the trunk with the narrow side. Do this firmly, but not enough to take off chunks of bark. On a solid, firm trunk the tap causes a ringing sound. Trees with some rot make a more hollow-drum, thumping sound.

If more than about 60 percent of the wood is dead or diseased, the tree may not have enough vigor to force new, healthy growth. In the winter when the tree is dormant, it is often difficult to tell healthy wood from dead wood. I look for peeling bark; a dull, instead of a glossy, sheen to the younger bark; beetle and borer holes; broken branches that expose dead wood; and dry, crumbly fruit buds and spur clusters, instead of firm buds that are green when rubbed off.

When in doubt, make a slight cut with your pruning saw. Then look for the distinctive green color of the cambium cells just below the bark's surface, which indicate live wood.

Pruning Diseased Trees

Some diseases, like fire blight, damage the tree much farther into the limb than is visible. Fire blight bacteria cause twigs to blacken and sometimes ooze dark brown sap. This sappy exudate is very different from that typical of injured bark; sap from a bark injury is usually a large, clear amber glob.

When removing branches destroyed by fire blight, cut 12 to 18 inches farther back into the older wood than the visible damage. Dip your pruning shears in a solution of 10 percent bleach and water after every single cut. Trees overcome with fire blight are best burned to destroy disease spores.

The first step in any pruning situation is to remove all of the dead, damaged, and diseased wood. Also, keep an eye out for branches that cross, as rubbing can produce an open wound that becomes an easy entry for pests and diseases.

I usually start by climbing into the center of the tree and removing limbs from the bottom up, cutting myself a hole in the thicket of branches as I go. That way I can throw down the limbs through the hole as they are cut.

If you set up a ladder and start at the top, the cut branches get hung up in the tree and you end up with a horrible tangle. Starting at the outside edge creates more work; you make lots of little cuts, only to discover that one big cut near the center would have done the job more quickly. I use a pole pruner to pull down branches that don't fall to the ground, so I seldom need a ladder.

When removing large branches, be sure to make 3 cuts. Make the first cut on the underside of the limb about 6 to 12 inches from its base; saw it halfway through. Make the next cut through the branch from the top, 2 to 4 inches out from the first cut. This will prevent the falling limb from stripping bark off below its point of attachment to the trunk or another limb.

After the limb has fallen, make a final cut to remove most, but not all, of the remaining stub.

Be very careful to leave the branch "collar" intact. There is a protective zone of chemicals in the collar that prevents rot from entering the heartwood of the tree. It also encourages healing of the wound without the use of pruning tars, waxes, or paints.

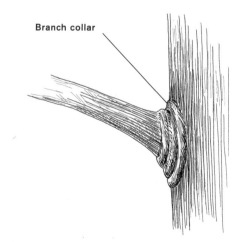

Take care not to cut into branch collar when pruning

Summer Timing

A renewal program for abandoned trees should begin with summer pruning, so as to avoid forcing too much new growth. Only after a year or 2 of thinning the canopy (by removing unwanted limbs in the summer) should you begin dormant (winter) pruning to force new wood that can be positioned for pruning.

Summer pruning is my personal preference. I like the dry, warm ease of summer pruning compared with the soppy wet, cold alternative. Like a good joke, "timing is everything" when you prune during the growing season. The removal of living leaves reduces the tree's carbohydrate production and storage areas. The following spring's growth is contingent on the amount of food stored during the previous year. When food storage is cut (literally) in the summer, the subsequent spring growth will be less.

The later you prune in summer, the less you restrict the following year's growth because more carbohydrates will have been stored away before the tree is cut.

With young trees—especially new dwarf fruit trees—excessive summer pruning results in stunted growth. The trees will never grow tall enough to support much fruit. On the other hand, abandoned fruit trees call for a healthy amount of stunting in order to lower the trees' height and allow more light to penetrate their canopies.

Summer pruning should be done as growth slows, because at this stage the flow of sap is reduced, preventing the formation of suckers. Where winters are early and severe, don't prune after the middle of August. In such climates, any new growth that might be stimulated by mid- to late August pruning

will be young and succulent when the first frosts occur and may freeze. Such dead wood becomes a possible entry point for insects and diseases. New shoots, formed earlier in the season, will have time to harden off enough to survive the winter's cold.

As with any pruning session, I first check for any dead, diseased, broken, or insect-riddled limbs that I may have missed during the previous pruning. Diseased or infested wood is burned. Always prune to leave those limbs that are already angling or arching on the outer fringe of the tree. This will encourage the tree to return more quickly to a fruitful state. Where there are hollow, open spots in the canopy, you will need to force new growth to fill them in. To do that, leave some large limbs unpruned and cut them back during the dormant season. When pruned in winter, even the oldest limbs will send out new shoots the next spring. The next summer, you can select 1 or 2 well-attached shoots growing into any empty, sunny spots to remain and prune out the extra shoots. If any new long shoot has already branched toward an open spot in the canopy, summer is the time to cut it off.

The last step is to look for any other dense spots in the foliage. I thin these with a pole pruner, which has both a clipper—operated by a long cord—and a saw. Whenever possible, use the faster, easier clipper rather than the saw to prune branches.

While walking around the tree, I look for places to trim the width of the canopy. Since standard-size trees need to have their limbs shaped to the side and toward a weeping form—curved and gracefully drooping—there is the risk that the tree will get too wide, causing the weight of the tree and its fruit to split the trunk apart. How wide is too wide? There is no rule. You will get a feel for it after looking at a lot of old trees, noting which have split.

After this first session of summer pruning, your tree should look noticeably shorter. The sky should be easier to see through the canopy and there should still be some limbs left over to be removed or thinned during the next season's pruning.

The tree's ideal form will not be entirely realized after the first 2 summer pruning sessions. It takes 2 to 5 years, trimming off roughly equal amounts of wood each year, to slowly shift your treasured tree back to its most beautiful and fruitful self.

Remember, successful pruning depends on timing, patience, and technique.

Christmas Shopping

Did you ever give any thought to growing a live Christmas tree?

Beyond the holiday consideration, there is much to be said for conifers. They add an air of permanence and maturity to the garden with height, depth, shelter, and privacy.

The trees are beautiful and functional, providing color in the landscape all year long, attracting birds to their shelter, and creating windbreaks. Once planted, conifers require little attention.

Before you make the leap to a living Christmas tree, however, you will have to do some planning. Select a planting site before you bring the tree home. Remember that most conifers grow extremely tall—up to 100 feet and more.

Don't buy a giant redwood if you live in the city with a small backyard, and don't plan on planting an evergreen tree near a house or neighboring property line. The roots could injure the foundation, drains, pipes, and walls. Keep in mind, also, that the tree might eventually shade your vegetable garden.

Ideally, you should plant the tree in a sheltered spot so that it won't be desiccated by winter winds. If you decide to plant in a windswept area, plan on erecting some sort of windbreak to protect the tree.

Dig a hole deep and wide enough to hold the root ball. If you like, pack the hole with leaves or mulch to keep it from filling with snow.

Expect to pay about the same for a potted tree as a premium cut tree. The ideal living tree should be 3 to 4 feet in height from the soil line to its crown. Although most nurseries sell potted conifers up to 15 feet tall, the smaller versions are much easier to move and plant.

Before you buy a tree, inspect the branches closely. You want uniformly distributed whorls (the rows of branches that encircle the stem) that are strong enough to support ornaments. Ideally branches should be dense with no large openings and the shape should gradually narrow from bottom to top.

If your kids are nagging you to get it into the house, even if Christmas is only a week away, don't give in to their demands. The tree should be acclimated slowly, spending a few days in the garage before being moved inside. A living tree should be indoors for no more than a week to 10 days. A longer stay in your warm living room could fool the tree into thinking that spring has arrived and new growth may begin to sprout. When you take it back out into the winter cold those new shoots will freeze, seriously damaging the tree.

I have found a way to satisfy the urge to decorate a new Christmas tree while it is still outdoors. Place the tree on the porch and trim it with popcorn and cranberry strings. Before you know it, your living tree will be decorated with living ornaments, too: birds.

Check the soil in the tree's pot at least once a week while it is outside. If it gets dry, add a little water—just enough to keep the root ball moist, but not soggy.

Once the tree is indoors, use a large plastic garbage bag to contain the tree's pot and to keep water from seeping onto the rug. The plastic also keeps the soil moisture from evaporating to some extent, but the tree still needs watering.

Once the ground is workable in the spring, plant the tree. That's it. You're finished. Your living Christmas tree requires little further care.

Unless your soil is especially poor, a 3- to 4-inch-thick layer of compost mulched over the root area should provide all of the nourishment that it needs for the first year.

Follow these instructions and one day early in the spring you will find new green growth at the tips of your conifer's branches. That will be a day that you will find almost as exciting as Christmas.

Attack on the Gypsy Moths

Is there any hope that nature will bring our woodland ecology back into balance before the gypsy moth spreads everywhere and annihilates the trees? The gypsy moth is an imported pest and has too few predators and diseases in America. Our woodlands are like an open field in which the gypsy moth is a wildfire.

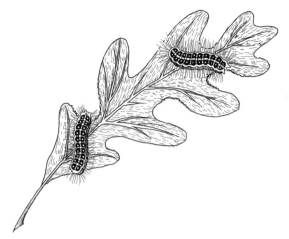

Gypsy moth caterpillars

Predators, many of them native, do play some role in reducing the population of the moth. Forty-five species of birds are known to include gypsy moths in their diets.

The best bird predators are the yellow-billed and black-billed cuckoos, crows, European starlings, redwing blackbirds, common grackles, brown-headed cowbirds, and chipping sparrows. Rodents like the white-footed mouse, chipmunk, mole, and squirrel also eat gypsy moth caterpillars. Clearly, these creatures aren't enough, but they do help.

Trees most likely to be attacked by the gypsy moth are oak, birch, willow, linden, basswood, apple, and other fruits and shrubs—more than 500 species in all. When mature, the caterpillars will eat evergreens, pine, spruce, and hemlock, if other trees are defoliated; but the mouths of young larvae are too small to penetrate evergreen needles.

From the time that the gypsy moths hatch until they are $1/2$ inch long, the caterpillars will swing by silken threads from trees and can be scattered by the wind to foliage as far as a mile away. The crucial control period is

ORGANIC GENERAL PREVENTIVE SPRAY PROGRAM FOR ORCHARDS AND FRUIT TREES

You will need the following supplies for this program: a sprayer device of at least 1-gallon capacity; lime-sulfur dormant oil; commercial insecticidal soap (Safer's Agrico-Chem™ is a recommended brand); a 20 percent fish–80 percent seaweed foliar extract (Kelp Plus™ is a good product); sulfur-copper–based or Bordeaux mixture fungicide; *Bacillus thuringiensis* (BT); Sunspray™ insect control; hydrated spray lime; baking soda; liquid copper; Basic H (a wetting agent); Epsom salts; and a surfactant (adhesive) to help materials stick to the leaves.

Late Winter

At least 3 weeks before the leaf buds begin to show, spray the entire tree with lime-sulfur dormant oil (3 ounces per gallon of water) to suffocate overwintering insects and any fungus diseases. Do not spray when temperatures are below 40°F, but trees should be sprayed by March 15.

Spring

Spray entire tree with insecticidal soap (3 ounces per gallon of water) to control aphids and scale. Also spray fish-seaweed extract (3 ounces to a gallon of water) to stimulate growth and reduce environmental stress; in fact, you can apply this fish-seaweed mixture after every time you spray your trees with dormant oil, soap, or anything else. At the least, give your trees an application of fish-seaweed extract the first and last week of every month from May to October.

When Blossoms Begin to Show Pink

Apply a sulfur-copper–based spray (1 ounce per gallon of water) to the entire tree. Use insecticidal soap with this mixture to make it stickier and to control aphids (add 3 ounces of insecticidal soap per gallon of spray). In addition, at this time spray trees completely with BT (1 tablespoon per gallon of water) to kill caterpillars. (Note: Do not mix sulfur-copper–based spray with BT or apply lime-sulfur when the tree is in blossom.)

During Early Bloom

About 7 to 10 days later, repeat above spraying technique.

During Bloom Period

Don't spray trees with any sulfur-copper organic fungicide. You can spray trees with BT (2 ounces per gallon of water) to control caterpillars.

At Petal Fall

About 7 to 10 days after full bloom, apply sulfur-copper–based spray (1 ounce per gallon of water). Two to three days later, spray BT for caterpillars. Use Sunspray insect control once a month from this point on to control insects (5 tablespoons per gallon of water) or whenever necessary.

Summer

Midseason

Spray trees completely every 10 to 15 days, using sulfur-copper spray (1 ounce per gallon of water) or Bordeaux mixture (2 ounces per gallon of water) to control fungal problems.

Before Harvest

Halt all spraying–except fish-seaweed mixture–30 days before harvest.

continued

Early Winter

Spray the entire tree with lime-sulfur dormant oil (3 ounces per gallon of water) to suffocate insects and destroy fungal diseases.

Pruning for healthy trees and high yields: Pruning is very important, and should be done during the winter months as long as the temperature is above 30°F.

ADDITIONAL PEST AND DISEASE CONTROL

Here are solutions for controlling other pests and diseases that are also detrimental to fruit trees and crops.

Apple Maggot

Hang up traps in June and leave until harvest. Set 2 traps per tree. The traps are red plastic spheres that can be purchased from most mail-order garden catalogs (such as Peaceful Valley, listed in the resources section at the back of this book).

Brown Rot Fungus

Apply a spray of 80 percent sulfur to entire tree, beginning when cherries are still green. Brown rot develops as the fruits begin to sugar. Reapply every 2 weeks until fruit is ripe.

Cedar Apple Rust

Blend 2 tablespoons of baking soda with 2 tablespoons of liquid copper and 2 drops of Basic H per gallon of water. Spray this solution once every 3 weeks, and after heavy rains.

Codling Moth

For maximum benefit, set moth traps out 2 weeks before bud break. Use 2 traps per tree. The traps are available through mail-order garden catalogs. Note: since codling moths hatch 3 generations per season, it is important to put out a new lure after 12 weeks.

Leaf Spot

Use a mixture of hydrated spray lime and 25 percent copper sulfate at a ratio of 6 tablespoons of lime to 3 tablespoons of copper per gallon of water. Begin at the appearance of the first leaf, then repeat every 2 weeks, continuing through harvest time.

Magnesium Deficiencies

If your soil test indicates a magnesium deficiency, every 6 weeks spray trees completely with a mixture of 2 tablespoons of Epsom salts and 2 drops of Basic H per gallon of water.

late April to early June, after the larvae reach $3/4$ inch long and begin eating leaves.

For those 6 to 7 weeks, spraying with BT (*Bacillus thuringiensis*) is extremely effective. Nontoxic to wildlife and people, this bacterial disease affects only caterpillars. Follow the label directions and apply to the leaves in liquid form at 10- to 14-day intervals, using a sprayer.

You may also want to try purchasing a batch of tachinid flies. The parasitic insects lay their eggs on leaves, which hungry gypsy moths consume. The eggs then hatch inside the caterpillars and the fly larvae eat their way out, killing their hosts.

In fall, winter, and early spring you can scrape off the tan-colored, furry, quarter-sized egg masses on tree trunks and limbs. Shape

FEEDING SCHEDULE FOR TREES

SPRING

Root feeding in the spring is crucial to a tree's health. Using either a soil auger or a hollowed-out pipe, make 4 holes approximately 12 to 15 inches deep at each point of the compass. Mix 3 ounces of Aggrand (a fish-seaweed micronutrient solution) or a similar product with 1 gallon of water. This will give you 4 quarts. Pour 1 quart down each of the 4 holes until they are filled, and pack them tightly with compost. Next, pile new mulch (straw or hay) 18 to 20 inches high around the dripline of the tree (make sure that the mulch does not touch the trunk). Apply Agway's Nature's Way Organic Fertilizer™ (4–5–4) at the rate of 2 pounds per tree around the dripline, plus a light dusting of dolomitic limestone (54 percent calcium and 42 percent magnesium), fish meal, bone meal, and kelp meal.

Note: According to spray program, spray entire tree with lime-sulfur dormant oil by March 15.

SUMMER

Foliage spray entire tree with Aggrand as recommended in organic spray program. Prune lightly if necessary. Keep the center of the tree open for good air circulation and sunlight penetration. Foliage spray with Epsom salts for magnesium deficiencies as recommended above.

FALL

Feed roots using the same method as in spring: Apply Nature's Way Organic Fertilizer (4–5–4), at the rate of 2 pounds per tree around the dripline, plus a light dusting of kelp meal, fish meal, and bone meal. Add winter mulch, maintained at a height of 18 to 20 inches around the dripline. Do not let mulch touch the trunk of the tree. After leaves fall, spray with lime-sulfur dormant oil to control insects and diseases.

WINTER

Prune trees before March 15—prune 2 inches off each branch to encourage fruit production. Keep the center of the trees open for sun and air circulation.

---

the open end of an empty coffee can to form a pointed lip. Use it to strip off egg mounds into the can. Destroy them in a mixture of detergent and water.

Although defoliated deciduous trees will grow a second set of leaves the same season, moth attacks heavily drain reserve nutrients in the roots. The new leaves grow in midsummer, when they should be full-sized and manufacturing food to be stored in the roots for the plants' survival during winter dormancy.

New leaf growth puts a second drain on the roots.

After several years of successive defoliation and draining of food reserves, trees become weakened and more susceptible to attacks by diseases and insects. If your trees were defoliated last year, fertilize them early next spring and again in July. Spread well-rotted manure, garden compost, or organic fertilizer over the root area and let the rain wash it in. Be sure that your trees get water during dry spells.

PART 5

Indoor Growing

Windows, kitchen counters, room dividers—even closets and cellar spaces—can, with the proper know-how, be converted into home mini-farms and gardens. Nature need not smile on you there, for neither season nor weather can affect your plants indoors. If you are a land-poor gardener you can also contribute to the health and nutrition of your family—as well as beautify your home. Resources and imagination cannot be limited by where you live.

CHAPTER 19

Interior Farming

In any season, but especially in winter, light is the prime factor that determines the crops that the indoor gardener can raise. Leaf and root crops need 4 to 6 hours of sun a day; fruiting crops should have 6 hours.

Not until the relatively recent introduction of special plant-growing lights has it been possible to grow vegetables indoors with any chance of real success. Even in the sunniest south window, the amount of light received during the winter's short days is inadequate for the heavy demands of annual vegetables, which must find sufficient energy to germinate, establish strong foliage, flower, set fruit, and bring it to maturity all in 120 days or less.

But artificial light can be a big help; even a north window will grow many kinds of vegetables, if a couple of fluorescent tubes are suspended over the plants and lit 16 hours a day during the darkest months.

Cherry tomatoes and long peppers can be grown in hanging baskets. Garden cress can be sown in shallow planters, and mustard can be grown the same way. Malabar and New Zealand spinach both stand heat and can grow well in overheated apartments. The European self-pollinating cucumbers are special indoor cukes that are long, slender, mild-flavored, and can be eaten skin and all.

Creating the Right Environment

One key to success with indoor vegetables is conditioning plants to interior use, if you wish them to respond favorably to abrupt changes in their surroundings. Certain physiological processes must be readjusted to reduce stresses during that transition period.

But conditioning alone is not the complete answer. You must also make every effort to provide an interior environment similar to the plant's natural environment. With proper conditioning and environmental engineering you can grow plants successfully indoors.

If you are bringing mature plants or seedlings in from your own garden or a nursery, select the time for the transition when your indoor conditions offer the least adverse environment—approximately 4 weeks before you turn on the heat. That way the plants adjust themselves to your home in two stages. The shock of going from outdoors directly into a heated house presents too many sudden stresses, often resulting in yellowing and drooping.

Examine outdoor plants for a healthy appearance and freedom from insects and disease. If a plant is very large and roots easily, try to root a cutting. Others with several crowns can be divided into smaller plants. Any that are small can be dug up directly. Large plants require some pruning to fit into containers of a reasonable size.

Once they are inside, pot them in good soil that drains well, has some established moisture retention, and releases nutrients slowly. Good drainage insures the entry of oxygen between soil particles for root respiration; moisture retention by soil particles supplies water to the roots and prevents rapid drying; and a slow release of nutrients produces the optimal nutrient level needed for growth. With balanced organic soil the plant will have one less stress on its system, thus helping it to cope better with other stresses.

Sunlight is not the only environmental factor that must be replicated. A daytime temperature in the neighborhood of 70°F and a nighttime temperature of 65°F, with a relative humidity of 50 percent will keep both you and your plants healthy.

Keep plants out of hot or cold drafts. If the humidity level is too low, consider a humidifier. Also, you can create a humid microclimate by grouping plants on wet pebbles so that the water level is not in contact with pot bottoms, but slowly evaporates around them.

Create a microclimate with pebbles on a tray

Water plants thoroughly until water seeps from the pots' drainage holes. Allow the top inch or so of soil to dry before watering the plant again, as would happen outdoors between rain showers. Fertilize plants weekly. You can use an all-purpose fish emulsion, mixed according to bottle directions given for houseplants, or you can feed them with a strong compost tea.

Germinating Seeds

Sprouting seeds don't need much light, at least until they grow their true leaves, so any out-of-the-way place that is cool and dim can serve as a germinating area. Succession cropping is the way to continuous peak production. Small sowings are advisable, and harvested plants should be immediately replaced with new seedlings, which take hold rapidly and are quickly ready for harvesting themselves.

Timing is the biggest challenge in indoor farming. The trick of serving heavenly home-farmed produce is harvesting most vegetables when slightly immature. Here is where the indoor grower has the advantage. Often, produce matures faster than the outdoor gardener can harvest or consume it, whereas the indoor plot can be tailored to produce the right amount at the right time.

Potted Tomatoes

You can start windowsill salads that last all winter by moving a tomato branch in a pot into your indoor garden. Just pot up 1 or more small, stocky tomato plants in the fall and bring them indoors to grow and bear all winter and spring.

Anyone with a properly mulched, weedless garden can create a stocky plant by cutting a branch off of a bearing tomato plant, placing it in a container of water and leaving it till roots appear, which takes about a week. The branch is then potted in a mixture of half compost and half garden soil. Alternatively, a branch still attached to the plant can be bent onto the ground with soil layered over a 3-inch section and left for 10 days. After roots grow, the branch can be cut from the larger plant and potted in the same compost–garden soil mixture.

I leave my potted tomatoes out in the garden for a few days, then bring them in on a warm day. It is best to bring them indoors for a week before the heat is turned on. The tomatoes are kept in a south window with flowering plants. They usually start blossoming in November and continue to bloom and bear tomatoes during the winter and spring.

I feed the plants with a diluted mix of liquid fish-seaweed emulsion every 12 days, but they do not regain their normal vigor until I open the inside south window, leaving only a ventilated storm window between the plants and winter weather.

The bane of most indoor tomato growers is an uninvited insect, the whitefly. There is a plant that repels this pest, though, and it is a good way to control it from the start. The plant is popularly called the shoo-fly plant or apple-of-Peru. A few kept in the house or greenhouse will dispel any whitefly infestation and discourage several other insects, too.

Blossoming and bearing tomatoes are heavy feeders. Mine require bone meal, mixed in near the surface of the soil during February and March. I water them with compost tea. Before they become too ungainly to move, I put them in the sink and shower them once a week.

When they show a tendency to grow too tall, I pinch the new growth or prune the plants. It is wise to remember that as houseplants, their root systems are quite limited compared to growth made in the outdoor garden.

To compensate for this, the tops should be pruned. By balancing stem and leaf growth, setting of fruit is encouraged and heavier bearing results. As the fruit becomes heavier, the plants need support. I tie them to a stake.

As for hand-pollinating, simply tapping the plants firmly so that the pollen scatters is generally enough. Do this several times as new blossoms appear.

My indoor-grown tomatoes do not bear very heavily, but the fruit is firm and has a good flavor and deep color. They are quite a contrast to the pale, tasteless tomatoes sold in the markets in winter. I pot 'Virginia Lady' (the vitamin C is double that of standard varieties) and sometimes 'Red Cherry', also high in vitamin C. Because of their delicious flavor, both are excellent in salads and the attractive fruit of 'Red Cherry' enhances the beauty of any fruit bowl. Cheerful yellow flowers, bright red tomatoes, and the green foliage of window plants show off strikingly against the cold skies just beyond the window.

In late spring, the plants can be transplanted into the garden, easily giving you the earliest tomatoes in the neighborhood. More vigorous plants, however, will result if branches are cut off to root in water. After they root, put them in flats filled with the potting mix to mature, and transplant them to beds when the weather is right. You then have a head start on your summer garden and do not have to sow or buy many new plants, if any.

A Windowsill for Watercress

Watercress is an ideal plant for windowsill culture for many reasons. It is easily grown from seed or cuttings, and does quite well even with limited sunshine. It does not need to float in water, as most people believe. Watercress may be cut back time and again and will always renew itself. It adds a very nice garnish to meats or may be used as a piquant addition to salads, and is rich in vitamins A and C, as well as calcium and iron.

Soil, obviously, must be extra nutritious, as the plant will depend upon only what you provide for it via the pot. Packed humus is a must. Woodstuff (a water-holding medium that can be purchased at garden centers) is excellent, but almost any kind of compost, leaf mold, or even peat moss will do. Watercress likes wet feet, and humus holds the moisture. In its native state, watercress usually gathers in pockets of leaf mold washed up along streams of moving water.

You can grow watercress easily from seed. Presoak the seeds for 18 to 24 hours before planting. Blot them on a piece of paper towel and sow thinly in a mixture of 60 percent humus, 10 percent sand, and 30 percent good garden loam. Also add several tablespoons of rock phosphate and 1 tablespoon of kelp meal or cottonseed meal. As watercress abounds in limestone regions, place a few small limestone rocks in the bottom of the pot.

After sowing the seeds, lightly sprinkle them with soil, gently water, then cover the whole pot with plastic kitchen wrap. Set the pot in a deep saucer to catch the excess water, and keep water in the saucer at all times. Place the potted seeds on the windowsill to germinate. When the seedlings are up, remove the wrap.

If you want faster results, use cuttings. Supermarkets usually have bunches of cress for sale. You can start your cress this way and it will grow quite rapidly.

Growing watercress from cuttings

Simply pick a bunch that looks fresh—no battered tops, bruised stems, or yellowed leaves. Make stem cuttings about 4 or

5 inches long and put in a jar filled with about $2^1/_2$ inches of water. If you can use well water or rainwater, by all means do so. Plants will root better in water minus the chemicals that are added to municipal sources for purification.

Change this water every day or so and keep the jar in sunlight or bright light. Some plants seem to make whiskers overnight and some make roots in 3 to 4 days. When the roots are about 2 inches long, pot the cuttings in the same mixture as you would for the seed. Water well and it won't be long before new growth starts.

The length of time before you can harvest your cress will depend on several factors, such as the size of the pot, soil fertility, and air temperature. They seem to do best in the cooler days of fall and winter. If the growth should start to slow down, a shot of fish emulsion or liquid seaweed fertilizer will revitalize it for a while.

Peppergrass (also called upland cress) will grow easily this way, too, with almost the same culture. The only differences are that it grows more quickly from seed, and does not require a constant saucer of water.

Try growing watercress—a plant for your windowsill that will cure the winter doldrums and can be eaten too.

Peppers Are Perennials

To prove that peppers are perennials, dig up the courageous plants and pot them into large juice cans with punched-in drainage holes. Place them in a sunny southwest window.

Transplanting will not set them back, and bell pods will continue to develop. As pollinizing insects are in short supply indoors, swirl a cotton-tipped swab lightly inside each blossom. To be sure to catch the pollen when viable, do each blossom twice. Those that are not successful will eventually fall over, while fertilized bells will display pea-shaped fruits. These will expand steadily like green balloons.

Once the green fruits start to turn red, they will cover the pod in a few days. Let the scarlet fruits hang for ornament, but not long enough to shrivel. Peppers can stay on the plant without losing flavor or freshness longer than any other ripe fruit.

Authorities list several reasons why pepper plants fail to bear fruit, including: an excess of nitrogen, too little light, bud drop caused by a prolonged dry hot spell, cold nights during flowering, or an insect bite on the blossom stem. Loss of leaf—caused by inadequate water, low light, and insects or disease—weakens the plant. New growth will appear when adverse conditions have been corrected.

White mites are a common problem with pepper plants. They usually appear without notice, announcing their arrival with silken webs that they weave all over the leaves, buds, and stem. Each industrious arachnid is the size of an ant's eyelash! To wash them away, place the plant under a flow of lukewarm water. Affected leaves lose their greenness, but plants eventually shed them and put out healthy new ones.

Whether indoors or out, peppers put forth a surge of bloom followed by pods, with blossoms reappearing before the first peppers are all harvested (not every blossom will produce fruit). A pepper grown indoors reaches $1/_2$ to $1/_3$ of the size it would attain in the garden, but it reaches that size fast and is edible from the beginning. Outside, it takes weeks longer for nature to ripen the fruit. Plus, the satisfaction you feel when you pick a fresh, homegrown pepper from your indoor garden (while looking out at snow-covered fields) is hard to surpass.

Mushrooms

Mushrooms are an ideal crop for organic gardeners. Mushroom boxes fit in small out-of-the-way spots, and, perhaps best of all, the main requirement for a good mushroom crop is expertise in compost-making.

The Common Mushroom

Cultural conditions for the common mushroom are best met by an indoor environment. A basement, a spare closet, or even a dark corner will do, as long as the space is well-ventilated and cool (below 70°F).

Many seed catalogs offer prepared trays or planters containing composted soil already impregnated with mushroom spawn (or mycelium, a mass of fungus threads), which are less trouble to care for than a bowl of goldfish.

Mushrooms don't demand total darkness. Though no direct sunlight should be on the beds, diffused light is often beneficial.

Humidity should be high and the beds always moist, but not soggy. The most desirable humidity level is somewhere between 70 to 80 percent and below 90 percent. Mushrooms will not thrive in dry, stuffy air.

Once you have grown your own mushrooms in these prepared trays or containers, you might want to try a more advanced project: building your own mushroom beds.

Mushrooms reproduce from spores, which are microscopic reproductive organisms corresponding to seeds. Unlike green vegetables, which manufacture their own starches from chlorophyll and sunlight, mushrooms must have a prepared medium containing organic matter and carbohydrates in which to grow.

Skillful composting provides a medium that is pasteurized as well as nourishing. The high temperatures created by the activity of bacteria in good composting kill off microorganisms that might otherwise compete with the desired mushroom species. Pasteurization is very important to success.

To make mushroom compost, mix fresh manure with equal parts of well-rotted humus. Add several handfuls of greensand, moisten it, and allow it to "cook."

Every 4 to 5 days, turn the pile and carefully check its heat with a thermometer. When the temperature is reduced to a steady 70°F and the strong ammonia odor disappears, fill the bed (see below), packing it firmly.

A good bed size for beginning production is 4 to 5 feet long, 12 inches wide, and 8 to 10 inches deep. Removable sideboards will provide an easy way of checking on the progress of the spawn growth.

Spawn for the common button mushroom is readily available in most reputable seed catalogs. It is a very specialized task to produce this product, and best handled by experts under strict laboratory conditions.

The spawn will often arrive in the form of a dried brick that can be broken into 1-inch pieces. These are planted at 2 inches below the surface of the compost, at 10-inch intervals through the bed. Beds are then leveled and tamped. From this point, the progress of the crop depends on careful regulation of temperatures.

The bed is ready for "casing" (a special type of soil used for mushrooms) when the mycelium that grows from the spawn appears in the manure along the side boards in spores shaped like half-moons, or when growth from the pieces of spawn meet. Then $1\frac{1}{2}$ inches of casing soil should be spread over the surface.

Casing soil should be a medium loam—slightly alkaline with low amounts of clay, sand, and organic matter. The loam must be kept slightly damp.

The mushrooms emerge in sudden groups, called "breaks" or "flushes," about a week apart. The highest yields come from these first 2 harvests, but 5 to 7 distinct flushes will break over a 2 to 3 month period. As stated above, mushroom production depends on temperature.

Temperatures slightly higher than the ideal (above 60°F) foster a fast but light total harvest. Lower temperatures (45 to 55°F) result in a longer cropping time and a larger harvest.

The mushrooms first appear as tiny pinheads, then grow to the button stage, and finally mature to full growth. A gentle watering from a nozzle with many small holes should be given to the bed as each flush is appearing.

The bed should be sufficiently moist by the time that the mushrooms reach the button stage, so that no further watering is needed until the break has been harvested. If the soil is too wet, air will be cut off from the spawn, preventing the production of mushrooms. If the soil is too dry, the mushrooms will die on the bed or develop under the surface and come up very dirty.

Mushrooms are harvested by grasping the cap lightly and twisting. A ripe mushroom twists off easily. If the mushroom is in a cluster, it is sometimes necessary to hold the cluster in place so that it isn't disturbed during picking.

Production of 2 pounds per square foot is considered good. One pound per square foot is poor productivity.

When all mushrooms are picked from a cluster, remove the cluster base from the soil.

All dead or improperly developed mushrooms should also be removed. This process is called "trashing" and is essential to producing a long crop. If this trash remains in the bed, it decays and sours, encouraging disease.

When the bed has ceased to produce in worthwhile quantities, it should be cleaned out. Scrub the wooden frames and dry them in the sun before reusing them. Spent compost is exhausted only for the production of mushrooms and is still excellent fertilizer for use in the garden.

The Prized Pleurotus

Pleurotus mushrooms are wild fungi highly prized in Europe and Asia, but little known here. They are not only delicious, but also good for you and easy to grow. If you have a north-facing window, some pots and pans, a stack of old newspapers, and some great spawn, you can start production in your home.

Unlike most mushrooms, which require a rich compost or manure medium to grow on, *Pleurotus* thrives on a number of common household and agricultural wastes including straw, corncob pieces, sawdust, newspaper, wood chips—even wastepaper. And the mushroom, which grows on dead trees in the wild, likes diffuse sunlight, so there is no need to hide your growing trays down in the basement.

There are several types of *Pleurotus,* but the most popular is the oyster mushroom (*Pleurotus ostreatus*). The name probably comes from the mushroom's shell-like shape, although some people swear it tastes like oysters. Another commercially available variety is sajor-cajou, a native of the Himalayas. Both types do well indoors.

To grow your own *Pleurotus,* first choose a growing medium. Straw works well, but, if

Oyster mushroom

you are unable to find any in your area, one of the mediums listed on page 38–39 will do.

You will also need trays to grow your mushrooms in. Just about any plastic or styrofoam tray that is about 1 by 2 feet and at least 6 inches deep will be adequate.

Pasteurizing the growing medium before planting the spawn will help kill any bacteria or fungi that could compete with the growing mushrooms.

Place a 4-inch layer of the medium in a metal tray or pan and soak it well with water. Cover the tray with tinfoil and place it in a 250°F-oven for 30 minutes. When the mixture has cooled for at least 8 hours, remove the foil and drain off any excess water.

The medium is now ready to be inoculated with mushroom spawn. Mix a pint of the spawn through the medium in each tray, saving a little to sprinkle over the top. Cover the trays with plastic and place them in a dark, warm (72 to 75°F) place.

Pleurotus is happiest when the humidity is up at about 80 to 90 percent. To achieve this, you will need to cover each tray with an opaque plastic tent to create a mini-greenhouse. Use wire or old coat hangers for the frame, then tape plastic film to it. Mist the inside of the tent every day or 2, but avoid spraying water directly on the medium, as it may damage the growing mushrooms.

Since mushrooms require very little oxygen for incubation, it is not necessary to perforate the plastic covering. The medium should be kept moist with regular watering and misting, but be careful not to overwater. Any standing water in the trays will encourage the growth of harmful bacteria.

Once you've tasted the rich flavor of these mushrooms, you probably won't care how good they are for you. Look at the nutritional benefits as an added bonus. *Pleurotus* is about 30 percent protein and is also a good source of iron, thiamin, riboflavin, phosphorus, and niacin. All that and only about 90 calories a pound!

The Simple Sprout

Did you know that there are vegetables that can be home grown in 4 to 6 days on any bit of shelf space you might have? Is this the latest miracle of modern biological science? Not at all. It is a miracle however, a simple phenomenon of nature known to man for thousands of years.

This miracle is nothing more than the sprouting of a bean or grain seed to create a nutritious and versatile food. Bean sprouts have long been an integral part of Oriental fare and have now gained great popularity among natural food enthusiasts in this country.

Growing sprouts in your own home is a simple matter. Mung beans, soybeans, lentils, or other dried beans can be used, as can rye or wheat seeds. The grains will produce a sprout with a sweeter, nuttier taste.

Germination is a process that involves hundreds of complex changes. Fortunately, Mother

Nature takes care of the whole thing without our having to know a single chemical formula.

Before a dry seed can sprout, it must absorb a great deal of water. This dissolves the chemicals in the seed, allowing growth to begin. It also causes the seed to swell to a much larger size. When you start your sprouts, remember that they will increase to as much as 10 times their original volume by the time they are ready to eat.

To grow your own sprouts, soak a teaspoon of bean, grain, or alfalfa seeds overnight in plain tap water. In the morning, drain them, place them in a clean glass canning jar, cover with a damp cloth, and put them in a dark place. Keep the sprouts moist, not wet, by rinsing them with tap water twice a day. This will also prevent mold.

In a couple of days the seeds will sprout and in another 2 or 3 days they will be ready to eat. The seeds should be from 1 to 2 inches long when ready. As with all fresh vegetables, store them in the refrigerator.

It is possible to buy commercial sprouting kits. The simplest of these is just a canning jar with a fine mesh screening fitted into the screw-on ring. This makes the daily rinsing of the sprouts more convenient.

What kinds of problems should you expect with your crop? If your seeds don't sprout, there is a good chance that they have been sterilized by heat treatment or are just too old. Get new seeds and try again.

Do not buy seeds intended for planting in the garden—they may have been treated with toxic chemicals. If your sprouts start to get slimy or moldy, then you are not rinsing and draining them thoroughly or often enough.

Otherwise, you should experience no difficulty as a sprout farmer.

Fresh-Started Herbs

You can start herbs from seed in late summer and enjoy them all winter long. Those best to include in your indoor winter herb garden are annuals such as basil and chervil, as well as parsley, a biennial. Sow them in a light, seed-starting mix in flats. Water gently, cover them with plastic wrap, and put them where temperatures will stay warmer than 60°F.

Remove the plastic after the seeds have sprouted; when the seedlings have their second set of true leaves, put them into 4-inch pots, and as they grow larger, 6-inch pots. Those should hold them nicely until next spring.

You can also propagate new plants from established ones by cuttings or layering. This works well for rosemary, thyme, oregano, and sage.

Take a 4-inch tip cutting, strip off the lower leaves, and stick the stem into a moist soil mix such as perlite and/or vermiculite (see more on soil mixes for herbs on page 283). To insure good humidity, cover with glass or clear plastic and keep the growing medium damp.

To propagate by layering, select a branch near the base of a parent plant. Strip the leaves where the branch touches the soil when you bend it over, and pin it down with a bent piece of wire.

Keep the soil moist until roots develop. When this new plant begins to grow, cut the connecting stem and pot it up.

Before the first frost, while the weather is still on the mild side, it is time to start moving your potted herb plants toward their winter home. Move them to an area with lots of sun (south-facing windows are the brightest), but protect them from heat and dryness.

Most herbs prefer daytime temperatures of about 65 to 75°F, although they can withstand climbs into the 80s. It is especially important that nighttime temperatures drop at least 10°F. Evening temperatures in the 50s are even better, as they simulate outdoor conditions. If the light is low, keep the temperature low as well. Temperatures that mimic May combined with the low light levels of a short December day will make for unhealthy plants.

Nearly all herbs like to be well watered, but don't like wet feet. That is why good drainage is important. Water when the top of the container feels dry or learn to judge the moisture in the soil by the weight of the pot. Choose the soil for your indoor herb garden carefully. For a good soil mix, blend one part potting soil with one part compost and one part perlite, vermiculite, and sand to ensure good drainage.

Learn to juggle water, light, and temperature. An herb in a south window in a clay pot will need more than one in a plastic pot in an eastern exposure.

Keep transplants separate from your other houseplants while you are gradually acclimating them to the indoors. If you see insects on a plant during this transition, quarantine it by leaving it outside. If, despite such defenses, your indoor plants do end up under insect attack, help them stay healthy by providing the correct mix of light and temperature and spray them once a week with liquid sea kelp. A plant weakened by hot, dry indoor conditions is even more susceptible to spider mites, whitefly, or aphid damage than a healthy one.

If you choose to control these with insecticidal soap spray, remember that the wet spray must come in contact with the insect to be effective. It takes 3 spray treatments at 5-day intervals to eradicate soft-bodied insects. Spray in the evening (never in bright sunlight) to prevent rapid drying and wash off residues the next day.

Treat your herbs like a mini-garden. Hold back on the water and organic fertilizer through December, but when the days start getting longer in mid-January, feed them with liquid fish-seaweed spray. Even potted soil gets compacted as you water it, so cultivate it with a little fork, then topdress it with compost.

February is usually a great month for indoor plants, because of all the bright light. By March they are starting to get buds. By April they are asking to be put outside on a warm day.

Environmental Conditions and Maintenance

Over the years, I've grown many kinds of fragrant herbs. The key, of course, is to find the right plants, soil mixture, and location; then, doing this, to give your potted garden the right maintenance. Indoor herbs need special attention. If you divide the major herbs into two groups there are those, like thyme, that thrive in slightly drier conditions than most garden vegetables; and those, like the mints, that need more humidity and moisture.

For both groups the first consideration is choosing a proper container. An unglazed pot is just about the best option, while those glazed on the inside with plastic and ceramic do not allow the plant to breathe.

Make sure that there are adequate holes in the bottom of the pot, then cover it with fine stones to facilitate drainage and aeration. Add your soil mix.

Herbs thrive on east-, west-, and south-facing windowsills. They will keep happy and healthy with about 5 hours of direct sun and

SOIL SOLUTIONS

In their natural state, thyme and many of the aromatic herbs, such as sage, oregano, marjoram, and winter savory, enjoy a soil that is more on the sandy side. For those plants make potting soil mix 1: 1 part sand, 1 part vermiculite, 1 part compost, and 1 part perlite.

Plants, including members of the mint family, which require moister, richer conditions for optimum growth, thrive on potting mix 2: 1 part sand, 1 part vermiculite, 2 parts compost, 1 part peat moss, and 1 part perlite. Both mixtures should also contain bone meal, greensand, and organic fertilizer. Fill all pots to within $1/2$ inch of the brim.

For plants that require an acid mix, such as rosemary, sage, and oregano, double the amount of peat moss. For those that need an alkaline soil, like yucca and bee balm, add either lime or ground eggshells.

a fairly cool atmosphere (below 75°F) with a humidity level of 30 to 50 percent.

You can't standardize a watering schedule for all of your plants. There are too many variables such as the size of the pot, the temperature of the room, and the thirstiness of the herb.

The best rule of forefinger to follow is to poke your finger into the soil to the first knuckle; if the soil is dry at that depth, water. If it's still moist, don't. As you become familiar with each plant, you'll learn its watering requirements.

For thyme in the sandy soil mix it is not unusual to water daily; for the mints in somewhat heavier, more humusy soil, every 3 days is about right. When the top $1/2$ inch of the soil is dry, it's usually time to rewater.

Once established, you can keep your herbs in the same pots for years by pruning roots and harvesting the foliage. When thyme starts growing out in all directions and the tiny leaves on the bottom begin to dry up, clip it down to the main stems and dry the leaves as an herb seasoning. After about a year of this treatment, remove the plant from its pot, trim off the roots that have wadded up along the sides and bottom, and, if necessary, transplant to a larger pot.

If the plant has grown too large, divide it and start the cuttings in new pots. Just about all herbs in the perennial class respond to this treatment. Annuals will have to be replanted every season. Wild herbs, like American ginger and yerba buena (a member of the mint family), can also be domesticated.

Most people who cook with fresh ginger root buy it at the store for premium prices; but with a minimum of effort, you can grow your own in a pot and have a fresh supply available whenever you want it. All you have to do is plant a section of the rhizome in a fairly shallow 8-inch pot with equal parts of garden loam, sand, and compost. Be sure to choose a firm, undamaged piece of root to plant and one that has a bud.

Fill the pot $3/4$ full of soil, then set the rhizome horizontally on top and cover it with an additional $1/4$ inch of soil. Water carefully and keep the soil evenly moist, but not soggy, throughout the life of the plant. Put the pot in a bright place out of direct sun and, when the first shoots are up, feed the plant with Kelp Plus™ fish-seaweed mixture once every 3 weeks.

In the fall the plant will go dormant. This is a good time to unpot it and harvest your crop. You will find that the roots have multiplied and you may find 8 or 10 new rhizomes

Herbs thrive under fluorescent lights

to harvest for cooking. Save one of the knobs with a bud to plant for a new crop.

A display of herbs can also be put under fluorescent lights. Keep them under the lights for 14 to 16 hours a day. Use 20 to 40 watt bulbs hung 12 to 16 inches above the plant. Artificial light is a great boon in cloudy months or in rooms that face north or have obstructed windows.

I have always had a curry plant tucked away in my fluorescent indoor garden, without fussing too much about its requirements. I like its narrow, $^3/_4$-inch-long silver green leaves and its untidy, yet compact, growth. Above all, I relish the smell of curry that emanates from the leaves whenever I brush them, a strange attribute since the plant is not an ingredient in the spice mixture called curry powder.

I add lime to the soil mix and make sure that the plant is never overwatered, resulting in better growth. I keep it in a sunny window

or under fluorescent lights. As the plant grows, the lower leaves die off and overlap each other. I cut them off and add them to potpourris.

Pineapple sage is one of my favorite mimic plants. Its fresh, clean pineapple aroma is strongest during the daytime. Like all sages, it has oval, gray green leaves with slightly pebbled surfaces.

Under fluorescent lights the plant produces brilliant red tubular flowers. Keep it trimmed back so that bushy, compact growth is produced.

Keep the plant well-watered and fertilize with fish emulsion every other watering. Add lime to the soil mix. Keep it on a south window or under the center of the fluorescent lights, where it will get plenty of warmth and sunshine.

Most indoor herbs are subject to the same pests that are problems for any other houseplant. For mites and whiteflies, I spray with insecticidal soap. I also wipe any scale infestations off the leaves and stems, using a cotton pad soaked with rubbing alcohol.

Don't hesitate to experiment with herbs indoors. Their uses are many and their tastes always a treat.

Fruit in a Flat

When Jack Frost clamps down on garden fun, satisfy the farmer in you by planting fruit seeds in flats and pots and watching them germinate.

Don't expect to raise grapes, peaches, or berries over the radiator by the window, but you can plant 10 date pits in a container and they will sprout. After a while, transplant them into pots and watch them grow into pretty and diminutive palm trees.

If everbearing strawberries are in your outside garden, pick a dozen of the biggest and heartiest berries, crush them between blotters, let them dry, and then sow the seeds in a flat. Keep the soil moist and eventually you will have some fine little strawberry plants. Incidentally, a date palm planted in the center of a container with strawberries surrounding it makes an attractive centerpiece.

There is almost no limit to the possibilities of indoor fruit culture. Seeds of orange and grapefruit can be saved from fruit bought merely for the eating. Soak the seeds overnight in a cup of water and plant in pots of growing soil. They will sprout and grow to form little green seedlings about 4 inches high.

Grapefruit, one of the common citrus fruits, is the most rewarding and easy to grow. A month after sowing seeds, you should have a few healthy young plants. Move them, putting each in its own pot, and they will all develop into really handsome foliage plants. You can produce the same with oranges and lemons, but they take longer to germinate and are a little harder to grow.

Pears and apples are most interesting and educational to cultivate. To make sure of successful germination, place the seeds in the refrigerator for a couple of months before planting. Later, after the young seedlings have taken hold and spring arrives, transplant them to the outdoor garden.

Growing fruit from seed is, in fact, remarkably easy, providing you are willing to follow the rules. Take a ripe-looking cherry in February and sow the seeds in a pot of sandy soil. Sprouting is rapid. The seedlings should be transplanted to a flat when the second pair of leaves shows, and put outside in the spring. Sometime during the growing season, pot up each seedling individually and bring indoors well before the first frost because they are rather tender plants. They will reward you by ripening fruit in time for the next holiday season.

To achieve success in starting fruit plants, 4 essential factors must be given every consideration. They are the same for indoor as well as outdoor gardening: soil, sunlight, temperature, and water. To these should be added humidity, because you are growing plants under artificial conditions that tend to rob the air of its natural moisture content.

Next to the actual soil, the most important factors are sunlight and temperature. All plants need good light to make their best growth. Flowering plants need at least 3 hours of sunlight a day, while fruiting plants need all the sunlight they can get.

Temperature is also important, and contrary to what you may have been told, need not be as high as in a greenhouse. During the day, 65 to 70°F is recommended with a drop to 55 to 60°F at night. This night drop is vital to the growing plant because it permits the seedling to rest and mature the growth made during the day.

Too much water is worse than too little, and you should be sure to keep the air as humid as possible. Water the plants amply at the root level whenever the surface soil begins to dry. This is better for the plant than frequent or scanty waterings. Misting the top growths at regular intervals maintains proper humidity, keeps the plants clean, and also discourages insect pests.

You owe it to your gardener's instincts to try your hand at planting fruit seeds. Your plants may or may not bear fruit, but they will provide you with real gardening fun and reward you beyond that with a really beautiful and interesting winter window garden.

CHAPTER 20

House-Happy Foliage

While white, powdery snows are blowing from the rooftops, there is no reason why you cannot have fantastic foliage blooming on your windowsills. All you have to do is follow the "rules of green thumb."

Light

As you probably already know, lighting is of utmost importance in indoor gardening because it furnishes energy for plant growth. Even those plants that thrive on filtered light will not set buds without some sun. Because most houseplants need sunlight in winter, they do best in a southerly exposure. An east window will do for plants that normally do not need direct sunlight. It must be remembered that plants will not grow or bloom as they should unless the amount of light they receive is approximately equal to that of their natural home.

In modern decor, large foliage plants are often used to set off pieces of furniture along inner walls or in dark hallways. To keep these foliage plants healthy and growing, place a 150-watt incandescent bulb within 4 feet of each. The light must be turned on throughout the day and extinguished after sunset.

Humidity

If the plant is expected to do its best, the relative humidity surrounding it night and day must be the same or close to that of its original habitat. Humidity is far more important to plants' health than one might think—low humidity is disastrous to flora. If the surrounding air remains hot and dry, evaporation takes place very rapidly, drying the leaves and causing more rapid transpiration (escaping of moisture through leaf pores).

A plant has been so constructed that there is a balance between the amount of moisture absorbed by the roots and the amount evaporated from the foliage. Plants will wilt in low humidity even though the soil contains sufficient moisture. If wilting continues over a long period, the plant will die.

Excessive humidity is not dangerous to most plants (except desert species—it causes them to become leggy and spongy). To maintain sufficient humidity, place pots on pebbles above the water level in shallow trays. Several plants grouped together will aid humidity levels through transpiration. Frequent spraying of the leaves with water also goes a long way toward keeping humidity at a high level.

Since all plants do not require the same amount of humidity, separate the plants into groups according to their air-moisture requirements, then situate each group in a suitable window. That way you can better control their humidification.

Temperature

The third important growing factor in plant growth is the air temperature. Again, each type of plant demands its natural temperature. Jungle plants require higher temperatures than other plants, although temperate-zone and desert plants can withstand 90 to 100°F for a short time without harm. Low temperatures are actually the demons that do plant growth real harm.

One of the biggest concerns that people have with their houseplants is watering. Most people think that more is better; but with respect to houseplants, overwatering is the main cause of plant demise.

Watering houseplants requires a skill that can be developed quickly, if the needs of the different plants are learned. In outdoor beds where plants grow all summer, you will notice that the soil remains moderately moist at all times. After rains drain away and the topsoil begins to dry, it absorbs moisture from the subsoil through capillary attraction. In garden

---

COOL CLAY POTS

It may surprise you to learn that the type of pots you are using has a great deal to do with the health of your plants' root systems. If at all possible, use only clay pots. They contain their own cooling systems: moisture is drawn from the soil through the side walls by force of evaporation. Actually, the clay pot is capable of evaporating twice as much through its walls than from the surface soil. This beneficial evaporation has a cooling effect on the soil and the roots, resulting in healthier plants.

---

soil only the soil particles are damp, with a multitude of air spaces in between.

Roots are designed to absorb moisture and plant nutrients from the moist particles and oxygen from air spaces. If the soil is too wet, these air pockets fill with water, thus shutting off the needed oxygen supply and hampering the natural growth processes.

It is wise not to water until the surface soil feels dry. Then, instead of watering from the top, plunge the pots in water to within an inch of the rim. When the surface becomes moist, remove them to the drain board to allow the excess water to drain off; then replace them on the sill. Three such dunkings a week are usually sufficient for most plants.

In reality, no one can say how often to water a houseplant. It depends largely upon the relative humidity and type of pot the plant is growing in. Clay pots may need watering every day, while others may get along with a drink once a week.

To grow successful indoor plants, know the conditions and needs of each plant and then supply them with the proper environment and care. However, a little care goes a long way. Give them proper light, soil, temperature, and watering, and your plants will send out new growth.

enough water to keep the leaves from shriveling and don't feed it.

Aloe

Because aloe is a succulent (a plant with thick, fleshy leaves or stems native to dry, tropical regions), you won't have to fuss over it. Just pot it in a light mix of 1 part garden loam, 1 part compost, and 1 part sharp sand in a 6-inch pot. Sharp sand is extra coarse, and can be purchased from a sand and gravel company.

The key to successful aloe culture is not to overwater. Its thick leaves store moisture, so let it dry somewhat between waterings.

Aloes are known for producing lots of babies—suckers that may be separated from the parent plant by cutting the underground runner that connects them. Each little plant can then be potted separately.

During the winter, aloe plants appreciate a rest. Reduce the amount of light your plant is getting and put it in a cool spot. Give it just

Azalea

Azaleas flower indoors from January to April, although no 1 plant will last that long. Practically any kind of azalea can be successfully grown in a flowerpot.

If your plant has large flowers, 2 or 3 inches in diameter, double or semidouble, growing on single stems resembling a little tree, then you may classify it as an *Azalea indica*. These come in tones of crimson-red, purple, pink, and white.

Azaleas that have myriad tiny flower clusters on each plant are known as Kurume hybrids. Frequently their flowers are so close that they conceal the leaves. These plants may be pearly white, or many tints of pink ranging from a creamy blush through rose and cherry-red to deep purple. When it is time to move pots indoors (before heavy frost), a larger container may be needed if growth over summer was abundant. Use only the next larger size, as azaleas bloom better if slightly pot-bound. For good results use a potting mix of equal parts good soil, leaf mold, and sand plus a handful of organic fertilizer.

When outside, azaleas pick the cool, bright days of spring to splash their exciting colors on the countryside. When you bring them in, you need to create a little of that springtime atmosphere in your home.

Azaleas should be placed as close to the windows as possible, where cool air coming through the glass will give them a touch of April. They are happiest with a temperature of 60 to 65°F in daytime and 50 to 55°F at night. Azaleas will keep their beauty longer if you pamper them by moving them to a cooler place at night (make sure temperatures are always above freezing).

Azaleas thrive in constant moisture. Their roots soak up water at a rapid rate, so make it a point to do 2 things: water them frequently from the top of the pot and keep the pot on a layer of fine stones that are thoroughly wet at all times. The evaporation of the water will increase humidity in the air closest to the plant, replicating the dewy, springtime air. Never allow the soil around an azalea to become parched; when even slightly dehydrated, it will drop all of its leaves and possibly die.

Your potted azaleas also demand light. Treat your plant to a place on your sunniest windowsill, where during the short days of winter it can bask in as much sunshine as possible. Peat moss will keep the soil acid and also serve to conserve moisture. One growing medium you can try is 1 part garden loam and 1 part peat moss.

Shortly after flowering, vegetative growth begins. At the bottom of each flower cluster several new sprouts appear and in approximately 10 days, the graceful foliage emerges: dark green glossy leaves that are simple and symmetrical. It is at this point that azaleas begin working on next year's flowers, so be very attentive. Feed with Seacure™ at least once a month.

When the weather becomes balmy and danger of frost is over, give your potted azaleas a taste of the great outdoors. Be sure to keep them in their pots buried to their rims in peat moss. Pick out a spot that will provide protection from beating sun rays during the heat of the day.

In early autumn prepare azaleas for winter by bringing them inside again, where the cool temperatures of the fall months will give them a chance to rest until January.

If at any time you notice your azalea's leaves turning yellowish green with dark green veins, they are not diseased. It is only a sign that your soil is not acid enough. If this happens, sprinkle about $1/2$ layer of pine needles under the branches. This increases soil acidity and the pungent aroma is very outdoorsy inside in the wintertime.

Azaleas are a delightful flowering species and their foliage is beautiful. Be sure to reserve a spot for them on your sunniest windowsill, where these charming garden aristocrats can add a breath of spring beauty to stark, wintry days.

Cacti

You can use any common plant container for a cactus, but clay pots are preferred for two reasons. First, they are porous and allow the soil to dry quickly. Second, they are heavy, and many cacti soak up water and become heavy themselves. Such plants easily tip over

will go far in developing healthy, blooming plants. One basic rule is to keep plants dry in fall and winter, wet in spring and summer. Cacti need a dormant period in which they harden growth and frequently set flower buds.

Cacti

when potted in light, plastic containers. A mature cactus needs replanting only once every 3 to 5 years. The pot should be at least as large as the largest diameter of the plant and its spines. The best replanting time is in late winter, before the dormant season ends.

What about the right kind of potting soil for a cactus? Well, here are two formulas that you might try. The simplest method is to use a commercial houseplant soil that you are happy with for other purposes. Mix it with an equal amount of clean, dry builder's sand (don't use sea sand). Another choice is to use equal parts of garden soil, compost, and builder's sand. To either of these mixtures add a tablespoon each of limestone and bone meal per quart.

The main point about the soil is that it should be quick-draining. Cacti don't like to sit in heavy, wet soil, as their roots will rot out.

Water is the single most critical factor. It is better to err in the direction of too little water, than to overdo. A little thought and scheduling

CACTI Q & A

Here are answers to the questions most frequently asked about the cactus.

(Q) *What kind of light is needed for my cactus plants?*

(A) Cacti are survivors. Even in a north window some plants will hang on for year after year. Desert cactus are basically light lovers, so by all means find a southern exposure for your plants, if you can.

(Q) *How do I know what temperature they need?*

(A) Most cacti can stand any temperature down to freezing. Generally, they are comfortable when we are comfortable. However, if you want them to bloom, try to find them cooler temperatures in winter. Warmer temperatures are preferred at other times.

(Q) *What should I feed my cactus?*

(A) Cacti like well-drained soil, but that doesn't mean poor soil. They appreciate nutrients, as does any other plant.

The key ingredient in their diet is phosphorous (P), the middle letter listed on most fertilizer bags. One good organic source is bone meal (1–20–0, N–P–K). Go lightly on it, though. Fertilize only during the season of active growth and then no more frequently than once a month. Also, use the fish-seaweed mix (4–4–1).

I follow this schedule:

In late February I step up watering to once a week. As spring goes on and the plants show signs of new growth, I water more frequently.

In August I find that new growth has slowed or stopped on most plants, so the water ration is cut. I extend the time between waterings from 3 to 5 days.

By early fall the growing season is over and the plants get water once a week.

The next step is the hardest, for it almost seems cruel. My plants get a good drink at the beginning of November. They get another one around Thanksgiving. That's it. They won't see another drop until mid-January. Then, in late February, they get another drink and the cycle begins again.

There are over 9,000 cactus plants to choose from. Their names are confusing, which can be frustrating to a serious amateur grower, but unimportant to the casual gardener.

By any name, a cactus is still a cactus and few plants can offer so much variety in shape, texture, and bloom for so little care.

Calendula

Calendulas aren't fussy; these hardy annuals will tolerate some neglect and grow even in poor soil. Plant them in 8-inch pots in an all-purpose potting soil with good drainage. Two parts garden loam and 1 part each of perlite and compost is a good basic mix. Calendulas like cool temperatures, no higher than 65°F during the day and between 40 and 50°F at night. They are good plants for a bright, unheated room. Give them full sun and plenty of air circulation. Keep the soil evenly moist, but not soggy. Calendulas also serve several medicinal purposes. The yellow 2- to

Calendula

3-inch flowers can be used either fresh or dried in a footbath to relieve the pain of a sprained ankle or sore foot.

Geranium

Geraniums have always been favorite house and garden plants. Less known and more

versatile are the scented geraniums, which are grown primarily for their fragrant foliage, but also reward indoor gardeners with small flowers in delicate shades of pink, white, and salmon. There is a wide range of fragrances to choose from, including rose, lemon, nutmeg, peppermint, ginger, apple, orange, almond, and pine.

Scented geraniums do fine in an all-purpose soil. Good drainage is a must, for the plants are prone to mildew. Give them bright light with 4 hours of direct sun a day; a south or east window is a good location.

Scented geraniums do best when they are pot-bound, so don't be in a hurry to repot large plants. Keep them in 6- to 8-inch pots. When the plants are in active growth, you can topdress them once a month with organic fertilizer.

Pinch back the plants often to encourage them to stay bushy and blooming. The prunings can be included in cut-flower arrangements. The plants bloom when days are long, in spring, summer, and fall. Scented geraniums live for 2 or 3 years. After that they lose their vigor, so take some tip cuttings and start new plants.

Scented geraniums are best used as an ingredient in potpourris and sachets. Dry the leaves on a screen, then mix them with flower petals. Store the potpourri in a covered jar. When the jar is opened, the mellow fragrance will drift throughout the room.

Nasturtium

If you miss the snappy taste of fresh cress in your winter salads, here is a longtime flower-bed favorite you can grow indoors for a continuous supply of fresh leaves with a familiar peppery flavor. If you can give these annuals a

Nasturtium

cool, sunny spot, they will do well inside. Nasturtiums come in a wide range of colors, and are vining plants. They need plenty of sun and a loose, well-drained soil. A mix of 3 parts garden loam, 1 part sand, 1 part peat moss, and 1 part perlite should give you good results.

As the plants grow, pinch back the tips from time to time to keep them bushy and to encourage more flowers. Picking off faded blooms will also promote continued flowering, but let some go to seed so you can use the unripe seedpods.

In addition to the tasty foliage that you can use in soups, salads, and sandwiches, the flowers make an edible garnish.

Ornamental Peppers

Ornamental pepper plants, with their brightly colored round or cone-shaped fruit, are popular gift plants during the winter holiday season. They are closely related to the green and red chili peppers grown in summer gardens; the small, fiery fruits of some varieties are

Ornamental pepper

Christmas. As they mature, the little peppers change color from green to creamy white, purple, orange, and finally, vivid red.

Ornamental peppers, like the garden variety, do best in a warm temperature. They also like lots of space; give them deep, 10-inch pots to grow in.

Sow seeds in spring and keep the soil evenly moist. When the seedlings are a few inches tall, give the plants lots of sun and constant warmth. Scratch a little bone meal into the soil to promote flower and fruit development.

When the plants begin to mature in the fall, move them to a cooler location to help keep the fruit on the vine. If kept cool, ornamental peppers may hold their fruit for several months. Ripe peppers can be picked whenever you need them, or they can be dried for use later on. You can use them in all the same ways you use hot chili peppers. Be sure to remove the seeds before using.

When the last pepper is picked, discard the plant and start over with fresh seeds.

edible, but not recommended unless you like very hot peppers.

Ornamental pepper plants grow to about 12 inches tall. If the seeds are sown in spring, they will produce lots of tiny white flowers, followed by fruits that will ripen in time for

Growing Questions and Answers

On Soil Management

(**Q**) *Gardeners frequently use the phrase "good fertile loam." I realize that this is a description of healthy, rich soil, but new gardeners like myself need a better explanation of what loamy soil is like. What characteristics do I look for?*

(**A**) The loamy soil which both farmer and gardener both aim for has a good deal of silt in it, plus organic matter, and enough clay and sand particles to give it good texture and structure. If the soil feels soft and oily when you rub it between your fingers, you have probably achieved a good fertile loam. Upon squeezing such soil, it will hold together for a minute when squeezed into a loose lump, but will fall as crumbly bits when you drop it back onto the ground.

Fertile loam is said to have good "crumbs" (granules or aggregates). What holds an aggregate together is not only the colloidal character of the surfaces of clay and humus particles, but also little bits of root and decayed leaves, threads, or pieces of fungi.

Earthworms, slug and snail secretions, residues left after the decomposition of vegetation, and the invisible bodies of the countless bacteria and fungi in the soil all combine to create loam.

(**Q**) *Perhaps you can settle an argument I am having with my neighbor. I say it's best to till in the spring, while he says it's best to till in the fall. Who is correct?*

(**A**) It depends. If your soil needs organic matter, you may want to till it under in the fall to condition your garden for the spring. Although organic matter tilled-in a few weeks before spring planting is more nutritive, it will not have the time to decay enough to aid soil structure the way fall-tilled organic material does.

Other than that, spring tilling is recommended. In the fall a cover crop of winter rye should be planted. Laying the soil bare to the elements over winter kills off many beneficial soil organisms in the layer that alternately thaws and freezes, and the soil could be recolonized by disease organisms.

A cover crop with roots that hold soil together—covered with mulch during the frozen months—is the best way to take a garden through the winter. Mulch or cover crops can be tilled in during the spring, adding lots of decaying organic matter to the soil.

(Q) *I recently saw an inoculant called* Azotobacter *in one of my garden catalogs. What is it and does it have beneficial effects in the garden?*

(A) *Azotobacter* are beneficial soil-dwelling bacteria that fix nitrogen and produce growth-stimulating, hormone-like substances. They are usually present in healthy soils that contain some organic matter.

Microorganisms exist in the soil in a remarkably stable ecological balance. They are highly competitive and will generally attack intruders that are introduced into their environment. Soils that don't contain any *Azotobacter* obviously don't have the right conditions to support them and, if added to such a soil, the bacteria will die. The best way to encourage *Azotobacter* and other beneficial organisms in your soil is to provide them with a steady diet of organic matter.

(Q) *I've always been curious about the different colors of the soil and wonder how to interpret them. Could you give me a basic explanation of soil color?*

(A) The changes in soil color that you see from one area to the next usually mean that there was a difference in mineral development somewhere along the way. Like people, soils inherit different deficiencies and different excesses of minerals that characterize their colors and consistencies.

White colors usually indicate that heavier concentrations of salt and lime deposits are present in the soil. The darker the soil color, the more organic matter it usually contains. Black soil can mean good humus content, but it may mean nothing more than manganese-bearing rock particles. Reddish soils usually denote a high iron content. Soils that display spots of different colors, particularly shades of rust, reveal a problem of insufficient aeration, caused by compaction. This type of soil experiences periods throughout the year when it cannot get enough oxygen.

If the soil suffers from periods of inadequate aeration due to waterlogging, the subsoil takes on bluish, grayish, or greenish colors. In general, tans, light grays, or light bluish grays usually indicate poor soil, but subsoils of these colors often contain good supplies of minerals.

(Q) *How important is soil aeration? How can I improve the aeration in my soil?*

(A) Air is needed in the soil for the proper working of bacteria and fungi. It aids in the breakdown of organic matter, such as the decomposition of roots from previous crops. With sufficient air, these roots turn to humus in time to feed the next crop. Air also aids in the oxidation of mineral matter. In an air-poor soil, many important minerals are not available for plant sustenance.

Another by-product of organic decay is carbon dioxide, too much of which is detrimental to plants. Air regulates the amount of carbon dioxide in the soil; better aeration encourages a larger root system, which is able to absorb more oxygen from the soil, leading to healthier plants.

A number of methods are used to increase the air supply in soil, including the addition of organic matter, the application of rock powders, soil drainage, sub-soiling (tilling with a certain type of plow), cultivation, and mixed cropping. By far the most important of all is to see that the soil is supplied with sufficient organic matter. It is axiomatic in agricultural literature that the more humus present in the soil, the better the aeration, and the more pore spaces it will contain.

(Q) *Some people say that you can tell the condition of the soil by the types of plants that grow in it. Could you tell me more about this relationship?*

(A) Plants can give you clues as to the soils they thrive in. Cattails, to use an obvious example, favor wet, marshy soil. Various grasses of the sedge family, like nut sedge, thrive in soil too wet for more desirable grasses.

Some of the plants that like wet soils include marigold, porcelain vineskunk cabbage, pin oak, red maple, swamp white oak, sour gum, weeping willow, starwort, and buttonbush. Where burdock, pigweed, lamb's-quarter, and purslane grow very lushly, the soil has good organic content and is fairly well-drained and fertile. The presence of sorrel, mayweed, and chamomile usually indicate a soil lacking in humus and fertility.

Where tiny mosses give the soil surface a greenish tinge that persists into the summer, the land is too wet for gardening and should be tile drained. Land is generally poor in places where broom sedge is growing. Bluegrass and alfalfa thrive on land that is not too acid.

You will always find good-sized walnut trees on rich ground, often near a well-drained river or creek bottom.

Some of the plants that indicate acid soil include scrub oak, white cedar, huckleberry,

hemlock, fir, azalea, blueberry, pine, mountain laurel, rhododendron, white birch, and red cedar. They will also grow on neutral soil (with a pH of 7.0).

(Q) *What are polysaccharides that are found in organically-enriched soil?*

(A) The soil bacteria break down green manures and other crop residues into a substance called polysaccharide. This glue-like material is a complex carbohydrate that helps soil particles clump together into the aggregates so essential for good soil structure.

The amount of these valuable polysaccharides can be tremendous. For example, decaying alfalfa and oat straw produce as much as 5,500 and 4,000 pounds of polysaccharides per acre, respectively, only 1 week after they are added to the soil.

(Q) *Will you please discuss the relative or comparative advantages of rotary tilling versus conventional tilling in various types of soil. Am I right to assume that rotary tilling breaks down soil aggregation too much in hard clays and ships so much air into sandy soil that humus decomposes too fast, and that it would not be recommended in either of these extreme types of soil?*

(A) The primary purpose of tillage is to prepare a seedbed by subjugating the plants that would compete with those you want to grow. Another purpose is to incorporate plant residues or organic matter into the soil.

Tillage performed to alter the soil structure is generally unnecessary and undesirable as far as seed germination and plant growth are concerned. A primary disadvantage of rotary tilling is the inability of these machines to completely incorporate a heavy mulch. In cases where heavy plant residues on the soil surface would interfere with the cultivation process, a plow is desirable to turn them under.

In situations where no heavy mulch is present or where it is desirable that this mulch remain in or on the soil surface, a rotary tiller works fine. The fewer trips required to prepare a seedbed reduce the compaction sometimes caused by conventional tillage methods. This serves to offset the increased cutting action of the rotary machine.

Any tillage method tends to work toward the destruction of soil structure. For this reason it is desirable to minimize the number of tillage operations required to prepare and maintain a seedbed.

Judicious use of a rotary tillage machine would not cause either of the conditions mentioned in your question any more than conventional tillage. The most important consideration when working clay soils is that they are not wet. The air movement in sandy soils should be quite free, whether rotary tilling or conventional tillage methods are used.

On Soil Amendments and Fertilizers

(**Q**) *People tell me that greensand is a good fertilizer and will improve my soil. What can you tell me about it?*

(**A**) Greensand is excellent for building and conditioning both hard and sandy soils. This undersea deposit contains most of the elements found in the ocean. It has been used successfully for soil-building for more than 100 years and is a fine source of potash.

The best deposits contain as much as 6 to 7 percent potash, 50 percent silica, 18 to 23 percent iron oxide, 3 to 7 percent magnesium, small amounts of lime and phosphoric acid, and traces of 30 or more other elements, most of which are important for plant nutrition.

Greensand is a valued gardening amendment because of its ability to absorb and hold large amounts of water in the surface layer of the soil where the plant's roots feed. It slowly releases the potassium necessary to stimulate photosynthesis and stirs up helpful soil organisms.

Greensand is so fine that it may be used in its natural form with no additional processing (except drying, if the material is to pass through a fertilizer drill). Because of its versatility, greensand may be applied directly to the plant roots (it never burns) and left on the surface as a combined mulch and compost. Combining it with a manure–phosphate rock mixture is often recommended. Apply no more than $1/4$ pound of greensand per square foot of soil at any time.

(**Q**) *I've read that adjusting the soil's acid-alkaline reaction by raising its pH with limestone where necessary helps to control some plant diseases. Can you explain how this is accomplished?*

(**A**) Several common plant diseases—including potato scab, beet rot, and tobacco, tomato, and cotton wilts—thrive in acid soil and are consequently reduced by the alkalinizing action of limestone. The microorganisms that produce penicillin, streptomycin, and other soil antibiotics (which in turn kill or make harmless the microbes causing these common diseases), must have calcium and magnesium to do their work. Liming acid soils supplies these nutrients and, therefore, increases production of the antibiotic-producing microbes.

(Q) *What is the difference between dolomitic and regular limestone?*

(A) Regular lime contains calcium, whereas dolomitic lime contains a rich supply of magnesium in addition to calcium. Both the classic and dolomitic forms are equally effective in raising soil pH. All plants need calcium to perform vital functions, and dolomitic lime provides magnesium. A good soil test should be your guide when determining what to use to provide extra lime additions.

(Q) *How does phosphorous actually function in plants?*

(A) Phosphorous is used as a form of energy by plants to help them synthesize carbohydrates (food) from carbon dioxide and water. Phosphorous plays an important role in photosynthesis, the process by which plants use the energy of light to transform carbon dioxide and water into glucose. The actual plant growth itself is fostered by aids in the energy flow within plants and produces good flower and fruit growth. When soil is deficient in phosphorous, rock phosphate or bone meal should be applied directly to the soil or mixed with compost.

(Q) *I have heard that bone meal that has been steamed is no longer of any value as a fertilizer. Since steamed bone meal is the only kind I can find in the store, is there any point in using it when I plant bulbs?*

(A) Bone meal consists mostly of calcium phosphate. The phosphorous and nitrogen content of bone meal depends mostly on the kind and age of bone used. Raw bone meal has between 2 and 4 percent nitrogen and 22 to 27 percent phosphoric acid. The fatty materials in raw bone meal somewhat delay its breakdown in the soil. Once the bones have been steamed, they can be ground more easily and are therefore considered in better condition for the soil. Steamed bone meal contains 2 to 3 percent nitrogen and up to 30 percent phosphorous.

(Q) *We used cottonseed meal at the bottom of the furrows in our garden, but every seed and plant burned up. What is the proper way to apply it?*

(A) Cottonseed meal is high in nitrogen and can cause a heat buildup if applied in excessive quantities. We recommend using a potful of meal (a 4-inch-diameter pot is ideal) per 15-foot row, applied with 2 inches of leaf mold in the fall. In spring, work the cottonseed meal into the soil a week or 2 before planting; water well at the time of application. This gives soil organisms a chance to digest the meal and lessens the danger of burn.

You may want to apply a little cottonseed meal at planting time and more when the plants are growing robustly. If you apply it as a midseason side-dressing, keep it away from stems and scratch it into the soil. Also, you should add the cottonseed meal before a predicted rain, or water heavily afterwards.

(Q) *How is dried blood beneficial in the garden? What does it contain?*

(A) Blood meal contains 15 percent nitrogen, 13 percent phosphorous, and 0.7 percent potash. It may be used directly in the soil or added to the compost pile. Use blood meal sparingly; because of its high nitrogen content, a sprinkling is enough. It is excellent in the compost pile, since the nitrogen stimulates bacterial action on woody, fibrous matter.

(Q) *I have access to manure from a horse barn. It has been there for 2 years. Is it composted manure? How should I use it?*

(A) Aging is not composting. If the manure has been protected and the weather hasn't leached out its nutrients, you can till it into your garden or layer it with other organic matter to make compost.

(Q) *What are the trace elements and how important are they?*

(A) Trace elements are minor mineral nutrients needed by all plants, animals, and humans in extremely small or "trace" amounts. Those known to be essential are boron, cobalt, iron, copper, manganese, molybdenum, and zinc.

Too little or too much of the trace elements produces deficiencies that result in plant or animal disease. On the other hand, an excessive quantity of any trace element similarly brings about a host of toxic conditions in plants, and sicknesses in animals and people.

Just how important these trace elements are can be seen by the fact that although trace elements may constitute less than 1 percent of the total dry matter of a plant, they are often the factor that determines its vigor. Even in farms and gardens with fertile soil, trace element additions to the soil can raise yields and improve crop quality.

The most reliable, safe method for assuring an adequate supply of trace elements is thorough organic fertilization, and growing certain plants which naturally accumulate these minerals. Compost, leaf mold, mulch, natural ground rock fertilizers, and lime help provide a complete balanced ration of both major and minor nutrients. Soil, like human beings, should have a varied diet. Other good sources of trace elements are seaweed and fish fertilizers, weeds that bring minerals up from deep in the subsoil with their long roots (such as dandelions and amaranth), and compost. Besides supplying trace elements themselves, when these materials decompose they release acids that make elements already present in the soil available to plants.

(Q) *Just what is vermiculite and why is it used for plants?*

(A) Vermiculite is a mineral belonging to the mica family, and is used as a medium for starting seedlings and root cuttings. Countless tiny air cells provide a high air-water holding capacity, which is an aid to germination and the development of dense root systems. Several times its own weight of water can be contained in vermiculite. Even when thoroughly wet, ample air circulates about plant roots, helping to avoid damping-off.

Vermiculite is also used for mulching or as a soil conditioner to lighten or aerate heavy clay soils, and to help sandy soils retain moisture. It does not perform these jobs as well as organic matter, which also feeds plants and improves soil ecology.

(Q) *I have noticed that there are different kinds of peat moss. How do the differences affect my gardening?*

(A) There are usually 2 types of peat for sale, peat moss (sphagnum peat) and sedge peat. Sedge peat is made from decomposed aquatic grasses like reeds and sedges. This peat is usually dark and thoroughly decayed. It looks like very fine, black soil and is a good ingredient in potting mixes. Sedge peat is often sold slightly moist in plastic bags under the name "humus peat."

Peat moss is derived from partially decomposed sphagnum or other types of moss. These decay more slowly than the aquatic grasses, although they are more absorbent. Peat moss is usually coarser, lighter colored (brown to reddish), and much more water-retentive than sedge peat.

For potting mixes, milled sphagnum (finely ground) is best. Cold water will run off milled sphagnum, but hot water soaks right in. For tilling into the garden or mulching, use the cheaper, coarser stuff that comes in bales. A 6-cubic-foot bale spread 1 inch deep will cover about 300 square feet.

Both of these peats are good soil conditioners. They lighten and aerate clay soils and help sandy soils hold water longer.

Peat is quite acidic, and is good for plants like blueberries or azaleas. If you don't have compost for potting soil, use peat. In potting mixes, peat is best mixed with topsoil and a little bone meal, which helps raise the pH.

(Q) *My professor in agricultural school does not put organic fertilizers down, but he says there is a common misconception that these fertilizers are immediately used by the plant. During the mineralization cycle, nutrients in organic fertilizers must break down into organic forms to become available to plants. Rock powders supply only a little of their phosphorous and potash the first few years after application. Nitrogen in organic matter is released slowly, too.*

How long does it take plants to access the nutrients in organic fertilizers?

(A) You are correct in observing that nutrients in organic fertilizers such as manure and rock phosphate are released slowly over a number of years, but organic farmers and gardeners are not misinformed. Quite to the contrary, the pivotal argument in favor of organic fertilizers is that they are slow to release nutrients.

Inorganic, chemical fertilizers are very soluble and immediately available to plants, and, while this has certain short-term economic advantages to farmers, the long-term disadvantages outweigh the presumed benefits. To continue to achieve the artificially high yields that chemical farmers have established as necessary for a profit requires increasing quantities of chemicals. This promotes soil-pollution hazards like nitrate poisoning and phosphate runoff into streams, and encourages economic inflation by demanding the kind of input from fossil energy that the world can no longer afford.

Slower-acting natural nutrients may not deliver record-high yields on large acreages, but they build fertility cumulatively, giving results over the years that transcend the mathematical analysis of mineral content. With a properly managed organic feeding program, the organic matter content of soil rises more steadily than in soil treated with chemicals. This matter provides a reservoir of fertility, which, along with increased soil tilth, water-holding capacity, and less erosion, yields more efficient production in terms of energy. Organically grown food is pound for pound richer in food value than food grown with chemicals.

The effects of rock phosphate may not show up much for 2 years, although some of the finer-ground colloidal types become available about as quickly as limestone (in about 3 months). Once the rock phosphate does become soluble, and if other nutrients are kept in balance with this comparatively low amount of phosphoric acid, crops make good efficient yields. But when you add a shot of high-potency superphosphate, you also get a shot of sulphuric acid, which kills the microorganisms, and your soil life.

(Q) *Since I live along the coast, seaweed is always easy to come by. What should I know about putting seaweed into my garden?*

(A) Seaweed is an asset to the compost pile, since it decomposes quickly and helps the pile to heat up. As for its fertilizing value, fresh seaweed is nutritionally similar to barnyard manure, except that it contains twice as much potassium. Because it is also high in iron and zinc and contains some iodine, seaweed is an excellent food source for citrus fruits and roses.

If you are using large amounts of seaweed, don't let it heap up and wait for it to decay. Nutrients leach out easily during the decaying process, so the seaweed should be dug into the soil before this happens.

Many gardeners feel it is necessary to wash the salt off seaweed before using it in the garden. It really isn't necessary, as the amount of salt that might cling to the plants is minimal.

On Composting

(Q) *Do I need to use a compost activator to start making compost?*

(A) Compost activators are usually described as high-powered, bacteria-saturated substances that stimulate biological decomposition in a compost pile. It is better to add high-nitrogen materials like cottonseed meal, fish meal, or manure along with any natural fertilizers. Large-scale waste composting research has recently supported this opinion.

(Q) *Gardening in my city yard has been a rewarding challenge. However, I wonder how I can keep my compost heap alive and hot throughout the winter months without creating a backyard eyesore for my neighbors?*

(A) The best way to keep your compost heap active and out of view is by making it in a pit.

During the winter, the pit sides keep compost warm and accelerate the decaying process. Even such resistant materials as ground corncobs and leaves will be ready for soil-building use by late spring with this method, especially if earthworms are used to do the mixing.

The depth of the pit can be 3 feet, the length and width about 4 feet. After placing the materials in the pit, cover them with soil, and then cover the pit with plastic to retain heat.

(Q) *Last summer I made my first compost pile. I used a compost starter and put kitchen scraps, grass clippings, and everything available into the pile. People told me they saw rats in it and there were flies all over the place. How do I keep these undesirables from thriving in my compost pile?*

(A) It doesn't sound like you had very much nitrogen in your pile; hence you did not have composting, but some sort of putrefaction—which would indeed attract rodents and flies. It is very important to remember that composting may well be the most natural of all actions, but when conducted in a controlled situation, it requires careful attention to detail or problems will arise.

Composting originated in China, and has been practiced for almost 2,000 years. In the early 1920s, Sir Albert Howard, in Indore, India, was responsible for the rebirth of composting in Europe as a method to recycle wastes and improve soil conditions. His method, which was further developed over the century, is commonly known as the "Indore" method. The Indore method is still the most widely used, practical, and productive method of composting. By layering different organic materials, decomposition takes place more quickly and more completely.

To layer, first place a 5- to 6-inch layer of green matter, then a 2-inch layer of manure, followed by a layer of rich earth, ground limestone, and rock phosphate. Repeat this layering process until the bin or pit is filled.

Compost is best started in the fall, when ample plant material is available. In the summer, piles may dry out; while in the winter, extremely cold temperatures will slow down the composting process. If you do start your compost during the winter, extra manure should be added to the heap to keep the temperatures high and an insulating layer of plant material should go around the whole pile.

Ventilation is crucial to a good compost pile. The soil organisms that break down the plant and animal residues and convert them into compost must have oxygen from the atmosphere to carry on their activities. If oxygen does not reach the inside of your pile, the process will turn anaerobic and odors may well develop.

Turn your pile regularly to keep it well-ventilated. Turning also mixes the ingredients to ensure that all items are exposed to the highest heat in the center of the pile.

The pile should be moist during the initial stages of composting. Later in the process, the pile may be somewhat drier, but should never dry out, nor become so wet as to be matted together.

The carbon to nitrogen ratio is the amount of nitrogen-containing material in your pile as compared to the amount of carbonaceous material. This ratio determines how well your pile will heat up. A good working pile should have 25 parts of carbon for every 1 part of nitrogen.

(Q) *I want to make compost fast. What is the best ratio to get a hot mix? Will rock phosphate and other additives help speed up the composting?*

(A) The proper ratio for fast, hot compost with leaves and horse manure is to alternate 3- to 4-inch layers of leaves with 2-inch layers of manure. Mineral additives like rock phosphate and bone meal are more for compost enrichment than activation. These substances increase compost's nutrient content. Add these rock powders or bone meal to compost only if a soil test indicates that your soil needs boosting.

(Q) *How can I hasten the decay of a large straw stack?*

(A) A good way is to make holes in it with a rod and pour in considerable quantities of manure water. Such water will supply the bacteria and nitrogen that the straw needs to decay properly and quickly.

On Chemicals

(Q) *In what way does a highly soluble chemical fertilizer harm soil organisms?*

(A) Highly soluble chemicals such as chlorides and sulphates are poisonous to beneficial soil organisms, but in small amounts act as stimulants. These chemicals stimulate the beneficial soil bacteria to such increased growth and reproduction that they use up the organic matter in the soil as food faster than it can be returned by present agricultural practices.

When chemical residues accumulate in the soil, the microorganisms are killed off by hydrolysis. The high salt concentration in the soil water pulls moisture from bacteria and fungi, causing them to collapse and die. Earthworms are also poisoned by swallowing the salty soil and humus particles coated with chemical residues.

(Q) *Is it alright to apply leaves or grass clippings that were originally treated with fungicides and pesticides to my soil? Should I use livestock manures from animals that have been treated with different chemical agents?*

(A) The kinds and amounts of chemical agents in plant residues and manure vary considerably. Organic chemicals, on the whole, are decomposed by microorganisms; heavy metals, such as copper, calcium, lead, and arsenic, are molecularly bound by soil humus and other complex substances produced by soil microbes. Very little of the pesticides and other chemical agents originally used to treat plants and animals are taken up by crops grown on the soil. The possibility of uptake can be minimized or eliminated entirely by composting such materials before adding them to the soil. Treated plant residues and manures can be added directly to the soil without composting, but the decomposition process will be slower.

(Q) *How long does it take to covert a chemical garden into an organic garden?*

(A) The answer depends mostly on the gardener, but the switch can be made in as little time as it takes to collect organic materials and apply them to the soil.

The main job at the start is to round up as much organic fertilizer material as possible. Some of these, such as commercial compost mixtures, dried manures, rock phosphate, greensand, kelp meal, and fish meal, can be worked directly into your soil to increase its humus content. Another portion of these materials, such as straw and sawdust, should be set aside for later use as mulches.

Plan on immediately setting up a composting area with the remainder of the materials you have collected. In about 6 weeks you can have high-grade organic compost that will be the real start of your organic garden.

(Q) *What is the chemical "captan" that is put on seeds?*

(A) Captan, a complex fungicide, is a chlorinated hydrocarbon compound that belongs to the same group of compounds as DDT. Because captan is antifungal and antibacterial by nature, it has a pathological effect on the beneficial bacterial inoculants that encourage nitrogen-fixing nodule growth. Captan can also harm many of the other beneficial organisms in your soil.

(Q) *I cruise through neighborhoods on garbage nights and collect bags of freshly cut lawn grass. Is it safe to mulch with grass clippings that have been treated with toxic chemicals such as herbicides?*

(A) Although the grass clippings you collect might be treated with any one of a dozen commercial herbicide preparations, the chemical that is most widely used by homeowners is the pre-emergent weed killer, 2,4-Dichlorophenoxyacetic, or 2,4-D.

This herbicide, which has been known to cause birth defects, is a fast-acting plant hormone regulator that causes broadleaf plants, not grasses, to literally grow themselves to death. A few hours after treatment, dandelions and other weeds that absorb this systemic poison shrivel and die.

Lawn grass does absorb traces of 2,4-D, too, but not enough to affect vegetable growth. Soil microbes usually break down the chemical weed killer in about 3 months. To be safe, compost suspect clippings.

You should never use clippings that may have spray still adhering to them from a fresh application. How can you tell? Ask your neighbors. If several rains and a mowing or two have passed since the spraying, there should be no 2,4-D residue in the clippings— it will have passed through the soil and into the groundwater that you drink.

Avoid spray residues completely by getting to know the lawns you are collecting from. Aside from knowing the practices of the people who are setting out the clippings, the surest sign of herbicide-free grass clippings is a healthy crop of dandelions.

(Q) *What vegetables and fruit trees can be grown over or close to a septic field?*

(A) A vegetable garden should not be situated over a septic system where the soil drains poorly. Since there is a risk of infection from pathogens found in septic tank effluent, choose another garden site, if at all possible.

(Q) *Is it safe to use chlorinated water to irrigate my organic garden?*

(A) When you use chlorinated water to irrigate your garden, some of the chlorine compounds escape as gases. Those that remain are washed into the soil. It is unlikely that these compounds would be taken up by plants.

Chlorine compounds break down when exposed to light, so the chlorine in water droplets on plants or near the soil surface degrades quickly on a sunny day. The soil acts almost like an activated carbon filter, destroying any chlorine that percolates through it, and preventing the element from forming compounds with soil minerals.

When watering flats, let chlorinated water stand overnight with as much surface as possible exposed to the air. The chlorine won't do the seedlings any good and will kill beneficial soil bacteria.

On Planting

(Q) *Should I start my plants from seed or buy them?*

(A) The craft of raising plants from seed is the very cornerstone of gardening independence. Practically speaking, the reasons for planting your own seeds are:

1. Your crops get a much earlier start in the garden.
2. Varieties of plants offered by commercial seedling vendors represent but a tiny fraction of the possibilities open to you as a gardener
3. Seedlings that you grow yourself can be super-seedlings, with well-developed roots and a good soil base untainted with chemicals.
4. By raising your own plants you minimize the chance of introducing soil-borne disease to your garden.

On a personal level, seed-starting provides a great deal of creative satisfaction and a cure for the winter doldrums.

(Q) *If I fertilize (with organic fertilizer) carefully, does it hurt to plant the same vegetables in the same spot each year? Is crop rotation really that important?*

(A) Regardless of how well you fertilize, you must rotate your crops every year. By doing so, your soil becomes exposed to diverse cultural activity and cultivation practices.

By growing one crop in the same space every year, a cultural timetable is established that may allow certain insects to acclimate themselves more easily to the area, thus increasing insect problems in ensuing growing seasons. If you practice good rotations, you will be cultivating the same ground at different seasons from year to year, disturbing the insects' cycles.

Additionally, by rotating legumes with nonlegumes, your fertilization requirements will be reduced, as the legumes leave nitrogen in the soil. Another advantage of a good rotation schedule is the buildup of minerals near the top layers of the soil by different plants. One plant may accumulate calcium in its roots, another, manganese. Through rotation, the crops that follow are able to take advantage of the accumulated minerals.

(Q) *I would like to know more about the French Intensive Method of gardening. How does it work?*

(A) Basically, the "Biodynamic French Intensive Method" involves adding organic soil amendments and nutrients to raised beds, and then literally covering them with plants whose foliages all touch at maturity (this is called a living mulch). The garden soil loses less moisture and maintains a more constant temperature.

Intensive gardening is particularly well suited to the organic grower. Few other methods make such efficient use of composted soil. The living mulch method of plant spacing means that every bit of rich soil will be producing nutritious edibles.

If you plan to try intensive gardening, prepare your soil by starting with a complete soil test. Measure and stake out the bed, making sure that you can reach the middle from either side without walking on it and compressing the soil. Double-dig the bed by digging out the first 2 feet of soil and laying it aside; then dig down another 2 feet and thoroughly loosen this soil with your spade. The next step is to add nutrients. A soil test will indicate the soil's need for potassium, phosphorous, magnesium, or calcium. Nitrogen can be added in the form of well-rotted manure or mineral fertilizer. Amend the dug-up soil with compost and sand to help improve its structure. After the bed has been worked, the soil will be 4 to 8 inches above the paths. At this point, mound the beds by raking the soil so that the sides slope up at a 45-degree angle and the top of the bed is flat.

Space your plants so that they virtually carpet the plot when grown. They will shade their own root zones, so that the bed retains soil moisture and grows no weeds. Try not to get the plants too close, though. They should all touch, but not crowd each other. Stagger your plantings for a prolonged harvest.

(Q) *Why is cultivation necessary and what does it do for plants?*

(A) Two types of cultivation are important to successful growing. Before planting, cultivation refers to preparing the soil, digging the top several inches lightly to loosen the earth, and breaking up clods to help aerate the growing site. For small areas, most gardeners use a spading fork. When turned and loosened, the planting location should be raked smooth to a depth of 2 to 3 inches.

Once seed is sown or plants set out, the main purpose of cultivating is to prevent competition between crops and weeds for both water and nutrients. This cultivation should be quite shallow (kept to about 1 inch deep), because damage to crop roots can easily result from deeper working.

The chore of cultivating during the growing season can be eliminated by using mulches. Besides being an effective method of keeping weeds down, mulches help to retain moisture and enrich the soil as they decompose.

On Mulching

(**Q**) *Someone recommended that I use salt hay as a mulch. Is it better than regular hay?*

(**A**) Salt hay comes from a grass grown abundantly in eastern coastal marshes. Unlike regular hay, salt hay is usually free of weed seeds and does not become matted, two big advantages. Although the grass grows only in saline conditions, it contains very little salt. Salt hay is harvested for use in coastal areas, and may be difficult to find farther inland.

(**Q**) *Can one leave a year-round mulch under fruit trees without encouraging insects, if fallen fruit and branches are removed?*

(**A**) A permanent mulch encourages insects. Renew your mulches every year by turning them into the top 2 inches of soil and using new material. Keep the ground within a foot of the trees clean. Avoid acidic mulches. Use straw.

(**Q**) *Is there any value in the use of coffee grounds as a mulch or mixed in with the soil? Might this be helpful to some plants or possibly harmful to others?*

(**A**) Coffee grounds are of value as a soil conditioner. I have not found or heard that they are good for some plants and not for others. Coffee grounds contain as much as 2 percent nitrogen, 1.3 percent phosphoric acid, and varying amounts of potash.

Coffee grounds sour easily because they preserve moisture well and seem to encourage acid-forming bacteria. Generally, it is best to mix them with other materials in your compost.

On Vegetables

(**Q**) *I love tomatoes, but have a small garden. What can I do to get maximum production from each plant?*

(**A**) Try varieties with an "indeterminate" growth habit, which yield more than "determinate" types, and stake the plants.

Most early varieties are determinate: They make their growth, then stop producing foliage and flowers while the fruit sets and ripens. The indeterminate types start producing a little later, but have higher yields because the vines keep growing and producing until the frost kills them.

Staking the plants saves space. Plant the tomatoes 2 feet apart in beds. They can also be planted in 18-inch intervals in rows that are 3 feet apart. To prevent the staked plants from becoming too top-heavy, they must be pruned. Pinch out all but a few stems that grow from leaf axils of the main stem. Plants with 2 or more stems produce the highest yield. After the soil has warmed up, mulch; staked plants dry out quickly.

(Q) *What vegetables can I plant that will be ready to harvest in spring?*

(A) You can harvest an early spring crop of spinach, lettuce, kale, garlic, and parsley. Protect young plants with a cold frame or thick mulch.

(Q) *The weeds always get ahead of my carrots. Is there some way to beat the weeds and get the seeds to sprout faster?*

(A) Try soaking the seeds overnight. When sowing carrot seeds, cover them with peat moss.

(Q) *At harvest time last year, I discovered that most of my onions had split. I found that they didn't keep well during the winter. What caused the splitting and how can I prevent it?*

(A) Bulbs are likely to split if the soil goes through repeated wet and dry periods early in the season or during bulb formation. Excessive nitrogen late in the season can also cause the problem. Under these conditions dormant growing points become active and produce more bulbs.

So, plant onions in well-drained soil, mulch to maintain even soil moisture, and compost early in the season.

(Q) *I have grown carrots for a few years, but they are always bitter. What's wrong?*

(A) Carrots exposed to an uneven supply of moisture or nutrients will become bitter.

Under these stressful conditions, the plants produce an acrid substance called isocumarin. Check for signs of insects and diseases, which can also stress the carrots and cause bitterness.

(Q) *My early broccoli didn't produce heads this spring. Does that mean that my plants were sterile?*

(A) Sterility in plants does not refer to head or flower formation, but to the production of viable seeds. Floret formation in broccoli (and cauliflower) depends on three factors: cool weather, plenty of water, and adequate calcium. Hot weather, drought, and/or a soil calcium deficiency can all produce non-heading broccoli plants.

To cure calcium deficiency, spread crushed limestone and bone meal over your future broccoli patch in the fall; then till it in. Early in the season, broccoli needs at least an inch of rain per week. Broccoli planted in August for fall harvest needs slightly less water, but the supply must be just as steady. In addition, broccoli requires cool nights. A sudden hot spell can produce button heads or no heads at all or cause the plant to bolt to seed within a few days.

(Q) *When is the best time of day for watering to keep my beans from blistering?*

(A) Blisters, brown papery spots on the pods and leaves of your beans, are burns caused by the effects of sunlight magnified by droplets of water.

If you water early in the morning, the droplets on the plant will have evaporated by the time the sun is strong enough to cause a problem. If you live in an area with scorching mornings, you can water in the early evening, but water early enough so that the leaves dry before nightfall. If the leaves stay moist through the night they will provide the perfect environment for disease to develop.

Plant your beans early in the spring to avoid the intense summer heat that causes blistering.

(Q) *How should I prune my tomato plants? Should they be staked or not? Should they be cultivated or mulched?*

(A) Indeterminate (vining) cultivars should be staked. For determinate (bush) cultivars that are not staked, strew a thick mulch of straw or grass clippings under them to help keep the fruit clean and the moisture content of the soil more uniform (thus preventing blossom end rot). Tomato plants permitted to sprawl without pruning will set and mature more fruit than plants that are pruned, but the fruit will be smaller and much of it may be lost by rotting on damp ground, damage from slugs and other insects, or overripening under a dense mass of foliage.

If allowed to go unpruned, tomatoes will make branches at each leaf node and sometimes fruit cluster stems will extend to form additional branches. Whether the vines are to be trained or not, these fruit cluster branches should be pinched off just beyond the cluster in order to throw all the nourishment from that stem into the fruit.

When vines are to be trained to only 1 stem, all side branches should be pinched back after they have made 1 set of leaves, thus preserving the plant's energy for fruit production. Suckers arising from the root after the main stem has made a good growth should also be removed. If 2 or 3 stems are permitted to grow, the branches on the first leaf nodes are allowed to develop. Each branch is then tied to its own stake and treated in the same

way as the parent stem. Once pruning has begun, it must be repeated every week throughout the growing season. If it is started and then abandoned, tops of the plants will develop heavily and many suckers will take the strength from the plants without providing much fruit.

Six weeks before the first expected frost, nip out all growing tips, including that on the main stem. This will stop vine development and permit the plant's nourishment to concentrate on maturing fruit. New blossoms may also be pruned out after this date, since fruit set late will not be large enough for use.

(Q) *My sweet potato plants produce mostly vines and few potatoes. Why?*

(A) Too much nitrogen in the soil promotes vine rather than root growth. The soil for sweet potatoes should be prepared with moderate amounts of compost and greensand, but don't add high-nitrogen sources like manures, cottonseed meal, and blood meal.

On Fruits

(Q) *We set out new strawberry plants last fall, after turning under a sod patch. Disappointingly, the berries wilted and died before ripening. What did we do wrong?*

(A) It is well to plan ahead for the area to be used as the strawberry patch by growing cultivated crops that need hoeing. These crops should be grown for at least 2 years and then the strawberry plants should be set.

Sod land very often contains white grubs and wire worms, which damage the roots of strawberry plants. Tilling the soil for 2 years will discourage the grubs.

(Q) *I grow strawberries in a 5- × 6-foot plot on a fairly steep slope behind my garden. I can't work nutrients into the soil because of severe erosion. Does this prevent me from gardening organically on a steep slope?*

(A) Strawberries like sun, moisture, good drainage, and soil loaded with organic matter. While a slight slope keeps cold air from settling on the patch, a steep slope is not recommended for either organic or strawberry growing because of the need for organically rich soil. Also, weeds and disease are encouraged by a nonrotation of crops, so many growers routinely redo strawberry beds and start new plants to eliminate these problems.

Terrace your slope to make adding organic matter easier. If you do decide to continue the patch on the slope, try creating a semipermanent bed by alternating rows each year. Let runners get established in rows next to the mother plants, which are then removed. Work organic matter into empty rows and mulch to prevent erosion.

(Q) *I have a number of everbearing strawberry plants. Would you please tell me how to take care of them so they will keep during the winter?*

(A) Strawberries should be mulched during the winter to prevent freezing injury from low temperatures, and, also, to prevent plants from being heaved out of the soil by alternate freezing and thawing. A mulch of straw to a depth of 3 to 4 inches will provide winter protection. Part of the straw is raked off the plants into the space between the rows in the spring just as the plants start growth.

(Q) *We planted 2 dwarf apple trees 4 years ago. They are both quite large (over 8 feet tall) and have never produced blossoms or fruit. What's wrong?*

(A) Your trees could be lonely. Some varieties are self-sterile or have very weak pollen and need to be planted close to one another in order to be able to set fruit.

To encourage good growth and abundant fruit, apple trees require a yearly application of nitrogen fertilizer such as fish meal, cottonseed meal, soybean meal, manure, or blood meal. Apply 6 to 8 weeks before the tree blooms, but never as late as June, as this may stimulate late growth that will not harden sufficiently before winter.

On Flowers and Herbs

(Q) *How can I tell the difference between French and Russian tarragon?*

(A) The crush and sniff test is the best way. The French has a distinct anise scent and the Russian smells more like lawn grass. The leaves of French tarragon are long, narrow, and glossy and the plants rarely grow taller than 2 feet. Russian tarragon is much taller and has lighter green, rough-textured leaves.

(Q) *I am interested in making up an organic fertilizer for the roses in my backyard. What components should be used and what is their function?*

(A) You can make up a beneficial rose fertilizer with the following ingredients: 2 parts fish meal, 2 parts blood meal, 1 part cottonseed meal, 1 part kelp meal, 1 part rock phosphate, and 1 part greensand. The fish meal, blood meal, and cottonseed meal are high in nitrogen, which forms a part of all proteins. Nitrogen is responsible for the vegetative growth, size of foliage, and flower color. The phosphate rock and greensand are sources of phosphate and potassium needed for root development and balancing nitrogen. Kelp meal supplies the trace minerals for healthy tissues.

When these organic soil amendments are used together, they work synergistically to enrich the soil and encourage vigorous plant growth.

On Insect and Disease Control and Prevention

(Q) *I have a question concerning the use of herbicides in my garden. Which ones are considered safe? I can keep the weeds under control by hoeing up to the time that the plants get large, but after that it is hard to work close to the plants.*

(A) The only two herbicides that can be recommended are cultivation and mulching. Chemical herbicides have a detrimental effect on the soil life and insect populations. By decreasing the number of soil microogranisms and insects, the chances for an insect imbalance or plant disease are greatly increased.

You would be better off to continue to hoe when the plants are young and then mulch heavily to prevent weed growth.

(Q) *Leaf miners devastated my spinach, Swiss chard, and beets last year. Can you please tell me how to prevent this from happening again?*

(A) The best way to keep leaf miners off is spraying with a natural control called Red Arrow™. Known as the spinach leaf miner, the larval form of this fly chews disfiguring tunnels in the leaves and can destroy over 75 percent of the foliage. There are 4 generations per season and the insects overwinter in the soil as pupae.

Check young plants for clusters of 1 to 5 small, white leaf miner eggs laid side by side on the undersides of the leaves. They usually appear in April or May. Destroy all eggs that you find so the larvae cannot establish a population.

(Q) *This past winter I covered my carrots with leaves to protect them from the frost. When I turned the leaves back, I discovered that the carrots had been eaten by slugs. How do I avoid slugs in the garden year-round and when covering winter vegetables? Is there an organic control for slugs?*

(A) Slugs seek an acid soil and a leaf mulch tends to acidify the soil. These soft-bodied animals cannot stand dry conditions and a moist, mulched garden provides welcome relief from the drying effect of the sun.

Two measures to help prevent a recurrence of this past year's disappointment would be to make sure that your soil has a rich supply of earthworms (whose castings are alkaline), and to mulch with oak leaves, which, though acidic, impart a bitter taste that the tender-bodied slugs cannot stand. Also, you may use diatomaceous earth (a penetrating powder that dehydrates slugs). This fluffy flour, mined in the west, is formed from the fossilized remains of one-celled fresh water algae called diatoms. Diatomaceous earth kills slugs in two ways: It pierces their skin as they crawl through it, and punctures their internal organs when they try to digest it. Diatomaceous earth works best when it is sprinkled around the base of plants.

(Q) *A few years ago, I took the advice of a friend and boiled some rhubarb leaves, saving the reddish-green water. Then I used the solution as a spray to control aphids. It worked, but why?*

(A) Oxalic acid kills aphids. Found in spinach, rhubarb, and many leafy vegetables, oxalic acid is poisonous in high concentrations. Although rhubarb contains negligible amounts of oxalates in its edible stems, its leaves are rich in the soluble substances and should not be eaten. The oxalates in the leaves make the aphids sick, too.

You can mix a simple rhubarb spray by first cutting up 1 pound of leaves and boiling them in 1 quart of water for 30 minutes. Then strain and bottle the liquid. To help it stick to leaves, squeeze in a dab of liquid soap when the solution has cooled. The vegetables will be safe to eat after harvesting.

(Q) *I would like to know how to control spider mites in my garden.*

(A) Mites thrive in stagnant, warm air, whether dry or humid. Good air circulation is often a problem in greenhouses and indoor gardens. Spraying a blast of cold water every 3 to 4 days on the tops and bottoms of leaves should end your problems.

Encourage ladybugs and lacewings. If you must resort to sprays, use pyrethrum. Mites can overwinter in perennials and weeds, so good garden sanitation is very important.

(Q) *How do I control corn earworms, which I understand are the same pests as tomato fruitworms?*

(A) They are one and the same. Fruitworm larvae not only damage tomatoes and corn, but also feed on alfalfa, grapes, okra, peas, squash, and other garden crops. The worm overwinters as a pupa 2 to 6 inches below the soil surface, but only if the soil does not freeze. As the larvae hatch from eggs laid on tomato leaves, they feed sparingly until they find the fruit. Then they cut a hole and burrow inside, usually at the stem end, and feed there for 3 to 4 weeks.

On corn, the worms feed on tassels first, disrupting pollination; but most of the damage is to the ear. Late-season corn is particularly susceptible.

Bacillus thuringiensis (BT), the bacterial disease that kills caterpillars, works well as long as you apply the spray while the insects are feeding. You can also plant a row or make up a spray of cosmos flowers near your corn and tomatoes, which deters the pests.

(Q) *Is there an organic method for eliminating the Colorado potato beetle?*

(A) Follow your normal planting schedule: Put the seed potatoes in the ground and cover the soil. Then lay a 1-foot-deep mulch of hay on the patch.

That is all there is to do. You are not likely to see even 1 potato beetle on vines mulched in this manner. The reason this method works so well is that the eggs of the Colorado beetles spend the winter in the soil. The potato vines, of course, will have no trouble pushing up through the heavy hay mulch, but the beetles, when they hatch, cannot make the same trip.

(Q) *My onions have been attacked by onion maggots. What can I do?*

(A) Adding fine sand to the top layer of your planting rows will deter onion maggots. Radishes can be used as a trap crop.

(Q) *Some of my tomatoes have small irregular white lumps under their skins. What's wrong?*

(A) The white lumps on your tomatoes are caused by stink bugs. Early in the season, this pest pierces the fruit when it feeds, leaving traces of saliva behind. The saliva in the wounds breaks down the tissue of the tomato, causing the spots. You can still eat the fruit by cutting off the damaged part.

Stink bugs prefer damp places, and generally attack the fruit closest to the ground. Control these pests by staking plants so they do not sprawl on moist soil.

(Q) *What do ladybug eggs, larvae, and adults look like? We handpick a lot and do not want to destroy this beneficial insect.*

(A) The ladybug usually lays its bright orange eggs in vertical clusters on leaves and stems. They are so similar to the eggs of the Colorado potato beetle and the Mexican bean beetle that you should wait until the larvae first start emerging before you consider squashing any pest eggs.

Fully mature ladybug larvae are $1/2$ inch long and black with orange spots. The adult beetle can be orange, red, pink, yellow, or even gray, and may have black spots or be solidly colored. Don't confuse the adult ladybug with the Mexican bean beetle, which has a golden luster and brown spots.

(Q) *I was told that soap flakes help keep the bugs off houseplants. I would like to use the solution on my plants, but I wonder if it is organic?*

(A) A solution of soap without detergent (such as Ivory, Octagon, or Safer's) acts as a mild insecticide against aphids and scale. Because it is gentle, it usually does not kill all of the insects on the plant, leaving a few stray pests to feed predators (like spiders) and parasites. Soap solutions also wash off dirt, dust, and insect eggs.

To make the solution, add 1 to 2 tablespoons of flakes to 1 gallon of tepid (70 to 85°F) water. Apply it to the plants by sponging leaves thoroughly, dipping them into it, or spraying. Leave the mixture on for 1 to 2 hours and then rinse it off well with lukewarm water. Don't use soap solution on hairy plants such as African violets and begonias.

(Q) *My tomato patch is full of hornworms. The majority of the hornworms have white tubes on their backs, which I understand are the eggs of a parasitic wasp. How long does it take for the wasp to destroy the hornworm?*

(A) The white tubes you see on the hornworms are the pupae of the brachonid wasp, a beneficial parasitic wasp. Once the wasps reach the pupae stage, they have done their feeding on the hornworm and considerably reduced its ability to destroy tomato and potato crops. However, a hornworm population can survive a quite sizable infestation of the wasp, so you need to keep reintroducing the wasps until the hornworms are under control.

If the wasps have reached the pupae stage in your garden, let the cycle continue, allowing as many wasps to reach adulthood as possible and to continue breeding in the remaining hornworms. If you have hornworms and see no wasp pupae forming, by all means, handpick the worms and destroy them. You can also use BT (*Bacillus thuringiensis*) spray, which is a biological insect control.

(Q) *Are June bugs harmful to my garden?*

(A) Full-grown June bug beetles can damage plants by feeding on foliage and flowers, including fruit trees and blackberry leaves.

However, greater damage is caused by grubs, the immature form of many common large bugs. Grubs harm corn by feeding on roots. They may also feed on the roots of bluegrass, timothy, and soybeans, as well as decaying vegetation.

Milky spore disease is effective against 43 types of white grubs, including those of the June bug.

(Q) *We have cedar galls (plant tumors) on our cedar and arborvitae trees and are wondering whether our nearby apple trees will be harmed as well. Is there anything that can be done about the galls?*

(A) Yes, your apple trees will be harmed. What your trees have is a curious disease called cedar apple rust. It starts when spores are blown from infected cedars to apple trees, where they cause bright orange spots on the foliage and to a lesser degree, on fruit.

The infections on apple foliage produce another spore stage, borne in delicate cup-like structures that reinfect the cedar and thereby keep the vicious cycle going.

There are many available disease-resistant apple varieties that you can plant, including: 'Baldwin', 'Delicious', 'Rhode Island', 'Franklin', 'Melrose', 'Red Astrachan', 'Staymen', 'Golden Delicious', 'Winesap', 'Grimes Golden', and 'Duchess'.

(Q) *As our asparagus sprouts came up this year, they looked strong and healthy at first. Then they started to get limp and wilted. It was just a matter of days until this wilt progressively hit each stalk after it reached 3 inches. What happened?*

(A) Stunting and yellowing or wilting are symptoms of asparagus wilt or root-rot caused

by fungi like *Fusarium* and *Verticillium*. These fungi invade the roots and stems of plants by interfering with the upward movement of water. In effect, the plant dies from clogged arteries.

The fungi build up in infested soil where asparagus is permitted to grow indefinitely. After the asparagus dies, the *Fusarium* fungus produces masses of spores that may live on humus in the soil for several years. The best way to heal the diseased section of your garden is to destroy it. For your next asparagus planting, start with healthy plants as far from the old beds as possible. The selected site should be rich and well-drained.

(Q) *Last spring I fertilized my apple trees with a commercial chemical tree food. Leaves curled and dropped. Insects ate everything. Apples were small, bitter, and wormy. For the last 3 years, I have been spraying with every poison I could get my hands on. Am I doing something wrong?*

(A) Overfertilizing with too much nitrogen can encourage certain blight diseases. It is hard to make an exact diagnosis, but it might be that after years of using all those chemicals, insects built up a resistance to them. There is probably an imbalance in your soil because of all the chemicals you have been using.

This year, start right with a dormant oil spray and follow as needed with rotenone, ryania, and pyrethrum (a natural plant derivative) and use *Bacillus thuringiensis* (BT), a bacterial control for codling moth. If you plant any new trees, choose more resistant varieties, get a complete soil test, and correct any deficiencies by using organic soil amendments and organic fertilizers. Orchardists who do not want to apply any of the poison sprays should plan to learn the life cycles of insects. Timely interception is key—early protection will definitely help your later crop.

(Q) *What causes the blisters on the trunks of my apple trees?*

(A) Water blisters on the outer bark of the trunk are caused by the uptake of excess manganese from very acid soils. It is normal for these blisters to burst, releasing a brown liquid that streaks down the bark.

The blisters do not penetrate to the cambium. Manganese toxicity in itself is not injurious to the tree, but the low pH it indicates leads to reduced growth and yield. An obvious control method is to raise the soil pH. This can be done by adding crushed limestone to the soil. Wood ashes or greensand are also very helpful and may be added to the compost pile.

USDA Hardiness Zone Map

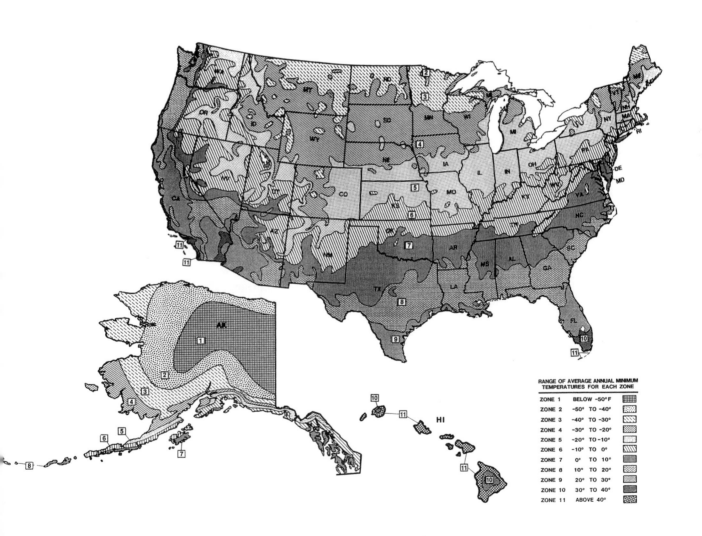

RANGE OF AVERAGE ANNUAL MINIMUM TEMPERATURES FOR EACH ZONE	
ZONE 1	BELOW −50°F
ZONE 2	−50° TO −40°
ZONE 3	−40° TO −30°
ZONE 4	−30° TO −20°
ZONE 5	−20° TO −10°
ZONE 6	−10° TO 0°
ZONE 7	0° TO 10°
ZONE 8	10° TO 20°
ZONE 9	20° TO 30°
ZONE 10	30° TO 40°
ZONE 11	ABOVE 40°

Organic Gardener's Yearly Plan

Here is a schedule of the gardening year, divided by growing season.

Winter
January

Go through seed catalog

Review observation notebook

Lay out garden plan

Order seeds

Prune fruit trees (weather permitting)

February

Mix potting soil

Set up indoor growing area

Spring seed in flats

Turn compost

March

Till in cover

Prune grapes

Harden-off indoor flats

Lime-sulfur fruit trees

Direct-seed peas and potatoes

Start summer crops in flats

Spring
April

Rough-till beds

Repair box gardens

Spread compost

Fertilize lawn

Feed and wood-mulch grapes

Prune, feed, and mulch roses

Transplant spring greens

May

Continue transplanting

Foliar-feed transplants

Mulch fruit trees and vegetables

Harvest spring greens

June

Direct-seed beans, corn, carrots, and squash

Transplant summer crop from flats

Check soil moisture

Cultivate between rows

Plant flower garden

Summer
July

Weed beds

Seaweed spray lawn

Check soil moisture

Mix potting soil

Seed flats for fall

Cultivate flower beds

August

Transplant fall crops

Spray organic fungicide on fruit trees

Replenish mulch

September

Harvest last of fall crop

Foliar-feed, cultivate, and mulch fall crop

Start new compost pile

Plant cover crops

Fall
October

Perform soil test

Dethatch and fertilize lawn

Root-feed trees

Transplant trees and shrubs

Add compost and soil amendments

Shred leaves and twigs

November

Add manure to beds

Lime-sulfur fruit trees

Mulch trees and shrubs

Burlap shrubs

Plant spring bulbs

December

Mulch beds

Lime lawns and gardens

Prune berries

Resources

Information Sources

Agri-Balance Organic Consultants
P.O. Box 3084
Sag Harbor, NY 11963
516-725-5725

ATTRA (Appropriate Technology Transfer for Rural Areas)
P.O. Box 3657
Fayetteville, AR 72702
800-346-9140

Bio-Integral Resource Center
Box 7414
Berkeley, CA 94707
510-524-2567

National Pesticide Telecommunications Network, Pesticide Hotline
800-858-7378

Sources of Gardening Supplies, Seeds, Pest Control Products, and Traps

AgriSystems International
125 West 7th Street
Windgap, PA 18091

Arbico, Sustainable Environmental Alternatives for Growers
P.O. Box 4247
Tucson, AZ 85378

D.V. Burrell Seed Growers Co.
P.O. Box 150
Rocky Ford, CO 81067
719-254-3318

Charley's Greenhouse Supply
1599 Memorial Highway #C
Mount Vernon, WA 98273
360-428-2626

Concept, Inc.
213 SW Columbia
Bend, OR 97702

Dalen Products
11110 Gilbert Drive
Knoxville, TN 37932
423-966-3256

Gardener's Supply Co.
128 Intervale Road
Burlington, VT 05401
802-660-3505

Gardens Alive!
5100 Schenley Place
Lawrenceburg, IN 47025
812-537-8651

Harmony Farm Supply
P.O. Box 460
Graton, CA 95444
707-823-9125

The Natural Gardening Company
217 San Anselmo Avenue
San Anselmo, CA 94960
415-456-5060

Ohio Earth Food, Inc.
5488 Swamp Street NE
Hartville, OH 44632
330-977-9356

Peaceful Valley Farm Supply
P.O. Box 2209
Grass Valley, CA 95945
1-888-784-1722

Seed Savers Exchange
3076 North Winn Road
Decorah, IA 52101
319-382-5990

Spalding Laboratories
760 Printz Road
Arroyo Grande, CA 93420

The Urban Farmer Store
2833 Vicente Street
San Francisco, CA 94116

Worm's Way Garden Supply and Home Brew Center
3151 South Highway 446
Bloomington, IN 47401

Grower's Glossary

Acid soil   Soil with a pH between 0 and 7.0.

Alkaline soil   Soil with a pH between 7.0 and 14.

Annual   A plant that flowers and sets seed within a single growing season.

Bolting   Producing seed prematurely.

BT   *Bacillus thuringiensis*, a bacterial bug-killer that causes paralysis of the digestive system of any leaf-eating caterpillar, resulting in death within days.

Brassica   *See* cole crops.

Biennial   A plant that completes its life in 2 growing seasons, making vegetable growth the first season; then flowering, fruiting, and dying the second.

Bulb   Essentially an underground leaf bud—masses of swollen plant tissue that store energy and food for the plant. Corms, rhizomes, tubers, and tuberous roots share many similarities with bulbs, and in fact the word "bulb" is often used interchangeably to describe all subterranean storage organs.

Cambium   The layer of developing cells between wood and bark on a tree.

Cloche   A covering, usually transparent, that is placed over plants for protection and allows in the sunlight.

Cold frame   A bottomless box that is higher in the back than in the front, usually made of wood and covered with glass or plastic. Cold frames are used for plant cultivation and protection.

Cole crops   Various species of the family that includes Brussels sprouts, broccoli, cauliflower, and kale.

Companion planting   The sowing of seeds in the garden in such a way that plants help each other grow instead of competing against each other.

   Vegetables should be planted as close as possible to their companions to reduce stress and prevent disease. Some examples of companion plantings include radishes and carrots, and lettuce and kale.

Compost   The collection of organic waste (such as leaves, kitchen scraps, or manure) to be digested and biologically decomposed by microbes and transformed into humus.

Cotyledon Plant embryos first develop a set of leaves called the "cotyledon," which are not true leaves, but a nutrient storage apparatus for the growing seed.

Cover crop Vegetation grown to protect and build the soil during an interval when the area would otherwise lie fallow.

Crop rotation The planting of a specific crop in a site different from the previous year. Rotation helps to control insect and disease problems, and lessens the depletion of the soil.

Cross-pollinator This type of plant is dioecious, meaning that the male and female sex organs are located in separate plants.

Crown The point where the stem and root join on a plant; or the leafy crest of a tree.

Cultivar A plant variety that is cultivated, not wild.

Damping-off A fungus disease of planted seeds due to overcrowding or poor plant conditions. Prevention is the cure.

Dioecious Refers to species with the male and female sex organs located in separate plants.

Direct seed To seed directly in the soil instead of starting in the greenhouse.

Drip line The area below the outermost circumference of the branches of a tree

Double-digging A method used to loosen uncultivated soil and maximize production. A series of trenches are dug into beds in 2-foot sections and soil is replaced with a 50–50 mix of soil and compost.

Embryo The incipient plant contained in a seed.

Espalier A plant trained to grow flatly on a lattice or trellis, or the technique of training a plant in such a way.

Everlasting Refers to certain flowers that, when air-dried, look almost as beautiful as they did when alive.

Floating row-cover A special lightweight covering used to protect rows of seedlings against insects and frost.

Greensand An undersea mineral deposit that contains 7 percent potassium and beneficial quantities of many trace minerals, including lime and phosphorous. It has the ability to thin dense, clayey textures, and also to fatten loose sandy aggregates.

Hardening off A process that slows down the growth of plants to make them gradually inured to outdoor conditions.

Hardy Refers to strong, healthy plants that are resistant to insects and diseases; also pertains to frost-tolerant plants.

Humus Any organic matter resulting from the decomposition of plant bodies. It acts as a sponge by holding water, aerates the soil, and feeds earthworms and beneficial microorganisms.

Green manure The growing of certain plants such as oats, buckwheat, and rye for the sole purpose of tilling them under to provide organic matter to the soil.

Inoculant A dry bacterial culture used to treat pea and bean seeds prior to planting. It encourages nitrogen-fixing bacteria growth on the roots, increasing yields and enhancing the soil.

Intensive garden A garden that produces high crop yields through organic methods.

Interplanting The practice of growing 2 or more plants in the same bed space is called interplanting or intercropping. By choosing plants that mature at different times, the net yield of both crops is increased and disease and insect infestation is greatly reduced.

Layering A propagation technique accomplished by selecting a low shoot that is easily bent to the ground, then making an inch-long diagonal cut through a joint about

1 foot from the tip of the shoot. The cut area is then buried in 3 to 6 inches of soil, its branch end remaining out of the ground to form the top.

Lesion nematode Also known as an eelworm; a microscopic parasite that attacks plant roots, stunting plants and causing leaves to yellow.

Living mulch Vegetables planted closely together so that the leaves of the growing plants eventually overlap at maturity are said to be a "living mulch." This practice makes maximum use of available sunlight, since none is wasted on the soil. It also reduces evaporation and the rate of weed seed germination.

Loam Fertile soil plentiful in silt, organic matter, and enough clay and sand particles to give it good crumbly texture and structure.

Mulch Along with compost, mulch is the organic gardener's most valued and versatile tool. Organic mulches like straw, hay, and pine needles protect plants from drought, extremes in temperature, and weeds, as well as provide food for soil microbes.

Mycelium A mass of fungus threads.

Nitrogen A major nutrient that feeds and sustains foliage.

Organic matter Improves the soil's tilth, good drainage, and moisture-holding capacities. The main sources of organic matter are animal manures, composts, mulches, and green manures.

Parasitic insects Beneficial insects, such as certain types of wasp, whose larvae feed on the larvae of pestilent host insects.

Perennial Plants that grow for 3 or more seasons. They are propagated from seed, but usually reproduced from cuttings or root division.

pH A symbol that indicates the degree of acidity or alkalinity (pH) in soil and other substances. The pH scale reads from 0 to 14, 0 indicating extreme acidity and 14 extreme alkalinity, while 7.0 is neutral.

Phosphorus A major element, needed for developing plants' root systems and producing flowers.

Pinching Just another name for pruning with your fingers to keep plants healthy and bushy.

Plug A cylinder of soil that is removed by an aerator or soil augur, and replaced with compost; or a small rooted piece of grass.

Potassium A major element, needed for the growth and development of healthy stems.

Pyrethrum A botanical insect control derived from a daisy-like flower.

Runner An extension from a plant's root system that develops into a new plant.

Seed The part of a flowering plant that contains an embryo, with food for that embryo and a protective covering.

Self-incompatible species Species that require pollination from other plants of their own species even though individual plants produce both male and female flowers.

Self-sowing plants A plant that produces its own seed and continues to grow.

Spawn The mycelium of fungi. *See* Mycelium.

Spores Microscopic reproductive organisms corresponding to seeds. Ferns, mosses, and fungi reproduce by spores.

Succession planting Refers to the procedure of making several sowings of the same crop 1 or 2 weeks apart or harvesting 1 crop and following it by another, in the same space in a single season.

Succulent A plant with thick, fleshy leaves or stems native to dry, tropical regions, such as aloe or cacti.

Sucker Or a water sprout; a shoot that sprouts from the trunk and roots of a tree and drains its energy.

Tender Refers to sensitive plants that are not as resistant to insects and diseases; or more susceptible to frost.

Top-dressing A process wherein compost and/or organic soil amendments are placed on top of soil around the base of the plant as a supplemental feeding.

True leaves The first leaves grown by a plant after the cotyledons.

Vermiculite A mineral belonging to the mica family, used as a medium for starting seedlings and root cuttings.

Water sprout *See* sucker.

Zone Plant hardiness regions determined by approximate annual range of lowest winter temperatures.

Index